*Perceiving and Remembering
Faces*

ACADEMIC PRESS
SERIES IN COGNITION AND PERCEPTION

SERIES EDITORS:
Edward C. Carterette
Morton P. Friedman
Department of Psychology
University of California, Los Angeles
Los Angeles, California

Stephen K. Reed: *Psychological Processes in Pattern Recognition*

Earl B. Hunt: *Artificial Intelligence*

James P. Egan: *Signal Detection Theory and ROC Analysis*

Martin F. Kaplan and Steven Schwartz (Eds.): *Human Judgment and Decision Processes*

Myron L. Braunstein: *Depth Perception Through Motion*

R. Plomp: *Aspects of Tone Sensation*

Martin F. Kaplan and Steven Schwartz (Eds.): *Human Judgment and Decision Processes in Applied Settings*

Bikkar S. Randhawa and William E. Coffman: *Visual Learning, Thinking, and Communication*

Robert B. Welch: *Perceptual Modification: Adapting to Altered Sensory Environments*

Lawrence E. Marks: *The Unity of the Senses: Interrelations among the Modalities*

Michele A. Wittig and Anne C. Petersen (Eds.): *Sex-Related Differences in Cognitive Functioning: Developmental Issues*

Douglas Vickers: *Decision Processes in Visual Perception*

Margaret A. Hagen (Ed.): *The Perception of Pictures, Vol. 1: Alberti's Window: The Projective Model of Pictorial Information, Vol. 2 Dürer's Devices: Beyond the Projective Model of Pictures*

Graham Davies, Hadyn Ellis and John Shepherd (Eds.): *Perceiving and Remembering Faces*

in preparation

Hubert Dolezal: *Living in a World Transformed: Perceptual and Performatory Adaptation to Visual Distortion*

Gerald H. Jacobs: *Comparative Color Vision*

Perceiving and Remembering Faces

edited by

GRAHAM DAVIES, HADYN ELLIS
AND JOHN SHEPHERD

Department of Psychology
King's College
University of Aberdeen
Scotland

1981

ACADEMIC PRESS
A Subsidiary of Harcourt Brace Jovanovich, Publishers
LONDON NEW YORK TORONTO SYDNEY SAN FRANCISCO

ACADEMIC PRESS INC. (LONDON) LTD.
24/28 Oval Road,
London NW1

United States Edition published by
ACADEMIC PRESS INC.
111 Fifth Avenue
New York, New York 10003

British Library Cataloguing in Publication Data

Perceiving and remembering faces.   BF
  1. Visual perception
I. Davies, G.   II. Ellis, H.   241
III. Shepherd, J.
152.1′4   BF241   P39
  ISBN 0–12–206220–5   1981
  LCCCN 81–66698

Phototypesetting by Oxford Publishing Services, Oxford
Printed in Great Britain by T.J. Press (Padstow) Ltd.,
Padstow, Cornwall

*For
Heather, Diane
and Jean*

Contributors

GEORGE W. BATTEN, Jr
  Department of Electrical Engineering, University of Houston, Houston, Texas 77004, USA

SUSAN CAREY
  Department of Psychology, Massachusetts Institute of Technology, Cambridge, Massachusetts 02139, USA

JUNE E. CHANCE
  Department of Psychology, University of Missouri, Columbia, Missouri 65211, USA

GRAHAM M. DAVIES
  Department of Psychology, University of Aberdeen, King's College, Aberdeen AB9 2UB, Scotland

KENNETH A. DEFFENBACHER
  Department of Psychology, University of Nebraska at Omaha, Nebraska 68182, USA

HADYN D. ELLIS
  Department of Psychology, University of Aberdeen, King's College, Aberdeen AB9 2UB, Scotland

HENRY HECAEN
  Unité de Recherches Neuropsychologiques et Neurolinguistiques (u.111) de L'INSERM, Centre de Recherches de L'Institut National de la Santé et de la Recherche Médicale sur les Maladies du Système Nerveux Central, 2 Rue D'Alésia, 75014, Paris, France

JULIE HORNEY
  Department of Criminal Justice, University of Nebraska at Omaha, Omaha, Nebraska 68182, USA

ALVIN G. GOLDSTEIN
  Department of Psychology, University of Missouri, Columbia, Missouri 65211, USA

KENNETH R. LAUGHERY
  Department of Psychology, University of Houston, Houston, Texas 77004, USA

ROY S. MALPASS
  Behavioral Science Program, State University of New York, Plattsburgh, New York 12901, USA

Contributors

BEN T. RHODES
  Department of Industrial Engineering, Cullen College of Engineering, University of Houston, Houston, Texas 77004, USA
ERIC A. SALZEN
  Department of Psychology, University of Aberdeen, King's College, Aberdeen AB9 2UB, Scotland
JOHN W. SHEPHERD
  Department of Psychology, University of Aberdeen, King's College, Aberdeen AB9 2UB, Scotland

Preface

When Academic Press suggested that we write a book on face research, we readily agreed to do so. We then decided that, rather than describe, often at second hand, the kinds of work being done in this area, it would be better to invite a selection of people prominent in this field both to discuss past research and also to describe any new and unpublished studies of their own. We felt that this approach would reduce the inevitable datedness of most textbooks, which so often lag by two or three years behind the work currently to be found in journals. This is a particular danger in an area, like face research, which has a rapidly growing literature, but we believe that this edited collection of contributions is as up-to-date and as representative as possible.

After the introductory chapter, the book is divided into two sections: there are seven chapters concerned with theory, and four devoted to applications of face research. However, any division into theory and applied fields in psychology is bound to be somewhat arbitrary and it will be obvious that they overlap quite considerably, producing mutually illuminating findings and sharing many common problems.

The section on theory and data contains chapters by the editors including topics such as feature saliency, individual differences in face memory and models of face recognition, all of which have been areas of research that have dominated work at Aberdeen University over the last decade. Henry Hécaen reviews related work on the anatomy of face-processing mechanisms, much of which he pioneered over twenty years ago. Alvin Goldstein and his wife June Chance have also long been engaged in face-related research. Their chapter, on laboratory studies of facial memory, represents only a small part of their extensive and seminal work. Susan Carey examines the development of face memory skills and relates this to theories of the processing of faces, arguing from her own work that changes in strategy occur at a critical period. The theory section also contains a chapter by Eric Salzen, who covers the field of emotional expression from a comparative standpoint.

In the applied section some aspects of forensic psychology are

examined. Graham Davies evaluates various methods for enabling witnesses to recall a suspect's face. The interdisciplinary group of Ken
Laughery, Ben Rhodes and George Batten looks at ways of storing and
retrieving mug-shots from a computer store, and in doing so report
results from their own recent work in this growth area. Kenneth
Deffenbacher and Julie Horney discuss some of the manifold problems
associated with identity parades currently attracting so much attention
from both psychologists and lawyers. The last chapter in the applied
section is by Roy Malpass who concentrates on methods of improving
memory for faces. This particular topic may be of importance for police
practice, particularly in training cross-racial identification strategies,
but it is relevant to anyone with a need to improve recognition.

This book covers most of the theoretical and applied aspects of
perceiving and remembering faces that are of contemporary interest.
Inevitably there are gaps and omissions. Doubtless other editors would
have made slightly different selections. However, we hope this will
prove to be a comprehensive survey that will apprize readers of much
existing knowledge in the area, and will encourage others to join us in a
worthwhile endeavour.

February 1981   GRAHAM DAVIES
                                                         HADYN ELLIS
                                                         JOHN SHEPHERD

Acknowledgements

Many hands have contributed to the production of this book, besides those of the Editors. Our first thanks go to our fellow contributors who have dealt promptly and courteously with our requests and queries. A major debt of gratitude is also owed to Jean Shepherd who took on the burdensome task of proof reading successive drafts of manuscripts and compiling the bibliography.

We would also like to take this opportunity of thanking all those who have assisted our own research efforts, the fruits of which are described in our individual contributions to the book. The Department of Psychology, University of Aberdeen, under Professors Fraser, Symons and Salzen has provided a hospitable home and excellent technical and secretarial services. The Police Scientific Development Branch of the Home Office, the Home Office Research Unit and the Social Science Research Council have all funded various aspects of our work. Our research has been greatly facilitated by the assistance of Sue Batt, Donald Christie, Martin Cooper, Janice Freeman, Rhona Flin, Douglas Forbes, Dennis Hay, Pat MacDonald, Mary McMurran, Jean Shepherd and Mary Simpson, all of whom have been associated with different projects over the years. It is only through such combinations of technical and administrative support, adequate finance and expert assistance, that psychologists can ever hope to understand how we perceive and remember faces.

February 1981   GRAHAM DAVIES
                                                            HADYN ELLIS
                                                            JOHN SHEPHERD

Contents

APPLICATIONS

1 Introduction[1]

Hadyn D. Ellis

No other object in the visual world is quite so important to us as the human face. Not only does it establish a person's identity, but also, through its paramount role in communication, it commands our almost continuous attention. The significance of the face has long been a topic for speculation by philosophers and artists concerned with character and aesthetics. When William Hogarth wrote in his "Analysis of Beauty" (1753) that "The face is the index of the mind", he was voicing a fairly common belief of the time. But Hogarth also acknowledged another aspect of faces and our ability to discriminate them when he advocated a "methodical enquiry" into the observation that "out of the great number of faces that have been form'd since the creation of the world, no two have been so exactly alike, but that the usual and common eye would discover a difference between them".

It was nearly 100 years before the physiognomy prevailing in Hogarth's time gave way to a more objective analysis of faces by men such as Darwin and Galton. However, even after their pioneering work interest in the study of faces largely waned, and, for another century, research into the topic was sporadic and unsystematic. Recently though, there has been a definite renewal of interest which has been brought about by several theoretical and practical movements in psychology that have made face related research quite popular.

An indication of this new interest is given by the number of published papers concerned with face recognition which has grown dramatically of late, from a pre-1950 average of about 20 each decade to well over 600 papers in the 1970s. As a result of all this activity we now have a great

[1] I am delighted to acknowledge the assistance of Colin Gray, Jean Shepherd, Suzanne Dziurawiec and Diane Ellis in the preparation of this introduction.

deal of information about various aspects of the processes of perceiving and remembering faces and the object of this book is to present reviews of some of the most significant directions of research in these areas and to indicate where they may lead over the next decade or so.

Contemporary interest in faces lies partly in the fact that they constitute a natural class of subjects, thus standing in contrast to the simple and artificial stimuli characteristic of so much psychological research in the past. In contrast, faces are complex, multidimensional and, above all, meaningful visual stimuli. In addition, they are plastic rather than rigid in form. As Gombrich (1972) in his discussion of "physiognomic constancy" points out, "We have not one face but a thousand different faces", a variability owing much to the fact that human beings have more separate muscles in their face than any other animal (Liggett, 1974; Attenborough, 1979). These considerations present the researcher with compelling questions regarding the range and stereotypy of facial movements; as well as provoking speculations concerning facial schemata that allow faces transformed by pose, changes of expression, or even the processes of ageing, to be correctly identified. Unfortunately perhaps, such dynamic aspects of face perception have largely been ignored by researchers who, for convenience, have used static two-dimensional photographs as research material and, in doing so, may have overlooked an important dimension of the underlying cognitive structures. An increasing use of moving films of faces rather than photographs will surely be a feature of future research. Nevertheless, even static snapshots of faces have provided valuable material for, as Brunswik (1956) remarked, "the face constitutes as tight a package of innumerable variables as might be found anywhere in cognitive research". This richness, together with their undeniable importance has made the study of human faces almost a discipline of its own. Although, like other common psychological stimuli, faces are employed as a means of uncovering underlying mental processes, they are also studied as an end in themselves.

Some of this research using facial stimuli has investigated the development of discriminative capacity, charting the limits of our aptitude for interpreting nuances of facial expression and our ability to recognize people after various intervals of time. Generally speaking, we show great facility in reading and retaining facial images and this confers obvious biological advantages to such a pre-eminently social being as Man.

Another approach to looking at the efficiency of face-processing mechanisms has been to investigate the conditions and situations in which people's ability to handle physiognomic information is reduced or impaired. This may arise from brain damage which can either entirely remove the ability to recognize previously familiar faces, or disrupt interpretations of facial expressions (Bornstein, 1963). Alternatively, the handicap may be caused by less specific disabilities, such as autism and dyslexia. (Autism appears to affect the way in which faces are examined and, in turn, minimizes the uptake of social information contained within them—Langdell, 1978; Pontius, 1976, claims that dyslexia is sometimes associated with a rather primitive perception of faces.) Interestingly, Levin and Benton (1977) used face discrimination tests to differentiate patients with psychiatric disorders from those with brain disease when the symptoms had been initially difficult to distinguish. While the performance of neurological cases was impaired in the face task, that of functional psychiatric patients was quite normal.

Most of us find it relatively difficult to interpret and memorize faces of people from other races. This highlights the probable importance of learning in the development of the skills involved in the efficient labelling and classification of faces to form effective facial schemata (Goldstein and Chance, 1980). Just how much these physiognomic information-processing skills owe to learning, however, remains to be established. The existence of universal facial expressions suggests that much of that part of the process may be largely innate (Trevarthen, 1980). Similarly, the fact that very young infants appear to attend to faces in preference to other stimuli, and soon learn reliably to discriminate among them has led some to suppose that the face-recognition mechanism is present at birth (Tzavaras *et al.*, 1970). There is a dispute, however, as to whether perceiving and remembering faces are truly innate cognitive capacities—an issue which is part of a larger psychological debate, and, as in other areas of inquiry, it is difficult to resolve.

One recent set of experiments is worth noting, however, not because their results necessarily resolve the nature/nurture issue—indeed they have proved difficult to replicate—but because they concern a much more dynamic interplay between a baby and another person. Meltzoff and Moore (1977) observed babies of a few weeks (and even as young as one hour) imitating facial gestures. This suggests that young infants not only can extract meaningful information from faces, but are able to link this information to some sort of internalized motor image of their own faces. It is difficult to see how this ability could be acquired by a process of learning in such a short time.

This leads me to anticipate the related question addressed by some of the contributors to this volume concerning the possibility that the ability to process physiognomic information is not only innate, but involves a special mechanism specifically designed to handle only facial images. This fascinating line of inquiry cannot yet be said to have reached a definite conclusion; but recent evidence for the presence of cells in the temporal lobe of the rhesus monkey that only respond to facial images (Perrett *et al.*, 1979), though not by itself conclusive, may provide a means by which the issue may eventually be resolved.

Indeed, the use of single-cell recording techniques may enable answers to emerge not only to questions of innate versus learned face-specific systems, but also determine the interdependence of face recognition and interpretation of emotional expression. It is known that, following organic brain damage, one faculty can be impaired while the other remains intact (Kurucz and Feldmar, 1979). Although the extent of their independence has not been fully explored, Walker-Smith (1980) has recently presented evidence to suggest that memory for face structure and memory for expression display different decay functions—thus giving some support for Lewis Carroll's whimsical notion in "Alice in Wonderland" of a cat without a grin and a grin without a cat!

It would be easy to over-emphasize the biological approach to face processing so I shall quickly move on to discuss some of the other cognitive, social and applied research activities that are currently attracting interest, and which are discussed more fully in later chapters of this book.

The cognitive approach to face processing has many aspects, some of which will be met in the chapters in the section on theory and data. There it will be apparent that, although no shortage of effort has been expended in this field, we have only a few undisputed facts to show for it. We know, for example, that facial images are quickly processed, with particular attention being paid to upper features; and that they can be later recognized quite well despite small transformations even after very long intervals. Furthermore, it has been observed that changes in the viewing context between presentation of a face and testing for its recognition may disrupt identification, a condition that in everyday life can give rise to the frustrating experience of knowing a face to be familiar but being unable to place it precisely—an observation with interesting theoretical ramifications (Mandler, 1980). Just how a facial image is matched to its corresponding internal representation remains a mystery, however, principally because we know so little about the organization of face memory.

The role of familiarity or repeated experience of a particular face is an important and related consideration and, despite the fact that some research has been published in which performance with familiar and unfamiliar faces has been contrasted, comparatively little effort has been directed at discovering what exactly is involved in becoming familiar with a face. The procedures whereby people get to know particular faces, and how throughout childhood they develop the cognitive strategies required for processing and storing large numbers of them, are also interesting topics of research. Similarly, the personal attributes of good face recognizers have long been of interest but the results of experiments on individual differences are rather inconclusive. What is not disputed, however, is that the act of judging a face along some social dimension such as honesty is a first-class way of improving face memory (Bower and Karlin, 1974). Why this should be so remains speculative, but implicit use of such strategies may underlie some of the individual differences reported.

The emotional or affective impact that a face makes on us may also determine the likelihood of subsequent recognition (Shepherd and Ellis, 1973). Such results may also arise because of storage and retrieval factors, but, equally they may reflect changes in our arousal level at the time of viewing, which in turn may affect memory consolidation. This factor in face research has received little attention and yet may well underlie some discrepancies between results from theoretical and applied investigations. For example, all too often experiments on the accuracy of eye-witness evidence reveal a somewhat lower level of performance than would be predicted from laboratory-based evidence. This problem which has important legal implications is currently undergoing investigation in numerous laboratories, and there is already some tentative evidence that the degree of excitement felt by witnesses to an incident affects their subsequent ability to select the person involved from a lineup (Shepherd *et al.*, 1980).

Another practical aspect of facial memory that has stimulated interesting research involves the quest for a suitable technique to help witnesses to a crime to recall a suspect's face. This has proved problematical—partly because our ability to recall faces is poor compared with our ability to recognize them, and partly because all existing systems require a piecemeal approach in constructing a facial image which may not be consistent with the holistic internal representation that some believe to be the basis for face memory (e.g. Baddeley, 1979). A topic that is related to this concerns ways of improving facial recognition ability. Leonardo da Vinci advocated a technique whereby the observer should pay attention to separate facial features. While this has been echoed by several contemporary writers, as mentioned earlier, there is some evidence that it may be better to consider the face as a whole rather than fragment it. This is but one example of a pervasive theme in this book: the interdependence of theoretical and practical aspects of facial research.

Theory and Data

2   The Development of Face Perception

Susan Carey

1   INTRODUCTION

A great deal of information is read from a face. Foremost, we tell who somebody is from his or her face (of course, there are other sources of relevant information, such as voice, clothing, gait, body size and shape). But much more than a person's identity is read from a face—mood and momentary emotion and a host of other properties such as sex, age, health and character. This chapter will concentrate almost exclusively on face recognition in the sense of identifying individuals by their faces.

Our capacity to recognize faces has two aspects—first, the productive ability to encode an unfamiliar face and second, the ability to recognize that face subsequently. I will use the phrase "encoding an unfamiliar face" to refer to the dual process of forming a representation of a new face and storing that representation in memory. Thus, "encoding" means roughly the same as "making familiar". "Recognition" will refer to matching a representation of a new instance with a representation already stored in memory.

Normal adults are extremely skilled both at encoding new faces and at recognition of those faces that have been encoded. Bahrick *et al.* (1975) asked subjects to pick the familiar face from among five. One of the five came from the subject's own high school yearbook; the rest were from other yearbooks of the same period. Recognition rates were not only over 90%, they were independent of class size (from 90 to 800) and of time elapsed between graduation and test (from 3 months to 35 years). Thus, in a 3- or 4-year period, and without conscious effort, high school students can make 800 faces familiar as easily as they can encode 90. Even more astoundingly, they can recognize those faces years later as well as they can a few months later, indicating that learning new faces does not interfere with the representations of those already in memory. The limits of this enormous but everyday capacity, if any, have not been found.

This chapter concerns the acquisition of face encoding and face recognition skills. Section 1 shows that the roots of the adult capacity are intact at least by 6 or 7 months of age, and considers the relation between the encoding of individual faces and the perception of faces as faces. Section 2 indicates that in spite of the impressive achievements in infancy, it is not until around age 10 that children approach the adults' level of ability to encode unfamiliar faces. Of most concern in section 2 is characterization of just what is developing between the ages of 7 months and 10 years. Section 3 shows a temporary decline in face encoding skills at around ages 12 and 13. Section 4 traces the acquisition of skill at recognition of familiar faces, reporting another anomaly occurring in adolescence. Section 5 traces the development of right-hemisphere specialization for face encoding. Finally, in section 6, explanations for the exact course of development are sought. The possibility is raised that genetic, maturational factors partially determine the details of the developmental curve.

2 FACE PERCEPTION IN INFANCY

Although most of this chapter will concern the psychological processes of encoding and recognizing individual faces, the beginning of the story in infancy inevitably concerns the representation of a face as a face. When does the child distinguish faces from other objects and on what basis does he or she first make this distinction?

A *Seeing a face as a face*

Very young infants reliably prefer to look at some stimuli over others. This fact allows psychologists to know which visual discriminations the child can make. Early studies using the technique of preferential looking demonstrated that infants as young as 2 weeks will look at a human face in preference to many other stimuli (e.g. Stechler, 1964; Fantz, 1966). Forty newborns (average age, 9 minutes) tracked a moving schematic face more than three similar stimuli (Gosen *et al.*,

1975)! However, mere preference for faces does not mean that the face is being seen "as a face". Differences in visual complexity, contrast within the stimulus, brightness, and a host of other properties might be responsible for the preference. Indeed, it is only at 15–16 weeks that the child clearly distinguishes the proper arrangement of features from a scrambled face (McCall and Kagan, 1967; Caron *et al.*, 1973; Haaf, 1977, but see also Thomas, 1973). And it is only at this age that an upright face is preferred to an inverted face (Watson, 1966; McGurk, 1970; Fagan, 1972). Haaf and Bell (1964) provide a particularly elegant demonstration of a change between 10 and 15 weeks. They constructed two sets of stimuli—one graded in complexity alone (by the addition of internal contour) and one graded in complexity and in face-likeness (by the addition of internal contour that matched the configuration of a schematic face). For 10-week-old infants, the increase in complexity within each series led to an *equal* increase of preferential looking; no effect of increasing face-likeness could be discerned in addition to the effect of mere increasing complexity. Thus, it appears that the whole configuration of a face is not represented (or at least is not governing preferential looking) until the fourth month of life. This conclusion is confirmed by results from a dishabituation paradigm (Caron *et al.*, 1973). Younger infants did not notice changes in mouth–nose configurations, while they did notice changes in hairline and eyes.

Let us grant that the child does not represent the entire internal configuration of faces until 3 to 4 months. Nonetheless, as stimuli with particular meaning, faces may be distinguished from other stimuli well before this time. Indeed, there is unequivocal evidence that they are. Tronick *et al.* (1975) showed that 8-week-old infants are disturbed by totally immobile real faces, but not by other unmoving stimuli. Presumably infants this young already expect faces to move. Monitoring eye movements, several studies have documented a change at around 8 weeks in scanning patterns as infants look at faces. Four-week-old infants, when they look at the face at all, tend to fixate edges. At around two months there is a shift to scanning the internal features of the face, especially the eyes (Bergman *et al.*, 1971; Maurer and Salapatek, 1976; Hainline, 1978). Hainline (1978) showed that this effect required that the eyes be part of a face, for no similar shift took place in the infant's scan of Fig. 1. In sum, at least by 8 weeks the face has special meaning to an infant, and eyes especially draw his gaze. This study, together with those reviewed above (especially Caron *et al.*, 1973), shows "eyes within a face" have meaning well before the child represents the total facial configuration.

FIG. 1. Non-face stimulus (redrawn from Hainline, 1978).

B *Recognition of a particular face*

When do infants distinguish the face of their mother figure from other faces? Maurer and Salapatek (1976) found that 4-week-old infants look significantly less at their mother's face than at the face of a strange male or strange female. In their study the faces were immobile; presumably gaze aversion from the mother's face was due to the infant's discomfort at seeing his or her mother stony-faced and unresponsive. Maurer and Salapatek comment that the infant's representation of his or her mother's face is probably based on hairlines and chins because the 4-week-old infants rarely look elsewhere. While Maurer and Salapatek provide evidence for the youngest age (so far)[1] at which a particular face

[1] There is evidence that the child distinguishes his mother from other people earlier than 4 weeks but on other bases than her face (e.g. voice, odour of breast milk).

is recognized, other paradigms also show the mother's face discriminated from other faces very early. Fitzgerald (1968) found differential pupillary dilation to videotapes of a mother's face compared to a stranger's at 17 weeks. Of course, we do not know what features of the mother's face are the basis of the 17-week-old's recognition.

Thus, forming a representation of at least one particular face parallels forming a representation of faces in general. Faces are distinguished from other stimuli in the first few months of life, and at the same time the mother's face is distinguished from other faces. But neither of these discriminations (faces from non-faces, mother's face from other faces) are first based on the total facial configuration. Indeed, since there is no evidence that the infant can distinguish scrambled from unscrambled faces or notice absent features until 14–16 weeks, it would be extremely unlikely that the infant could distinguish individuals from each other on the basis of differences within internal facial configuration before that age.

C Encoding new faces

A young infant has had hours and hours of exposure to his or her mother's face. Here we will be concerned with the baby's capacity for encoding new faces from relatively brief exposures. As I will show in this section, the 5-month-old is quite competent at face encoding, but on the basis of relatively superficial properties of faces. By 7 months there is no doubt that new faces are encoded in terms of some aspects of internal facial configurations. In the period from 5 to 7 months the roots of all of the salient characteristics of the adult face encoding capacity emerge.

Dirks and Gibson (1977) presented 5-month-old infants with six or seven 20-second exposures to a live face during which habituation was obtained. These exposures were followed by a 20-second exposure to a life-size coloured photograph. They found no dishabituation if the photograph depicted the same person, or a person of the same sex, hairstyle and hair colour. Dishabituation was observed, in contrast, if the photograph depicted a person of a different sex, hair colour and hairstyle. This study shows that a still colour photograph is sufficient for recognition of a face that has been encoded from a moving person. It also demonstrates that exposure for approximately 120 seconds to such stimulation is sufficient for encoding a face, but that the face is represented in terms of gross features (probably hairstyle), not on the basis of subtle properties of the facial configuration.

Many other studies of 4- and 5-month-old infants establish that infants of this age can discriminate photographs of highly dissimilar faces. Fagan (1972) and Cornell (1974) showed a man's face could be discriminated from a woman's; Miranda and Fantz (1974) showed a woman's face could be discriminated from a baby's. The infants in these studies were 5-months-old, and the stimuli black-and-white stills. Cohen *et al.* (1977) showed that a colour slide of a woman was distinguished both from that of a man and that of a baby by 18-week-old infants. These studies demonstrate that a representation can be encoded from a still photograph by these young infants, a representation at least adequate to distinguish that face from very different ones. Presumably, as in the Dirks' and Gibson study (1977), features such as hairstyle are the basis of the discrimination. Fagan (1976) showed that 5-month-old babies could discriminate 3/4 view (black-and-white stills) of two men judged highly dissimilar by the adult subjects of Goldstein *et al.* (1971). Babies of the same age cannot discriminate 3/4 views of two men judged highly similar, but 7-month-olds can.[1] The highly dissimilar faces differed in many ways—one man was thin, long-nosed, with a full head of black hair; the other was fat, round-faced, and bald. The highly similar faces shared the same overall head shape and hairstyle. Thus, by 7 months, infants apparently are able to encode unfamiliar faces from black-and-white photographs on the basis of the internal features of the face.

Photographs of unfamiliar faces seem to be encoded by 5-month-old infants in terms of features such as hairstyle. The question arises whether the fact the stimulus is a face plays any role in its representation—after all, a thick head of curly hair might be discriminable from straight, pulled back hair even when not in the context of a face. Observations of Fagan's (1972) suggest that "face-ness" matters. Under conditions in which upright photographs of men, women, and babies are discriminated by 5 months, inverted photographs are not. And under the conditions in which upright 3/4 views of highly similar faces are discriminated by 7-month-old infants, the same stimuli inverted are not (Fagan, 1979). (The difficulty with inverted faces is not absolute—with longer inspection times both 5- and 7-month-olds could distinguish inverted stimuli.) As meaningless stimuli, upright and inverted faces present equal complexity, symmetry, even the same relations among the parts. That young infants find it more difficult to encode inverted than upright faces may have one of two interpretations. First, all stimuli

[1] Fagan's technique is a little different from a pure habituation paradigm; an infant looks at a face for some time and then is presented with that face paired with another. Preference for the novel stimulus is evidence that the infant successfully encoded the original face and that he or she can distinguish that face from the one it is paired with.

may tend to be scanned from top to bottom, and the distinguishing features the infant uses to tell the faces apart may just happen to be at the top of the upright face. Second, the infant may use what he has represented about faces (in general) in encoding a new one, and be unable to bring to bear this knowledge for inverted faces. An inverted face, in some sense, is not a face. Several considerations favour the second interpretation. We know from the preference literature that upright, unscrambled faces are preferred and missing internal features noticed by 15 weeks. This means that the infant has represented the configuration of an upright face, and thus it is available in the encoding of a particular new face. Also, eye movement data do not indicate differential scanning of the tops of faces even by children under 7 weeks. Finally, Fagan's highly similar faces could not be discriminated on the basis of hairstyle (a salient top-of-the-head distinguishing property). Yet the inversion effect was found with these stimuli too. In conclusion, then, it seems that even when an infant is capable of distinguishing unfamiliar faces only when they are grossly different, 'faceness" plays a role in the encoding.

An adult encodes a face seen in a still photograph in sufficiently abstract terms to be able to recognize other photographs of that face taken from different angles of view. Results from two types of para-digms indicate that 7-month-old infants also have this ability. Fagan (1976) showed that infants habituated to either a profile or a 3/4 view of a person's face preferred to look at a different person when presented with two front views (see also Cohen *et al.*, 1977). Fagan (1976) also showed that for 7-month-olds, seeing two different views of the same face facilitates telling that face from another. This effect demands that the baby represented the two different inspection poses in terms of some common features.

Once an adult has mentally represented a face, that representation is stable in two related senses: it is fairly permanent and is interfered with little, if at all, by the representation of new faces. The roots of these two characteristics of the adult's encoding capacity are also found in very young infants. Fagan (1973) used his preferential looking technique to show relative permanence—5-month-olds retained a representation of a photographed face for 1, 2, 7, and 14 days. Cohen *et al.* (1977) showed non-interference—once 18-week-olds were habituated to a colour photograph of a woman's face, they remained habituated to that face even after viewing a man's face and a baby's face. Fagan (1977) also demonstrated conditions under which viewing new faces did not inter-fere with faces already represented, although there were conditions under which interference was observed.

In summary, by 4- to 5-months of age the infant can encode still photographs of faces, such that the resulting representations are stable. While faces are encoded in terms of very crude distinguishing features at this age (similar faces cannot be distinguished), nonetheless, the faceness of the stimulus plays a role in the encoding process (inverted photographs are less successfully encoded). By age 7 months, highly similar faces can be distinguished and facial invariance across different poses represented. Strikingly, then, most aspects of human face encoding skills are present by 7 months of age.

3 FACE ENCODING—AGES 2 TO 10

A *Measures of improvement*

The very impressive achievements by infants as young as 5–7 months must not be misinterpreted. Development of face encoding skills is far from completed in infancy. The performance of young children (8 years and under) on face encoding tasks, relative to that of 10-year-olds and adults, is very poor,

When the child is past infancy, standard recognition memory paradigms can be adapted for the study of face encoding. In the prototypical experiment, several photographs are each presented for some fixed time and the subject is told to study them because he will have to recognize them later. There follows a series of recognition trials in which photographs are presented either one at a time or in pairs and the subject instructed to indicate the people who were pictured in the inspection series. For young toddlers this procedure must be modified somewhat. In our work the child is shown a desired object hidden in an envelope with a particular picture on it. He then must find that particular envelope again among two with similar pictures. This procedure removes the requirement that the child understand complicated instructions.

It does not make sense to ask how good (in absolute terms) people at different ages are at encoding new faces. Performance at all ages is affected by a host of variables, including the exposure conditions (length of inspection, still versus moving faces, single versus multiple views), the size of the inspection set, the transformations in the targets between inspection and recognition trials, and the characteristics of the distractors. It *does* make sense to hold all these variables constant and ask how performance changes with age. When this is done, percentage correct (or d') increases markedly in the years from 5 to 10 (e.g.

Goldstein and Chance, 1964; Kagan and Klein, 1973; Carey and Diamond, 1977; Diamond and Carey, 1977; Blaney and Winograd, 1978; Carey, Diamond and Wood, 1980; Flin, 1980).

Another quantitative indication of developmental improvement at face encoding is obtained when performance level is held constant and other variables manipulated so that children at different ages may achieve the particular performance level. For example, Carey, Diamond, Ginsburg and Jaaskela (unpublished data) held forced-choice recognition level at 85% for still photographs of male MIT faculty members. Two- and 3-year-olds could achieve this performance level only at set-size 1 (one inspection item followed immediately by the forced-choice item). Four-year-olds managed at an average set-size of 2·5; 5-year-olds at set-size 6; 6-year-olds at set-size 7 and 10-year-olds at set-size 10.

Still another dramatic indication of poor performance by 6-year-olds relative to adults is obtained when set size and performance level are held constant and exposure times during inspection varied. Six-year-olds exposed for 5 seconds to each inspection photograph failed to match the d' of adults exposed to each inspection photograph for 250 ms (Carey, Diamond and Jaaskela, unpublished data).

In addition to recognition/memory paradigms, face encoding skills may also be assessed in simultaneous matching tasks. Subjects are required to judge whether two photographs of faces differing in clothing, angle of lighting, expression, angle of view, and so on, depict the same person. Such judgements require that the photographs be encoded sufficiently abstractly so that the identity of the models can be seen in spite of the differences. Several studies of this sort confirm the improvement in skill between ages 6 and 10 (Saltz and Sigel, 1967; Benton and Van Allen, 1973; Diamond and Carey, 1977; Carey, Diamond and Woods, 1980). Diamond and Carey (1977) also showed the simultaneous matching performance and immediate recognition memory for the same materials were virtually identical in pattern of errors and overall error rates, suggesting that both tasks involve face encoding in the same ways.

In summary, children of 8 and under are very bad at encoding unfamiliar faces. By 10 they approach, if they do not actually achieve, the normal adult level. Performance steadily improves from 2 to 10 years of age. So far there are no surprises. For any skill whatsoever, there will be some age at which performance will be poor, compared to that of adults, and some age at which the adult competence is approximated. It would be surprising if face encoding did not improve in the years between 2 and 10.

The data summarized so far leave open just what is developing. As reviewed above, a 6-year-old recognizes few (e.g. 60%) of the inspection faces under conditions in which a 10-year-old recognizes many (e.g. 95%, Carey and Diamond, 1977). Clearly, the older child encodes the faces in terms of distinguishing properties more adequate to the problem of discrimination than does the younger child. The 6-year-old's performance on these same faces improves with smaller inspection set sizes, even though the distractors in the forced choice pairs are the same. Therefore, the poor performance of young children must be partly due to interference effects. Interference effects are greater the more similar the stimuli to be encoded are to each other. But similarity of stimuli is relative to the features in terms of which those stimuli are encoded. The set-size effect, then, reflects the same developmental fact as does the simple improvement in performance level at a given set size. For younger children, still photographs of faces are more similar to each other than they are for older children, and this must be because the younger child encodes unfamiliar faces in terms of less adequate distinguishing properties. The simultaneous matching results point to the same conclusion: young children are less able than older children to encode unfamiliar faces in terms of the properties that reflect identity across various changes in the stimulus (angle of view, clothing, hairstyle, lighting, and so forth).

The point being made here may seem vacuous—performance improves because the stimuli are encoded in terms of more adequate properties, where "more adequate" means nothing more than yielding better performance. Obviously, to go any further we must try to specify more fully the developmental changes in properties in terms of which faces are encoded. Are these qualitative changes? To what extent do the changes reflect the development of general pattern encoding and memory processes and to what extent do they reflect the acquisition of knowledge of faces, *per se*? I will take up the latter question first.

B *What is developing?*

The period from 5 to 10 is clearly one in which memorial and metamemorial abilities develop (e.g. Brown, 1975; Flavell, 1977) and appears also to be a time when the efficiency of pattern recognition is increasing (e.g. Vurpillot, 1976). Perhaps, improved face encoding during childhood is due entirely to acquisition of such general skills. The developmental course of the encoding of inverted faces is relevant to this hypothesis. As abstract meaningless patterns, inverted and upright faces do not differ and thus both present the same problems for an all-purpose pattern encoding mechanism. A recognition paradigm with inverted faces as stimuli provides the same scope for general memorial and metamemorial strategies as does the same paradigm with upright stimuli. Goldstein (1965) showed that face-letter paired associates were less readily learned by 7- and 8-year-old children than by adults overall, but that adults differed from the children far more when the faces were upright than when they were inverted. Using a simple forced-choice recognition paradigm, it has been found in two studies that 10-year-olds do not differ from 6-year-olds on the encoding of inverted faces, even though usual improvement on upright faces was observed (Carey and Diamond, 1977; Carey *et al.*, 1980). The acquisition of face encoding skills during these years is reflected in more accurate processing of upright faces alone. Presumably, this processing recruits knowledge of faces, *per se*, knowledge that cannot be efficiently applied to the encoding of inverted faces.

As students of child development well know, it is dangerous to interpret a young child's failure to recruit some knowledge in a particular task as indicating that he or she lacks that knowledge. Perhaps 6-year-olds could encode upright faces as well as 10-year-olds, but the instruction "Look at the faces carefully, so you'll be able to tell which ones you've seen before" fails to elicit their most efficient encoding strategies. This is unlikely, given the range of paradigms yielding relatively poor performance by 6-year-olds, but a direct test of the hypothesis is warranted. Encoding efficiency in adults can be manipulated by instructions that direct attention to the whole face, requiring judgements of character (e.g. honesty, likeableness, of whom the person remind one) rather than judgements on the basis of piecemeal properties (e.g. sex of the person). Later recognition is better for faces judged for the former type of property during encoding than for those judged for the latter (Bower and Karlin, 1974; Warrington and Ackroyd, 1975; Patterson and Baddeley, 1977; see also Goldstein, this volume). Instructional manipulation that induces efficient encoding strategies is known to improve performance of young children on verbal memory tasks, greatly decreasing differences between younger and older children (cf. Flavell, 1977, for a review). If poor face encoding in young children results from the failure to exploit knowledge the child in fact possesses, then requiring the child to judge faces for likeableness during encoding might decrease the differences in encoding success between 6- and 10-year-olds (relative to their performance in a task which involved discriminating between male and female faces). This experiment has now been done twice; both studies found the expected effect of encoding instructions (models judged for likeableness during

encoding were subsequently better recognized than models judged for
their sex). And both studies found no age by instructions interaction.
Likeableness judgments during encoding did *not* decrease the developmental differences between 6- and 10-year-olds relative to judgments of
sex (Blaney and Winograd, 1978; Carey *et al.*, 1980).

Thus, two different kinds of results support the proposition that
knowledge of faces, *per se*, is acquired before the age of 10, and that the
acquisition of this knowledge accounts for most of the improvement in
face encoding during these years. General pattern encoding, memory,
and metamemory development would be reflected in improvement in
the encoding of inverted faces, but such improvement is very slight
compared to that in encoding upright faces. Also, instructions that
maximize efficient encoding of upright faces did not diminish the
comparative advantage of 10-year-olds over 6-year-olds, suggesting that
young children actually lack the requisite encoding skills, rather than
that they merely fail to exploit them in standard recognition paradigms.

How might we conceptualize the encoding skills acquired in these
years? In encoding a previously unfamiliar face, a representation must
be formed adequate to distinguish that face not only from all others
already represented in memory but from other faces one might encounter in the future. Properties that distinguish one face from another
vary in the degree to which they involve the entire face. Relatively
piecemeal distinguishing properties such as "bushy eyebrows" or
"moustache" contrast with relatively configurational properties such as
"large, wide-set eyes for such a long, narrow face". Several lines of
evidence suggest that young children differ from older children and
adults in terms of what kind of information from an unfamiliar face is
represented during encoding, such that young children represent relatively more piecemeal properties and relatively fewer configuration
properties. There is reason to believe that the encoding of configurational properties is more likely to be adversely affected by stimulus
inversion than is the encoding of piecemeal properties (see Carey,
1978). If the young child relies more on relatively isolated information,
his performance should be affected less by inversion than is the older
child's, as is the case (Goldstein, 1975; Carey and Diamond, 1977;
Carey *et al.*, 1980). Further, Diamond and Carey (1977) provided direct
evidence that 6- and 8-year-olds encode unfamiliar faces in terms of
such relatively isolated features as hats and eyeglasses. Identification
problems were constructed in which facial expression and garb were
confounded with identity of the models. Reliance exclusively on either
expression or on paraphernalia as a basis for person identification would
lead, therefore, to a distinctive pattern of errors. When photographs of

two different persons matched in paraphernalia were presented, 6- and 8-year-olds judged them the same person. By age 10 this tendency was less frequent, and by age 12 it had disappeared. At no age was expression used as a basis for judgements of person identity. Even though they had been explicitly warned that sometimes two different people would be wearing the same clothes, glasses, hats, or hairstyles, it is possible that the young children had not understood the task. To make sure, a second study was run in which the children themselves participated as models for the stimuli. They then practised on the problems in which they and their classmates were models. When models were the child's familiar classmates, 5- and 6-year-olds showed no tendency to be fooled by confounding hats, glasses, and so on. But even after such practice, when the models were unfamiliar the results were as before; previously unfamiliar faces were represented in terms of paraphernalia. When faces are already familiar, hats, hairstyles, and so on, are irrelevant to person identification, but when the task is the encoding of an unfamiliar face, young children cannot ignore such salient piecemeal features.

If the input to the encoding is a still photograph, the problem of forming a representation adequate for later identification is compounded by the ambiguity of the stimuli. For example, those aspects of the stimulus contributed by permanent facial characteristics must be distinguished from those contributed by momentary expression—is that a wide mouth or a grin? In all of the studies reviewed so far, the unfamiliar faces presented for encoding have been depicted in still photographs. The hypothesis that young children are simply bad at interpreting photographs of faces is ruled out by the study just cited; photographs of faces already represented in memory (familiar classmates) are readily identified. Rather, young children have not yet developed encoding mechanisms that are adequate to represent unfamiliar faces from still photographs. Such encoding power is available to 10-year-olds. It has been suggested that the encoding deficits of young children relative to 10-year-olds may be restricted to the artificial case of still photographs as inputs. This hypothesis is under test in our laboratory; preliminary data oppose it. A difficult face encoding task was constructed by introducing various kinds of changes between the inspection and recognition photographs of each model. In some cases clothing was changed, in other cases facial expression, and in still others, both. Angle of view was sometimes varied. Performance of 6- and 7-year-olds and adults was equated for a baseline condition by variation in set size. The adult's performance at set size 40 ($d' = 0·92$) was matched by the child's at set size 10 ($d' = 0·74$). As can be seen, performance was low. Video tapes of the target models were

TABLE 1
Improvement in d' from baseline (5-second exposure to still photograph)

	Short video	Long video
Adults (set size 40)	0·98	1·61
6–7 year olds (set size 10)	0·50	0·58

constructed. In one type (long video) each model told a joke, put on different hats, pulled his or her hair back, mugged for the camera, and turned his or her head side to side and up and down. The total time for all this was about 40 seconds. The second type (short video) consisted of the joke section of the long video and required about 10 seconds. We then examined how performance improved (relative to the baseline) when the input was video segments. Not surprisingly, both adults and children were better at recognizing models which they had seen in video segments than those they had seen only in still photographs, and the long videos improved performance relatively more than did the short videos. But, most important, video presentation improved adult performance markedly more than children's performance (Table 1, Carey, Diamond and Jaaskela, unpublished data). These are pilot data; the study is being repeated with more conditions. But the lesson is clear—young children are worse than adults at encoding unfamiliar faces from moving rich input as well as from the impoverished input of still photographs.

Young children differ from adults (and older children) in how much input is required in order to form representations with equal potential for future recognition. Whether the child's representations of highly familiar faces differ from the adult's will be discussed in section 4 and two alternative accounts of the late development of a powerful encoding schema will be contrasted in section 6.

C *The inversion effect—a puzzle resolved*

Data from two studies have shown that the increase in encoding efficiency during ages 6 to 10 is limited to upright faces as stimuli; in both studies no significant improvement over this age range was observed for the encoding of inverted faces (Carey and Diamond, 1977; Carey et al., 1980). In addition, in both studies, 6-year-olds performed equally well on upright and inverted faces. That is, at age 6 there was no inversion effect.

At first glance, this is a puzzling result, since there is a well-documented inversion effect for encoding unfamiliar faces in 5- and 7-month old infants. In section 1, the data from infants were interpreted as showing that the encoding process for unfamiliar faces recruits knowledge of faces *per se*, even at this young age. There is no reason to doubt that knowledge of faces is recruited in the 6-year-old's face encoding processes. And, indeed, Mehler (personal communication) and Bertelson (personal communication) have found inversion effects in face encoding tasks with 6-year-olds and with preschool children as subjects. The question then becomes why there was no inversion effect in the two studies cited above.

The answer is simple. Performance levels in the two studies were very low (under 65% correct for both upright and inverted faces). Performance levels were low because the inspection sets were large (12 faces mixed with 12 houses in one study, 10 faces in the other) and the stimuli similar to each other (adult male MIT faculty members with no glasses, moustaches, or beards). While performance was clearly better than chance in both studies on both upright and inverted faces, each child might have successfully encoded only a few faces in each orientation, responding randomly on most of the forced choice items. If a floor effect due to large set sizes is masking the inversion effect, then it should emerge if the same stimuli are used in smaller sets. Table 2 shows this to be the case (Carey, Diamond, Ginsburg and Jaaskela, unpublished data). For each age we determined the set size at which an 85% level of performance for upright faces was attained. From age 3 onward, a significant inversion effect is obtained at that set size. Preschool children and 6-year-olds are better at encoding upright faces than inverted faces.

In summary, the presence or absence of an inversion effect is influenced by performance level. If the encoding task is made hard by requiring the child to encode several faces that are very similar, in terms of the features the child uses for representing faces, performance on upright faces drops, and can drop to the level of that on inverted faces. Equally obvious, ceiling effects would obliterate an inversion effect at set sizes so small that performance is very high for inverted faces.

Two facts remain. There is a dramatic improvement within this age range in encoding efficiency for upright faces and this is greater than the improvement in encoding efficiency for inverted faces. To reiterate my interpretation of these facts: unfamiliar faces are encoded with respect to knowledge of faces *per se*, at least from 5 months on. Nonetheless,

TABLE 2
Inversion effect when performance on upright faces is at 85% level

Age in years (number of subjects)	Set size	Performance on upright faces %	Inversion effect %
2(8)	1	85	8
3(8)	1	84	13
4(16)	2.5	86	19
5(24)	6	85	19
6(24)	7	81	16
10(22)	10	86	16

there is a developmental change in the features in terms of which fixed input (still photograph or moving face) is represented. For any given input, older children and adults are better able than young children to encode relational distinguishing features. The developmental change primarily reflects acquisition of further knowledge of faces, *per se*, as opposed to general pattern encoding or memory changes.

4 FURTHER DEVELOPMENTS DURING ADOLESCENCE

Very few studies include adults as subjects along with children from a wide range of ages. Benton and Van Allen's simultaneous matching task was developed as part of a neuropsychological test battery, and normative data were collected for 6- to 11-year-old children as well as for normal adults. Ten- and 11-year-olds did not differ from each other; both were in the "normal adult range" (74%) although they did not reach the normal adult level of performance (84%, Benton and Van Allen, 1973). A natural assumption might be that progress between age 10 and the adult level is further steady development, albeit slower than the progress between ages 2 and 10. This assumption is wrong. Carey *et al.* (1980) found that there was no change on this task between the ages of 10 and 14, and then there was a significant improvement between the ages of 14 and 16, at which point the adult level of performance was attained.

The Benton and Van Allen task requires systematic scanning of six photographs to find three that depict the same model as a target photograph. Five studies using simple recognition memory paradigms further underscore that ability at face encoding does not progress steadily between age 10 and adulthood. In all five the same developmental pattern was observed—improvement up to ages 10 or 11, followed by an actual decline in performance, again followed by recovery to the adult level (Carey *et al.*, 1980; Flin, 1980; Flin, personal communication). As Fig. 2 shows, not all of these dips actually reach statistical significance, and there are slight differences in the exact ages at which the decline is seen. In some of the studies, the decline has begun by age 11; in others by 12. In some recovery is complete by 14; in others by 16. Nevertheless, every study shows the decline.

It is possible that the developmental function for the Benton and Van Allen matching task (improvement until age 10, a plateau between ages 10 and 14, attainment of the adult level by age 16) is a variant of that observed in the simple recognition tasks.

General information processing skills such as those required to scan systematically a complex array are tapped by the Benton and van Allen matching task, but not by simple recognition tasks. The effects of declining efficiency in encoding faces (Fig. 2) could be cancelled by improved efficiency in such skills (see Vurpillot, 1976). The result of these two developmental processes would be the curve found for the Benton and Van Allen task. The ages at which developmental discontinuities are found are the same in the two paradigms (continuous improvement until age 10, followed by a decline or by a period of no improvement, with another improvement sometime before age 16).

One assessment of the development of face encoding, Diamond and Carey's (1977) confounding paraphernalia task, did not yield a variant of these curves. Rather, a performance level of 90% correct was reached by age 12 and maintained through age 16. Like Benton and Van Allen's task, this procedure provides much scope for metamemory strategies. Just what conditions yield the developmental functions of Fig. 2 is a question for further research.

Another important question is the degree to which the disruption of face encoding skills reflects the disruption of pattern encoding in general, as opposed to the disruption of that aspect of face encoding that deploys knowledge of faces *per se*. One study compared the encoding of upright faces with that of inverted faces, upright houses and inverted houses (Carey and Diamond, unpublished data). A decline in performance was found only for upright faces, but there were only 12 children at each age and neither the decline on upright faces nor the materials by subjects interaction was significant. Thus, this question remains very much open.

In sum, the steady improvement in face encoding skills between

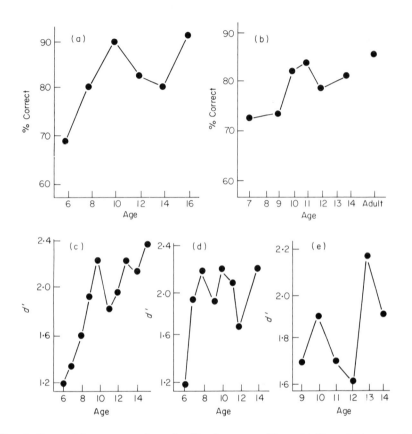

FIG. 2. Recognition memory for unfamiliar faces: age effects. (a) 12- and 14-year-olds not significantly different from 10- and 16-year-olds (Carey *et al.*, 1980); (b) 12- and 14-year-olds significantly worse than both 11-year-olds and adults (Carey *et al.*, 1980); (c) 11- and 12-year-olds significantly worse than 10-year-olds (Flin, 1980); (d) significance not available (Flin, personal communication); (e) significance not available (Flin, personal communication).

infancy and age 10 is followed by a brief period of disruption before the adult capacity is reached by age 16. This disruption is small in absolute quantity, sometimes manifesting itself as a mere levelling in the rate of improvement on the way to adult performance. Nonetheless, a disruption in performance, however small, suggests some kind of reorganization of encoding processes during these years. Exactly what kinds of reorganization may be involved will be discussed below.

5 REPRESENTATION AND RECOGNITION OF FAMILIAR FACES

So far we have seen that young children differ from adults in the efficiency with which they encode new faces. Given the same exposure to an unfamiliar face, a young child encodes it in terms of relatively isolated, piecemeal distinguishing features while an adult encodes it in terms of more relational distinguishing features. The development of the capacity to form more adequate relational representations of faces from little input is due primarily to advances in knowledge of faces *per se*, rather than improvement in general pattern encoding, memorial, or metamemorial processes. Finally, we have seen that during early adolescence face encoding efficiency is slightly (and temporarily) disrupted.

These generalizations about the development of the ability to encode unfamiliar faces raise questions about the young child's representations of highly familiar faces. Certainly, the knowledge about faces *per se* that enables the child to become a more efficient encoder of new faces is abstracted from the representations of familiar faces already in memory. Merely an increase in the number of familiarized faces could provide the basis for the improvement of encoding skills in the years before age 10. Alternatively, it is possible that changes in the representations of familiar faces occur during development. I will argue in this section that there is no evidence in favour of one over the other of the two hypotheses. That is, there is no conclusive evidence for or against developmental change in the representations of highly familiar faces, at least after age 5.

At first glance it seems that the processes of recognition of familiar faces become more efficient during the years after the age of 5. Chi (1977) found that 5-year-olds took more time to name classmates that they had known for three years than adults required to name colleagues they had known for three years (1531 ms versus 666 ms). Of course, slower retrieval times for the names, rather than slower recognition times for the faces, may account for this difference. But Chi also assessed the threshhold for recognition of 1, 2, or 3 familiar faces presented tachistoscopically. For adults, the 50% recognition thresholds were 26 ms, 42 ms, and 320 ms respectively, compared to 138 ms, 280 ms, and 692 ms for 5-year-olds. This is a large difference in favour of the adult.

The most straightforward interpretation of these results is that the retrieval and matching processes that constitute recognition of a familiar face are more powerful in an adult than in a child. But there is a problem: we know that young children encode unfamiliar faces much less efficiently than do adults (section 2). Three years' experience with a face between ages 2 and 5 may not produce as adequate a representation as an adult's three years' experience with a face. In order to see whether recognition times are really slower for children, given equally familiar faces, some independent measure of face familiarity is needed, so that stimuli for children and adults can be matched for familiarity. Only then can recognition times for familiar faces be compared across children and adults.

Another approach is to make the recognition task difficult and then chart the developmental course of coping with that difficulty. If the young child experiences the same level of difficulty and makes the same kinds of errors as the adult, we should conclude that there is little developmental change in the representations of and in the recognition processes for familiar faces. One way to introduce difficulty in face recognition problems is to photograph different models with identical clothing, glasses, or hairstyles. When asked to pick which two of three photographs of unfamiliar faces depict the same person, young children cannot ignore such confounding cues. The same types of problems can be constructed with familiar faces (the child's own classmates). Presented with these, young children (5- and 6-year-olds) appeared hardly to notice the very same confounding cues that determined their choices when the models were unfamiliar (Diamond and Carey, 1977). By age 10, these confounding paraphernalia were largely ignored even on unfamiliar models. It seems then, that there is much less developmental change during these years in the representation and recognition of familiar faces than in the encoding of unfamiliar faces. While I believe this conclusion to be true, the pattern of results under consideration has another interpretation. When the faces are unfamiliar, the child must compare the photographs to pick the two that depict "Mary". But when the faces are familiar classmates, once one has been identified as Mary, the others need only be scanned to find another photograph of Mary. No active comparison of the photographs is required, and so the fact that Jean has a hat like Mary's is less likely to interfere with the correct choice.

Goldstein and his colleagues have studied the developmental course of coping with recognition of familiar faces made difficult in two different ways. The developmental results are equivocal. First, they have studied the recognition of parts of familiar faces, ranging from half faces to just eyes, noses, or mouths. Second, they have studied the recognition of inverted familiar faces.

In the case of recognition of parts of familiar faces Goldstein and Mackenberg (1966) found that 6-year-olds were as proficient as 10-year-olds, although 4-year-olds were consistently poorer than both. On the same task, Chance *et al.* (1967) found kindergartners to be worse than first and second graders, who in turn, were worse than sixth graders. Thus, there seems to be improvement between the ages of 4 and 11 at recognition of a familiar face from just a part, although the amount of change between ages 6 and 10 is minimal. Chance *et al.* further showed that differences between younger and older children are *not* due to the older children's greater experience with their classmates' faces. The first, second and sixth grade samples included children who had been in the school only 8 to 12 weeks. Children who had been in the school for over a year did not do better on old classmates than on new classmates, and the new children did not differ from old children on either old or new faces. It seems, then, that the degree of familiarity with a face required for optimal performance on this task is achieved by first to sixth graders in at least 8 to 12 weeks. But the story is still more complex, since the performance on neither old acquaintances nor new acquaintances was optimal. For kindergarten, first, and second graders, friends' faces were better recognized from parts than were faces of classmates who were not friends. By sixth grade this was not the case. A possible explanation is that friends' faces have been attended to more, and therefore better encoded. Only by sixth grade, then, are all class-mates' faces automatically familiarized to the same degree as are friends' faces. In sum, during the ages 4 to 11 there is slight improvement in the capacity to recognize a classmate from just a part of a photograph of his or her face, but this improvement may be due to the older child's more adequate encoding of acquaintances' faces, rather than differences in the recognition process itself.

Goldstein and Mackenberg (1966) showed that the portions of the face that are most informative to 10-year-olds are exactly the same as those most informative to 4- and 6-year-olds. This further suggests that the representations of familiar faces and the retrieval processes by which these representations are found during recognition do not change much over this age range.

Two different studies with very slight procedural variations have charted the developmental course of recognizing inverted faces. Before discussing the results, some distinctions among inversion effects should be highlighted. From at least 5 months on, there is an inversion effect for encoding unfamiliar faces. Faces presented during inspection up-side down are relatively poorly recognized when presented for recog-nition, still upside down. Here there is no mismatch between the encoded stimulus and the stimulus to be recognized; both are in the same orientation. The inversion effect reflects relative inability, during encoding, to recruit relevant knowledge of faces. The inversion effect for familiar faces, in contrast, involves a mismatch between mental representations (of upright faces) and stimuli to be recognized. Since these are quite different effects, it would not be surprising for the developmental histories for each to differ.

According to Goldstein's 1975 study, the 5–6-year-old child is as able to recognize inverted photographs of peers (88%) as is the 9–10-year-old (89%) and both are slightly better than the 13–14-year-old (81%).[1] Not only are young children as good at recognizing inverted familiar faces as older children, but they do not show the large inversion effect characteristic of adult performance on this task. Goldstein went on to trace the acquisition of the usual inversion effect: 17–18-year-olds' performance fell to 76% and 19–20-year-olds to a staggeringly poor 62%. Thus, performance is steady through some point in the early teens, at which time children begin to get worse at recognizing inverted familiar faces. Only further study with just this paradigm would reveal whether the normal adult level has been achieved by age 20.

Goldstein's (1975) data, then, indicate no developmental change in the age range from 5 to 10. A very different picture of the course of development in the years before age 9–10 emerged from Brooks and Goldstein's (1963) earlier study. Rather than steady performance, accuracy at identifying inverted photographs of classmates increased from 67% at age 3–4, to 80% at 5–6, to 84% at 7–8, to 100% at 9–10. The only source for the dramatic disagreement in results of the two studies that I can think of hangs on a procedural difference. In Brooks and Goldstein's procedure, subjects saw the photographs upright a week before they were shown the same photographs inverted. In Goldstein's later study, in contrast, the inverted faces were shown first and only later were upright photographs presented in order to provide the baseline against which recognition of upside down faces would be compared. Perhaps older children are more able than younger ones to use a memory for particular photographs in recognition of inverted faces. This hypothesis could easily be tested; in any case, the purer assessment of recognition of inverted familiar faces provides no prior experience with the particular photograph, and in such a procedure there was no change after ages 5–6 until the beginning of the decline at ages 13–14 or 17–18.

Why are 20-year-olds worse at recognizing inverted familiar faces than 5- and 10-year-olds? Goldstein (1975) attributes the decline

---

[1] Percentages are the proportion of photographs recognized upright that can be identified upside down.

(already begun by ages 13–14) to "overlearning of a mono-oriented configuration". His idea is that with such drastic overlearning as results from seeing thousands upon thousands of upright faces flexibility is lost in the recognition procedures that permit compensation for mismatches in orientation between stimulus and mental representation. An alternative explanation is that there are developmental changes in the kinds of distinguishing features in terms of which familiar faces are represented and in terms of which recognition processes compare stimulus and mental representation. Perhaps in the years before age 13–14, both piecemeal and configurational distinguishing features of familiar faces are richly represented, but in the years following 13–14, there is an increased reliance on configurational distinguishing features alone. On the assumption that configurational distinguishing features are harder to represent from an inverted face, Goldstein's (1975) results would be expected.

A serious methodological problem is relevant to the interpretation of all developmental studies involving familiar faces. It is extremely difficult to equate across age groups for familiarity with the stimuli, given that young children are dramatically less efficient at encoding new faces than are adults. What appears as developmental differences across ages in recognition processes for familiar faces may reflect the failure to equate for degree of familiarity. Adults' representations of familiar faces clearly change with increasing exposure. We have all had the experience of failing to recognize a casual acquaintance who has changed hairstyle or shaved a beard. We have also had the experience of noticing something is different, but not even knowing quite what, when a close friend has changed hairstyle or shaved a beard. Within an adult's store of familiar faces, then, there are probably changes toward more abstract, relational representations of individuals as their faces become more familiar. It is difficult to be certain, when we compare children and adults, that we are not simply tapping different levels of familiarity.

The question we would like an answer for is when during development the child's representations of the faces most familiar to him become the same as the adult's representations of the faces most familiar to him. In the absence of a moderately well confirmed theory of exactly how highly familiar faces are represented in memory by adults, it is clearly impossible to ask how young children differ from adults in this regard. The data presented here suggest that between the ages of 5 to 10 there is relatively little developmental change in the representation and processing of highly familiar faces. This is in marked contrast to the dramatic improvement during these years in efficiency at encoding unfamiliar faces (section 2). Section 3 demonstrated a temporary decline in encoding efficiency for upright faces around ages 12 and 13. And in this section we have seen some evidence for a change in the representations and recognition processes involving highly familiar faces beginning at around age 13 or 14. Quite clearly, the developmental course of face recognition is a protracted process.

6 RIGHT HEMISPHERE INVOLVEMENT IN FACE ENCODING

Studies with patients with brain damage have shown that an intact right hemisphere is required for the normal encoding of unfamiliar faces. Patients with right hemisphere damage are impaired at encoding tasks that demand subsequent recognition of identical photographs (e.g. Warrington and James, 1967; Milner, 1968; Yin, 1970) as well as at encoding tasks that demand simultaneous matching of photographs taken under different lighting conditions and angle of view (e.g. Benton and Van Allen, 1968). The right posterior cortical region is especially implicated.[1]

Data from patients with commisurectomies (split-brain patients) underscore the greater involvement of the right hemisphere during face encoding (Levy *et al.*, 1972). So, too, do data from normal adults from a variety of paradigms where faces are tachistoscopically presented to either the left visual field or the right visual field. Under most conditions, performance on faces presented to the left visual field, which projects to the right hemisphere, is superior (e.g. Hilliard, 1973; Klein, Moscovitch and Vigna, 1976).

The right hemisphere is specialized for the processing of many kinds of complex visual configurations (e.g. Gross, 1972; Fontenot, 1973). Faces must be distinguished from each other on the basis of subtle configurational properties. Perhaps the right hemisphere involvement in face encoding reflects nothing more than its general specialization for processing relational patterns. This is unlikely. Yin (1970) showed that patients with right posterior lesions were impaired, relative to normals and other lesion groups, on the encoding of upright faces but not on inverted faces. In addition, with normal adults as subjects, there is a visual field by orientation interaction, such that the left visual field advantage for upright faces is larger than that for inverted faces (Leehey

---

[1] There is some evidence that aphasic patients with lesions in the left posterior cortex are also deficient on at least some face encoding tasks (for reviews see Benton, 1980, and Hécaen, this volume). But the majority of studies, by far, agree that right hemisphere damage is the most debilitating for face encoding.

et al., 1978).[1] As mentioned before, as meaningless patterns, upright and inverted faces are identical. The interactions between visual field and orientation (Leehey *et al.*, 1978) and between patient group and orientation (Yin, 1970) indicate a right-hemisphere specialization for face encoding beyond its specialization for processing of visual configurations in general. A functioning right hemisphere seems required for the deployment of specifically facial knowledge in the encoding of novel faces.

Young children (8 and younger) resemble patients with right hemisphere lesions. Just as these patients differ from normal controls only on the encoding of upright faces, so do young children differ from older children and adults more on the encoding of upright faces. The two populations may be compared directly on Benton and Van Allen's standardized test of face encoding. Children 8 and under performed at the level of patients with right hemisphere damage while 10-year-olds were in the normal adult range (Benton and van Allen, 1973; Carey *et al.*, 1980). Dricker *et al.* (1978) found patients with right hemisphere damage were impaired relative to normals on the confounding paraphernalia task on which 6- and 8-year-old children perform so badly (Diamond and Carey, 1977). On this task, the patients did not resemble the children in their pattern of errors.

In sum, children 8 and under are poor at face encoding, just as are patients with right hemisphere damage. In the case of the comparison of upright and inverted faces, the similarity between the two groups extends beyond mere low performance levels; both groups are impaired relative to normal adults more on encoding upright than inverted faces.

The periods in childhood when face encoding is poor are associated with less strong lateralization on face encoding tasks. In two separate studies with different stimuli and different subjects, Leehey (1976) found no left visual field advantage for face encoding at age 8 and the normal left visual field advantage at age 10. There was no change in the right visual field between ages 8 and 10; the emergence of the normal left visual field advantage for encoding faces at age 10 was due entirely to improvement in the left visual field. Also, the left visual field advantage decreased at ages 12 and 14 (Leehey, 1976). All of the subjects in Leehey's studies, ranging in age from 8 through adulthood, showed the normal right visual field advantage for words. In addition, subjects at all ages tested, including age 8, showed a left visual field advantage for

Ellis and Shepherd (1975) failed to find such an interaction. But the exposure times they used were so low that it is unlikely that the faces were being processed as faces (see Leehey *et al.*, 1978 or a discussion).

familiar faces. Thus, the change with age in left visual field advantage for encoding unfamiliar faces does not reflect a change in hemispheric specialization.

Leehey's results conflict with a number of reports of a left visual field advantage for encoding unfamiliar faces as early as age 5 (Young and Ellis, 1976) or 7 (Marcel and Rajan, 1975; Broman, 1978). In the case of Young and Ellis, we have elsewhere (Leehey *et al.*, 1978) questioned whether their paradigm actually involves face encoding, since the durations of stimulus presentation are below those for recognition of an already familiar face (Chi, 1977). In the case of Broman, the task was not encoding unfamiliar faces but discriminating four faces that had previously been familiarized. As just pointed out, faces already represented in memory (classmates) are recognized better in the left visual field than in the right at least by age 8 (Leehey, 1976). In the case of Marcel and Rajan, the face presented had to be chosen from an array of only two, an easier encoding task than that used by Leehey, and data from 7- to 9-year-olds were grouped. The conclusion from Leehey's studies of importance here is that there is an increase in left visual field advantage in the age range from 6 to 10, and a subsequent decrease at ages 12 and 14. At every age task variables will influence the presence or absence of a right hemisphere advantage for faces as well as its absolute magnitude.

7 EXPLANATIONS OF THE COURSE OF DEVELOPMENT OF FACE ENCODING

In previous sections we described the course of the child's acquisition of face encoding skills. In spite of the impressive beginning evident at least by 7 months, the developmental process is protracted. Dramatic improvement between the ages of 2 and 10 is followed by a few years of no gain or actual decline. The adult capacity appears intact by age 16. In this section I will briefly discuss the question of what would count as an explanation for this developmental pattern.

At one level there will be an explanation in purely information processing terms. The improvement in the years before age 10 most certainly reflects the acquisition of knowledge gained from increased experience with faces. I assume that this knowledge is abstracted from representations of familiar faces. Obviously, as children get older, more familiar faces are represented in memory. In section 4 I raised the question whether not only more faces have been made familiar, but also whether the representations of familiar faces themselves change during these years. The data on this question are inconclusive; the answer is an important step in the explanation of the dramatic improvement in encoding unfamiliar faces.

What of the decline in the years after age 10? Dips in performance during development have now been documented in many domains of cognitive, perceptual, and motor development (for reviews, see Bower, 1976; Strauss, 1978). Such dips are usually thought of as "growth errors". Reorganization of the processes underlying the skill, on route to better functioning, yield, temporarily, poorer performance. Thus, we would want to know, for face encoding, exactly what kind of reorganization is involved and, also, just why it occurs around age 10.

Between the ages of 10 and 12, many children leave relatively small elementary schools for much larger junior high schools. They are now in classes with different children and different teachers every hour. A consequence of this change is dozens, even hundreds, of new faces to encode. Many partially encoded faces in memory may well interfere with the recognition processes for faces encoded in the experimental session, yielding poorer performance. This hypothesis could easily be tested with a comparison of children in the same school through grade 8 (age 13–14) and children who switch schools between grade 6 (age 11) and 7 (age 12).

A related possibility is that the decline reflects a growth error. Perhaps driven by the pressure of many new faces to encode, the child may systematize his face encoding processes. The first steps of such systematization may involve awareness and use of relatively superficial distinguishing properties, resulting in poorer performances. Such a strategy shift might also result in less right hemisphere advantage for encoding unfamiliar faces, since it is likely that the left hemisphere is relatively specialized for piecemeal (as opposed to relational) processing.

In sum, both salient aspects of the developmental course for face encoding—the extremely poor performance of young children relative to 10-year-olds and the decline in performance around 12—are amenable to explanation at the information processing level. Further research is clearly necessary to decide among alternative information processing accounts. Finally, in the few remaining pages of this chapter I will consider the possibility that another type of explanation is also relevant—that genetically determined maturational factors also contribute to the exact shape of the developmental curve for face encoding.

What is meant by maturational? No genetic programme, including any genetic programme for development, is carried out in the absence of environmental input. Nonetheless, behavioural development (perceptual, motor, conceptual) involves change in neural substrate, and some changes in neural substrate are constrained by the genetic programme for neural development. Several different types of maturational constraints on behavioural development have been validated in animal models (e.g. Carmichael, 1926; Goldman, 1972, Hubel and Wiesel, 1970; Nottebohn, 1970; see Carey, 1980, for a discussion of these and still other types).

A hypothetical example might clarify the discussion. Suppose that all genetically programmed developments in the nervous system are completed by the second decade of life. Suppose then that a blind man regains his sight and learns to discriminate faces. We could describe his acquisition of face-recognition skills in terms of changes in his representations of faces and in the processes by which he recognizes familiar faces and encodes previously unfamiliar faces. By hypothesis there would be no maturational component to this development, since all maturational changes in the state of his nervous system are complete. As outlined above, we must also describe a child's acquisition of face-recognition skills in these same terms. But in the child's case it is possible (but only possible) that some maturational changes affect this developmental course. The challenge, of course, is to specify reasonable hypotheses about the maturational factors that might contribute to development and then to bring relevant evidence to bear on those hypotheses.

The shape of the developmental course of face encoding suggests two maturational hypotheses. First, immaturity of some aspect of neural substrate may limit the face encoding skills that children under age 9 or 10 can achieve. Second, maturational events associated with the onset of puberty may actually disrupt, temporarily, face encoding processes. The similarities in performance of young children and patients with right posterior lesions, along with evidence that the magnitude of the left visual field advantage for face encoding shows the same relation to age as does overall recognition performance, point to the right hemisphere as a prime candidate for the locus of both maturational effects.

None of the data presented thus far establishes that these (or other) maturational factors constrain the development of face encoding skills. The limiting factor before age 10 may simply be insufficient experience with enough faces. Similarly, an information processing account of the dip around age 12 may be its total explanation. Even Leehey's lateralization results do not compel an appeal to maturation. The right hemisphere might be differentially involved in face encoding only to the extent that relational distinguishing properties are computed. If the child has not yet developed an encoding schema powerful enough to compute relational distinguishing properties of a face from a still photograph presented for 150 ms, then the right hemisphere will not be differentially exercised. Thus, the lesser right-hemisphere advantage in encoding faces at ages 8, 12, and 14 could simply reflect the strategy for face encoding the child is using at those ages. Developmental changes in strategy could well be explained in information processing terms without implicating any maturational events.

A maturational contribution to the poor performance of children under 10 could be evaluated by the study of young children with focal brain damage. If immaturity of right posterior cortex limits the performance of normal children under age 10, then before 10 there should be relatively little difference between children with focal lesions in this area and normal children. The effects of the brain damage should emerge clearly around age 9 or 10. I know of no face encoding data relevant to this prediction, although Goldman's (1972) studies on the effects of early frontal lesions in monkeys validate its logic. The prediction should be tested.

Regarding the second maturational hypothesis: if the decline in face encoding skills is associated with the onset of the adolescent period, prepubescent children should encode faces better than children of the same age who have already begun adolescence. Since girls reach puberty earlier than boys, one would expect the decline to be earlier than for boys. Leehey (1976) found that the left visual field advantage shown at age 10 by both sexes was absent at age 12 in girls but not absent until age 14 in boys. However, in our studies and in Flin's, this sex difference was not found, suggesting that the decline is not related to maturational status. But sample sizes in these studies have been small (from 12 to 30 per age group compared to 40 per age group in Leehey's studies), and age of onset of puberty is extremely variable within both sexes. A more sensitive test for a relation between the decline in face encoding skills and maturational status requires knowledge of each child's pubertal stage. A pilot study comparing 7 prepubescent and 6 pubescent 11-year-old girls yielded a significant difference in the expected direction; pubescent girls were worse on a face encoding task (Carey and Diamond, 1980). A full study, comparing children matched for age, sex, and IQ, but differing on Marshall–Tanner indicators of puberty, is in progress in our laboratory. We hope to replicate our pilot study and extend the results to boys and to older children. For older children the prediction is that pubescent children will be worse than matched controls who have completed pubertal changes.

Diamond and I have thought of one other type of evidence that would bear on the two maturational hypotheses. If both hypotheses are true, then at least some other skills that exercise the relevant neural substrate should show the same course of development as does face encoding. For a few years now we have been collecting developmental norms for clinical tests used for diagnosing focal lesions in all parts of the brain. Carey and Diamond (1980), report our findings as of 1979; the norms we have added since do not change the picture. The available data are incomplete, and within single instruments we have often had to combine data from different sources, an admittedly dangerous practice. Nonetheless, the preliminary results are clear: most clinical tasks, by far, do not have the same developmental course as does face encoding. In most cases there is no hint of a temporary plateau or decline in the years after age 10.

We have found only two tasks that share the developmental course of face encoding. One is voice encoding (Mann *et al.*, 1979). Voice encoding shares neural substrate with face encoding (cf. Assal *et al.*, 1976). It also shares experiential influences with face encoding, since both are bases of person identification. Thus, the results for voice encoding do not help us pin down a maturational contribution to the developmental course of face encoding. The second is the Seashore Tonal Memory test. Patients with right temporal lesions perform at the level of 8- or 9-year-old children on this task, and its developmental course is characterized by a plateau between the ages of 10 and 14 that is significantly worse than the adult level of performance, achieved around age 16 (see Carey and Diamond, 1980). Tonal memory shares no obvious experiential base with face and voice encoding, but it does share an aspect of neural substrate. This pattern of results is consistent with the maturational hypothesis. Of course, characterization of those skills that develop as does face encoding and those that do not has barely begun. As long as most skills do not, then it is possible that there will be common elements among those that do that will allow us to evaluate the maturational hypotheses.

In conclusion, I have argued in this chapter that the development of face recognition skill is a protracted process, extending throughout all of childhood at least. Gradual improvement in the years before age 10 is followed by a period of reorganization both of face encoding processes and of the processes underlying recognition of highly familiar faces. I have argued that full explanation of this developmental pattern may well include maturational considerations in addition to information processing considerations. The data now available are inconclusive; I have tried to indicate some kinds of studies that might be done to refine and evaluate both information processing and maturational hypotheses concerning the precise course of the development of face recognition.

3 The Neuropsychology of Face Recognition

Henry Hécaen[1]

1 HISTORICAL INTRODUCTION

The isolation of the disorder of face recognition or prosopagnosia as a specific form of visual agnosia is relatively recent. In the course of describing complex visual agnosias in earlier periods of neuropsychological research, some authors had observed that certain patients were not only unable to recognize objects, pictures, colours, or to orient themselves in familiar surroundings, but they were also incapable of identifying or visualizing even the most familiar people's faces. The most famous observations of these types of cases are those of Charcot (1883) and Wilbrand (1892).

Charcot published his case under the title "Abrupt and isolated suppression of the mental vision of signs and objects (forms and colours)". A very well educated man who was renowned for his remarkable visual memory demonstrated an abrupt loss of the ability to recognize and visualize places, colours, forms and human faces. He no longer recognized his familiar acquaintances—even his wife and children. It seemed to him that he saw new traits and characteristics in their physiognomy (physical appearance). He no longer recognized his own face; he saw the passage in a public gallery being blocked by a person that he was going to excuse himself to, but who was only his own reflection in a mirror. Charcot explained this trouble as a non-specific loss of mental imagery.

[1] Directeur d'Etudes Honoraire à l'Ecole des Hautes Etudes en Sciences Sociales Directeur de l'Unité de Recherches Neuropsychologiques et Neurolinguistiques (U. 111) de l'INSERM.

Wilbrand (1892) cites the case of a 43-year-old woman who, after a loss of consciousness, demonstrated bizarre behaviour which caused her to be considered blind, even though she insisted that she was not. For example, she remembered having confused her dog with the doctor who was treating her; and her maid with her table. This despite the fact that she was able to read. Upon examination, several years later, she presented an incomplete left-lateral homonymous hemianopsia. She explained that after her attack, everything that she looked at had a strange character. She was incapable of recognizing the streets of her native city Hamburg, and of revisualizing them. As to physiognomies, she declared "I recognize people very well that I knew before my illness; but those that I have just met don't leave a trace on my memory. I recognize their voices and their accents but not their faces." Post mortem examination revealed a bilateral involvement of the occipital lobe, but the lesion was more marked on the right side.

Other similar observations were reported by Heidenhain (1927), Milian (1932), Hoff and Pötzl (1937) and Donini (1939).

These disorders of visual recognition of human faces were thus present in a complex symptomatic ensemble and were not considered to represent a specific agnosic syndrome until 1947. In that year Bodamer, basing his conclusions on the study of three cases, isolated the defect of facial recognition from other disorders of visual recognition (of objects, forms, and colours) and provided the new syndrome with a name—prosopagnosia. He attributed this particular deficit of visual recognition to an inability to appreciate the "visual category, which is the most profound and genetically the most primitive in our perception". According to Bodamer recognition of general facial expression preceded vision of objects in the infant. Therefore, prosopagnosia was a regression to an infantile stage of perception of the external world in which visual attention cannot separate itself from the region of the eyes or the faces of other people.

However debatable Bodamer's interpretations may be, their publication in 1947 marked an important date in neuropsychology because it demonstrated the possibility of a selectivity within the disorders of visual recognition. Agnosia for objects could become manifest without agnosia for faces. Bodamer only cites the case of Lissauer (1890) in support of this dissociation. In fact, since this date, several observations of visual agnosia of objects, with conservation of face recognition, have been published. The inverse dissociation found in cases of prosopagnosia appears more frequently.

On the anatomical level, Bodamer believed that lesions to the bilateral posterior region were critical for the occurrence of this condition, whereas Hécaen *et al.* (1957) and Hécaen and Angelergues (1962) emphasized the importance of damage to the right posterior junction of the brain.

2 CLINICAL DESCRIPTION

Essentially the disorder in prosopagnosics consists of an inability to identify people who they have known previously. The patient is still capable of distinguishing and naming the different parts of the face but can no longer identify what makes a face individual. Differences between faces are recognized but the identification of a particular face cannot be achieved. So the patient can neither recognize the people he knew well before his illness (parents, close friends), nor those he has recently met (doctors, nurses). He may even fail to recognize his own face in a mirror, if positional cues are suppressed, or the face recorded on videotape. According to Bodamer (1947) the difficulty in recognizing faces is especially marked for the region incorporating the eyes and the bridge of the nose. Subsequent studies by Gloning and Quatember (1966, 1967) have provided experimental support for this clinical intuition. However, for some patients, eyes are the easiest features to recognize (Hécaen and Angelergues, 1962). Details that are not an integral part of the face (e.g. colour of hair, hairstyle, moustache, beard) are well perceived and may occasionally form the basis for identification.

If photographs of familiar acquaintances are mixed with photographs of unknown people and presented to a patient, he fails to recognize them. A picture of the investigator is not recognized as such when placed before the patient, and he is also incapable of indicating the picture of this investigator in a multiple choice test. The disorder extends to include impaired recognition of pictures of famous people.

Although some case reports indicate an impairment in recognition of facial expressions (e.g. anger, joy, sadness), in our own experience these expressions are identified.

Very quickly the patients learn to compensate for this defect, identifying people who were known to them either by visual cues, such as hairstyle or colour, a scar or wart or other distinguishing mark on the face, clothing and accessories (e.g. glasses), silhouette and gestures or by non-visual cues, such as the voice, the sound of footsteps, and so forth.

Patients often complain of not being able to form a visual image of a remembered face. If they do succeed in imagining it, they provide a verbal description that is shallow, inadequate, and focused on elements extrinsic to the face itself, even for members of their own family.

In addition to this typical form, other forms of defective facial recognition exist in which a distorted perception of faces (and only faces) occurs. This form may coexist with the preceding one. But the deficiency in face identification is often less marked. These metamorphosias which are limited to faces are the most often paroxystic; they range from slight deformations (such as hazy faces, cross-eyed people, eyes too close together) to dislocations of the face, features no longer being in their proper place as if one were looking at a face by Picasso.

In one case where these changes were permanent, this facial distortion only occurred with actual faces and not with pictures of them. As the patient said herself, this was because the features were immobile (Hécaen *et al.*, 1957).

Another patient, having undergone an occipito-temporal removal for epileptogenic scar, complained of always seeing deformed faces and of having trouble recognizing even the faces of his parents. Identification was almost achieved, but as the patient stated: "I always have the impression of meeting a double, someone who strangely resembles the person that I remembered but I am not aware that it is that person." He also said: "Looking in a mirror, my face gives me the same impression, but obviously I don't doubt it." The difficulties also extended to animal faces.

3 ASSOCIATED CLINICAL FINDINGS

When the lesion that produces prosopagnosia is bilateral, it is not unusual to find other types of visual agnosia (objects, pictures, colours) in the total clinical picture. A statistical study evaluating 22 patients with facial agnosia compared with 395 patients with unilateral retrorolandic lesions without prosopagnosia found the following associations. Spatial dyslexia, spatial dyscalculia, visual field defects, dressing apraxia, and distortion of visual coordinates were all correlated with prosopagnosia. A negative correlation was found between aphasia and acalculia. No significant difference in sensory disorders and intellectual deterioration were found between these two groups (Hécaen and Angelergues, 1962).

Thus, approximately the same complex of symptoms and associated defects is found for prosopagnosia as for the spatial agnosias, which themselves are frequently associated with prosopagnosia. The association with loss of topographic memory may be of particular importance. But the most frequent association is with the visual field defect and the left hemianopsia or left superior quadranopsia. Meadows (1974) in reviewing 42 cases which were either reported in the literature or personal observations, states that the visual field was intact in only 4 cases; in 15 cases the defect was bilateral; in 19 cases it was situated uniquely on the left, and finally a right unilateral defect existed in 4 of the cases.

4 LATERALIZATION AND LOCALIZATION OF LESIONS

As for the anatomic correlates of prosopagnosia, Bodamer (1947) believed that the lesion was necessarily bilateral. In 1957, on the basis of anatomical studies associated symptoms and statistical data, Hécaen *et al.* emphasized the role of right hemispheric lesions in the production of prosopagnosia. Nonetheless no anatomoclinical case has ever been reported with unequivocal prosopagnosia in which the lesions have been limited to the right hemisphere; they have also always been bilateral.

However, it must be noted that in the 9 cases with postmortem examination given by Meadows, although there was always a right-sided lesion affecting the occipito-temporal region, the corresponding area in the left hemisphere was injured in only 7 of these cases. In effect, in the case given by Pevzner *et al.* (1962) the left lesion consisted only of mild atrophy, gliosis and rarefaction of the cells in the areas of both the angular gyrus and the upper part of the superior temporal sulcus. In the case of Hécaen *et al.* (1957), there was invasion by glioma from the right hemisphere through the posterior part of the corpus callosum, but only as far as the ventricular wall. Thus, Meadows concluded that, although in the majority of cases, prosopagnosia depends on bilateral occipito-temporal lesions, in some cases the right occipito-temporal lesion is not accompanied by a corresponding lesion in the left hemisphere.

With respect to intrahemispheric localization, anatomoclinical observations point to a right temporo-occipital involvement. Meadows (1974) has argued more specifically that the crucial structure in the right hemisphere is the inferior longitudinal fasciculus. A lesion here, he contends, may spare the visual association cortex while isolating it from necessary mnestic associations.

While accepting the necessary role of the right inferior longitudinal fasciculus, Benson *et al.* (1974) argued that a lesion in this area is not sufficient, additional pathology must be present. On the basis of a clinico-anatomic study in addition to a review of the literature these researchers proposed that prosopagnosia is the result of a combination of lesions affecting both the right inferior longitudinal fasciculus and the splenium of the corpus callosum. This latter type of lesion would prevent visual memories from passing from left visual association cortex to right.

5 EXPERIMENTAL NEUROPSYCHOLOGICAL STUDIES

The legitimacy of prosopagnosia as a syndrome and the proposed right hemispheric lateralization of lesions responsible for the symptom complex have been subjects of dispute. Because the syndrome in its purest form is relatively rare, it is necessary to find other means of studying deficiencies in face recognition. This consisted, for the most part, of testing large numbers of patients with unilateral hemispheric lesions but without prosopagnosia on a variety of tests of facial recognition (matching or immediate memory). The supposition was that these tests might uncover a clinically silent defect.

De Renzi and Spinnler (1966) administered to groups of brain-damaged and normal subjects a test of immediate recall of photographs of faces previously unknown to the subjects. On this test, it was found that the ability to recognize faces is much more impaired following right than left hemispheric lesions. No correlation was found between performance on a test of recognition of items in groups of similar objects and performance on the facial recognition test.

In a subsequent study, De Renzi et al. (1969) further evaluated the role of memory in performance on facial recognition tasks. They found no significant differences between results on a test of immediate recall and one of delayed recall. On both tests, performance was significantly impaired in the group with right hemispheric lesions with visual field defects.

On two tests of facial recognition, one with photographs of people unknown to the subjects, the other with photographs of famous people, Warrington and James (1967) also found a prominent right hemispheric effect. Between the two tests no significant correlation existed in patient performance. Additional support for right hemispheric involvement on a test of matching faces (in photographs) was provided by Benton and Van Allen (1968), Tzavaras et al. (1970) and by Yin (1970).

Milner (1968) administered tests of immediate recall and delayed recall of photographs of faces to subjects with right or left cortical ablations, especially of temporal lobes. She found that subjects with right temporal lobectomy had severe impairment of memory for photographs of the human face. In the delayed recall task, even when the delay period was not filled, the subjects were no better than when the period was filled. This observation suggested that right temporal lesions caused a specific defect in visual memory. By contrast, subjects with right frontal lobe ablations performed about as well as those with left-sided lesions. Too few subjects with parietal lesions were studied to allow comment on this anatomic region.

A series of supporting results which were obtained with normal subjects must be added to these experimental results in favour of the predominant role of right hemispheric lesions in producing face recognition difficulties.

Rizzolatti *et al.* (1971), and Suberi and McKeever (1977), using photographs, Geffen *et al.* (1971) using life-like stimuli made from the Identikit, and Patterson and Bradshaw (1975) using face drawings, have all demonstrated faster recognition when the facial representations are projected to the left hemifield. According to Hilliard (1973), Ellis and Shepherd (1975) and Klein *et al.* (1976) the exact recognition scores should be higher for the left-hemifield, a finding which was not supported by Rizzolatti *et al.* This greater ability should even be found in a long-term recognition task (Jones, 1979).

These various statistical studies all point to the same conclusion: that the right hemisphere plays a special role in determining deficits in facial recognition, at least on these tests. Hamsher *et al.* (1979) found the usual relationship between right lesions and performance deficits on the Benton and Van Allen test (1968), but they stated also that patients with left-hemisphere lesions and verbal comprehension trouble were also deficient on their test.

Thus, there is agreement between the lateralization of the lesion site in the case of clinical prosopagnosia and deficiencies in performance on different types of face matching or face recognition tests, and results with normals. This gives evidence for the preferential processing of this type of recognition by the right hemisphere. However, it is difficult to ascertain that the deficient performances on these different tests represent a latent form of gnostic disorder. Of course, De Renzi *et al.* (1969) stated that the only one of their subjects who had clinically demonstrated this disorder also performed very poorly on their matching test. Since then, however, it has been shown that prosopagnosic patients could have very near, if not perfectly normal scores on this type of task (Benton and Van Allen, 1972; Tzavaras *et al.*, 1970; Lhermitte and Pillon, 1975; and a personal unpublished case). These patients had been examined at a fairly long interval after the onset of their trouble and it should be admitted that, with experience they were able to develop new recognition strategies which permitted them to compensate for their difficulty with these tasks. But in the cases described by Assal (1969) and in Tzavaras et al.'s (1973), the matching test had been given in the acute period and the performance was not deficient even in this period.

6 NEUROPSYCHOLOGICAL CONSIDERATIONS

The hypothesis put forward by Bodamer in 1947, according to which prosapagnosia represents a perceptual disorder that affects one particular category of objects in the external world, rapidly met with opposition.

Stollreiter-Butzon (1950) and Bay (1950) considered prosopagnosia to be the result of a visual sensory defect that interfered with simultaneous face perception. For these authors it did not matter if the sensory defect was peripheral or central, although they did accept the role of a "general disorder of psychic synthesis" in explanation of the gnostic problem.

For Faust (1955) prosopagnosia was neither a disorder of a specific visual category nor an elementary sensory defect. Although the defect was selective, he thought that the disorder was not limited to the human face. Rather, the disorder consisted of the difficulty in appreciating the element in any figure that provides individuality. Thus in his view, prosopagnosia is not a specific perceptual disorder but rather is a general neuropsychological defect related to the inability to abstract the essential elements of a given category. There are some cases in which the deficit goes beyond simple face identification, but nonetheless the deficit remains specific. The subject is incapable of differentiating objects with similar morphologies and of the same category, such as different makes of car, different animals, monuments and food (Bodamer, 1947; MacRae and Trolle, 1956; Gloning et al., 1966; Bornstein, 1963; Lhermitte et al., 1972; Lhermitte and Pillon, 1975).

However, the experimental results of De Renzi and Spinnler (1966) are not supportive of Faust's hypothesis as they have not found any correlation between recognition scores for similar items of a given category (photographs of chairs, line drawings) and those for facial recognition. The same thing was found in Tzavaras et al.'s (1970) study. In contrast, because of the positive correlation that they found existed between other perceptual tests, De Renzi and Spinnler concluded that the disorder of facial recognition was nothing more than a manifestation of a general disturbance of recognition of any relatively complex perceptual pattern.

But before discussing the nature of the perceptual problem, it should be taken into consideration that the prosopagnosic subject no longer remembers even faces that are most familiar to him. The perception of familiar faces cannot be related to the memories of these faces. Agnosia for faces would thus be a specific form of mnesic trouble as Hécaen *et al.* have suggested since 1957. Even the words of one of their patients evokes a problem of this type: "it is the forgetting of physiognomies" (*comme un oubli des physionomies*). The frequent association between prosopagnosia and loss of topographical memory, the possibility of global problems in revisualization, along with the frequency of temporal lesions would all serve to reinforce an interpretation of this type.

In their 1967 study, Warrington and James used two facial recognition tests: one for photographs of celebrities, the other for unknown faces. These authors concluded from this that the two tests evaluated different functions. Following right temporal lesions, failures on the test of famous faces implied involvement of a mnestic factor; defective performance on this test approximated to prosopagnosia as it is seen clinically. With the test of unfamiliar faces, mean errors were greatest with right parietal lesions; defective performance on this test depended perhaps on a general perceptual disorder. The syndrome of prosopagnosia, thus, may result from two disturbances (mnestic and perceptual) due to two different lesions (temporal and parietal) in the right hemisphere.

One of the findings that also seems to come out of Marzi and Berlucchi's (1977) results with normal subjects is a different treatment for information concerning faces according to whether they are known or unknown. However, these results cannot be assimilated with those of Warrington and James, as in their subjects the recognition deficit for faces, whether known or unknown, was always more marked when the lesions were on the right. Perhaps even the differences in stimulus presentation, either with or without time limitations, prevents any meaningful comparison to be made between these two series of results.

In Moscovitch *et al.*'s experiment (1976) there was a left visual field advantage only when the subjects had to discriminate a face that had been memorized from faces that had not. When the task did not involve memorization, there was no visual field advantage. (It should be added that the stimulus presentation is particularly long—300 ms—for this type of experimentation.)

Ellis *et al.* (1979b) have shown that face recognition can be based on different facial features according to whether the faces are familiar or unknown. In the case of familiar faces, recognition seems only to depend on internal features (eyes, nose, mouth), while for non-familiar faces it seems to depend just as much upon external features (hair, ears, contours).

The studies of Milner (1968) also seem to support the postulation of a mnesic element, for patients having suffered a right temporal lobectomy, in their difficulties in recognizing photographs of faces. The fact that some prosopagnosic patients demonstrate no difficulty in face matching tests could also be used as an argument in support of the not entirely perceptual nature of the disorder.

Meadows (1974) although not refuting the hypothesis of a mnesic deficit, remarked nonetheless that patients with Korsakoff's syndrome generally recognize people with whom they were very familiar before the onset of the disease. Dricker *et al.* (1978), however, have stated that Korsakoff subjects are just as deficient as patients with right hemispheric lesions on tests of both memory and face matching. In addition, it seems that for matching, they fix upon external characteristics of the faces, such as expressions or paraphernalia.

However, Meadows admits that the association that was previously described by Hécaen *et al.* (1957) between topographical memory loss and prosopagnosia supports the mnesic character of the deficit. According to Meadows, either of the syndromes could result in a discontinuity between the posterior parietal areas, which are devoted to spatial discrimination, and the anterior temporal areas, which are implicated in learning.

In regard to this association between topographical memory loss and prosopagnosia, it is quite important to note that in a large series of cases with unilateral hemispheric lesion, the frequency differs according to whether it is the group of prosopagnosic cases that is being considered (38%) or the group with topographical memory loss (77%) (Hécaen and Angelergues, 1963). Thus, in the case of loss of topographical memory, it is much more likely that the association with prosopagnosia is reported than the reverse. It could be that only one form of prosopagnosia—the form in which a mnesic aspect predominates—is associated with topographical memory loss.

Even though we cannot therefore exclude a mnesic component, it is necessary to discuss the characteristics of the perceptual aspect of the defect. Many authors disregard the real specificity of the disorder, emphasizing either the complexities that often accompany prosopagnosia, or the failures in performance of patients on other visual discrimination tests. The disorder only covers the problem that is caused by right hemisphere posterior lesions in discriminating complex perceptual patterns (De Renzi and Spinnler, 1966); or, as Lhermitte and Pillon (1975) have stated, "the difficulties in processing ensembles of visual information whose elements are morphologically very similar to each other or to extract the patterns that underlie either the identity or the individuality of these ensembles".

The general perceptual superiority of the right hemisphere over the left, and its holistic mode of processing information, would both tend to favour its treatment of perceptual facts concerning faces—permitting immediate recognition without recourse to an analysing process of the diverse elements of which they are composed. Levy *et al.* (1972) have demonstrated right hemisphere superiority for processing of visual data in split-brain subjects. This effect takes place as long as the response is not verbally solicited. The same superiority exists for faces and meaningless designs, as well as for meaningful and familiar images.

There are, however, some observations which seem to assume a much larger specificity of the recognition deficit. For the cases described by Whiteley and Warrington (1977) for example, the very precise test for perceptual capacities that was used only revealed deficits when the discriminations involved facial representations.

Tzavaras *et al.* (1970) attempted to investigate the specificity of the recognition disorder by submitting unilateral lesion patients to a series of visual matching tests. The tests involved faces (photographs or line drawings) that were modified either by changes in facial expression, lighting, or associated elements (hair, hat, etc.). Objects were either meaningless line drawings, photographs of objects in the same semantic category but differing according to individual details, or objects that were shown with varying degrees of shading. Results confirmed previous studies that suggested the predominant role of the right hemisphere in recognition deficits of the human face. A high correlation was found among deficits on all tests of facial recognition; no correlation was found between results on tests of facial recognition and results of the other tests. These results, according to Tzavaras *et al.*, favour a recognition deficit exclusively for faces which leads them to hypothesize a specific function for human facial recognition.

Ellis (1975) remarked that this conclusion remains uncertain because the degree of difficulty of the different matching tests had not been equated. For example, control subjects only committed errors on tests that involved faces. Subjects with right lesions, who were deficient on these tests, could thus be equally deficient on other recognition tasks if these later tests had caused difficulties that were comparable to those concerning faces.

The specific characteristics of face perception, and its related difficulties have also been discussed by Yin (1969, 1970, 1978). It is generally known that, for both children and adults, recognition of faces is more difficult when the faces are presented upside-down (Kohler, 1940). Taking this fact into account, Yin (1969) showed that this recognition difficulty was much greater when a subject had to select in a multiple choice task an upside-down face that had previously been presented in the normal position. This upside-down recognition defect also existed for objects that normally have a single orientation, but the defect was more severe for faces. In this task of delayed identification, Yin concluded that two factors were relevant. The first, a factor of familiarity, related to all visual representations, facial or otherwise. The second, which was specific for human faces, may have been a loss of the "general impression" of the normally oriented face, when the face was upside-down. An additional piece of evidence was provided by the same author to suggest that the human face is a specific perceptual complex. Photographs of faces were much more difficult to remember than photographs of objects under conditions of rapid presentation.

Yin (1970) continued similar research with post-traumatic brain-injured subjects. On a test of facial recognition, performance of subjects with right posterior lesions was inferior to that of subjects with unilateral lesions in any other part of the brain and to that of a control group. When the faces were presented upside-down, the test performance of subjects with lesions in all other locations was inferior to those of subjects with right posterior lesions and to controls. This dissociation between normal and inverted positions of presentation was not found with photographs of other familiar items.

This dissociation, in Yin's view, demonstrated that the defect is specific to facial recognition. The recognition of "expression" implies both an appreciation of the face as a social object, and, at the same time, memory for the people that are represented. Thus, presentation of inverted faces does not affect the performance of patients with right lesions since they are incapable of distinguishing expressions.

Later, these conclusions were disputed. According to Rock (1974), if presentation in the inverted position makes face recognition more difficult, it is because the more components a figure has the more difficult it is to make compensating corrections when it is presented in the wrong position. Ellis and Shepherd (1975) found no such disparity between the recognition of upright and inverted faces by normal subjects, according to the hemifield of presentation. Of course, recognition was superior in the left hemifield, but this advantage was similar for both upright and inverted presentation. Thus either the hypothesis of system specificity must be rejected, or it must be admitted that the system is not orientation sensitive.

However, Yin's results have been confirmed by Leehey et al. (1978), who found a highly significant left visual field advantage, but only for faces in the upright position. Ellis and Shepherd's negative results may be due to the fact that their stimuli were presented too briefly for them to be encoded as faces. The results of Leehey *et al.* also revealed a left hemifield superiority for inverted faces, but it did not reach a significant level. Therefore these authors concluded that the right hemisphere is specialized for recognition of faces that are presented in the normal position, as well as having a general specialization for visuo-spatial patterns.

In their presentation of three cases of prosopagnosia, Whiteley and Warrington (1978) emphasized the integrity of visual and spatial discrimination in two of the three patients. In recognition tests for objects that were presented in an unusual perspective, and for uncompleted letters, all three patients showed different patterns of difficulty. In contrast, their below average performance in face matching was marked and constant. According to these authors, the selectivity of the disorder depends upon a perceptual classification defect, the effect of which is constant only for human faces. In the same sense of this interpretation, it can be noted that Landis *et al.* (1979) demonstrated an asymmetry of the association process accomplished by the two hemispheres. Their experiment, using tachistoscopic presentation of stimuli to normal subjects' hemifields, revealed a superiority of the left hemisphere for recognizing the category to which different objects belonged, while the right hemisphere was superior in visual recognition of the expression that was common to two faces that were very different from each other (one schematic, and the other a photograph in profile).

A study by St John (1979) also shows that there is a significant left hemifield advantage for judgments of identity or difference between two face representations—one in the normal position, and the other a mirror image. But this advantage does not exist for a similar task dealing with objects (shoes, in this case).

7 CONCLUSIONS

The different data given by the anatomo-clinical observations, along with the experimental results in pathological subjects as well as in normals, and attempts at interpretation which these diverse studies have permitted, all serve to affirm a certain cohesiveness. Yet, at the same time, important discordances arise. It seems to us that these discordances merit study in spite of the general unity which marks the perceptual problem, and the different conditions both anatomic and functional that can be taken into consideration. Prosopagnosia can thus be manifest under several different forms.

Considering the diversity of the associations that are recognized in prosopagnosia, one can easily conceive that the anatomical conditions which produce it are diverse. For example, when it appears in the midst of a cluster of perceptual problems (colours, objects, graphemes), then the syndrome results from bilateral lesions, and can even be a stage in the recovery from cortical blindness (Beck *et al.*, 1978). It is equally possible that the left hemisphere also participates in facial discrimination, but by means of different mechanisms. Such a notion is supported by the results of Hamsher *et al.* (1979). Face recognition is a bi-hemispheric process, even though studies with normal subjects seem to exclude any process of verbal coding for faces. If the symptom is present in a strong and persistent form, then bilateral lesions are probably present. In the case of right unilateral lesion, the recognition deficit could be compensated for through the intervention of the other hemisphere. Thus, one of our patients (Hécaen *et al.*, 1972) could recognize the doctor he saw daily only after verbally describing his face. But this procedure did not always suffice for the identification of other people or for photographs of celebrities whose faces the patient said he knew.

If the right hemisphere lesion is predominant, although not totally isolated, then the difficulty is seen to be clinically isolated. But when the perceptual capacities are experimentally tested, defects are seen in other discrimination or recognition tasks.

Where the lesion affects only the posterior region of the right hemisphere, besides difficulties in identification of faces there would only be the defects in spatial function commonly associated with lesions in this area of the brain.

Finally, there are some particularly pure cases such as those described by Whiteley and Warrington (1977). It seems such cases do exist although they are extremely rare. Perhaps this unusual condition depends on anatomical factors; for instance a focal lesion in the right hemisphere associated with a callosal lesion, as Benson *et al.* (1974) suggest. Because of the mnesic component, the specificity could also be due to a lesion of the connections between the hippocampus and the right posterior cortex.

But it seems to us that several different forms could exist under the general rubric of prosopagnosia.

a. Forms in which the mnesic component predominates. The subject's perception of faces is not related to his store of memories for them, even though he can distinguish their characteristics well or can mimic them. In spite of this identification problem, the subject can perform well on face matching tests. It is in such cases that there is often also a loss of topographical memory.

b. Usually transitory but sometimes permanent metamorphosic forms. The subject can identify faces in spite of the variant of changing expression. These changes are much less pronounced in the cases of photographs than real faces. The association with spatial problems without a mnesic component is predominant.

c. Almost purely perceptual forms, where the difficulty is confined purely to human faces. This may be due to loss of detectors specialized for the recognition of human faces. It could also be due to a defect in the ability to recognize any complex figure. Performance on face matching tasks would be affected in the same way as recognition of real faces. In contrast emotional expressions are recognized without difficulty. Thus face identification and recognition of emotional expressions can be dissociated—a conclusion to which a number of clinical observations would lead (Suberi and McKeever, 1977; Berent, 1977; Ley and Bryden, 1979).

We certainly do not have enough data to prove the existence of these three types of prosopagnosia—a syndrome rare in itself and often modified by other gnostic disorders due to extension of the lesion. The division into types is only proposed as a model to be tested by analysis of the clearest cases.

It seems to us in fact, that these forms are closely associated with the specific and fundamental deficit, according to the predominance of one or another of their components: mnesic, visuo-spatial or figure organization. But the essential problem still remains of the identification of the human face. Perhaps it is necessary to consider the defect as a single perceptual disorder that involves any multiple-component structure, and whose selectivity stems from the particularly complex organization of the human face.

However, the human face could be represented as a species-specific stimulus which is apprehended precociously by the infant. Yin (1978) summarized the arguments which support a special capacity for face recognition utilizing the following three criteria:

1. the attraction which manifests itself very early for this type of stimulus and not for other visual objects;
2. its different evolution in the course of development;
3. the appearance of an earlier and more precise perception of the differences between human faces and other classes of visual object.

Although he admits that no definite conclusion can be formulated, Yin tends to consider the results as pointing in this direction. In contrast, Haith (1978) and Ganz (1978) both concluded that recent results are opposed to such a conceptualization. In fact it seems these results are inconsistent with a precocious recognition ability in the infant for any visual configuration, as visual experience seems absolutely necessary for such perception.

In addition, in relation to other objects, the capacity for face recognition seems to appear in the child only rather late when the perception involves faces that are not familiar to him up to that point. Moreover, the advantage of the left hemifield for unknown face discrimination only appears at ten years of age, according to the results of Reynolds and Jeeves (1978) and of Leehey (1976), although Young and Ellis (1976) seem to have found it starting at age seven.

The ability to recognize familiar faces, as well as the superiority of the left hemifield for this purpose are both found much earlier (Leehey, 1976). According to Carey (1978), if these results are kept in mind, along with the considerable capacity for adults to encode new faces—a capacity which is greatly diminished when photographic negatives of faces are used, or when faces are presented in the inverted position— then it can no longer be considered that encoding is accomplished by an analysis of the various facial features. A canonical store of the different facial features would be established at a relatively late stage, and it is by means of reference to the canonical face, that is constructed by experience, that a particular face is identified. This recognition is accomplished in spite of modifications in the face that are made by different expressions, by the cut of the hair, different paraphernalia, or age.

Thus, a certain number of results seem to imply a different mode of development, not only for face recognition in relation to that for other objects, but also between familiar and non-familiar faces. This specific character of faces as visual stimuli for members of the same species does not seem to be exclusive to humans, if the results of Rosenfeld and Van Hoesen (1979) are taken into consideration. These authors have demonstrated that rhesus monkeys were particularly adept in discriminating photographs of other monkeys' faces. This capacity persisted in spite of modifications of position, size, colour, or the lighting that was used in the photographs.

4 Social Factors in Face Recognition

John Shepherd

1 INTRODUCTION

People differ in the personal histories and social experiences they bring to any task, and these differences may be especially important when the task involves socially relevant stimuli (Tajfel, 1969). For example, estimates of the physical properties of culturally valued materials such as coins or precious metals may vary with the characteristics of subjects (see Tajfel, 1957, for review), and subjects with opposing attitudes may differ in the attitude relevant material they can recall (Jones and Kohler, 1958).

The most obviously "social" stimulus is another person, or, at one remove, his photograph. Many of the studies of the effects of social factors on responses to faces have been carried out in the tradition of "person perception" research. Here, interest has centred on the ways in which personal characteristics of the perceiver are related to his perception of character traits or emotional states of a target, whom it is convenient to present in the form of a photograph. The "accuracy" of the subjects' judgments about these attributes of the target, or the pattern of inferences which he makes have been the major dependent variables investigated (Shrauger and Altrocchi, 1964). Since the mid 1960s, however, facial stimuli have been increasingly used in studies of recognition memory, and in line with the major theme of this book, this chapter concentrates on research investigating the effects of social and personal factors on memory for faces.

In order to recognize a face, a subject must first have had to encode or categorize it on the basis of some attributes. The categories available to a subject will depend upon his particular experiences, and the effectiveness of his categorization for subsequent recognition will depend upon the appropriateness of the categories for the stimuli.

A unique characteristic of faces compared with other classes of stimuli is that the categories in terms of which they may be described are also appropriate to describe subjects. A person's performance on a face-related task may thus be related to the degree of similarity between his own social category and that of the facial stimuli. One such instance is race, and the first section of this chapter deals with the ways in which the racial category of faces may interact with the race of the subject in face memory. Another important social category is sex, and the second section examines the effect of the sex of the subject, and of the stimulus faces, on recognition performance. In the third section, evidence concerning a number of individual difference variables is reviewed briefly. Finally, in a fourth section, the criteria for judging attractiveness of faces and the effect of attractiveness on memorability are discussed. Each section is thus concerned with a social characteristic of either the subjects, or the faces, or both, and the effect of variations in this characteristic on facial memory.

Two important social factors which are not discussed in this chapter are age and emotion. Both of these are dealt with in detail in other chapters of this book.

2 RACE EFFECTS IN THE RECOGNITION OF FACES

A *Attitude and the identification of race*

Although anthropologists may question the validity of the concept of race, in the popular mind there is little doubt that peoples of the world can be identified as belonging to distinct physical types. The lack of precision in defining the criteria of "race" has not reduced the psychological reality of the phenomenon, nor its significance as a basis for social discrimination. Psychological research has typically been directed towards "racial prejudice" involving groups who have suffered some degree of social disability as a result of this discrimination.

One example is the tradition of research on the ability of anti-Semites and Jews to distinguish between photographs of Jews and non-Jews. Generally, this work has accepted the implicit assumption that there are physical differences between Jews and Gentiles, even though the stimulus material has been selected on the basis of religious affiliation rather than that of physical anthropology, and, indeed, it would appear that the assumption was justified in that a number of researchers found a better than chance identification of Jews (Allport and Kramer, 1946; Lindzey and Rogolsky, 1950; Himmelfarb, 1966). The overall level of accuracy, however, presumably will vary according to the groups from which Jews have to be discriminated. Tajfel (1969) has pointed out that high efficiency in identifying Jews has occurred under some social circumstances, for example, where there has been a large Jewish minority who have differed from the majority in speech, gesture and physiognomy. However, where there has been less physical distinctiveness perceptual discrimination between groups has been less reliable. When Carter (1948) instructed his American subjects to make a threefold classification of faces into Northern European, Mediterranean and Jewish, instead of a twofold classification of Jews and non-Jews, the level of accuracy was diminished, though still above chance.

The prediction can be made that both Jews and anti-Semites will show greater accuracy than others in identifying Jews, but the reasons for superiority will differ for the two groups. Jewish subjects, through their greater contact with Jews, should have a greater opportunity to learn the distinguishing physical features of their own group. Anti-Semites, on the other hand, supposedly regard Jews as a threat and might be vigilant for cues which indicate membership of this group (Lindzey and Rogolsky, 1950).

The evidence for the superior accuracy of Jews in identifying photographs of Jews is inconsistent. Lindzey and Rogolsky (1950) failed to find any evidence for the superiority of Jews, a negative finding replicated by Himmelfarb (1966). These findings have been challenged by Toch *et al.* (1962) on the grounds that the task explicitly set the subjects was one of racial discrimination, with its underlying premise that there are real, detectable differences between Jews and others. Such a task may have been distasteful to Jewish subjects who may have refused to commit themselves to their discriminations. For their own study, Toch *et al.* embedded the task of distinguishing Jews in a wider context of identifying religious groups such as Jews, Catholics and Protestants, rather than a racial task of discriminating between Jews and non-Jews. They found with two sets of stimuli that Jews were more accurate than non-Jews in identifying Jewish photographs, though the effect was significant for only one set of stimuli.

An interesting aspect of this study worth noting in passing is the reasons given by subjects for sorting faces into religious categories. Jewish faces were identified by Jews on the basis of global features, and similarity to a known Jewish person, while non-Jews also used reference to a known Jewish person, but most often used hair colour. Catholics were selected mainly on the basis of similarity to a person known to be Catholic or because of Italianate appearance, but Protestants were selected by a process of elimination. Thus subjects used stereotypes or prototypes for identification of minorities (Jews and Catholics) but appeared to have no stereotypes for the majority category (Protestants). If Jews are superior to non-Jews in recognizing Jewish faces, the reason may be "motivational", with Jews presumably finding it advantageous to be able to recognize co-religionists, or it may be due to familiarity as a result of frequent experience with a large number of Jews. In the case of any demonstrated superiority of anti-Semites at the same task, the latter explanation would seem improbable. When a difference between pre-judiced and non-prejudiced subjects has been found, the result has been interpreted in terms of a "vigilance" hypothesis (Lindzey and Rogolsky, 1950). Those who have found higher recognition rates for anti-Semites have also found an associated response by these subjects to label faces "Jewish" (Lindzey and Rogolsky, 1950; Elliott and Wittenberg, 1955; Himmelfarb, 1966), which provides an alternative explanation. If subjects call more faces "Jewish", then they may identify more Jewish faces by chance. When Himmelfarb (1966) re-quired subjects to identify the Jewish member in pairs composed of one Jewish and one non-Jewish face, anti-Semites were no more accurate than controls, though identification was above chance level for both groups.

More recently this problem has been attacked from the point of view of signal-detection theory (Green and Swets, 1966). This theory was originally developed in the context of measuring psychological thresh-holds but the principles are applicable to other areas. In the "ethnic discriminability" case, the "sensitivity" of the subjects to differences between Jews and non-Jews can be distinguished from the "criterion" or response bias of the subjects. Using a rating procedure, Dorfman *et al.* (1971) found that prejudiced subjects did show greater sensitivity to Jewish faces but no response bias towards calling faces Jewish. These results were contrary to most previous findings, and Quanty *et al.* (1975), using similar methods though slightly different indices, failed to replicate them. In their study anti-Semites did identify more Jewish faces, but when false alarms were included, they showed no greater sensitivity.

The hypothesis that a preoccupation with the threat of Jews leads to a "vigilance" response by which anti-Semites are sensitized to differences between Jews and non-Jews gains little support from these findings. On the other hand, the response category of "Jews" is more "available" to such individuals, and is coordinated to particular cues in the stimuli (responding is not random). Accuracy generally is above chance, so cues of moderate validity must exist.

There have been few studies of the effect of attitude on perceiving "racial" characteristics in faces which were not Jewish. The ability to distinguish Chinese Americans from Japanese Americans was tested in two studies by Farnsworth carried out in 1943 and 1965. Accuracy in the first study was found to be slightly above chance, but faces which were Caucasian or Malay in appearance were more likely to be called Chinese than Japanese, though, in fact, they were more often Japanese. In 1965, when the diplomatic relations between the United States and China and Japan had undergone a transformation, discrimination was at chance level, and the response bias to call faces of Caucasian appearance Chinese, though still present, was much reduced. These results could be interpreted as showing that the group which evoked a hostile response were perceived in terms of a stereotype, an effect which diminished as attitudes softened.

B *Race effects in face memory*

People generally find it easier to recognize faces of members of their own racial group than those of a different racial group. The effect is extremely robust, having been demonstrated with American black and Caucasian college students (Galper, 1973; Chance *et al.*, 1975; Brigham and Barkowitz, 1978), American black and Caucasian grade school children (Feinman and Entwistle, 1976) and with black Rhodesian adults and white Scottish 16 year olds (Shepherd *et al.*, 1974). In one or two cases the expected difference has not been found. Malpass and Kravitz (1969) used black and Caucasian college students, but only the Caucasian students showed the "other-race" effect. Black students recognized black faces and white faces equally well. By contrast Brigham and Williamson's (1979) elderly black subjects showed much better recognition scores for black than for white faces, but their elderly white subjects did equally well with faces of both races. In a study using 7, 12- and 17-year-olds and non-student adults, Cross *et al.* (1971) obtained more complex results. Using per centage correct recognition as a measure, they found that white subjects had higher scores for white faces than for black faces, while black subjects had equally high scores for both races of face. However, both white subjects and black subjects made more incorrect identifications (false alarms) for black faces than for white faces. If these two measures are combined into A', a non-parametric measure of sensitivity, the pattern of errors shows a superiority in recognition of white faces for both groups, although the difference for white subjects is much greater than for black subjects.

While the "other-race" effect is fairly easy to replicate, it is less easy to explain. One simple hypothesis is that black and oriental faces are more homogeneous than white faces, and are therefore more difficult to discriminate on recognition trials. Although some studies using both black and white subjects have found a main effect for race of face with superior scores for white faces (Malpass and Kravitz, 1969; Cross et al., 1971; Shepherd et al., 1974), others have found no difference (Chance et al., 1975; Feinman and Entwistle, 1976), and two, which used the same stimulus set, found an advantage for black faces (Brigham and Barkowitz, 1978; Brigham and Williamson, 1979). The hypothesis is a difficult one to test because difficulty in discrimination may not be due to physiognomic homogeneity but to inappropriate cue utilization. Direct measurement of physiognomic variation within different ethnic populations runs into the problem of selection of appropriate indices. Many anthropometric surveys have selected facial measures from different racial groups (Goldstein, 1979a,b) but these may not be relevant for perceptual discrimination, and hair colour and hairstyle may be used more readily as discriminating cues (Ellis et al., 1975). Indeed, the dramatic effects which changes in hairstyles have on face recognition (Patterson and Baddeley, 1977) are testimony to the importance of these cues.

Goldstein and Chance (1978b, 1979) have carried out a series of studies on Japanese and Caucasian faces to test perceptual differentiation by white subjects within these two classes of stimuli. For the most part they have found little difference in performance on a variety of discrimination tasks, although there are marked differences in recognition memory for these two kinds of faces (Chance et al., 1975).

Races may not differ in the overall variability of their physiognomy, but they may differ in the variability of particular features. Individuals may use for other races the same cues as they use for discrimination within their own race, and these may be less appropriate. For example, hair colouration may be a dominant cue in recognizing Caucasian faces, where considerable variation occurs, but if used for black faces, it may yield little information.

Some support for the notion that members of different races use different features to describe faces comes from a study by Ellis et al. (1975). Twelve adolescent male Bantu and 12 British male adolescents were asked to describe in turn colour photographs of a white woman, a black woman, a white man and a black man. The frequency with which each feature was mentioned was tabulated, and these were compared for the two races of subjects. White subjects more often mentioned hair colour (particularly for white targets), hair length and texture and eye colour. Black subjects more often mentioned hair position, eye size, eyebrows, chin and ears. There is also evidence from this study that black and white faces were described by different features. For example, hair colour was more frequently used in descriptions of white than of black faces, while hair texture, nose and lips appeared more frequently in descriptions of black faces.

In a subsequent study, Shepherd and Deregowski (1981) applied multidimensional scaling techniques to judgments which African and Scottish subjects made of black and white women's faces. The results indicated that when dealing with racially homogeneous faces, African and European subjects did not differ in the attributes on which their judgments were based. Both groups of subjects, however, used different attributes for judging the two sets of faces. For black faces the most important features were texture and colour of skin, face shape, thickness of lips and breadth of nose; for white faces, length, texture and colour of hair, eye shape, fatness of face and skin texture were the most salient features.

Thus it would appear from these results that the facial features appropriate for discriminating among black faces are different from those appropriate for white faces, but that there is no evidence for differential usage of these between African and European subjects.

However, the subjects were asked to make comparisons among triads of faces within a racial group, which may have led to them searching for cues relevant to this specific task. By contrast, when faces are presented singly for purposes of memory, subjects may encode these in terms of habitual responses to faces they most frequently encounter. Presented with individual black faces, white subjects may use attributes customarily used for white faces for encoding these faces.

If this were the case, the effects of training might be expected to differ according to the race of subjects and of the faces involved. For white subjects training on white faces should bring little improvement in recognition performance because the most appropriate attributes for encoding would have been learned; white subjects trained on other race faces should improve their performance.

The literature on training effects is reviewed in detail by Malpass in a later chapter in this volume. Here, it is sufficient to mention that three studies, Elliott *et al.* (1973), Malpass *et al.* (1973) and Lavrakas *et al.* (1976), have attempted to train Caucasian subjects to recognize Asiatic or black faces. The results have been generally disappointing, for neither Malpass *et al.* nor Lavrakas *et al.* succeeded in gaining long-term improvement in the recognition of black faces by white subjects, although Elliott *et al.* did obtain some improvement in recognizing Japanese faces after training on Japanese faces. Taken together, these experiments have yielded little information about the basis of the

"other-race" effect. They also have the disadvantage of being performed as "cognitive" laboratory tasks. In a social context in which
learning to discriminate among members of another race is of functional
value, more effective learning might occur.

C "Contact" versus "attitudinal" hypotheses

Differential frequency of visual contact with faces of different races
should provide varying opportunity for developing appropriate cognitive schemata, whether these be feature based or holistic, for encoding
faces. The use made of these opportunities may vary according to the
individual's attitudes towards members of particular groups. However,
the relationship between frequency of contact, attitude and recognition
is likely to be richly confounded. For example, one possible relationship
which might be tested is that increased contact with a race may lead to
improved recognition. This effect could be explained by the subject's
exposure to more instances of the other race and the development of a
more efficient schema (Elliott *et al.*, 1973), but the increased contact
may lead to more favourable attitudes towards the other race, and these
attitudes may lead to improved performance. Unfortunately, evidence
for the relative importance of experience and attitudes is difficult to
evaluate because frequently these are not measured separately.

Two measures which may be taken as indices of experience of other
races are degree of reported contact with members of other races, and
racial composition of locality or institution. If these measures are
accepted, there is conflicting evidence for the "frequency of contact"
hypothesis. In Cross *et al.*'s (1971) study, white and black children from
integrated neighbourhoods showed less of an "other-race" effect than
that found for children from white segregated and black segregated
neighbourhoods. Similarly, Feinman and Entwistle (1976) found that
children in mainly integrated schools tended to have smaller "other-
race" effects than children from segregated schools. Further analysis of
results of children from integrated schools revealed that "other-race"
effects were related more strongly to proportions of other races in
census tract of residence than integration status of school.

The results of Chance *et al.* (1975) may also be interpreted as supportive of the differential experience hypothesis, since black and white
subjects scored highest on faces of their own race, and lowest on
Japanese faces. Against these results, Malpass and Kravitz (1969),
Brigham and Barkowitz (1978) and Lavrakas *et al.* (1976) found no
relationship between reported contact with other race and recognition
scores for faces of that race; indeed in the latter study, white students

who had attended integrated schools had poorer recognition scores on black faces than those from segregated schools.

If "frequency of contact" does not predict recognition performance, perhaps attitude toward minorities might. People who are favourably disposed towards another race may try to discriminate among its members more than those with unfavourable attitudes. Experiments on perception of other-race faces attest to the influence of attitude on responses to physical qualities of black faces by white subjects. Anti-Negro subjects perceive blacks as more Negroid in appearance than do neutral subjects (Secord *et al.*, 1956) and anti-Negro subjects set black faces farther away than do pro-Negro subjects in an Ames "thereness-thatness" apparatus (Beloff and Coupar, 1968).

In the face memory literature, however, the evidence is less clear. Galper (1973) found a positive relationship between attitude and identification of black faces by white subjects, in that white students in black studies courses made fewer errors on black faces than on white faces, and white subjects in psychology courses made more errors on black faces than on white faces. Further weak support comes from a study by Seeleman (1940) who reported that prejudiced subjects were inferior to tolerant subjects on one of her measures of recognition but not on the other.

Two published studies which directly measured anti-Negro attitudes in white subjects failed to find any relationship with other race recognition (Brigham and Barkowitz, 1978; Galper, 1973), and the claim of Pulos and Spilka (1961) to have shown a relationship between anti-Semitism and recognition of Jewish faces compared with non-Jewish faces appears not to be supported by their data.

Probably the strongest variable relating to recognition performance with other race faces is the racial integration of locality. Where this has been directly assessed, the findings have been consistently positive (Cross *et al.*, 1971; Feinman and Entwistle, 1976), and results from other studies could be claimed to support it. For example, Shepherd *et al.* (1974) found a smaller other-race effect for their African than for their European subjects. The African subjects were members of or connected with the Rhodesian army in which most of the officers are white, and the proportion of whites in the community is much higher than are blacks in Scotland, where the European subjects lived.

The effect of having a substantial proportion of members of another race in the community would be to render less useful a categorical, stereotyped response to the minority as "Blacks" or "Orientals", and to encourage a more individual mode of responding. This may involve the elaboration of schemata in which cues of high criteriality (Bruner *et al.*,

1956) are developed, or where frequent encounters in interpersonal relationships lead to greater "depth of processing" (Bower and Karlin, 1974) of other-race faces. It has been suggested (see Goldstein and Chance's chapter in this volume) that white subjects make fewer attributional responses to black faces than to white faces, and are more likely to perceive black faces in terms of physical features alone.

So far there has been no direct test of this possibility, or whether making "attributional" judgments such as honesty or likeableness about black faces will increase their recognition of white subjects. The previously mentioned study by Shepherd and Deregowski (1981), however, has some indirectly relevant evidence to offer on this point. In addition to the groups of subjects who were run with racially homogeneous faces, Shepherd and Deregowski also ran a group of Africans and a group of Scots with a set of faces comprising 15 black African and 15 white Caucasian women's faces. INDSCAL analyses were run on these data and 6-, 5-, 4-, 3- and 2-dimensional solutions accounted for 67%, 63%, 57%, 47% and 42% of the variance respectively. The four-dimensional solution was retained for interpretation and single and multiple correlations were run using ratings by independent judges and the coordinates of the stimuli on the dimensions. The first dimension was clearly a racial dimension, with no overlap between black and white faces, the highest correlations being with skin colour, hair length and hair texture, nose length and lip thickness. On the other three dimensions black and white faces overlapped considerably, the second dimension being primarily one of facial expression, the third hair colour and the fourth skin texture. When the weights given to the various dimensions by subjects were compared, a marked difference emerged between Scottish and African subjects: of the 10 Scottish subjects, 9 had their highest weights on the first dimension, and 1 on the second dimension; the Africans' main weights were on the first dimension for 3 subjects, but for the other 7 subjects the weights were distributed across the other three dimensions. Thus the Scots responded primarily in terms of racial category, the Africans in terms of a number of attributes some of which were independent of race. The African subjects were students at a fully integrated University with 40% white and 60% black students; the Scottish subjects were at a University with less than 1% black students. One possible explanation for the result is that the Africans had learned more useful criteria than race to discriminate between individuals in a mixed race context, but the Scots had not had the opportunity or the need to acquire such criteria.

The "other-race" effect in face recognition may be due, then, to an encoding strategy in which the availability of a "race" category related to salient physiognomic cues, prevents the use of more differentiating and individualizing categories, which are used for "own-race" stimuli, for whom a "race" response category will be less available. Increasing familiarity with the "other-race" will lead to modification of this "race" category as more functional modes of responding are adopted for individual encounters.

3 SEX OF SUBJECT

In their extensive survey of sex differences in behaviour, Maccoby and Jacklin (1974) concluded that very few psychological differences between males and females had been unequivocally demonstrated. In particular they concluded from their review of performance on memory tasks that few sex differences had been revealed, with the exception of verbal memory where girls tend to be superior to boys. However, only one of the articles reviewed concerned sex differences in memory for faces (Witryol and Kaess, 1957). Now there are more than 20 published papers in which sex differences in facial memory have been examined.

Only a minority of these studies have set out explicitly to examine sex differences; in most cases sex of subject has been incorporated as an incidental factor in the design. One possible consequence of this is that more negative results may have been published than would have been the case for other factors.

Studies in which sex of subject may interact with an experimental variable should reveal some of the mechanisms underlying sex differences, although so far this is more of an expressed hope than an even partially fulfilled reality.

Table 1 summarizes the results of experimental studies in which sex differences have been tested. Two features of the Table immediately stand out. First, sex differences have not been found consistently. Secondly, on those occasions where differences have been significant, they have mostly favoured females. The reasonable conclusion is that women are at least marginally superior to men in face recognition memory.

In a number of cases there is a sex of subject by sex of face interaction. Where this occurs it is usually attributable to females showing greater facility on women's faces than on men's, while males usually perform with equal facility on male and female faces.

The superiority of women is believed to stem from their greater interest in other people, and their tendency to look at faces more than is the case for men. Sex differences have been reported as early as the first

TABLE 1
Studies in which sex differences in face memory have been tested

Author(s)	Year	Age of Subject	Sex with higher scores	Comments
1. Studies in which sex differences were found				
Bahrick, Bahrick and Wittlinger	1975	Adult	F	
Brigham & Barkowitz	1978	College	F	
Cross, Cross and Daly	1971	7, 12, 17 years	No main effect	F superior on female faces, M on male faces
Deffenbacher, Leu and Brown	in press	College	F	
Ellis, Shepherd and Bruce	1973	12 and 17 years	F	
Feinman and Entwistle	1976	8–11 years	F	Four-way interaction involving sex
Going and Read	1974	College	No clear effects	F superior on female faces
Goldstein and Chance	1971	College	F	
Goldstein and Chance	1978	College	F	
Kaess and Witryol	1955	College	F	
Laughery, Alexander and Lane (experiment 2)	1971	College	M	Only 1 target used
McKelvie (experiments 2 and 3)	1978	College	F	Superior on F faces only
Marx and Nelson	1974	College	F	
Witryol and Kaess	1957	College	F	
Yarmey	?975	College	M	When judgments of attractiveness made
			F	When other judgment made
Yarmey and Paskaruk	1974	College	F	

2. *Studies in which no sex differences were found*

Borges and Vaughn	1977	College	3 experiments
Carey, Diamond and Woods	1980	6–16	2 experiments
Chance, Goldstein and McBride	1975	College	
Flin	1980	6–15	
Goldstein and Chance	1964	5–14	
Howells	1938	Adult	
Laughery, Alexander and Lane (experiments 1 and 3)	1971	College	One target
McKelvie (experiments 1 and 4)	1978	College	
Shepherd, Deregowski and Ellis	1974	16, Adult	
Shepherd and Ellis	1973	College	
Yarmey	1978	College	
Yin	1969	College	2 experiments

year of life. Fagan (1972) using an habituation paradigm (see Carey's chapter in this volume for discussion of this technique), reported that girls were superior to boys in face discrimination at the age of 5 months, while Lewis *et al.* (1966) found that infant girls, but not infant boys, showed a preference for faces over other stimuli. The tendency for women to engage in mutual gaze during interaction to a greater extent than males has been shown by Exline (1963). As a result of their interest, women may learn to identify the parts of the face which carry most information and are more likely than men to look at these (Going and Read, 1974).

In an attempt to explain the interaction of sex of face with sex of subject, it has been argued that women are more interested in women's faces than in men's, because they make implicit comparisons between themselves and other women. Men do not make implicit comparison, so do not show a differential effect. In a test of this idea, McKelvie (1978) used British and Canadian students' photographs with Canadian student subjects. He argued that Canadians would make comparisons with fellow Canadians, but not with the seemingly dour-looking Britons, and hence he predicted an interaction with the Canadian photographs but not with the British. His hypotheses were partially supported in one experiment, but not in a replication.

Yarmey (1975) tried explicitly to manipulate interest in his male and female subjects. Using the report of Coombs and Kenkel (1966) that men place more emphasis than women on physical attractiveness in making dating choices, Yarmey argued that if men were asked to judge women's photographs for attractiveness, their interest would be heightened and they would show superior retention to women given the same task. His results bore out this prediction, but he also found a superiority by men on male faces which had been judged for attractiveness, a result not anticipated from his argument. When other attributes were judged, women were consistently better than men at recognition.

The studies by Yarmey and by McKelvie are of interest because of the apparent contradiction in their initial premise. McKelvie argued that women made implicit self-comparisons on attractiveness with other women and predicted women would therefore be superior in recognizing female faces; Yarmey contended that men are more oriented towards attractiveness judgments of women and should be superior to women when given this orientation.

In spite of the conclusion of Maccoby and Jacklin (1974) that the sexes show few differences in "attachment, affiliation and positive interactions of all kinds", it is the case that women are expected to show more interest and more skill in interpersonal relations than men (see

Hoyenga and Hoyenga, 1979, for a review). Induction into a role with such expectations might lead one to expect increasing ability in girls and women to recognize faces, and to recognize emotions.

Studies which vary the age and the sex of subjects should provide evidence relevant to this question. Results of studies with children, however, have been even less consistent than those with adult subjects. Neither Carey *et al.* (1980) nor Goldstein and Chance (1974) found any sex differences. Carey *et al.* conducted four separate experiments with children aged from 6 to 16 years, while Goldstein and Chance used kindergarten, third grade and eighth grade children. Flin (1980) also failed to find any sex differences among British children aged from 6 to 15 years using children's faces as stimuli.

Two other studies which sampled children of different ages did report sex by age interactions in recognition memory, but the findings are entirely contradictory. Feinman and Entwistle's (1976) results indicate that boys are superior to girls in grade 1, but girls are superior to boys in grade 6. By contrast, Cross *et al.*'s sex by age interaction may be attributed to an early advantage for females (at ages 7 and 12 years) and a later superiority of males (17 and adults). These two studies used very different methods, but it is doubtful whether these can account for the inconsistencies, and the overall conclusion from developmental studies of sex differences in face memory must be that the sexes do not develop differentially in their recognition ability.

The inconsistent nature of results, together with the small overall absolute values of significant differences when they are found, have led some commentators to dismiss sex differences as being of minor importance (e.g. Yarmey, 1979a). A similar standard applied to other aspects of face memory research would lead to a similar dispiriting conclusion. Adult competence in face memory is generally of a high order, and even slight differences in performance, if consistently replicable, may shed light on the process involved in perceiving and recognizing faces. It is possible that the nature of the task and of physical parameters of the stimuli may effect sex differences, as Yarmey's (1975) study indicated. Studies of testimony and observational accuracy have shown that own-sex related details are retained better by each sex (McCall *et al.*, 1974; Powers *et al.*, 1979), and that women's recall of a violent incident is more impaired than men's by high arousal (Clifford and Scott, 1978).

Women are more responsive than men to affective aspects of faces. Beloff and Beloff (1961) used an Ames "thereness-thatness" apparatus in which male and female subjects were asked to set a number of well-known faces at a given distance. They found that the placement of faces by women was influenced by the affective value of the stimuli more than it was for men. More recently, Yarmey (1979b) has found that women show superior recognition memory for self-poses of "sociable" and "true self" than do men, which he interprets as reflecting the greater sensitivity of women to subjective processes.

Greater emotionality is part of the female stereotype (Broverman *et al.*, 1972), and there is some evidence that women may be superior expressors of emotion when asked to communicate an emotional state (Gitter *et al.*, 1972a), but the same study by Gitter *et al.* failed to find sex differences in identifying emotions. The evidence for sex differences in emotional judgments is as inconsistent as that for face recognition (Tagiuri, 1969; Gitter *et al.*, 1972a).

One possible line of research into sex effects in recognition memory for faces could be the role of verbal mediation in face encoding. In everyday social intercourse faces are not simply remembered in isolation, but are normally associated with a name. Women have been found to be consistently superior to men in remembering face–name associations in laboratory tasks (Kaess and Witryol, 1955; Witryol and Kaess, 1957), and when required to identify previous school classmates (Bahrick *et al.*, 1975). There is also some tentative evidence that women make different verbal associations from men to pictures of faces, being more likely to use pleasant–unpleasant and warm–cold (Hurwitz *et al.*, 1975), while Mazanec and McCall (1975) report that women have more "cognitive categories" available for the categorization of visual and verbal aspects of every observation of persons.

These findings would suggest that in tasks which permit or encourage affective responses to faces, or seeking verbal labels or categories, women should show superior recognition to men. The longer the exposure time, the more likely it is that these verbal associations will occur, and one would thus predict females will be more superior in performance to males the longer the inspection period. It is also possible, of course, that women will have different attentional strategies during the longer durations (e.g. more fixations) which would improve their performance.

In sum, then, studies of sex effects in face memory have led to some inconsistent and some provocative findings which show a slight tendency to favour women. However, so far, little progress has been made towards explaining differences when they occur.

4 INDIVIDUAL DIFFERENCES

People differ in their ability to recognize faces. This apparently trite observation is not altogether self-evident. The residual variance in memory experiments may reflect simply transient lapses in attention and other extraneous events which produce random variation in performance, rather than consistent individual differences in recognition ability. Only one study appears to have directly addressed the question of intra-individual consistency in face recognition (Goldstein and Chance, 1978a), and has reported generally significant positive correlations in performance across sessions. However, the tasks required of subjects were very similar on the different occasions, comprising the usual recognition memory paradigm of using multiple targets presented serially. Deffenbacher *et al.* (1978) correlated performance on this paradigm with performance at an identification parade and found a positive but non-significant correlation across the two tasks. Intra-subject consistency thus seems to be limited to tasks involving a similar paradigm.

Demographic variables, race and sex, may explain some of this variability, but within race and sex groups measures of individual differences might be expected to account for some variance. However, in view of the gaps in our knowledge of the process involved in face memory (see Ellis's chapter on theoretical aspects, this volume), it is not surprising that the theoretical basis for using some of the measures is rather tenuous.

A Field dependence

The concept of field dependence–independence, introduced by Witkin (Witkin *et al.*, 1962) has been related to a wide range of social and cognitive behaviours. Field independent subjects generally have a more differentiated style of structuring experience and can, for example, more easily segregate relevant elements from a visual pattern and disregard distracting aspects. This is the basis of the principal measures of field dependence, the Embedded Figures Test (EFT), and the Rod and Frame Test (RFT).

Although the Embedded Figures Test was developed to test for field dependence in cognitive and perceptual tasks, it has also been extended to "social" field dependence. Subjects who show "cognitive" field dependence on the EFT are also considered to be socially dependent, and reliant upon others for support and guidance. Using this line of argument, Witkin *et al.* predicted that field-dependent subjects would be attentive to facial characteristics of other people, and would be superior in recognition memory for faces to field-independent subjects. This prediction was supported in a study by Messick and Damarin (1964), who found a significant negative correlation between scores on

EFT and incidental memory for faces in a predominantly male sample. However, as Messick and Damarin themselves pointed out, this finding was something of an anomaly in the field-dependency literature, where field independents usually show superiority on perceptual and cognitive tasks.

The result remains an anomaly. Subsequent research has failed to replicate the finding. Biejk-Docter and Elshout (1969) used four measures of field dependence, and on three of these they found no relationship with face recognition.

More recently Hoffman and Kagan (1977) reported a positive correlation between field independence and face memory. However, the correlation was significant only for Rod and Frame test with male subjects. Correlations with EFT for men, and with EFT and RFT for women were in the same direction but were not significant. Lavrakas *et al.* (1976) also used EFT in a study with white subjects and photographs of blacks. They found a significant positive correlation between field independence and recognition memory, a correlation which held for testing at three different sessions.

In summary, then, it seems that Witkin's initial hypothesis has not been confirmed, but Hoffman and Kagan and Lavrakas *et al.* claim their results are consistent with the theory of field dependence. However, their results suggest that there is nothing special about facial stimuli in memory tasks which distinguishes them from any other kind of pattern. Thus "social" dependency is irrelevant for predicting face recognition. One procedural point may be worth noting. In both of the more recent studies cited above, the paradigm used to measure face recognition required subjects to select the target faces from a matrix of distractors, a task which may involve more structuring of the perceptual field than the usual serial presentation procedure.

B *Anxiety*

Recently a few papers have examined the relationship between self-reported anxiety and face recognition. Generally, one would expect anxiety to interfere with cognitive performance as a result of restricted task-relevant attention (e.g. Mandler, 1979). Siegel and Loftus (1978) report a negative correlation between eyewitness testimony scores and scores on anxiety items of the Multiple Affect Adjective Check List, and on the Sarason and Stoops self-preoccupation scale. The effect of test anxiety on face memory was tested by Mueller *et al.* (1979), who found that high anxiety subjects had a higher false alarm rate, but did not differ on hit rate from low anxiety scorers. These results were not replicated in a study by Nowicki *et al.* (1979), who found a negative correlation between Spielberger's Trait anxiety measure and hit rate, but no correlation with false alarms in an unstructured face memory task. Furthermore, the significant correlation held only for female subjects. In a second experiment, where the subjects were given an orienting task during initial presentation, no significant correlations were found between recognition performance and anxiety scores. As with field dependence, the effects of anxiety, where they occur, appear to be related to general cognitive efficiency rather than to any interaction with faces as a special class of stimuli.

C *Other measures*

Sporadic attempts to find other individual difference measures which predict face memory performance have been reported.

One might expect intelligence, verbal or non-verbal, to be associated with memory ability, but neither Witryol and Kaess (1957), nor Feinman and Entwistle (1976) found any relationship, although Howells (1938) did report a low but significant correlation of $+0.27$.

Messick and Damarin (1964), in addition to measuring field dependence, also administered Pettigrew's category-width test to their subjects. Factor 1 of this measure had a higher correlation with the face recognition score than did field dependence, narrow categorizers being superior to broad categorizers. This superiority was due mainly to the lower false alarm rate of the narrow categorizers, who also outscored broad categorizers on Messick and Fritzky's memory for designs test.

The previously mentioned study by Nowicki *et al.* (1975) was designed primarily to examine a locus of control measure as a predictor of face memory. Two experiments were conducted, one an unstructured memory task, the second, one in which subjects were required to make a specific judgment during the inspection period. Only male subjects produced a correlation between locus of control and recognition scores, and this was true only for the unstructured task. Women's scores on locus of control were not related to face memory.

A study which related measures on interpersonal variables to face memory was that of Schill (1966). He reported that high need approval subjects, assessed on the Marlowe–Crowne scale, showed greater recognition of faces than low need approval subjects, particularly for stimuli associated with positive reinforcement.

There have been too few studies on the basis of which to draw any general conclusion about individual differences in face recognition. In almost every study there is some indication that the requirements of the specific face memory task interact with individual measures. There is clearly a need to explore these interactions more extensively, as with studies of sex differences, and so provide some account of the mechanisms by which these individual differences in performance come about.

5　AFFECTIVE ASPECTS OF FACES

Possibly more than any other class of stimuli, faces evoke an affective response in the observer. In part, this is no doubt due to the face itself being an important means of communicating emotion, but affective and evaluative judgments are readily made about faces which are "neutral" in expression. One affective aspect of faces particularly relevant to face memory is their rated "beauty" or "attractiveness".

Although people have attached great importance to the aesthetic qualities of faces since at least early historical times, this particular aspect of faces has only recently been extensively investigated by psychologists. Lindzey (cited in Berscheid and Walster, 1974) has argued that this neglect has been rooted in some of the philosophical assumptions underlying American psychology, but this reluctance has not been a feature of philosophers and poets who have sought to define beauty in the human face, and to see its relevance to character.

In spite of obvious changes of fashion in "beauty" which dictate the use of cosmetics as beauty aids, there appears to be a remarkable consistency over the millenia since Classical Greece in the attributes which define beauty in faces. According to Plato's theory of the golden section, the length of the face should be divided into thirds by lines drawn through the eyes and the mouth, while the width of the face should be two thirds of its height. A similar standard has been found to hold for modern American aesthetic judgments. Taylor and Thompson (1955) constructed line drawings of faces some of which conformed exactly to these classical proportions and some of which departed from this ideal on various features. For each feature they found that American college-age students preferred the classical proportion, and that there was an age development in the strength of this preference from second grade, where the preference was not found, through 4th, 8th and 12th grades.

If there is some commonly shared criterion of "beauty" or "attractiveness", one would expect to find a consensus in the judgments of beauty among a wide range of people. Indeed, unless this can be demonstrated, research using "attractiveness" as an independent variable would face difficulties of generality, since each individual' standard of beauty would have to be established. It is generally true, however, that even in studies where only photographs of the faces of unknown women and men are used, high levels of agreement among subjects may be found in ratings of physical attractiveness. Murstein (1972), for example, reported a correlation of 0·80 between male and female judges in ratings of "good looking" carried out on 99 couples.

Consensus in the evaluation of attractive faces has been found across age, social class and nationality. In a nationwide survey conducted through a British newspaper, Iliffe (1960) asked his subjects to rank in order of prettiness black and white photographs of twelve young women. Professional "beauties" and extremely unattractive girls were excluded from the stimulus pool. The 4355 respondents were divided into age, sex, class and regional categories, and mean ranks for each category were computed and intercorrelated. All correlations with two exceptions, fell between 0·80 and 0·98. In general, there was considerable consensus among subjects of different age and social background.

Udry (1966) replicated Iliffe's study in the United States and found even higher agreement between categories of subjects and within categories than existed in Great Britain. Furthermore, the correlation between United States males and British males was 0·88, and between United States females and British females 0·87. The pervasive influence of cinema, television and cosmetics manufacturers may account for the widespread norms, an hypothesis supported by Udry's discussion of the relatively low agreement of lower working class and older people with the general standard. Udry suggests that these groups are more isolated from general social values than most other groups.

The pervasiveness of Caucasian standards of facial beauty is revealed even more notably in Martin's (1964) work on judgments of attractiveness of photographs of black American women. He asked 50 United States blacks, 50 United States whites and 40 Nigerian blacks to rank in order of attractiveness 10 photographs of black American women. The ranking of United States blacks and United States whites correlated 0·86, but the rankings of United States blacks and Nigerian blacks though positively correlated, were not significantly so ($\rho = 0·44$). The rankings of each group were also correlated with a ranking of Caucasoid/Negroid appearance which had been carried out by 15 "social scientists". All three sets of subjects' ratings correlated positively with Caucasoid appearance, though only the American blacks' ranking reached a conventional significance level ($\rho = 0·60$). This preference for Caucasian over Negroid appearance was also shown by Cross and Cross (1971), although methodological weaknesses in this study preclude confident generalization about preferences for facial categories (see also Parrott and Coleman, 1971).

In spite of the wide consensus about standards of attractiveness, little formal description of the attributes which define an attractive face has been carried out. Some initial steps have been taken by Brooks and Hochberg (1960), Jones and Hirschberg (1975), and Milord (1978). The two more recent of these studies used multidimensional scaling analysis of similarity and preference judgments among faces to identify the dimensions along which faces were discriminated and evaluated. From their analysis of the judgments of black men's and white men's faces by women from each race, Jones and Hirschberg (1975) identified attractiveness as one of the six dimensions emerging along with race, maturity, masculinity and more specifically physiognomic dimensions. The attractiveness dimension was related to anthropometric measures of chin length, nose profile, hair length and chin type.

Milord (1978) used similar methods in experiments using two samples of faces. In the first experiment, 16 faces were selected on the basis of a 2 (sex) × 2 (race) × 2 (age) × 2 (expression) factorial design, and subjects were asked to state their preference and degree of preference between all possible pairs. Analysis of preference judgments resulted in a four-dimensional solution with most variance accounted for by the expression variable; a second dimension was related to age and race, running from young white to old black; and a third dimension age and sex running from young females to old females with old males and young males undifferentiated in the middle. Degree of preference judgments were also analysed and a four-dimensional solution was adopted. These dimensions were associated with expression (dim.1) and with race, unfamiliarity and "uncertainty" (dim.3). The other dimensions proved to be difficult to label.

6 ATTRACTIVENESS AND MEMORY

In spite of the salience of attractiveness as an attribute in the perception and judgment of faces, remarkably little research has been conducted to relate it to memory. The earliest work appeared in 1917 when Peter reported that the more pleasant or unpleasant a face was rated, the more readily it was subsequently recognized, but it was not until 1971 that the next paper reporting a similar effect was published. Cross *et al.* (1971) found that faces previously judged as attractive were more often correctly recognized than faces not judged as attractive. The initial presentation task was given as a beauty judgment exercise, and there was no control of allocation of attention to different faces, although the authors rule out this as an explanation on the grounds that subjects often spent more time scrutinizing faces of "doubtful beauty". It is also likely, however, that subjects would give little attention to faces clearly not beautiful, so that overall less time could have been spent on the non-attractive faces. The possibility that attractive and unattractive faces might be recognized better than faces of moderate attractiveness was tested by Shepherd and Ellis (1973), who found the predicted effect but only after a delay of 35 days. However, it is possible that this attractiveness by delay interaction was due to a ceiling effect, since only 3 faces in high, medium and low categories were tested at each delay interval. For delay intervals of 1 day and 1 week, the task may have been too easy for any differential forgetting to occur.

Yarmey (1975), found that faces rated low in attractiveness and on degree of liking had higher recognition rates than faces rated medium on these characteristics, but that faces rated high did not differ significantly in recognition from the medium rated faces, although the difference between the means was in the appropriate direction.

Taking these studies together it would appear that faces which depart from a medium or neutral value on attractiveness are more likely to be recognized than faces rated at the medium level. An explanation for these results is not immediately apparent.

One hypothesis is that unattractive faces have physiognomic characteristics which make them more distinctive than "neutral" faces. The apparent simplicity of this hypothesis, although it leaves open the question of how "distinctive" features are to be specified, is spoiled by the evidence that attractive faces tend not to be rated as distinctive. Milord (1978), in a second series of experiments, used only young, male white faces as stimuli for a multidimensional scaling analysis. He found that the dimension accounting for most variance in an INDSCAL analysis of similarity judgments correlated positively with ratings of "pleasing" and "beautiful", and negatively with ratings of "unique". For this sample of faces, uniqueness was characteristic of unattractive, unpleasing faces.

Indeed, the evidence that the distinctiveness of faces facilitates memory is stronger than that for attractiveness affecting memory. Going and Read (1974) originally showed differences in memorability between faces of low and high uniqueness, and more recently, Light *et al.* (1979) have demonstrated the same effect for typicality (defined in terms of ratings of usual to unusual appearance) under a variety of conditions. If the effect of attractiveness on memory could be shown to be mediated by the distinctiveness of the faces, it would reduce the range of effects to be explained. What is lacking at present is any clear evidence of the relationship between attractiveness and distinctiveness. Since the concept of unattractive implies some departure from a norm or modal value, it seems plausible that very unattractive faces should be judged as unusual or unique. However, it is not so intuitively obvious how attractive faces would be rated. To the extent that beautiful faces also depart from the norm, they may also be judged as unusual, but they may also be seen as approximating an ideal, and so be more similar to each other than are unattractive faces. This would lead to the prediction that unattractive faces would be easier to recognize than attractive faces, and both would be easier to recognize than faces of medium attractiveness. In addition, attractive faces should produce more false alarms than unattractive faces because of their greater similarity.

There is little in the way of evidence to support these speculations, but some of Milord's (1978) results are intriguing. In particular, he took looking time measures for his subjects who were allowed to inspect, one at a time, each of the faces for as long as they wished. These looking times were then correlated with subsequent ratings by these subjects and with INDSCAL analyses. Generally, looking times were more strongly related to scales reflecting uncertainty, uniqueness and information than to scales indicating pleasantness or desirability. Loftus (1972) has shown that numbers of eye fixations given a picture is a good predictor of recognition performance, and that a greater number of fixations are given to areas of high information content. Thus more information may be "picked" up from distinctive, unique or unattractive faces as a result of a greater number of fixations (Going and Read, 1974).

Attractive faces, by this reasoning, should not transmit as much information as unattractive faces, and hence should not be as memorable.

7 CONCLUSIONS

The investigation of social factors in face memory is still in its early stages. Nearly all the studies reviewed in this chapter were carried out within the past ten years. Yet already race of subject, attractiveness of faces, and to a lesser extent, sex of subject have been shown in a number of studies to be important variables in face recognition. Some measures of individual differences have also been found to be related to face memory, although not with sufficient consistency to lead to any firm conclusions.

Perhaps the most promising questions for future research concern the interactions between subject characteristics and face characteristics which have been found, particularly in race and sex effects. A more refined psychological taxonomy of faces, such as that attempted by Jones, Hirschberg and Rothman (1976) should provide a more detailed and systematic description of the stimuli; and a finer grained study of the subjects' responses to these faces, as Goldstein and Chance have discussed in their chapter in this volume, may give us important clues about the manner in which individuals process facial stimuli.

Current theories of face recognition tend to be based on traditional memory models (for review see Ellis's chapter, this volume), which typically take little account of social factors. It may be that a return to some of the social judgment models (Eiser and Stroebe, 1972) would provide fruitful areas of exploration.

5 Laboratory Studies of Face Recognition[1]

Alvin G. Goldstein and June E. Chance

1 INTRODUCTION

The title of this chapter implies that it might cover almost the entire range of existing investigations of face recognition. For the most part, however, we have interpreted our mandate to exclude studies in which the independent variable was not, strictly speaking, under the experimenter's control. Although in the interests of continuity, the reader will see that this rule was breached on occasion. This review focuses mainly on adults' recognition performance with live faces or photographs of faces. With two exceptions, theses and presentations at scientific meetings were not cited. Selection of articles was also strongly influenced by consideration of topics to be covered in other chapters of this book.

Development of a coherent organization for the material was difficult, in part because of the rather broad scope of potential content inherent in the title, but also because of the relative dearth of systematic investigation of many problems within the field. Only a few problems have had more than a small handful of investigations directed at them. Perhaps interest in face recognition is too recent to expect a great deal of system and organization in investigations, but a reviewer's job becomes very difficult when the amount of information on a topic is enough to suggest that it ought to be mentioned, but scarcely enough to warrant extended comment or criticism. The topics finally dealt with seemed to us to capture the maximum number of studies in the net while avoiding large overlap with other chapters of this book.

[1] The authors gratefully acknowledge the support of the Graduate Research Council of the University of Missouri, Columbia, in the preparation of this chapter.

We will examine the effects of eight variables on face recognition performance. These eight are effects on face recognition of: transformation of face stimuli; singularity of faces; contexts; retention interval and related factors; depth of processing; verbal coding; intention to learn; and familiarity with the experimental situation and the stimuli. A concluding section will offer a few comments on the state of research in the field.

2 TRANSFORMATIONS

In much face recognition research, stimuli viewed in study trials are also viewed without modification in test trials. Discussed in this section are experiments measuring the effects of modifying stimuli from study to test session. Transformation may be major, as when photographic negatives or inverted photos are used, or minor, as when details of pictures are changed.

We will begin with black-to-white reversals, a transformation familiar to nearly all photographers except Polaroid camera users. Photographic negatives have been shown to be more difficult to recognize than photographic positives (Galper, 1970; Galper and Hochberg, 1971; Phillips, 1972), but in our opinion, subjects' performances were somewhat less disturbed by this transformation than subjective judgments of difficulty might have led us to expect. Taken together, these data show that recognition memory suffers when we match (if that is what we do) a positively encoded portrait with its negative image and also when we encode negative portraits without transformation.

Although Phillips (1972) tried unsuccessfully to show that difficulty experienced when looking at negatives is related in some way to presence of greys in photographs, his hypothesis never clearly spelled out the relationship between greys and perceiving negatives. Nevertheless, Phillips' subjects experienced difficulty when identifying portraits of then famous people from both positive *and* negative pictures lacking tones of grey (lith film was used; it produces black and white images only). Perhaps greys are important after all. As we will see, line drawings of famous faces, which lack greys, are also relatively difficult to recognize (Davies *et al.*, 1978b).

In sum, research on black-to-white reversal in photographic stimuli would profit from a thoughtful analysis of the problem. For example, why is black-to-white reversal used? The real perceptual world for normally sighted people is a rainbow of hues. Looking at achromatic negatives may tell us something about how we perceive portraits, but will it tell us anything else? Are faces the only stimuli which suffer from black-to-white reversal?

By inverting photographs of stimuli performance can be disrupted in a variety of learning and recognition tasks, although the extent of disruption depends on the stimuli and the task. Inverting portraits of faces almost always has large effects on memory performance in naive subjects. Inverting portraits makes them less easily learned if they have not been seen before, and less readily recognized if they are already familiar. Performance differences in these tasks also have been shown to be age-related (Goldstein, 1975).

Many researchers in this area have been intrigued less with the effects of inverting faces on recognition *per se,* than with the question: Is perception of faces affected more than perception of other stimuli when they are turned upside down? Subjectively, inverted faces appear to be more "distorted" or less recognizable than pictures of houses or boats rotated visually by 180 degrees. This subjective experience, in addition to results of recent research on infant's perception of faces, has stimulated speculation concerning the "unique" role of the human face for human beings.

Yin's (1969) investigation is an example of research addressing the problem of face uniqueness. His findings, which are widely cited, were obtained in a series of studies which utilized photographs of faces, houses (including some surrounding scenery), sideview silhouettes of aeroplanes, and cartoon stick figures engaged in various "everyday" movements ("men in motion"). Yin interpreted his results as showing that all mono-oriented objects are more difficult to recognize when upside down, but that faces are disproportionately affected by inversion.

The logic underlying Yin's experiments is that if faces are "special" stimuli, inverting them will affect recognition performance to a greater degree than inverting "non-special" (and non-face) mono-oriented stimuli. Both logical and practical difficulties are involved in this approach to the question at issue. Why would the stimulus uniqueness of the face be proved if faces *are* more affected than non-face stimuli by inversion? Even if the experiment finds a difference between inverted faces and inverted non-face objects, is it not just as plausible, for example, to explain the difference as a function of the discrepancy between the degree of "mono-orientedness" inherent in the two classes of stimuli, as it is to explain the outcome as being related to the "uniqueness" of the face stimulus? Unless non-face stimuli are equated with face stimuli along various meaningful dimensions, any conclusion based on the findings of the experiment is seriously faulted. Principles of good experimental design dictate that non-face stimuli should be equated with face stimuli on all critical dimensions, otherwise recognizability differences caused by inverting the stimuli could be a function of uncontrolled factors. Apparently no attempt was made to equate face stimuli with stimuli of equal configural complexity, class familiarity, or psycho-social importance.

The most critical dimension probably is mono-orientation, and although Yin attempted to "equate" faces with control stimuli also "mono-oriented" (houses and aeroplanes), in fact no real equivalence of "mono-orientation" was ever approached. Mono-orientation has at least two distinct meanings in the present context. First, it means that the object is seen almost always in one orientation (and this feature implies that the object is *not* amorphous, but displays a distinct topside, bottom side, etc.), and second, the class of objects has to have served in past experience as a discriminatory stimulus. The latter quality is critical. Faces are discriminative stimuli from birth. Almost every face we see forces us to make a discrimination; do we know this person or is he/she a stranger? Thus, subjects in Yin's experiment probably had vast discrepancies in amount of "mono-oriented" experience with faces as discriminative stimuli compared with control stimuli. Houses can not be considered seriously to be equal to faces as "mono-oriented" stimuli for a variety of reasons. For instance, houses are seldom if ever pure discriminative stimuli. Houses are identified not by unique structure alone, as are faces, but also by relative location (e.g. near a corner, next to the large red house; the one set back from the street, etc.) along with other cues involving non-house stimuli (e.g. shrubs, trees, number, etc.).

If mono-orientation is a critical factor in the answer to the question: Are faces "special"?, and if the frequency of discriminating upright faces is many orders of magnitude greater than the frequency of discriminating (or even *seeing*) houses, then it follows that faces are special only because, compared to houses, they are more frequently seen, learned, memorized, and discriminated. It is one thing to attribute unspecified special properties to a class of stimuli; it is quite another thing to show that a class of stimuli has become special because of massive overlearning.

Yin's position suffers further erosion from the work of Toyama (1975). Her research, essentially a replication and extension of Yin's investigation, offers almost no support for Yin's results or conclusions. Unfortunately, Toyama's work, an unpublished doctoral dissertation, has had little impact on investigations within this area of psychology.

Scapinello and Yarmey (1970) recognized some of the problems alluded to in the present discussion of Yin's work, and tried to introduce corrective procedures in their study of the effects of orientation on recognition. Pictures of human faces, canine faces, and buildings were selected as stimuli. Picture similarity within each category was assessed and to some extent controlled. Moreover, "familiarity" was manipulated in one experimental condition; half of the stimuli were presented only once, and half were presented for 7 successive inspection trials. More about that in a moment. In agreement with Yin, their results indicated that recognition performance declined for all stimuli as a function of both stimulus inversion and of delay (20 minutes versus immediate testing) in testing, but the decline was greater for faces than for the other stimuli under all conditions.

Although Scapinello and Yarmey included a number of valuable innovations not found in Yin's design, interpretation of their results is still open to question for the following reasons. Within-series similarity may have been effective in controlling for relative ease of discriminability, which is an important consideration. Unfortunately, the real problem lies not in within-series similarity but in the equality of the psychological distance between a pair of human faces compared to a pair of canine faces, for example. If dog faces differ more one from another on the average than human faces differ among themselves, canine faces should be easier to learn, and remember, all other things being equal. Also other things are not equal in this study; stimulus-class familiarity could not possibly be controlled adequately by just adding 6 extra trials in which the houses or the canine faces were repeatedly shown to the subjects. Stimulus familiarity, in the context of the larger problem, specialness of the human face, *cannot* be an *experimental* variable, but of necessity has to be an experiential one. Familiarity is something the subject brings to the experiment, not something the experimenter manipulates.

Are faces "special" stimuli? It depends on what is meant by the term "special". Is there a special factor, as Yin suggests (1969, p. 145), which makes the face an unusual stimulus, and which affects the way in which it is processed by our memories? Clarification of these questions, in addition to some sharpening of the methods used to test the questions, would improve greatly the chances of obtaining answers. "Special factor" is too vague a concept to be helpful.

Findings pertaining to recognition of inverted faces, as well as the data concerning effects of transformations of photo positives to negatives, or effects of removing shading from pictures, can all be subsumed under a hypothesis that humans develop a face schema. The schema results from our multitudinous exposures to upright, detailed visual images of faces found in our particular environments. The development of the face schema can account for the effectiveness with which we process familiar kinds of faces; however, a schema also could hinder processing of faces perceived as different—foreign, in the "wrong" orientation, represented in a degraded form, etc.

In the conclusion of this section consideration will be given to minor transformation studies in which the stimulus itself is altered between the study and test sessions. Studies of this type might be expected to provide information about the nature of memory traces—what is or is not stored or represented in memory. Ellis *et al.* (1978b) observed that recognition of Photofit faces, which contain several lines representing the boundaries of the transparent plastic pieces bearing the various facial features, is more difficult than recognition of ordinary photographic portraits. Although those thin lines seem unlikely reasons for reduced performance, this is exactly what these investigators report. Photographs, when marked with a few irrelevant lines, are more difficult to recognize than when unlined.

The above result, surprising as it may appear, is consistent with other research concerning disguises. Patterson and Baddeley (1977) report that adding or subtracting wigs or beards has markedly deleterious effects on recognition. Even the presence or absence of spectacles reduced performance under some conditions. In accord with these findings, Davies *et al.* (1978b) also report impaired recognition memory performance when photographic portraits used in the study session are changed in the test session to detailed line drawings. In this same investigation, correct identification of detailed line drawings of the faces of male celebrities were far less frequent than identifications of photographs of these same celebrities. These findings suggest that the difficulty experienced by the subjects in this experiment is of a general nature. In other words, not only unfamiliar faces (i.e. target faces) but also well-known faces are made much less recognizable by changes of presentation mode which are quite modest and still preserve many of the attributes of the original face. In contrast, Davies *et al.* (1978b) and Patterson and Baddeley (1977) find small changes in pose (position in relation to camera) do not affect recognition.

A bit removed from this discussion, but still relevant is Diamond and Carey's (1977) curious finding that paraphernalia changes (hats, scarves, glasses, wigs) confuse young children when the faces are unfamiliar, but have little effect when the faces are familiar. Although direct comparison between the studies just cited and Diamond and Carey (1977) is not possible for a variety of reasons, it is intriguing to wonder if adults are really affected so much more than young children by seemingly small changes in stimuli.

Finally, Egan *et al.* (1977) demonstrated that, after looking at live study faces, recognition performance in the test session (2, 21, or 56 days later) is better when live faces rather than photographs are viewed (overall, 97% versus 85% correct identification). The latter finding, if confirmed by replication, suggests faces in photographs are processed differently from live faces.

The sum of work to date on minor transformations would indicate that faces are made more difficult to recognize by any manipulation which reduces the amount of detail present when recognition is demanded: photographs are less easy to recognize than live people, but photographs are better than line sketches of faces. Accuracy is also impaired when the face to be recognized has undergone additions or changes like glasses, beards, wigs, hats, etc. Even addition of a few non-face related lines can impair recognition. In contrast, small changes in pose seem not to have an effect. Work on major transformations suggests that photographic negatives (or other markedly degraded photos) are harder to recognize than good photographic positives. Inverted faces are harder to recognize than upright faces, and may be harder to recognize than other inverted objects. The claim that faces are unique stimuli is open to serious question; if they are special, the reasons for this characteristic are by no means clear. In a recent paper (Goldstein and Chance, 1980) we have suggested that learned face schemata, which facilitate face recognition under many circumstances, may impede the same performance when faces are modified as by inversion or in photographic negatives.

3 SINGULARITY EFFECTS

In 1917, Peters (cited in Ellis, 1975) reported that among her subjects perceived pleasantness was related to correctness of recognition memory in a U-shaped fashion; the best memory performances on the average were associated with faces rated either high or low in pleasantness, whereas faces rated intermediate in pleasantness were recognized less frequently. In the intervening years, surprisingly little new information has been added to this early finding. In fact, if the dimension "pleasantness" were considered to be a special case of a more general category, "singularity" (or "typicality"), Peters' work sums up most of what we know today about recognition memory for unusual faces: on any continuum, faces judged as near the extremes are better remembered than faces judged in the middle. Exactly why is still unclear.

Since Yarmey (1979a) has recently reviewed the relatively small number of studies of the effects of singularity on recognition memory for faces, only a brief sketch of the findings will be given here. Face recognition performance has been shown to be affected by stimulus distinctiveness (Going and Read, 1974; Cohen and Carr, 1975; Light *et al.*, 1979), attractiveness (Shepherd and Ellis, 1973; Fleishman *et al.*, 1976) and beauty (Cross *et al.*, 1971).

In one of the most comprehensive studies of the phenomenon under discussion, Light *et al.* (1979) demonstrated that recognition memory for unusual faces was better than for typical faces ". . . under both intentional and incidental learning conditions, with presentation rates varying from 3 sec to 15 sec/item, and over retention intervals varying from 3 hr to 24 hr" (p. 223). In the final experiment of the series, a strong relationship was found between interitem similarity and typicality, suggesting the basis for obtaining better recognition performance with unusual faces: typical faces are more alike and thus are more frequently mistaken for each other.

In two relatively comprehensive studies, Yarmey (1979a, p. 119) demonstrated, depending on the sex of the observer, memory for faces is differentially (and somewhat complexly) affected by perceived attractiveness, distinctiveness, and likeability. Effectiveness of these variables is detectable over relatively long periods of time (up to one month) even with a 2-second encoding period.

The speed at which humans appear to be able to extract the dimensions just cited is also astonishing. For instance, in our laboratory we have collected data on judged attractiveness as a function of length of inspection interval (Goldstein and Papageorge, 1980). Ratings obtained from subjects following a single 150-ms look at each of a series of faces were highly correlated with ratings of the same faces made by judges who had unlimited time for their judgments; short exposure and the consequent lack of eye movements had almost no effect on attractiveness judgments. Since a visual mask did not follow the face stimulus, the exact length of processing time is debatable, but surely no more than a few milliseconds were added to the total processing time.

What mechanism could be responsible for the effects of singularity on recognizability? Are the findings related to the von Restorff isolation effect? Surely there is common ground here, even if the homogeneous list in face experiments is in the perceiver's head and not, as in von Restorff's experiment, in the laboratory memory task. Though von Restorff studied recall, not recognition, his work might still be relevant although weak as an overall explanation of the singularity effect. Thus, the atypical face is perceived to be atypical because it is compared to the observer's memory store (schema) of faces. Possibly scalar judgments are made automatically with every encoding, and atypical faces compared to typical faces might be encoded differently. This leaves several questions unanswered: In precisely what way is a singular face encoded differently? And even if an unusual face is specially treated at encoding, how does its memory trace survive and win acceptance in the recognition test when some distractor faces are also atypical?

Changes in arousal level also have been suggested (Shepherd and Ellis, 1973) as an explanation of the effects of at least one kind of singularity, attractiveness. (Another form of the arousal hypothesis has been offered to explain variations in face recognition memory performance under conditions of situationally caused stress, e.g. fear induced by a person holding a gun. For the time being, confusion between the two forms of the hypothesis should be avoided.) Arousal as an explanation of singularity effects is, on the one hand, an attractive hypothesis since it seems so plausible, but on the other hand, it presents several problems which could reduce its effectiveness. To begin with, arousal changes evoked by attractive and unattractive faces would have to be equal in order to explain the U-shaped memory curve. It is unlikely that attractive and unattractive faces are equally arousing. Moreover, the apparent complexity of the arousal–memory process raises questions about its applicability to face recognition findings. Some evidence suggests that arousal interacts with retention interval. Also, recent reports (Schulz and Straub, 1972) of the effects of "high priority events" (HPE) on memory suggest that changes in arousal influence memory for events preceding and following the arousal-inducing HPE, and these effects both enhance and reduce memory performance. These considerations suggest the need for additional research, and the first place to begin the work should be a test of the assumed relationship between perception of different kinds of faces and arousal level changes.

Differences in eye movements might shed some light on the effects of singularity on recognition memory. Almost by definition atypical faces are more "interesting" than typical faces, and therefore they could elicit more attention, in turn promoting longer looking times and increased total number of eye movements. All these factors should improve retention, but number of eye movements is one of the easier ones to study in the laboratory. Frequency of eye fixations during inspection of other pictorial material has been demonstrated to be related to information acquisition (Loftus, 1972). Given the usual imprecisely controlled, several-second study time used in face recognition studies, unusual faces might be effectively looked at for slightly longer periods of time and therefore are scanned by more frequent eye movements than are ordinary faces. The total difference in eye movement frequency need not be large at all; recognition memory performance differences between unusual and ordinary faces, although consistent, tend to be fairly small. A few additional eye fixations and slightly more information about atypical faces could be processed, thereby enhancing memory performance for these stimuli.

So far as we know, solid evidence for this information processing approach has not been reported. In a preliminary attempt to study this question, we have measured recognition memory performance as a function of facial attractiveness with eye movements reduced to a single fixation per face. Under these conditions, if the eye movement interpretation were correct, all faces, irrespective of attractiveness rating, should have been equally memorable. Unfortunately, for reasons still unclear, the results of several small studies of recognition were inconclusive (Goldstein and Papageorge, 1980). The problem deserves further investigation.

Several other studies not yet cited also seem to be related to the issue of effects of singularity on recognition. Why, for example, are some distractor faces frequently chosen as targets—i.e. false alarms—while other distractors are *in*frequently chosen as targets (Goldstein *et al.*, 1977)? We have not yet answered this question in our laboratory, but we have recently found (unpublished data) the phenomenon to be highly reproducible. In two studies where only the subjects differed, frequently misidentified faces were misidentified in both studies. In a few cases, the frequency of false alarms exceeded the number of correct responses made to any single target face. It is tempting to speculate that there is something unusual about these faces despite their seemingly "normal" appearance. (Obviously, target-distractor similarity could easily explain these results. Simple visual inspection gives little support for this interpretation. See, however, Davies *et al.* (1979b) for a more sophisticated treatment of this topic.)

Shoemaker *et al.* (1973) also have reported findings which are interpretable within the context of singularity effects. Subjects in that study who were asked to find a murderer, a rapist and other "deviants" in an array of portraits of middle-aged genetlemen, selected individual faces for each deviant category with significant between-subject agreement. In order to infer these "impossible" character traits with a significant degree of consensuality from portraits alone, subjects must have accessed their memory stores for shared prototypes of normal, typical people and of murderers, rapists, etc. On the basis of Shoemaker *et al.* (and our own unpublished data collected on a related problem), we speculate that subjects did these "selection" tasks "successfully" and willingly because they had done something like them in earlier extra-laboratory situations. We infer that people in daily life categorize and judge new, unfamiliar faces along one or more impressionistic continua fairly automatically.

Carrying this point further, it suggests a possible explanation for singularity recognition effects. Unique atypical faces evoke responses which differ from responses to typical faces. In other words, they are coded differently. Average faces compared to atypical faces might be coded less distinctively, or average faces might evoke coding responses less consistently often than unusual faces. How many things can you say about Mr Average, anyway? Both possible coding differences would lead to poorer retention for average faces. Missed codes could not help and less distinctive codes would be more susceptible to all forms of interference. It could be hypothesized that however the coding differences arise, that singular faces are more likely to be remembered because the code or codes they evoked the first time are also more likely to be evoked when they are seen again. This hypothesis is readily testable.

One last incidental observation and speculation may be of interest. We have initiated work in our laboratory on the problem of perception of facial beauty. In this research, literally thousands of good-to-excellent quality portraits of college students have been rated for beauty using standard rating techniques. From these ratings, one fact stands out clearly; beauty is much rarer than its opposite; judgments of facial beauty are not normally distributed. Although judges rate many faces at the extreme low end ("ugly") of the rating continuum, almost never is a face given the highest or even next to the highest rating. If we disregard the unlikely possibility that the skewness is caused by a massive sampling error, this finding suggests that ugly faces should be more difficult to recognize than beautiful faces because our memory store should be less cluttered with beautiful faces. In addition, beautiful faces should be more arousing (both meanings intended) than ugly faces because they are more unique. Past analyses of data concerning atypicality and recognizability of faces may not have been sensitive to this possibility.

4 CONTEXT EFFECTS

Consider the following observations. Verbal material learned in one situation (context) is best remembered if performance is tested under conditions similar to those present during learning. Pavlov's trained dogs salivated as they were placed in the experimental apparatus, but before either the bell was sounded or food was made available to them. A familiar face may not be recognized when seen unexpectedly in a strange setting (e.g. foreign country). These two examples of learning–performance relationships are connected by an underlying theme: They illustrate that learning involves the complete situation experienced at the time of acquisition. The learner becomes responsive to stimuli which are apparently "irrelevant" to the main task or to the material to be learned, but these seemingly irrelevant stimuli affect performance.

Face recognition should also be susceptible to context effects. Thus, when Bower and Karlin (1974) reported that memory for faces did not seem to be related to the context in which they were learned, several investigators set out to check the validity of that report. Bower and Karlin had studied the effects of context by using pairs of study faces. Recognition was tested when both members of the pair were identical in study and test (same context), when only one face was presented (deletion of context), and when a new face was substituted for one of the study faces (changed context).

With some variations, this paradigm has served as a model for the studies which followed Bower and Karlin, all of which found evidence for context effects in face recognition. Watkins *et al.* (1976) showed in a series of studies that faces are better remembered when the contexts provided during study are also provided during test, and that this facilitation takes place when the context is either randomly assigned descriptive phrases accompanying the faces at study or other faces (i.e. pairs). Winograd and Rivers-Bulkeley (1977) had their subjects judge the "compatability" of male–female couples in order to enhance the probability that the faces would be encoded as pairs and found increased recognition for same context pairs as compared to changed context pairs.

In a slightly different approach to the effects of contextual variables, Brown *et al.* (1977) presented two different sets of study faces, each set presented in separate rooms 2 hours apart. After a retention interval of 2 days, testing took place in a third room. Subjects' memory for faces was excellent (96% correct). In contrast, memory for the room in which the face had been seen turned out to be no better than chance. A similar finding has been reported by Deffenbacher *et al.* (in press).

It would appear from these two studies that while faces themselves are affected by contextual variables, it is even more likely that the context in which a face is learned will be forgotten, at least when the context is no more interesting than a room. Only additional research will tell us if the situation in which a face is seen is remembered when that situation is characterized by more arousing features than would be found in a classroom. Real-life errors of identification, especially those made in connection with eyewitness identification of criminals offer support for the laboratory findings reported by Brown *et al.* (1977) and Deffenbacher *et al.* (in press). Witnesses sometimes report that they see a "familiar" face in the police line-up but the familiarity is a result of a previous encounter with the face either in a mug book or in the police station, not at the scene of the crime (see, for example, Ellis *et al.*, 1977).

Since this kind of error is not unique to culprit watching, it suggests that *where* a face is first seen is not always remembered as well as the face. Although this conclusion is not all that surprising (Bahrick *et al.*, 1975), it does emphasize the difference in memory processing involved when a face is recognized compared to remembering where the face was seen. Faces are recognized, contexts have to be recalled, or at least the connection between the face and the context must be recalled. A particular context could enhance or reduce recognition memory depending on its actual relevance to the conditions present at encoding, but the observer need not be aware of the true relationship between context and face for this effect to occur.

Broadly defined, as the term is used here, contextual variables were also manipulated by Leippe *et al.* (1978) in an attempt to assess the influence of perceived seriousness of a (simulated) criminal act on eyewitness accuracy. They report that if subjects were aware at the time of a theft of the value of the object stolen, they were more likely to identify the culprit correctly when the object taken was expensive ("serious crime") than when it was inexpensive ("not serious crime"). If subjects became aware of the value of the object taken only after the incident occurred, accuracy of identification was not affected. The results of this study are not only statistically significant, but also psychologically impressive in that the disparity between the findings in the serious and not serious conditions was quite large. Knowledge of crime seriousness may have enhanced recognition accuracy by enhancing attention paid to the scene or by increasing chances that the subject would engage in immediate rehearsal of the face.

5 RETENTION INTERVAL AND RELATED FACTORS

When one thinks about memory the most likely association evoked is time. Memory is something that happens over time. The history of psychology contains uncounted examples of studies of remembering or forgetting as a function of amount of delay between encoding and retrieval. Therefore, it comes as a surprise to discover that systematic laboratory research about the relationship of face recognition perform- ance and delay interval is sparse to non-existent. Why there has been a lack of investigation is not immediately obvious. Could it be that researchers, like the proverbial man in the street, "know" that faces are never forgotten, so they have little incentive to explore the effects of time on face memory? Perhaps the work of Nickerson (1965), which demonstrated almost unbelievably huge and persistent recognition memory capacity for pictorial materials, convinced investigators that length of delay interval was unlikely to have much effect on face memory performance. Whatever the reason for the lack of research, one thing is clear. It is quite difficult to get scientific answers from the current literature to questions as "simple" as: How many of a set of faces learned can be recognized after 1 minute delay? Five minutes? Five days?

Memory load also has been neglected by investigators. In short, we do not know the answer to some fundamental questions pertaining to memory for faces because pertinent studies are lacking. Research on faces and our memory for them has started from the middle of the problem instead of from the beginning.

Although the Bahrick *et al.* (1975) study is not, strictly speaking, a laboratory study of face recognition, it would be foolish to omit it from this review since it represents the only available systematic information about face recognition memory over long delay intervals. This study is an impressive attempt to get answers to a variety of truly difficult questions regarding human information retention. Bahrick *et al.* addressed the problem of the fate of face recognition over delay intervals as short as 2 weeks to as long as 57 years using as memory stimuli yearbook portraits of high school graduates' classmates. After statistic- ally adjusting retention scores for other measured variables such as original learning and rehearsal opportunities (e.g. the fact that some subjects looked at their yearbook one or more times in the years inter- vening between graduation and the recognition test), the investigators concluded that visual information can be retained almost unimpaired for at least 35 years. In fact, per cent correct recognition varied from 89% at about 3 months after graduation (the value the investigators took as "original" learning) to 73% for the group who graduated on the average almost 48 years earlier. Since the recognition tests consisted of one target picture (a classmate) and 4 foils (non-classmates) the reported retention scores represent solid evidence that the faces were truly recognized by the subjects. Other data from this investigation confirm this conclusion.

These data confirm anecdotal reports, and subjective impressions that human memory for visual information, acquired by prolonged and repeated exposures, is inordinately tenacious. Note that the data from other retention tasks included by Bahrick *et al.* (e.g. identification and matching of names and faces) also showed surprisingly slow forgetting over long periods of time; however, among those aspects of memory included, face recognition memory was the winner, although not by a large margin.

The importance of the Bahrick *et al.* investigation can not be disputed, nor can the problems associated with extremely long-term memory research be underestimated. Until additional research on this topic is conducted, it appears reasonable to conclude tentatively that well learned faces can be routinely remembered for periods of time in excess of 30 years. We wonder whether other overlearned stimuli would be as well remembered as faces.

We turn now to more conventional laboratory studies of retention. As in most kinds of learning, the longer the acquisition period for faces the better the retention (Scappinello and Yarmey, 1970; Wallace *et al.*, 1970; Laughery *et al.*, 1971; Light *et al.*, 1979). Also the advantage conferred by longer looking time is not materially changed whether the subject is intentionally or incidentally learning the faces or when delay intervals vary from 3 to 24 hours.

In a series of studies, where essentially one target face (instead of many faces) served as the memory stimulus, and 149 faces served as distractors, Laughery *et al.* (1971) found that longer total exposure time to the target improved memory performance. Also if subjects viewed many faces during the test trials before arriving at the target face, their performance suffered in comparison to subjects who viewed only a few faces prior to seeing the target.

In another series of studies, again using the single-target method of testing for retention (analogous to an eyewitness situation), Laughery *et al.* (1971) found that varying study–test delay intervals from 4 minutes to as long as one week made little difference in hit rate. Similar findings attesting to the apparently robust nature of the face memory trace have been reported by other investigators (e.g. Egan *et al.*, 1977).

Wallace *et al.* (1970) also reported that increasing inspection time increased recognition rate, but they also found that increasing the length of the delay interval may not always decrease memory perform- ance. They found, as Milner (1968) had earlier, that sometimes memory performance improved instead of declining as delay interval increased from immediate to 45 seconds (Wallace *et al.*, 1970) or to 90 seconds (Milner, 1968). This unusual and poorly understood phenomenon, called *reminiscence*, is quite similar to hypermnesia (Erdelyi and Becker,

1974) for pictorial (not faces) material. Yarmey (1971) has also reported reminiscence for faces with memory improvement occurring 20 minutes after encoding. Notice, however, these memory "improvements" although theoretically significant, are in actuality quite small.

Interference during the retention interval apparently affects face recognition performance (Laughery *et al.*, 1971; Laughery *et al.*, 1974), and interference is especially likely to occur in recognition if decoys are quite similar to the target. Yarmey (1974) collected other evidence for the effects of interference in a study using proactive inhibition as a tool to investigate whether male and female faces are encoded differently. Face recognition memory performances declined over 5 successive study–test trials (analogous to the method used by Peterson and Peterson (1959) in their study of short-term verbal memory) in which subjects saw a total of 75 same-sex portraits (60 different faces).

These results suggest that face recognition may be susceptible to all the infirmities commonly afflicting other memories, but they also make one wonder why faces seen in a laboratory setting for only a few seconds seem to be identified so well either a few minutes or one week after encoding. Why does not much more interference take place over the week-long period during which subjects surely must see many dozens of faces? A direct answer is not possible, but some guesses are. Careful measurement of false alarms must be included in any test because increased error arising from interference effects may not be evident in hit rate alone. Thus, in a study which simulated some aspects of the task facing the eyewitness to a crime, Egan *et al.* (1977) found that as the retention interval increased, correct identification was not affected, but false alarms increased remarkably.

Another speculation worth further investigation is the following: faces are not all equal in proactive inhibition value. Faces seen in natural settings may not interfere with those seen in the context of laboratory settings. This prediction may have special relevance when photos are used as targets in the laboratory study. Context effects are discussed elsewhere in this chapter.

6 DEPTH OF PROCESSING

Craik and Lockhart (1972) have suggested that kind of activity performed at the time of encoding of memory material is a significant determinant of later performance. In terms of verbal material, they theorized that deeper processing at encoding, involving greater semantic meaning extracted from the stimulus, leads to more effective memory than does shallow processing, which deals only with the stimulus as presented, i.e. its physical attributes. Thus, words in which subjects counted the number of letters were less well recalled than words rated for their pleasantness (Hyde and Jenkins, 1969), or a word was better recalled when the subject had inserted it appropriately into a sentence than when the subject had been instructed to find a rhyming word for it (Craik, 1973).

Bower and Karlin (1974) used faces to explore the usefulness of levels of processing in relation to pictorial material. They found that subjects better recognized faces they had judged earlier for either honesty or likeableness than those they had judged for sex of pictured person. The effect was obtained whether or not subjects made their judgments anticipating a recognition test to follow. Strnad and Mueller (1977) confirmed Bower and Karlin's findings, utilizing a highly similar design. Warrington and Ackroyd (1975) also found faces judged for pleasantness to be better recognized than those judged for height of face, and better recognized than faces studied with only the intention to remember them. Winograd (1976) found no difference in subjects' recognition performances when faces were characterized in terms of personality traits (e.g. anxious) and when they were characterized as occupational stereotypes (e.g. teacher). Both these conditions yielded performances superior to conditions where subjects answered questions about whether the faces had straight hair or large noses.

In contrast, Winograd found that answering a question, "Does he look heavy?" was associated with recognition performance levels more similar to those associated with making personality trait or occupational stereotype judgments than those associated with answering questions about hair or noses. Mueller *et al.* (1978) found that inferences drawn about the pictured person's body (height, weight, etc.) from a photograph of the face and processing judgments about personality traits (generosity, friendliness, etc.) were equivalent in their effects on face recognition memory. Both these sets of inferences produced recognition superior to a form of shallow processing in which subjects were asked to rate such facial characteristics as height of forehead or thickness of lips. This finding was in contrast to another one (Mueller *et al.*, 1979) in which personality traits yielded better later recognition performance than inferences about body size.

Taking the outcomes of all of the above studies into account there seems to be strong support for the empirical conclusion that making inferences about personal characteristics of pictured persons rather than assessing the physical characteristics of the faces shown is a useful mnemonic strategy. Nonetheless, it would be very strained logically to assert that judgments of personal characteristics made in response to facial photographs is extracting meaning from stimuli in the same sense as meaning can be extracted from words. Whether deep processing as conceptualized in these studies parallels semantic deep processing in verbal learning situations and enhances memory in a similar way, or whether the task of making judgments about personal characteristics from photos of faces induces other behaviours which enhance memory is a question awaiting further analysis and research.

Apart from the issue of whether processing means the same thing with faces as it does with words, the use of the concept of levels of processing with face memory data encounters many difficulties similar to difficulties found in connection with its use in verbal learning (Baddeley, 1978; Eysenck, 1978). Specifically, the data from investigations of face recognition employing the levels framework demonstrate small, albeit statistically significant, differences in memory associated with operations which are quite grossly characterized as *shallow* or *deep*. Although the data concerning face recognition where inferences were drawn about the unseen body might represent a level between *shallow* and *deep*, it seems more likely that the conflicting findings obtained thus far reflect sources of error in the experimental data. In order to talk productively about levels of processing with faces it is necessary to demonstrate that more than two degrees of performance result.

Until recently application of the Craik and Lockhart framework to faces had not led to attempts to define *depth* independently of its effects on memory. Chance and Goldstein (in press) devised a tentative scale for rating depth of processing of natural ("give your first response to the face") responses to faces. They had judges rate responses given by subjects who had been asked to react to faces. Chance and Goldstein showed that natural responses made to faces of persons belonging to different ethnic groups—shown elsewhere (Chance *et al.*, 1975) to differ in recognizability—differ in "depth of processing" responses elicited. The relation of the rated depth of responses to subjects' memories for the same faces has not yet been tested.

Alternative, or overlapping, explanations for effects of making personal characteristic judgments on recognition memory for faces might involve the possibility that these orienting tasks induce the subject to spend more time looking at the face and/or induce scanning more features in the face. Bower and Karlin (1974) attempted to control functional looking time by informing subjects in their second experiment of the memory test to follow the judging procedure, reasoning that subjects, so instructed, would use all the available time to look. Under these conditions, Bower and Karlin found still that faces judged for likeability and honesty were better recognized than those judged for gender.

A study by Patterson and Baddeley (1977) also bears on the question of looking time. They had subjects look at portraits for 28 seconds each and make four judgments of either facial or personal characteristics for each portrait. They found that recognition memory for the faces was better among those subjects making trait judgments than those judging facial features. The relatively long study interval used here for both sets of judgments, coupled with subjects' knowledge that a memory test would follow, appears to preclude differential looking time as an explanation of the memory effect.

Although not one of the judgments typically employed as a deep processing task, Goldstein and Papageorge (1980) find that reliable (i.e. consensual) judgments of beauty or attractiveness of faces can be made in 150 ms—a very short looking time for what is probably a deep processing response. Hall (1976) in an unpublished dissertation compared times taken by subjects to make various sorts of judgments about faces. He found that easy physical characteristics (e.g. gender, hair colour) took least time, personality attributions (e.g. likeable) and stereotypic descriptions (e.g. homosexual) took intermediate times, while difficult physical judgments (e.g. width of forehead, thickness of lips) took the longest times. Curiously, these latter hard physical judgments have been among those employed by Mueller and his associates (Mueller *et al.*, 1978; Courtois and Mueller, 1979) to induce shallow processing—and poorer recognition memory—in subjects.

If not looking time, then what could explain why judgments of inferred personal characteristics of pictured persons should lead to better recognition later on than does careful study of the real face and its stimulus characteristics? A shallow orienting task may restrict what features of the face are attended to, and, in contrast, a deep orienting task, such as how honest is this person, may increase the number of features scanned by subjects attempting to answer this impossible question. Studies by Winograd (1978) and by Courtois and Mueller (1979) designed to get subjects to scan all facial features, utilize an instruction to "find the most distinctive feature". Both studies showed that such instructions were followed by levels of recognition performance comparable to instructions to judge the pictured people for personal characteristics.

In summary, adoption of the levels of processing view in the study of recognition memory for faces has led to a variety of studies which demonstrate a small, but very consistent, advantage in face recognition memory when subjects make inferential judgments about personal characteristics of pictured persons. More research will be necessary, however, before we understand the mechanism by which this memory advantage occurs. Evidence currently available argues more strongly for the hypothesis that instructions to make judgments about personal characteristics lead to scanning of a greater number of facial features. Much less supportable is the suggestion that increasing looking time strengthens memory thereby.

7 OTHER FACTORS

A *Verbal coding*

The reader should note that while depth of processing studies with faces involve responses registered in verbal or quasi-verbal terms (e.g. rating scales), the concept of levels of processing does not require that processing has to take place verbally. Also when average accuracy measures are examined for many studies of faces, one sees that although deep processing increases performance accuracy relatively, the increase actually represents a very small absolute increment over what subjects do without processing instructions—and even without warning that a recognition test is in the offing. Human recognition memory for faces, at least on the short term and under the kinds of conditions provided in most experiments, is excellent; hit rates average 70 to 85% in the majority of studies.

The "deep processing increment" thus appears to be only one of many factors responsible for the level of performance displayed by humans in face recognition memory. We can raise the question of the role of verbal coding in this highly effective form of memory. Do verbal codes help face recognition? Are all kinds of verbal descriptors equally helpful? (Extrapolation from the evidence concerning depth of processing would suggest not.) Under what conditions are verbal descriptors about faces likely to be used by subjects? If verbal descriptions of faces are made, how accessible are they to subjects when later recognition occurs? Are subjects who are good verbal describers better at face recognition tasks than others? Unfortunately, studies bearing directly on these questions are not plentiful.

Goldstein and Chance (1971) found that faces as visual stimuli were a great deal better recognized than were inkblots or snow crystals. They proposed that faces were more "familiar" leading to their greater recognizability. A possible consequence of faces' greater familiarity might be an increased repertory of verbal descriptions available to code them with. Goldstein and Chance did find that faces as a class elicited greater numbers of verbal descriptors than inkblots and snow crystals; however, when the recognizability of particular stimuli, within each type, was correlated with the number of verbal responses elicited by those particular stimuli, no significant relationships were obtained. They concluded that while verbalizations may often be made by subjects in response to visual stimuli like faces, such verbalizations probably play a relatively weak role in visual memory for them.

Chance and Goldstein (1976) contrasted face recognition performance of subjects asked to respond verbally—either to describe or to associate to the faces—with that of subjects who were instructed merely to look-to-remember and other subjects who judged the faces for age and did not anticipate a later memory test. One week later, the four groups differed little in recognition performance, except that the group asked to describe some one thing that might help them to remember each face later showed a small superiority in performance. (This latter instruction is quite similar to the instruction to find the most distinctive feature in the face which yields good recognition in the depth of processing studies.)

When face recognition was tested a week later, those subjects who had made verbal responses to the faces viewed earlier were also asked to recall their verbalizations as well as to recognize the faces. To a striking degree subjects were unable—even fairly generally and when simultaneously they were positive that they recognized a face—to recall what they had said about the faces a week earlier. Or looked at another way, the faces very infrequently called up the same verbal responses on second presentation. It is difficult to see how such non-retrievable verbal descriptions aided recognition. Both the recognition data and the "recall of verbalizations" were interpreted by Chance and Goldstein as providing little evidence of an important role of verbal mediation in face recognition.

In another study, Goldstein *et al.* (1979) showed that persons assessed by an independent measure as very capable of making accurate descriptions of faces from memory do not necessarily recognize faces presented in a standard recognition study any better than other subjects. In another approach to the question of verbal mediation, Cohen and Nodine (1978) utilized an interference paradigm and showed that other visual tasks interfered more than an intervening verbal task with face recognition.

The above studies suggest the availability or use of verbal codes has little or no effect on face recognition. The evidence concerning face recognition is consistent with other experimental literature concerning the role of verbalization in recognition of other visual stimuli (Baddeley, 1976, pp. 215–217).

B *Intention to learn*

An incidental learning paradigm has been employed by a number of investigators in this field. Chance and Goldstein (1976) found that incidental learning of faces—making age judgments purportedly as a reason to look at faces—does not lead generally to worse recognition than occurs in conditions where a subsequent memory test has been announced; nonetheless, incidental exposure is slightly inferior to a condition where subjects both anticipate a later test and have been asked to describe something memorable about each face studied. Studies of the effects of depth of processing on face memory frequently utilize incidental learning instructions because investigators assume that expectation of a later test might induce the subjects to do un-controlled forms of processing apart from the processing the experimenter wants to induce. Albeit, a series of studies within this framework have failed to obtain different outcomes when processing takes place under intentional or incidental instructions (Bower and Karlin, 1974; Strnad and Mueller, 1977; Light *et al.*, 1979). Recog-nition memory for other sorts of materials besides faces also has been found to be uninfluenced by intention to learn (Seamon, 1980, p. 186), thus the findings pertaining to faces are also consistent with other data in the general field of learning.

C *Familiarity with experimental situation and stimuli*

Chance and Goldstein (1979) showed that when subjects performed three independent face recognition tasks separated by intervals of a week, both percentage of correct choices and false alarms tended to decrease; false alarms, especially, dropped dramatically. These findings suggest that increased subject familiarity with the experimental situ-ation itself can be a variable influencing performance. In other contexts, these investigators have suggested that the relative familiarity of faces as a class of stimuli may account for: subjects' higher levels of recognition for faces as contrasted with other visual stimuli, e.g. snow crystals (Goldstein and Chance, 1971); the greater memorability of own-race versus other-race faces (Chance *et al.*, 1975); and the difficulty experienced by subjects in recognizing otherwise familiar faces when they are presented in an inverted orientation (Goldstein, 1975). In a recent paper (1980), Goldstein and Chance have argued that familiarity, established by repeated encoding of members of a class of stimuli, serves to develop schemata which facilitate further interactions with stimuli of the class, but which may hinder encoding of stimuli of different classes.

Where Goldstein and Chance inferred differing degrees of familiarity for stimuli based upon their ecological occurrence, Wiseman and Neisser (1974) had their subjects attribute familiarity to stimuli from the Mooney Faces Closure Test. They found that ambiguous pictures seen by subjects as faces (familiar class) were better remembered than similar pictures from the series not seen as faces. Wiseman and Neisser propose that recognition of a stimulus as belonging to a familiar class—face—enables the subject to access consistent encoding dimensions which facilitate perception and memory. These findings have been replicated and expanded by Freedman and Haber (1974).

8 RESEARCH IN FACE RECOGNITION

In this concluding section, we will make a few comments about the state of laboratory research in face recognition. As has been indicated several times throughout this chapter, more research is needed—research into particular questions and research generally of a more systematic and comprehensive nature. Parametric studies of variables affecting recognition such as study time, context, retention interval, etc., while perhaps not the most exciting sort to do, are nonetheless much needed.

Because psychology has few standard laboratory procedures or techniques, except in the areas of psychophysics and psychobiology, psychologists seem to experience great methodological difficulties each time we open "new" research areas. We often uncritically adopt methods from other areas, and we quite as often fail to profit from the errors which our predecessors have made. Our review of the literature suggests that the use of d-prime and related signal detection measures is increasingly widespread. Frequently, results of investigations are reported in terms of these measures alone, omitting both hits and false alarms from the account. Assumptions implicit in the use of d-prime— that hits and false alarms are positively related to each other, that the effect of guessing on total accuracy is the only thing being corrected for—may not be justified when applied to responses to faces. Even apart from whether these assumptions can be satisfied, we suggest that a clearer understanding of face recognition performance would be forthcoming if false alarms and hits were reported and given careful attention by investigators along with the signal detection measures. An illustration of this point can be found in the study of Egan *et al.* (1977), where false alarms, but not hits, were shown to change as length of retention interval increased. While d-prime would reflect the increase found in false alarms, perhaps it is of more interest to focus on the source of the decline in accuracy.

Our review of the literature also suggests that many investigators carry over from other areas of research in psychology attitudes and practices influencing selection of face stimuli and experimental subjects in ways that may give rise to non-repeatable outcomes. Faces appear to vary along an almost infinity of dimensions. So far as we know, except for identical twins, probably no two faces are exactly alike; nor is it safe to assume that the diversity among faces is homogeneously distributed. Until we have the means to describe characteristics of faces—much as Ebbinghaus could describe his nonsense syllables or words can be described in terms of their usage frequencies or their semantic relationships—it is dangerous to assume that every face is equivalent to every other face in selecting targets and distractors for a study. A sample can turn out unexpectedly (and unknowingly) to be unique. The danger is especially great when a small sample of targets and/or distractors are used. We suggest that multiple sets of stimuli be used in any face-related research problem as one way of decreasing the risk of obtaining outcomes which are dependent upon a particular set of faces.

A related problem arises when all subjects are treated as equivalent to each other. Especially with faces as stimuli the recognition process can be influenced by social factors pertaining to the subject and those pertaining to the social attributions made to the face stimuli. If these two sets of factors interact fortuitously, a misleading finding may be obtained. Samples of subjects should be carefully described and generalizability of results needs always to be questioned.

Finally, face recognition researchers as a group are open to criticism for the single-minded way we have tested recognition memory. Except for confidence judgments (a problematic dependent variable), rarely are any measures used other than frequency of right and wrong responses. While correctness is a perfectly legitimate measure, it may be too insensitive to get at the root of many face recognition problems. Latency measures, eye movements, physiological arousal, reactions times, looking times are examples of other information which might profitably be collected in addition to the usual accuracy measures.

6 Studies of Cue Saliency

John Shepherd, Graham Davies and Hadyn Ellis

1 INTRODUCTION

In recognizing an object, not all aspects or attributes of the stimulus receive the same attention: certain elements appear to be more critical for identification purposes than others (Vernon, 1955; Bruner, 1957; Dodwell, 1971). This is almost certainly true for faces. A recent opinion poll, for instance, asked respondents: "What facial features draw your glance and hold your attention?" Eyes (62%) were the overwhelming choice followed by hair (22%) and mouth (8%) with the remaining 8% distributing their choices over a variety of other features (Jones, 1977).

In referring to "features", the survey questions may have excluded responses relating to other sources of information in faces. Garneau (1973), for example, has distinguished, in addition to *features information, contour cues* provided by the shape of the face, and *relationships* reflecting the relative distance between features or contours. More global characteristics, although ultimately based on physical features, may also be used as a distinctive source of information. Judgments of age, intelligence, character and mood are confidently made from faces (Davies, 1978), though whether these are inferences made from feature information, or ways of encoding feature information is not clear.

A variety of different experimental techniques have been used to provide information on cue saliency in faces. If some convergence could be found in the results of such studies it might be of importance in resolving such theoretical issues as the piecemeal/configurational processing controversy (see Ellis' contribution, this volume) as well as of practical significance for forensic science. For the purposes of review, studies have been grouped into four categories: (i) studies which have relied upon subjective reports or on verbal descriptions; (ii) experiments which have examined the ability of subjects to detect changes in facial cues, or the effect of such changes on recognition of faces; (iii) investigations of subjects' eye movements when examining faces; and (iv) studies which examine the dimensions underlying subjects' assessments of the relative similarity of faces. In this last category we report the results of a number of unpublished investigations by the Aberdeen group.

2 SUBJECTIVE REPORTS AND VERBAL DESCRIPTIONS

A *Subjective reports*

An apparently simple method for assessing saliency is to ask subjects what cues they employed in recognizing a given face or set of faces. This technique was pioneered by Howells (1938) who administered a questionnaire to subjects following an experiment involving face recognition. He reported that subjects found the question a difficult one to answer and there appeared to be little agreement among them.

The same technique was also employed by Laughery and his colleagues (Laughery *et al.*, 1971; see also Zavala and Paley, 1972) following three separate experiments concerning face recognition. Overall, subjects rated eyes as most important followed by nose and facial structure; the skin, hair and the lip/chin region were perceived as less important but all were more salient than the mouth. However, the degree of agreement across experiments was not impressive, given that the experiments shared some common target faces; indeed, for the cues ranked in all studies, the coefficient of concordance was a modest $+0 \cdot 61$ ($p < 0 \cdot 10 > 0 \cdot 05$).

A further difficulty with relying on subjective report is that there is little evidence that it is a reliable guide to the cues subjects actually attend to in the experimental situation. Nash (1969) asked his subjects to rank the degree of (i) distinctiveness and (ii) differentiation of different regions of the face. Noses were perceived as more distinctive than mouths or eyes, followed by ears, chins and foreheads, but eyes were seen as more differentiated than the mouth or nose areas. However, neither subjective distinctiveness nor differentiation was significantly related to the subjects' success at identifying the relevant features in photographs of themselves and others.

A similar finding emerged from a study by Friedman *et al.* (1971) using schematic faces. Again, ratings of perceived saliency were not closely related to actual performance at discriminating changes to the features concerned in successive pairs of faces. Interestingly, subjects frequently detected that members of a pair of faces were different, but then incorrectly attributed the difference to a feature perceived as subjectively salient. This ability to detect change without insight into its source is interpreted by Friedman *et al.* as consistent with a wholistic processing strategy. Whatever the merits of the latter interpretation, it is clear that for face recognition, as for other cognitive tasks (see Nisbett and Wilson, 1977), introspection alone cannot provide a simple answer to the problems of the area and may, on occasion, be misleading.

B *Verbal descriptions*

Another simple method of exploring how people attend to faces is to ask them to describe a face and see which features they mention.

This technique was adopted by Ellis *et al.* (1975a) as a convenient method for examining any differences in feature extraction by Europeans and Africans looking at both white and black faces. It was also more extensively employed by Shepherd *et al.* (1977) in a series of studies of facial feature saliency and the results of these later investigations will form the basis for discussion in this section.

In the first experiment 40 subjects were each asked to write descriptions from black and white prints of white male faces. There were 100 faces ranging in age between 16 and 60 years, and each subject wrote descriptions of 10 of them. The resulting 400 descriptions were then tabulated and frequency counts made of the number of times each feature was mentioned, the number of faces for which each feature was mentioned, and the number of subjects who used the particular feature description.

Thirteen facial features were identified in this way. In order of frequency they were: hair, eyes, nose, eyebrows, face shape, chin, lips, mouth, ears, face lines, complexion, forehead and cheeks. The total number of times hair occurred as a descriptor was 1135; at the other end of the continuum, cheeks were mentioned 53 times. Similarly, the category hair was divisible into 10 subsections (e.g. length, colour, texture), whereas cheeks subdivided into three description classes.

The frequency tables indicated that upper face features attracted more attention than did others. Hair, forehead, eyebrows and eyes together accounted for almost half of the total number of feature descriptions given. Not surprisingly, most subjects gave a hair- or eye-related description, and most faces attracted at least one description of their eyes and hair. Figure 1 illustrates the relative frequencies with which different features were mentioned.

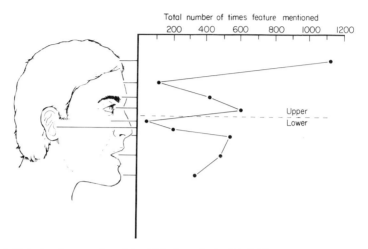

Fig. 1. Relative frequencies with which the principal facial features were mentioned in free descriptions (from Shepherd *et al.*, 1977).

It could be argued that the distribution of descriptions across facial features depicted in Fig. 1 is limited in generalizability. The faces were shown as black and white prints and descriptions were made in the presence of the pictures. In the next experiment (Ellis *et al.*, 1980) colour prints of just two male faces were employed. Subjects were required to make a description of one face immediately following a 20-second inspection period and the other face after a delay of an hour, a day or a week.

The detailed results of this experiment need not concern us here. What is striking about the data, shown in Table 1, is the fact that the proportions of features in the descriptions made from memory of just two faces is remarkably like those derived from descriptions made of 100 faces while each was present.

There is considerable agreement between the two sets of figures shown in Table 1, and it may therefore be reasonable to infer that there is a consistent pattern of attention to different facial features. Regardless of whether the face is described from a picture, or from some sort of memory image, upper face features attract more attention.

Interestingly, this pattern was not found for descriptions of faces given by black African subjects (Ellis *et al.*, 1975a). Presumably then, we learn to attend to distinguishing facial features. In Caucasian faces hair and eyes vary among individuals sufficiently for reliable discriminations to be made largely on the basis of these features alone. Negroid faces,

TABLE 1
Proportion of descriptors allocated to various facial
features in two different experiments

Feature	Faces absent (from Ellis *et al.*, 1980)	Faces present (from Shepherd *et al.*, 1977)
Hair	0.27	0.24
Eyes	0.14	0.13
Nose	0.14	0.12
Face structure	0.13	0.9
Eyebrows	0.8	0.9
Chin	0.7	0.7
Lips	0.6	0.6
Mouth	0.3	0.4
Complexion	0.2	0.4
Cheeks	0.1	0.1
Forehead	0.1	0.2
Others	0.4	0.9

however, are less easily differentiated by hair colour and texture and eye colour and so Africans may develop a more diffuse deployment of attention across more areas of the face.

3 EXPERIMENTAL STUDIES

Experimental studies of saliency have generally adopted one of two approaches to the problem. In *face fragmentation* studies, only a part of the face is presented for recognition trials; any feature which enables the subject to identify the target is said to be salient. In *face distortion* experiments, the whole face is retained, but alterations are made to one or more of its features; if the subject detects a change the amended feature is assumed to be salient. Published results are summarized in Table 2 and some of the methods illustrated in Fig. 2.

A *Face fragmentation studies*

A variety of regions of the face have been contrasted for their ability to serve as cues for recognition. Studies are reviewed under five headings based on the areas examined: (i) upper versus lower; (ii) left versus right; (iii) inner versus outer, and (iv) isolated features: recognition; (v) isolated features: reconstruction.

TABLE 2

Summary of major experimental studies on cue saliency. Measure is recognition accuracy unless otherwise stated. Race of subject is white unless otherwise stated

Author(s)	Subjects	Method	Results	Comments
a. *Upper versus lower*				
Howells (1938)	Students ($n = 47$)	Novel faces, obscured at study	Lower > upper	No error data
Goldstein and Mackenberg (1966)	Children aged 4.5, 6.5 and 10 years ($n = 76$)	Friends' faces, obscured at test	Upper > lower	
Fisher and Cox (1975)	Public ($n = 400$)	Celebrities: progressive exposure	Upper > lower	Large sample
Garneau (1973)	Students ($n = 60$)	Novel faces, obscured at test	Upper > lower	
Wayman and Scott (1974)	Youths ($n = 36$)	Novel faces: upper, middle and lower regions obscured	No difference on accuracy	
Langdell (1978)	Groups of children aged 5, 8, 9 and 13 years ($n = 40$): autistic and subnormal samples aged 10 and 14 years ($n = 20$)	Friends' faces, observed at test	Upper > lower	Trend reversed in younger autistic sample
b. *Left versus right*				
Fisher and Cox (1975)	Public ($n = 400$)	Celebrities: progressive exposure	No difference	Large sample
Harris and Fleer (1972)	Retardates ($n = 24$) and normal children ($n = 24$)	Unknown faces; half versus whole faces at study and test	Half faces no different from whole faces for normals; retardates worse on half faces	

c. Inner versus outer

Study	Sample	Task	Result	Notes
Ellis et al. (1979b)	Students (n = 69)	Famous faces: inner or outer features only shown	Inner > outer	
	Public (n = 54)	Uknown faces: inner versus outer at test	No difference	
	Public (n = 48)	Famous faces; inner versus outer at test	Inner > outer	
Phillips (1979)	Students (n = 32)	Unknown faces: inner versus outer at study and test	No difference	
	Students (unknown)	Famous faces; inner or outer features only shown	No difference	

d. Isolated features: recognition

Study	Sample	Task	Result	Notes
Goldstein and Mackenberg (1966)	Children aged 4.5, 6.5, and 10 years (n = 76)	Friends' faces: selective exposure of facial fragments	Eyes > mouth > nose	
Nash (1969)	Children aged 12 (n = 26) and 14 (n = 20)	Own faces: recognition of isolated features	Forehead > mouth > eyes ≥ chin ≅ ears > nose	Small sample
	Students (n = 10)	Recognition of own and friends' isolated features	Eyes, mouth > nose, ears and eyebrows	
Fisher and Cox (1975)	Public (n = 200)	Celebrities' faces: progressive exposure	Expansion from eyes > expansion from mouth	Large sample
Seamon et al. (1978)	Students (n = 120)	Unknown faces, recognition of fragments, front and profile	Eyes ≅ mouth > nose	
Langdell (1978)	Groups of normal, subnormal and autistic children (see above)	Friends' faces: eyes and nose only exposed	Eyes > nose	Trend reversed in younger autistic samples
McKelvie (1976)	Students (n = 115)	Eyes or mouth masked study and test on unknown faces	Eyes > mouth	
Garneau (1973)	Students (n = 36)	Eyes, mouth or nose masked on unknown faces	Eyes > mouth ≅ nose	

TABLE 2 (cont.)

Author(s)	Subjects	Method	Results	Comments
e. *Isolated features: reconstruction*				
Ellis et al. (1975b)	Public (n = 32)	Making Photofit faces: accuracy of selection of features	Forehead > eyes ≈ mouth > nose ≥ chin	Differences between face composites
		Order of selection of features	Forehead > eyes > nose > mouth > chin	
Ellis et al. (1977)	Public (n = 32)	Introspective accounts during Photofit construction	More time and trouble on upper than lower features	
Laughery et al. (1976)	Students (n = 182)	Time and number of changes: Identikit and Sketch artist representation of white target faces	Upper > lower	
	Students (n = 60; 20 were blacks)	As above black target faces	Upper > lower; eyes more prominent than for white targets	
f. *Disguise*				
Patterson and Baddeley (1977)	Female members of the public (n = 62)	Unknown faces: presence or absence of wig, beard or glasses	Wig or beard more disruptive than glasses	Long exposure
Laughery and Fowler (1977)	Students (n = 480)	Unknown faces: presence or absence of wig, beard or glasses	Beard more disruptive than wig; wig worse than glasses	
Baker (1967)	Students (n = 47)	Identikit faces: moustache or glasses	Glasses more disruptive than moustache	
Patterson (1978)	Female members of the public (n about 100)	Unknown persons: presence or absence of wig or beard	Wig as disruptive as beard	

g. *Feature alteration*

Study	Subjects	Task	Results	Notes
Friedman et al. (1971)	Students (n = 49)	Sequential discrimination task with schematic faces: nose length, eye distance, brow height, mouth height altered	No difference	
McKelvie (1973)	Students (n = 64)	Labelling and attribution with schematic faces: eye-brow, mouth, nose, eye height and shape manipulated	Labelling and expression a function of brow and mouth orientation	
Matthews (1978)	"Volunteers"	Simultaneous discrimination task with Identikit faces; hair, eyes, eyebrows, nose, mouth, chin altered	Hair ≈ chin ≈ eyes > eyebrows > nose ≈ mouth	
Baker (1967)	Students (n = 47)	Similarity ratings, Identikit faces, varying in hair, eyes, nose, mouth, chin	Hair > chin > eyes ≈ mouth > nose	
Garneau (1973)	Students (n = 60)	Recognition of Photofit faces from memory: faces varying in hair, chin and eyes + nose + mouth	Hair > eyes + nose + mouth > chin	Very brief presentation
Davies et al. (1977)	Students (n = 40)	Recognition of Photofit faces in presence or absence of target; faces varying in hair, eyes, nose, mouth and chin	Hair > eyes ≈ mouth > chin > nose	
Walker-Smith (1978)	Students (n = 8)	Sequential discrimination of Photofit faces varying in hair, eyes, nose, mouth and chin	Hair > eyes ≈ mouth > chin > nose on errors	Mouth and eyes less salient with 20-second delay

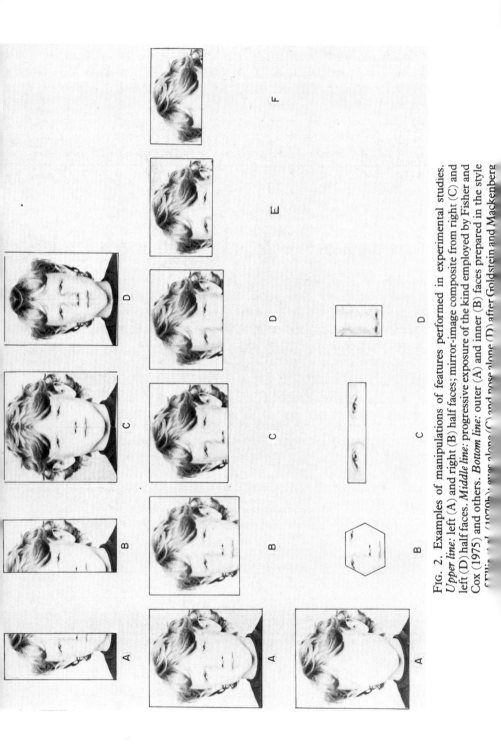

FIG. 2. Examples of manipulations of features performed in experimental studies. *Upper line*: left (A) and right (B) half faces; mirror-image composite from right (C) and left (D) half faces. *Middle line*: progressive exposure of the kind employed by Fisher and Cox (1975) and others. *Bottom line*: outer (A) and inner (B) faces prepared in the style of Ellis *et al.* (1979); eyes alone (C) and nose alone (D) after Goldstein and Mackenberg

i Upper versus lower

Howells (1938) appears to have been the first to split photographs of faces in half and examine the relative potency of upper and lower features for identification. His subjects saw half of the face for 10 seconds and then attempted to pick out the relevant individual from a photographic array. Recognition was superior for the lower half of the face and Howells concluded that the latter contained the more important features. However, Howells reports all findings in terms of hits and no reference is made to false alarms. At least one study has reported a higher positive recognition rate for lower features compared to upper, which disappeared once differential false alarm rates were taken into account (Wayman and Scott, 1974). Howell's results should therefore be interpreted with caution.

This result may be contrasted with those from more recent studies. Goldstein and Mackenberg (1966) examined the ability of children aged 4½ to 10 years to recognize their classmates from a variety of facial fragments. Irrespective of the subjects' age, upper half-faces yielded significantly better results than lower half, and upper quadrants better than lower quadrants. Subtraction of the eye region from the upper half-face significantly reduced the identification rate, but it was still better than for the lower half of the face.

The superiority of upper features for identifying friends was replicated by Langdell (1978) using groups of both normal and mentally subnormal children. Langdell also reported that this effect was absent among a sample of autistic children, a result attributed to the unusual patterns of social interaction exhibited by the latter group. Adult members of the public showed a similar superiority for upper features in a study reported by Fisher and Cox (1975). They progressively exposed the faces of celebrities either beginning at the hair and moving down or starting at the chin and moving up. A particularly large increment in identification occurred under both conditions when the eyes were exposed: a jump from 11 to 64% identification in the case of chin-up. A similar superiority for recognition based on upper features was found by Garneau (1973), this time using faces previously unknown to the subjects.

It thus seems safer to conclude, from modern research, that upper face features are likely to be favoured in encoding faces.

ii Left versus right

It has been repeatedly demonstrated that the face is not symmetrical around its vertical axis. Subjects consistently rate the right side of the face (i.e. the left side as it is observed in a photograph) as being more representative of the appearance of the person than the left. This preference for the right side appears to be associated with normal processing strategies in that preferences are reversed if the original face is seen as a mirror image (Gilbert and Bakan, 1973). This has led to speculation that the right side of the face will be better recognized than the left (Coltheart, 1975).

There are, indeed, a number of accounts of subjects being unable to recognize themselves from composite "faces" made up from photographs of the non-dominant side of the face and its mirror image (Wolff, 1942; Lindzey *et al.*, 1952). However, such effects may be very specific to the special type of stimuli employed. There is accumulating evidence that subjects are highly efficient at recognizing others from half faces and that the two sides elicit no discernible difference in rates of identification. Goldstein and Mackenberg (1966) included a condition involving recognition from the left face in their study of the identification of school friends; performance under these conditions was as good as for the whole-face condition. Fisher and Cox (1975) exposed the faces of celebrities, starting either from the left- or right-hand side of the faces; no marked differences were found in recognition accuracy. Harris and Fleer (1972) did find the recognition performance of the mentally retarded was impaired relative to that of controls matched for mental age, if only half faces were employed as stimuli as either study or test. However, later research suggested that the effect was due to the emotional impact of the disembodied stimuli rather than to the cue-value of the half-faces as such (Harris and Fleer, 1973). In all, Ellis' (1975) speculation that the asymmetries in the two sides of the face are insufficient to prevent recognition from either half under normal circumstances seems to be supported.

iii Inner versus outer

Many theorists have emphasized the expressive and communicative function of such features as the eyes and the mouth (Argyle, 1967). One might, therefore, predict that the central area of the face containing the eyes, nose and mouth would be a better cue to subsequent recognition than the peripheral area taking in the hair, ears and chin. Ellis *et al.* (1979b) contrasted the cue value of central and peripheral facial elements in a series of studies using both well-known and unknown faces. For the well-known faces, subjects exhibited higher recognition rates for central features, but for novel faces the two areas were functionally equivalent. The authors speculate that the contrasting results may arise from the differing strategies associated with the two classes of stimuli: expressive elements of the faces of actors and politicians are frequently attended to, whereas photographs of unknown faces do not assume the same communicative function. Goldstein and Mackenberg (1966) also concluded that the peripheral facial area was an ineffective cue in their study of children's identification of school friends.

These results may be contrasted with those of Phillips (1979) who could find no differential rates of recognition for either known of unknown faces from inner and outer features. His failure to find an effect for the faces of celebrities may arise from the small number of faces sampled; Ellis *et al.* noted that while the majority of their famous faces produced increased recognition for the inner features, there was a minority where the effect was either not present or reversed.

iv Isolated features: recognition
Newspaper competitions often invite their readers to recognize the faces of the famous from pictures of isolated features; psychologists have been quick to adopt a similar strategy in an attempt to ascertain the cue value of different features. Goldstein and Mackenberg (1966) reported that school friends were better recognized on the basis of the eye region than the mouth, and that the latter in turn was a better cue than a front view of the nose. Nash (1969) replicated their study, using a wider range of features, but failed to find a consistent superiority for the eyes over the mouth region. The forehead area emerged as the best cue and the chin, nose and ears were generally poor for identification purposes. A further study by Langdell (1978) confirmed the finding that children recognize their friends more readily from their eyes than their nose. This pattern was, however, reversed in his group of young autistic children, though the older group showed the normal superiority for the eyes. Surprisingly, no positive relationship has been reported between length of acquaintance and ease of recognition (Chance *et al.*, 1967; Nash, 1969).

The nose in isolation emerges as a relatively poor cue for recognition purposes, even when profile, rather than full-face pictures are employed (Seamon *et al.*, 1978). However, Fisher and Cox (1973) noted that when the nose area was added to the eyes there was a doubling of the effective recognition rate for full-face pictures of celebrities. The same authors noted that while the eyes alone served as better cues than mouths, eyes in isolation were not particularly well recognized: only some 12% of their stars were recognized on the basis of eyes alone.

The superiority of the eyes to the mouth region has also been found in those studies which have selectively deleted these two regions from the face. McKelvie (1976) reported that omission of the eyes at study or test lowered recognition performance on unknown faces more than taking out the mouth. A similar effect was found by Garneau (1973) who also investigated omission of the nose; the latter produced results similar to that of mouth deletion. One problem about such studies is that the area of the face masked is not equivalent for the two features; given the importance of context to recognition it may be that the results are explainable in terms of the latter factor alone, larger masks obliterating more of the surrounding context.

v Isolated features: reconstruction

Face reconstruction systems such as Photofit and Identikit rely to a great extent on the witnesses' ability to recognize features in isolation (see chapter by Davies, this volume). The extent to which subjects experience difficulty in selecting appropriate features also provides an indirect source of information on saliency.

Ellis *et al.* (1975b) examined the order and accuracy with which their subjects constructed two Photofit faces. They discovered that, in general, the subjects preferred to select first the hair and forehead, then the eyes, followed in turn by the nose, mouth and chin.

Because the original target faces were themselves made up from Photofit pieces it was also possible to examine the accuracy of choices for each feature. Again, the hair and eye features were most accurately selected followed by mouth, nose and chin—an order not too different from the ranking for selection. Taken together these data support the idea that upper face features are more salient than lower face features. A further piece of evidence in support of this conclusion was presented in a subsequent Photofit experiment (Ellis *et al.*, 1977). In this study subjects were asked to verbalize their deliberations and strategies when selecting Photofit features to construct a face from memory. It was noted that they took much more time and trouble selecting hair and eyes than for any of the remaining features. This, of course, may explain the superior accuracy for hair and eye selections, or may instead reflect the disproportionate significance that subjects attached to these features.

Laughery *et al.* (1977) examined the behaviour of subjects using Identikit and sketch artists to reproduce faces. They observed that both recall techniques involved more time being spent on upper face than lower face features; that is to say selection of these features took longer when using Identikit and more time was required to instruct the artist when he was sketching hair and eyes. This pattern was observed where subjects were constructing white faces but a slightly different one emerged when the target faces were black. Then the hair features received rather less attention and the mouth region became more important.

vi Conclusions

While some scattering of results is perhaps inevitable, certain consistencies do emerge from this survey of face fragmentation studies. Upper features are generally better cues for redintegrative purposes than lower ones. Eyes in particular emerge as powerful aids, though eyes in isolation are not particularly effective. This latter finding underlines one deficiency of all fragmentation studies, namely the way in which the normal facial Gestalt must be broken up, giving rise, perhaps, to abnormal or unusual processing strategies. Before drawing any more general conclusions regarding the saliency of various aspects of the face, studies which have striven to retain a normal whole-face at all stages of study should be surveyed.

B *Face distortion studies*

Two procedures have been adopted to manipulate the appearance of the face between study and test. These are (i) the use of different types of disguise and (ii) selective amendments to the facial image by means of such systems as Photofit and Identikit.

i Disguise

Baker (1967) appears to have been the first systematically to investigate the effects of disguise. She reports that the addition of spectacles to an Identikit composite had a more deleterious effect upon recognition than adding a moustache, a finding consistent with the reported saliency of the eye region. However, two later and more comprehensive studies have not supported these results. Laughery and Fowler (1977) examined the effect on the recognition of male targets of the addition or deletion of spectacles, full beards and wigs. They reported that, irrespective of the direction of change, wigs and beards had a more detrimental effect upon recognition than spectacles. The same changes were also examined in a study by Patterson and Baddeley (1977). They reported that the addition of spectacles had a minimal effect upon recognition accuracy, unless combined with a change in orientation of the face. The essential equivalence of wig and beard changes were confirmed in a later study by Patterson (1978), who concluded that changes to all three features were sufficient to reduce identification to chance levels. From the point of view of ascertaining saliency, these studies provide only the grossest information in that the relative distortion produced by disguise was not equated across features. Nevertheless, they show no positive evidence for the disproportionate significance of the eye region.

ii Feature alteration

Studies which have used intact faces to study cue saliency may usefully be distinguished by the nature of the stimuli employed. Friedman *et al.* (1971) used schematic faces in a successive discrimination task where changes were confined to forehead height, eye distance, nose length or mouth height. They reported no difference in the relative saliency as assessed by accuracy at detecting change in the feature concerned. McKelvie (1973) examined the ease with which subjects attached verbal labels and attributed expressions to a series of schematic faces. He concluded that a combination of brow and mouth were critical to both labelling and emotional attribution, eye size and nose length playing no part. However, the limited range of feature change inevitably qualifies such a conclusion. This illustrates a more general problem with schematic faces: their inevitable lack of realism. More realistic stimuli may be constructed from forensic tools such as Identikit and Photofit.

Matthews (1978) constructed a series of faces from Identikit, using different combinations of hair, eyes, eyebrows, nose, mouth and chin components. Subjects made same/different judgments on simultaneously presented pairs of faces. The reaction time data suggested that changes to the hair, eye, and chin region were detected most rapidly; nose and mouth changes produced the slowest reactions, with eyebrows falling midway between. Matthews interpreted his data in terms of a "double take" strategy involving an initial comparison with hair–chin–eyes template followed by a detailed examination of the eyebrow–nose–mouth area. He was able to discount any explanation of his findings in terms of the relative discriminability of the components employed.

Baker (1967) also systematically varied the components of an Identikit composite, this time using alternative hair, eyes, nose, mouth and chin pieces. Subjects made similarity ratings on pairs of composites which differed in a single feature. In agreement with Matthews, hair changes were rated most distinctive, but the mouth was given equivalent weighting to eyes and chin; nose alterations were again least rapidly detected. Baker claimed that the sex of the observer influenced judgments: men gave greater weight to hair and chin, whereas women accorded more importance to the eye and mouth region.

Data less in accord with Matthews' hypothesis emerges from discrimination studies which have used Photofit composites. Garneau (1973) asked subjects to provide same/different judgments on successive pairs of composite faces; changes were restricted to the hair, the chin, or the eyes–nose–mouth complex. Hair changes were more rapidly detected than those to the eyes–nose–mouth complex, with changes to the chin least often noticed. Such an ordering is indicative of a "down-through" scanning strategy rather than the "double-take" model proposed by Matthews, though the very brief presentation interval (a half or a third of a second) employed may have encouraged the former strategy.

Davies *et al.* (1977) asked subjects to identify a target face composed from Photofit in an array where each distractor differed from the target in one feature. Features changed were the hair–forehead region, eyes, nose, mouth and chin. Discriminability was controlled by including sets of distractor faces composed from features of high and low rated similarity to those in the target. Irrespective of whether judgments were made in the presence or absence of the target, hair–forehead changes produced fewest confusions, followed by mouth, eyes, chin and nose.

This same order of saliency was replicated by Walker-Smith (1978) in a discrimination task involving Photofit composites. However, the introduction of a 20-second delay produced an interesting reversal in ordering: eye and mouth changes were now less likely to be detected relative to other features. She attributed this latter result to the lack of utility of expressive information in the absence of the target (see also Walker-Smith, 1980).

Thus, the saliency data derived from studies of Identikit and Photofit are more impressive in their homogeneity within, rather than across, composite techniques. Matthews' own evidence for a "double-take" interpretation of cue saliency is impressive, but fails to explain why, when Photofit rather than Identikit is employed, the mouth is as salient as the eyes, and the chin little better than the nose. Nor can the theory readily explain fluctuations in saliency with delay noted by Walker-Smith, or the apparent changes found by Garneau with brief exposure intervals. Taking the composite studies as a whole, hair emerges as the dominant cue while the nose consistently attracts least attention. However, in considering such results, one reservation noted by both Davies *et al.* and Matthews needs to be emphasized: the restricted range of change which such kits allow. It may well be that there are other cues in faces, such as inter-feature distance, texture or contour information which are critical to face identification but not represented in existing kits.

4 EYE MOVEMENTS

It could be argued that the most direct way of determining which features of a face are most important to the viewer is simply to look at his eye movements; if his gaze consistently falls on certain areas of a face it might be reasonable to infer that those areas are of greatest interest (Berlyne, 1958) and provide most information (Loftus, 1972).

Yarbus (1967) was one of the first to show typical eye-movement patterns superimposed over the face being examined. The pattern of movements in his illustrations indicates that the eyes and mouth receive most attention and that the left half of the face is looked at more than the right half. Yarbus was himself not particularly interested in relating such eye movements to processes of face recognition, but in recent years there have been at least three attempts by others to do this (Walker-Smith *et al.*, 1977; Luria and Strauss, 1978; Cook, 1978).

Luria and Strauss (1978) found that, when initially viewing positive prints of faces and when attempting to recognize them, subjects spend most time fixating the nose followed by the eyes and mouth. They concluded that the central region of the face conveyed most useful information but admitted that, because all of their photographs were of military personnel wearing caps, it was not possible to assess the attention-catching potential of the hair.

In Cook's (1978) first study the photographs were of unfamiliar faces and included hair, but nonetheless there was little evidence that the hair, or indeed any peripheral features, were looked at very much. Cook's data indicate the eye region to be most salient followed by nose and mouth. In his second experiment Cook presented famous faces for identification and again found that the central region of the face commanded most attention.

Cook did find small individual differences in fixation patterns, however, and observed that some of his subjects preferred to begin viewing a face by fixating some featureless area such as a cheek. Walker-Smith *et al.* (1977) also discovered quite marked individual differences in scanning but again found that the central facial features attracted the majority of eye fixations. They suggest that, although fixation may first be directed at a fairly central point on the face, this may serve to allow the general framework of the face to be determined which may be a prerequisite for a sequential scan of individual features. It is clear from the experiments reported by Walker-Smith *et al.*, however, that not only do individuals differ in the ways they scan a face, but the nature of the task also affects scan patterns: simultaneous comparison of two faces produces a different pattern from that observed when subjects attempt to match successively presented faces. Rayner (1978) discusses other evidence showing how eye-movement patterns may vary as a function of the task, and has therefore argued that the proposal of Noton and Stark (1971), to the effect that pattern recognition may be causally related to consistent eye movement is not tenable. However, Luria and Strauss do report that eye movements for faces printed in negative are less organized than for positive prints and suggest that this finding may have a bearing on the fact that negatives are harder to remember than positive prints of faces.

In addition to assessing the direction of eye movements, the amount and duration of fixations have also received attention. Loftus (1972) has aruged that memory for a picture is a positive function of the number of fixations made to it. This has been disputed by Tversky (1974), and as far as face memory is concerned there seems to be no support for the idea that more fixations necessarily lead to an improvement in performance.

In conclusion it should be said that eye movements are not a particularly reliable method for studying saliency in faces, and that, furthermore, their exact interpretation is equivocal.

5 SCALING STUDIES

The attractive simplicity of the free description method described in section 2, is offset to some degree by the possibility that the data may be biased as a result of task demands. Subjects may provide descriptions of minutest detail, but these may not represent the features to which they normally attend. Quite possibly, for purposes of everyday identification, only one or two features may be utilized. On the other hand, the experiments in which facial features are isolated, omitted or distorted pre-empt the subjects' own normal strategies, since the manner in which the experimenter divides the face may not accord with normal perceptual analyses.

In recent years, the development of techniques of multidimensional scaling (Shepard *et al.*, 1972; Carroll and Arabie, 1980) has provided methods to overcome some of these objections. The data for multidimensional scaling (MDS) studies usually take the form of a measure of similarity or association between pairs of stimuli, often obtained from direct judgments by subjects. Dimensions underlying the subjects' judgments may then be revealed by the application of MDS, often augmented by independent external measurement of the stimuli to assist in interpretation of the dimensions (see Kruskal and Wish, 1978, for a more detailed account).

Apart from the requirement to judge the similarity, or some other general relationship between stimuli, subjects are left free to adopt their own basis for their judgment. Hopefully, this method should reveal what aspects of faces subjects use spontaneously in judging similarity.

A *Previous research using multidimensional scaling*

One of the earliest studies of faces using MDS was reported by Groner in 1967. His stimuli were 20 black and white photographs of Caucasian males which were selected from a larger pool of photographs. Subjects judged the similarity between all pairs of stimuli, and the resulting matrix was analysed by Torgerson's (1958) classical procedure. The resulting solution produced 12 dimensions. Groner also asked his first 25 subjects to nominate the features they used in making their judgments, and a further 24 subjects then rated all the photographs on the 17 attributes which were most frequently mentioned. Ratings on the scales were then related to the dimensions obtained in the MDS solution.

Only eight of the dimensions could be interpreted in terms of the scales used, and, for the most part, the relationship between dimensions and scales was not strong. Nevertheless, the first seven dimensions were labelled respectively, length of lower face, length of middle face, distance between eyes, width of middle of face, tidiness of hair, hair colour and forehead height. The eighth dimension was interpreted as a "light-heartedness" dimension.

Groner's stimuli were homogeneous in age, sex and race, and in expression, which, as the author himself pointed out, may account in part for the relatively few mood or personality attributes mentioned. The dimensions he obtained may be summed up as relating to face shape (height and width of the face) and hair style and colouring, which is of interest in view of results to be mentioned below. It should be pointed out, however, that the individual scales associated with the dimension Groner labelled "width of middle of face", were breadth of nose, and size of mouth. A more appropriate label for this dimension might therefore be "size of inner face features".

In a more recent study, Hirschberg *et al.* (1978) used photographs of 9 male blacks and 9 male whites, which were also known to vary on a previously developed Face Differential Scale. Subjects judged the degree of similarity between all possible pairs of stimuli, and in addition rated all faces on a number of physical attributes and personality characteristics. In a separate procedure, physical measurements were taken of a number of facial features on each photograph.

Matrices of similarity ratings by 33 white female subjects and 30 black female subjects were analysed using the INDSCAL program (Carroll and Chang, 1970). Six dimensions were retained for both the white and black subjects. These dimensions were interpreted using simple and multiple correlations between coordinates of stimuli on the dimensions, and mean ratings on the scales assessing physical and personality characteristics.

The first dimension was a race dimension, highly correlated with physical features, like skin colour, nose breadth and thickness of lips—features associated with race differences. No personality-trait ratings correlated with this dimension. By contrast, the second dimension, labelled "desirability" by the authors, was related to ratings on a number of scales such as "likeable", "attractive" and "pleasant". The only substantial correlations with physical features were with "chin type" (double chin versus normal chins), and "nose profile" (hooked versus ski jump noses). The third dimension, labelled "masculine maturity", was correlated with ratings on "strong", "masculine" and "mature", and with ratings of physical features of "moustache", "beard" and "side burns". Only one rating scale and one physical measurement correlated with the fourth dimension, namely "face shape" which contrasted long, narrow faces with wide and flat faces. The fifth dimension was associated with ratings on "relaxed–tense" and with physiognomic ratings of eye shape, while the sixth dimension was related to face fatness and neck thickness for white subjects, but not for black subjects.

An interesting feature of Hirschberg *et al.*'s results is that in some cases dimensions were related to global aspects of faces but not to specific features, while other dimensions were associated with a specific physical feature but not with any personality characteristics. It is possible that subjects may switch from global to more analytic judgments, or that different subjects use different dimensions (as Hirschberg *et al.* went on to show) but any general statement about wholistic or feature processing would be unjustified from these data. It is also apparent that the dimensions depend upon stimulus sampling. The inclusion of both black and white men's photographs, and of hirsute and clean shaven faces made appropriate dimensions salient.

In a series of studies concerned primarily with aesthetic questions, Milord (1978) had subjects rate similarities between all pairs of 16 facial stimuli varying in sex, age, race and expression in a factorial design. The subsequent INDSCAL analysis resulted in four dimensions, although the sex and age dimensions accounted for quite small proportions of variance compared with race. However, he also carried out a similar analysis with 16 faces of young, white males. This resulted in five dimensions of which four were interpreted by relating them to independent ratings. "Pleasantness" and "ordinariness versus uniqueness" were related to dimension 1, "expression" to dimension 2, "aesthetic affect" to dimension 4, and "lightheartedness" and "maturity" to dimension 5. The third dimension was found to be the result of a photographic artefact.

Milord's results, like those of Hirschberg *et al.*, show that race is a potent cue in face discriminations, as is "expression". The "light-hearted" dimension obtained in Milord's analysis of homogeneous faces recalls the finding of Groner.

B *The Aberdeen studies*

An investigation by Shepherd *et al.* (1977) had the objective of identifying features of the face which should be incorporated into a face construction system. They began by photographing some 200 male students, faculty and conference visitors to the University campus. As a result, their samples varied considerably in age and general appearance. A set of 100 full face, black and white prints were selected from this pool, and presented to 48 subjects who were asked to sort them into groups of faces similar in appearance. The number of times each pair of faces was sorted into the same group was used as a measure of similarity, and the resulting similarity matrix was analysed using the MINISSA program (Lingoes and Roskam, 1973). Although the degree of fit of the data to the solutions was only moderately good, as assessed by Kruskal's Stress measure, the three- and four-dimensional solutions appeared to be most easily interpreted. Ratings were independently obtained on a set of scales describing a number of physical features of the faces. The regressions of the coordinates of the faces on the dimensions on to these scales were used to label the dimensions, by fitting vectors to the solutions.

The first dimension was strongly associated with features reflecting the age of the targets, with scales measuring degree of baldness and linedness of the complexion prominent. At one end of this dimension were balding men in late middle age, with lined or even wrinkled faces, and at the other extreme were smooth-faced youths with thick hair. Almost orthogonal to this dimension was a "face shape" dimension, described by scales relating to face length and fatness of face. The third dimension, while distinct, was partly related to the "age" dimension. This was a "length of hair" dimension; the extremes of which, however, were marked by two groups of young men, with long-haired students and workers contrasted with a group of closely shorn police cadets. The fourth dimension was associated mainly with hair texture, and, less directly, with hair coloration.

This initial study once again indicated that face shape and attributes of the hair are among the most salient of features for subjects when they are asked to make judgments of similarity among photographs of faces. In all cases, the main scales had multiple correlations of 0·80 or greater with the four dimensional solution, this solution thus accounting for well over 65% of the variance on these scales.

A second study, replicating the first, was conducted with a different sample of 100 photographs drawn from the same original set of 200 targets. The results were remarkably similar to those of the first study, with "age" (baldness and skin texture), hair length and face shape emerging as the major dimensions, but with hair coloration rather more salient than in the first solution.

Not surprisingly, the dimensions which emerge from these analyses depend very much on the heterogeneity of the stimuli. Although no dimensions were "built in" to the sample, the method of collecting the photographs threw up groups which were distinctive in appearance, particularly in their hair style. However, men with beards or moustaches were excluded from the sample, as were non-Caucasians. Thus facial hairiness and race did not emerge as dimensions as they did in Hirschberg *et al.*'s (1978) study, though they are obviously salient facial cues.

To examine the response of subjects to a more homogeneous set of faces, Christie (1979) prepared colour prints of photographs of male students aged 18–22 years, who were photographed under standard conditions, wearing a green surgical gown to cover clothing. A group of 40 undergraduates were asked to sort 24 of these faces into groups on the basis of similarity.

The co-sorting of faces was used as a measure of similarity for the input matrix to the MINISSA program, and solutions in one to six dimensions were obtained. To assist in interpreting the solutions, multiple correlations were computed between the coordinates of the stimuli on the axes and the mean ratings of the faces on a set of scales, for which a separated group of subjects was used. Four dimensions appeared to be the optimal solution with a stress value of 0·09, and interpretable dimensions.

An examination of the multiple correlations shows a remarkable similarity with the studies of Shepherd *et al.* (1977), except that the age-related scales were not included. The highest relationships were again with face shape and hairstyle, with multiple correlations of 0·80 and higher. The first dimension is primarily a face shape dimension, contrasting short, fat and round faces with long, thin and oval faces; the second dimension is related to hair length, the third to hair colour, and the fourth to hair texture (straight versus curly).

The priority of face shape and characteristics of hair is apparent, but the addition of colour information in the photographs made hair colour more salient than in studies in which black and white prints were used.

In addition to the scales assessing isolated features, three other scales were included in the rating task in an attempt to assess more global aspects of the face. These scales were "strong features" versus "weak features", "very attractive" versus "very unattractive", and "masculine appearance" versus "feminine appearance". Of these, only the "strong features" versus "weak features" had a multiple correlation of above 0·60 with the four-dimensional solution, this value being 0·63. It would thus appear that judgments involving these attributes were not salient in the sortings carried out by these subjects.

So far, most of the work on scaling has used male faces, or sets in which both male and female faces occur. Christie followed his study of male faces with one using only female faces. He photographed young women under the standard conditions used before, and prepared full face coloured prints. Subjects were asked to sort 34 of these with similar instructions to those used for the male study. The MINISSA program was run followed by multiple correlations with independent ratings.

Stress values for solutions in 2–6 dimensions were similar to those for male faces, with the four-dimensional solution seeming the most optimal. From the angles of the vectors fitted to the space on the basis of regression weights, it was clear that the first dimension was related to hair length, and the second to hair colour. The third dimension was not clearly related to any specific feature, but to a more general assessment of attractiveness, while the fourth dimension was related to hair texture.

The surprising aspect to the solution for female faces was the apparently small importance of measures to face shape, which had been so prominent in the solutions for male faces. One can only speculate on the possible reason for this. No simple facial feature appears to substitute for the face shape measures, although "attractiveness" is closely associated with the third dimension. "Attractiveness" ratings in turn are highly correlated with "femininity–masculinity" ratings, which suggests the subjects may have been responding to a general coarseness or delicacy of the facial features. For the male faces, attractiveness was of only minor importance in subjects' judgments.

The women whose photographs appeared in Christie's sample were young Caucasians. It is possible that samples drawn from other populations would have different relevant attributes for similarity judgments. Evidence for this comes from a study by Shepherd and Deregowski (1981), who used a different sample of faces from those used by Christie, and a different method of obtaining the dimensions. A set of 30 full-face colour photographs of European women aged 18 to 60 years were used. Triads of faces were selected from these and were presented to the subject who was asked to select the two faces which were most similar among the three, and to identify the feature on which they were similar. Five attributes were elicited in this way, and the subject then rated all 30 faces on the 5 attributes. From these ratings a matrix of similarities was derived for each subject, and used as input for INDSCAL. An independent group of subjects also rated the faces on the 15 most commonly identified attributes. Multiple correlations were run between the mean ratings on these scales and the coordinates of the faces on the INDSCAL dimensions.

The results confirmed the prominence of hair as a feature in judgment with hair length, hair colour and hair texture all correlating with different dimensions. Age was also a major attribute, together with skin texture and fatness of face. Face shape, measured on a round–oval scale, was only weakly related (multiple correlation of 0·61 with five-dimensional solution), which is consistent with the results of Christie's analysis.

A further condition run by Shepherd and Deregowski had photographs of black African women as the stimuli. Analysis of judgments on these faces resulted in a set of dimensions different from those found for the sample of European faces. Hair colour and texture were of relatively minor significance, and hair length was less important than with European faces. By contrast, skin colour, fatness of face and breadth of nose were more salient for African faces than for European faces.

One surprising outcome of this experiment was that black African and white European subjects did not differ in the dimensions emerging from their judgments. In view of the consistent "other-race" effect in face memory which has been found with these populations, it was anticipated that they might use different attributes from those used by members of the other race to judge faces of their own race. Indeed, when presented with a set containing both black and white faces, the two groups of subjects did differ in the dimensions they used. With homogeneous sets of faces, however, the groups of subjects used the same attributes for their judgments.

It is apparent that we cannot make any general statement from MDS studies about what features of the face are most often used for discriminating among faces. The population of faces within which the discrimination has to be made affects the attributes used. Where physiognomic differences associated with race occur, these will be used; where the race is homogeneous, different features will be used according to the race. There also appears to be some difference in the features used for women's faces and for men's, although characteristics of hair are important for both. Sex-linked features may also be important in a group comprising both sexes, although Milord's (1978) data suggests this may not be very salient. Indeed, long-haired young men may not be easily distinguishable from long haired young women in a full-face photograph, and, given the importance of hair as a distinguishing feature, this may reduce the salience of sex under these conditions. However, for faces of Caucasian males, the major features emerging from studies using scaling techniques have consistently been hair length, colour and texture, and face shape. Internal features (eyes, nose, mouth) are seldom found to be of any significance in these studies.

6 CONCLUSIONS

Virtually all the studies mentioned in this review have been concerned with one of two questions. Either they have asked, which parts of the face are most important for enabling a subject to identify a face as being one he has seen on a previous occasion? Or they have asked, what parts of the face are most important in judging that two faces are similar? For the most part, these studies have used static photographic stimuli to answer these questions, and the answers have been shaped very much by the method and the materials used.

Probably the most consistent finding has been that the hair is the most important single feature for the purposes of these studies. Studies involving fragmentation of the face for recognition (e.g. Goldstein and Mackenberg, 1966), alteration of features (Matthews, 1978; Davies *et al.*, 1977), face description (Ellis *et al.*, 1980) and multidimensional scaling (Shepherd *et al.*, 1977) have all demonstrated the salience of the hair in detection of faces. Face shape has consistently emerged in scaling studies as an important feature, but the techniques adopted in feature fragmentation or substitution have not manipulated this aspect of faces.

Ironically, perhaps, the hair is the facial characteristic most easily altered. The length, colour, style and texture of the hair can be modified without recourse to a plastic surgeon, and for men, at least, beards, moustaches and sideburns can conceal face shape. The nose, eye shape and colour, and mouth are less salient in the experimental tasks reviewed, although changes in these features are more difficult to accomplish.

However, we should pause before dismissing these inner features as of minor importance compared with hair. For one thing, these features may be important in identifying people from other racial groups than Caucasians. More basically, however, faces are encountered in forms other than still photographs, and for purposes other than memorizing for future identification or looking for similarities. Generally, we look at the faces of others to pick up signals relevant for social intercourse, and in particular for when those others wish to speak, or want us to speak. For such purposes, the hair is a cue of no value, and the eyes are by far the most important feature (Argyle and Cook, 1975). We also use the face as a source of information about the emotional state or mood of a person, and the parts of the face yielding this information are the brows, eyes and mouth (Ekman *et al.*, 1972, see Salzen's chapter in this volume). Different parts of the face are attended to according to the task confronting the individual, and generalization from one kind of task, say recognition memory, to another task, say emotional labelling, cannot be made.

Nevertheless, within the domain of face recognition, there is an impressive consistency in the findings. At the applied level, these should be of value in the design, development and use of face construction and face recognition procedures. To the experimentalist, they should be useful for indicating those areas of the face most likely to reveal evidence about face processing in identification. In themselves, the studies reviewed here do not contribute to the issue of whether processing is piecemeal or wholistic, since their design often imposed a piecemeal strategy on subjects. However, we have the beginnings of a taxonomy of faces for psychological purposes (see, for example, Jones *et al.*, 1976) which could provide the basis for greater precision in research design.

7 Perception of Emotion in Faces

Eric A. Salzen

1 INTRODUCTION

Our understanding of the nature and limits of the perception of emotion in the face rests largely on studies of the identification of specific facial expressions as representing specific emotions or emotional state intensities. It is generally accepted that the foundation of modern studies was laid by Darwin (1872) in his book "The Expression of the Emotions in Man and Animals". Not only did Darwin propose three major theoretical principles which, either explicitly or implicitly, have formed part of most subsequent theories of emotional expression, but he also employed all the investigatory methods that have subsequently been exploited, viz. the comparative method particularly with non-human primates, cross-cultural studies, developmental studies, photographic recognition studies, consideration of the muscle patterns involved, and the study of the insane. Although the comparative method which underlies these approaches reflects Darwin as the supreme natural historian, he was very ready to test his observationally based inferences with experimental data. Thus he rejected the possibility that the opening of the mouth in surprise gave more acute hearing via the Eustachian tube because of evidence that a watch held inside the open mouth could be heard less distinctly than when outside. His own experiment of approaching his baby son backwards, in order to present a strange stimulus which could be transformed to a familiar one simply by turning round, has yet to be bettered or even copied in numerous modern studies of the stranger-reaction in infants (see Darwin, 1877, for the results of this experiment and Décarie, 1974, for a modern equivalent). Some idea of the importance and influence of Darwin's ideas and methods can be obtained from the review of facial expression

studies published 100 years later as a tribute to Darwin and edited by
Ekman (1973a). Darwin (1872) reviewed his predecessors in the study
of facial expression of emotion, and subsequent studies in the intervening century have been critically reviewed by Jenness (1932a),
Ruckmick (1936), Davitz (1964), Frijda (1969), Izard (1971), Dittman
(1972), and Ekman et al. (1972). The recent review by Ekman and Oster
(1979) brings the story up to date. Much of this work has been on the
expression of emotion in the face but at the same time, through the use
of human judgments of the emotion seen, has also been studying the
perception of emotion in the face, i.e. impression as well as expression.
Indeed one of the points that this chapter may make clear is that failure
to separate these two aspects may have led to a self-substantiating body
of data and beliefs.

2 RECOGNITION OF EMOTIONAL EXPRESSIONS

The usual procedure in facial expression studies has been to ask for
judgments of facial expressions in still photographs, much after the
manner of Darwin, and much less frequently in drawings, motion
pictures, or live subjects (cf. Table 1). The problems inherent in these
different representations and the inadequacies of the sampling of the
emitters and receivers (expressers and perceivers) and of the expressions themselves have been thoroughly detailed, reviewed, and discussed in a definitive manner by Ekman et al. (1972) for almost all the
studies contained in Table 1. Also shown in this Table is an indication
of whether the data have been collected, analysed or interpreted in
terms of the perception and recognition of discrete categories of
emotion or of a limited number of dimensions of emotion, i.e. whether
the researchers have sought for or found categories or dimensions of
emotion. Of course, particular categories and dimensions may or may
not be regarded as emotional traits according to one's view of the nature
of emotion. Thus some studies include "interest" as an emotional
category and others include "activation" as a dimension of emotion.
Neither of these conceptual terms, whether referring to behaviours or
internal states, refers only and necessarily to emotional phenomena;
both can be non-emotional concomitants of drive or need motivation. In
their critical and exhaustive review of face studies Ekman et al. (1972)
selected five of the methodologically most adequate studies of still
photographs which had used specific categories of emotion (Woodworth, 1938; Plutchik, 1962; Tomkins and McCarter, 1964; Osgood,
1966; and Frijda, 1969) and proposed that the categories which they

TABLE 1
Major studies of the categories and dimensions of emotion seen in the human face

A list of studies of recognition of emotion in facial expressions. The majority are studies that explicitly or implicitly examine the range of emotions that can be accurately identified from facial expressions alone. Column 1 lists the nature and source of the stimulus materials. Column 2 lists the corresponding studies in which discrete categories of emotion were identified. Column 3 lists the corresponding studies that identified a limited number of underlying dimensions of emotion. The Table does not include studies designed to examine limited and specific aspects of the recognition of emotions from facial expressions.

Stimulus series	Category studies	Dimension studies
A. *Drawings and schematics*		
1. Rudolph (1903) drawings: artist drawings from photographs of an actor	Langfeld (1918); Allport (1924); Jenness (1932b)	
2. Boring and Titchener (1923) model: profiles made from the Piderit (1867) diagrams	Buzby (1924); Fernberger (1927)	
B. *Photographs*		
1. Feleky (1914): posed by herself	Feleky (1914, 1924); Kanner (1931) *Scaled categories* Woodworth (1938) (re-analysis of Feleky)	
2. Ruckmick (1921): posed by an actress	Ruckmick (1921); Hanawalt (1944)	Schlosberg (1952, 1954)
3. Landis (1924): elicited and posed expressions from 25 people	Landis (1929) (negative results)	
4. Frois-Wittman (1930): posed by himself (see also Hulin and Katz, 1935)	Frois-Wittman (1930); Schlosberg (1941); Ekman (1972); Ermiane and Gergerian (1978)	Schlosberg (1952, 1954); Royal and Hays (1959); Kauranne (1964)
5. Dusenbury and Knower (1938): posed by a man and woman	Dusenbury and Knower (1938); Dickey and Knower (1941)	

TABLE 1 (*cont.*)

Stimulus series	Category studies	Dimension studies
6. Lightfoot (Engen *et al.*, 1957): posed by an actress	Ekman (1972) *Scaled categories* Levy and Schlosberg (1960); Triandis and Lambert (1958) *Hierarchy of categories* Frijda (1969)	Engen *et al.* (1957, 1958); Triandis and Lambert (1958) Abelson and Sermat (1962); Gladstones (1962); Saha (1973)
7. Ristola (Nummenmaa and Kauranne, 1958): posed by an actor		Nummenmaa and Kauranne (1958) (re-analysed by Nummenmaa, 1964)
8. Tolch (1959): posed by a man and woman		Williams and Tolch (1965); Williams and Sundene (1965)
9. Plutchik (1962): movements of specific muscles by an actor and actress	Plutchik (1962)	
10. Nelly (Frijda and Philipszoon, 1963): posed by an actress	*Clusters of categories* Stringer (1967) *Hierarchy of categories* Frijda (1970, 1973); Stringer (1973) (re-analysis of 1967)	Frijda and Philipszoon (1963) (re-analysed by Frijda, 1969)
11. Tomkins and McCarter (1964): posed by 11 people	Tomkins and McCarter (1964); Ekman (1972)	
12. Hastorf *et al.* (1966): posed by Osgood		Hastorf *et al.* (1966)
13. Ekman and Friesen (1968): mental patient interviews	Ekman (1972)	

14. Jerome (Frijda, 1970): posed by an actor

15. Izard (1971): posed by several people

16. Ermiane and Gergerian (1978): posed by authors and others, normal and abnormal   Ermiane and Gergerian (1978)

17. Magazine photographs:
   14 pictures   Munn (1940)
   20 pictures   Hanawalt (1944)
   21 Caucasian faces   Vinacke (1949)
   8 Oriental faces   Vinacke and Fong (1955)

Hierarchy of categories
Frijda (1970, 1973)
Izard (1971)

C. *Film/video sequences*

1. Posed by a man and woman   Dusenbury and Knower (1938)

2. Posed by 25 men and 25 women   Levitt (1964)

3. Six interviewees   Dittman (1972)

D. *Live models*

1. Posed by 22 men and 28 women   Thompson and Meltzer (1964)

2. Posed by 24 men and 24 women   Drag and Shaw (1967)

3. Posed by 10 women   Gitter et al. (1972b)

4. Posed by 50 subjects   Osgood (1966)   Osgood (1966)

found could be labelled more or less adequately by the seven terms—
(1) happiness, (2) surprise, (3) fear, (4) sadness, (5) anger, (6) disgust/
contempt, (7) interest (cf. Table 2). Ekman *et al.* conclude that these
are the primary emotions recognizable in still photographs of posed
facial expressions. They believe that a wider range of expressions and
modes of presentation, especially of spontaneous expressions and
motion pictures, might permit perception and recognition of a wider
range of emotions including blends of these "primary" categories. It is
perhaps interesting to note that the earliest explicit scheme of basic
categories for the faces of emotion was devised by Allport (1924) and
consisted of six groups which, as can be seen in Table 2, column 3, have
an obvious correspondence with the primary categories of Ekman *et al.*
Implicit in Darwin's book (1872) are equivalent groupings of emotional
expressions and these are given in Table 2, column 4. Darwin also had
three other groupings—(1) affirmation and negation; (2) helplessness,
patience; (3) self-attention, shame, shyness, modesty/blushing—but
these may be seen either as non-emotional expressions (1), or as blended
expressions (2), (3).

Allport (1924) considered that the basic expression categories were
manifestations of two underlying emotional states with corresponding
facial patterns—pleasant and unpleasant. The notion of underlying
common dimensions of emotions and facial expressions has led to the
study of the number and nature of dimensions that can be perceived and
recognized and the relevant studies are indicated in Table 1. Dittman
(1972) has listed and reviewed these studies and Ekman *et al.* (1972)
have made a definitive analysis of six that they considered methodologically most adequate (Schlosberg, 1954; Osgood, 1966; Hastorf *et
al.*, 1966; Frijda and Philipszoon, 1963; Frijda, 1969, 1970). The
conclusion seems to be that there is evidence of 4 or 5 dimensions, of
which pleasantness/unpleasantness is invariably one and activation/
intensity and interest/attention are others commonly identified.
Dittman (1972) reviewed 13 face studies and noted that 10 found
pleasantness/unpleasantness dimension, 10 identified a level of
activation dimension, and 6 obtained a dimension describable as
attention/rejection with a possible equivalent in the control dimension
(surprise/disgust) of Osgood (1955, 1966). Interestingly Dittman cites
Wundt (1907) for the earliest dimensional approach to emotion with the
three dimensions of pleasurable/unpleasurable, arousing/subduing
and strain/relaxation.

It seems reasonable to conclude that both the category and the
dimension interpretations are reflecting real characteristics of facial
expressions and of their perception and recognition/impression. It

TABLE 2
Emotions and facial expressions

The Table lists the equivalent categories of emotion postulated by various workers as being recognizable from facial expressions. The last column gives possible functional expression elements that may contribute to the expressions interpreted as these emotional categories.

Ekman et al. (1972)	Izard (1971)	Allport (1924)	Darwin (1872)	Facial actions (cf. Table 4)
1. Happiness	Enjoyment/joy	Pleasure	Joy, high spirits, love, tender feeling, devotion	Relax and incorporate
2. Surprise	Surprise/startle	Surprise/fear	Surprise, astonishment, fear, horror	Attend and incorporate or Reject
3. Fear	Fear/terror			Attend and reject or protect
4. Sadness	Distress/anguish	Pain/grief	Low spirits, anxiety, grief, dejection, despair, suffering, weeping	Protect and reject or tire
5. Anger	Anger/rage	Anger	Hatred, anger	Attend and attack and protect
6. Disgust/ contempt	Contempt/disgust	Disgust	Disdain, contempt, disgust, guilt, pride	Reject and retreat
7. Interest	Interest/excitement	Attitude	Reflection, meditation, ill-temper, sulkiness, determination	Attend and incorporate or reject
8.	Shame/humiliation		Self-attention, shame, shyness, modesty	Attend and retreat

perhaps not surprising, therefore, that Osgood (1966) found clusterings of judgments which could represent equivalent category judgments and which were distributed in a three-dimensional space or pyramid, while Stringer (1967) obtained clusters that seemed to be ordered in several dimensions. More recently Stringer (1973) and Frijda (1970, 1973) have presented hierarchical orderings of such clusters which more effectively represent the experimentally obtained pattern of judgments of facial expressions of emotion. Unfortunately no consistent pattern of hierarchy has been obtained even using photographs of the same actor (Frijda 1970) and the ordering of major clusters may differ. Frijda (1973) gives the higher-order hierarchy of clusters for four experiments using separate sets of photographs of faces of an actor and an actress. It is apparent from his Table 2 (p. 337) that the agreement is good at a level of clustering roughly equivalent with the familiar emotion categories (Frijda's clusters agreeing for unhappy, anger, happy, fear/ surprise, attentive/calm, self-confident, and distaste).

The problem with both category and dimension approaches to the perception of emotion in the face is that the results may simply reflect the experimental approach and the cognitions of the experimenter. Thus, in discussing such studies, Dittman (1972, p. 71) has written: "The experiments we have been surveying here, and the methods of analysing the data they produce, have predestined the results to support either the categorical or the dimensional points of view." Earlier, in the case of categories of emotion, Ruckmick (1936, p. 456) noted that ". . . terms which we use, like fear, love, and anger (or rage), are names which we have for centuries applied to certain social expressions. The whole matter then revolves about a common point and the argument becomes circular. The names are designations of certain well-known overt responses: therefore the certain well-known overt responses give us the names". Is this what has been happening with studies of perception of emotion in the face? Many involve the selection of photographs on the basis of the "well-known responses" (explicitly or implicitly chosen by the experimenter or by "judges" or by the subjects themselves) to be recognized by others (the subjects) often using "well-known names" of the "well-known responses". What is being tested is the degree of agreement with others, and the adequacy of the "typical" facial postures as partial representations of the whole body response patterns. Where classes of photographs have not been chosen a priori the subjects have been effectively choosing them. Where class names have not been provided the judges choose them by concordance of their labelling responses. Hulin and Katz (1935) considered this problem and got judges to sort the 72 Frois–Wittman photographs into related groups. They found wide differences in judgments of similarity but unfortunately were not able to compare their results for individual photographs with the results of Frois–Wittman's recognition study (1930). Similarity judgments were also used by Gladstones (1962) with 10 Lightfoot photographs and he obtained three factors—pleasantness/unpleasantness, sleep/tension, and expressionless/mobile—but the photographs were a highly selected set. Stringer (1967) used 30 Lightfoot photographs for similarity judgments and through cluster analysis got five groups which he labelled—worry, disgust/pain, surprise, thoughtfulness, and happiness. These obviously correspond with the familiar emotion categories but subjects varied in the number of groups (4–13, mean 8·4) which they used and over half the subjects reported that they consciously used verbal labels while forming their groups. A study by Coleman (1949) used motion film and required identification of the emotion-provoking situation. The judges had to select from a list of situations which can be roughly labelled neutral, effort, surprise, shock, threatened shock, disgust, fear, and joke. Coleman found that the joke situation was the best, and threatened shock the least well judged. More recently Buck (1976) has used videotaped expressions of slide-viewing subjects for judgments of the eliciting stimulus slide and of the pleasantness/unpleasantness of the elicited affect. Curiously, judgments of the slides were reliable while those of the affect were not; but only four broad categories of stimulus were used (sexual, scenic, unpleasant, and unusual) and the affect ratings were only for a single pleasant/unpleasant dimension. It remains likely that tasks requiring similarity judgments or situation identification involve intermediate cognitive classification and verbal labelling and that these processes are reflected in the resulting judgments. Concordance between individuals will simply reflect development in a common culture and environment.

Ekman *et al.* (1972) have critically analysed studies that allow assessment of the accuracy of recognition of emotional facial expressions, i.e. where the agreement between the perceived and the intended or situationally defined category of emotion can be assessed. These studies included the earlier elicited expression studies of Landis (1924, 1929), Sherman (1927) and Coleman (1949) as well as studies of spontaneous and posed expressions. The reviewers concluded that there is good evidence for accurate recognition of six of their primary emotion categories in posed behaviour and weaker evidence for four of the categories (happiness, surprise, fear, and sadness) in spontaneous expressions. The concordance of categories of posed and judged expressions could result from the individual's developmental experience. The concordance of spontaneous and judged expressions could be the result of centuries of cultural experience operating through the language of the culture and it is interesting therefore to look at some explicit studies of the use of verbal labels for emotions. Using factor analysis on similarity ratings of emotional state words in Swedish, G. Ekman (1955) obtained factors which he interpreted as states of pleasure, discomfort, agitation, longing, animation, fear, affection, disgust, and anger. Nummenmaa (1964) factor analysed both verbal responses to, and similarity judgments of, facial expression photographs and identified two independent sets of factors. For the verbal response study they were—an attention-like factor, surprise/fear, anger, pleasure, and rejection. For the similarity grouping study they were—pleasure, anger, surprise/fear, and rejection. Clearly there was some isomorphy of language and facial categories, but Nummenmaa points out that these could simply be aspects of Schlosberg's pleasant/unpleasant, and attention/rejection dimensions.[1]

Dimension-like factors of pleasantness/unpleasantness, level of motivation, and interpersonal relatedness, were identified by Block (1957) from a semantic differential analysis (Osgood, 1952) of 15 emotional terms. Plutchik (1962) also used this analysis on 20 words representing his 8 primary emotions at different intensities. He obtained clusters of adjectives for each term but these were shared and increased in number with intensity of affect. By plotting his terms in paired dimensions, represented by five scales (good/bad, pleasure/pain, exited/depressed, active/passive, excitable/calm), Plutchik calculated intercorrelations for the five scales and demonstrated at least two independent dimensions, pleasure/pain and active/passive. Finally Osgood (1962) himself concluded that the semantic differential gives three factors—evaluation, potency, and, less clearly, activity; that these are affective in nature and that they are comparable with Wundt's three dimension and Schlosberg's face dimensions. A later study by Davitz (1969, 1970) used a checklist of 556 phrases obtained from a large sample of people asked to describe their emotional experiences. This list was then used by 50 people to describe the particular experiences which they remembered in response to each of 50 emotional terms. Cluster analysis of th resulting data gave the 12 clusters or emotional elements which ar listed in Table 3. Davitz noted that these clusters appeared differentially in the descriptions of experiences elicited by different emotion words and so could be regarded as components of the emotional significance of words. Six of the emotional category terms used by Ekman

[1] Perhaps it should also be noted that the Ristola photographs used by Nummenmaa were posed using the list of dimensions of emotion constructed by G. Ekman.

TABLE 3
Dimensions in the language of emotion (after Davitz, 1969)

The upper part of the Table shows the results of Davitz' analysis of verbal descriptions of emotional experience. Phrases used in these descriptions fall into the four dimensions shown in column 1. Within these dimensions the phrases can be grouped into the cluster categories shown in the following three columns. The lower part of the Table lists six of the emotion category terms obtained in studies of facial expression and the corresponding clusters of descriptive phrases of emotional experience which Davitz obtained in response to these terms. Thus the Table gives some information on the relation between categories and dimensions of emotion in language and cognition.

Emotional dimension	Clusters of descriptive phrases for experienced emotion		
Activation	Activation	Hypoactivation	Hyperactivation
Relatedness	Moving toward	Moving away	Moving against
Hedonic tone	Comfort	Discomfort	Tension
Competence	Enhancement	Incompetence/dissatisfaction	Inadequacy

Emotional category	Clusters prominent in descriptions of category
Happiness	Activation, comfort, enhancement
Surprise	Hyperactivation
Fear	Inadequacy, hyperactivation, tension
Sadness	Discomfort, hypoactivation
Anger	Hyperactivation, move against
Disgust/contempt	Move against, tension

al. (1972) are among the 50 words used by Davitz and the primary underlying components for these terms are also listed in Table 3. There is little evidence from Davitz' language analysis in support of the existence of specific categories of emotional experience isomorphic with specific facial categories of emotion. In fact the 12 clusters of descriptive phrases in Table 3 fall into four triplets of dimensions labelled Activation, Relatedness, Hedonic tone and Competence. These obviously have some similarity with the dimensions of facial recognition studies, i.e. with level of activation, attention/rejection, and pleasant/ unpleasant dimensions respectively. Competence represents a new dimension which Davitz himself feels is related to feelings of efficacy and to the competence motivation concept of White (1959). Davitz also relates his other three dimensions to comparable constructs in a variety of theories of emotion. More recent work has also been analysed and interpreted in terms of dimensions of emotion. Bush (1973), using multidimensional scaling of 264 adjectives for feelings, obtained three dimensions which she called pleasantness/unpleasantness, level of activation, and level of aggression. Russell and Mehrabian (1977) used 42 different verbal-report emotion scales for 200 written descriptions of emotion-eliciting situations. Regression analyses of the results against ratings on the authors' three semantic-differential scales for pleasure/ displeasure, arousal/non-arousal, and dominance/submissiveness, and a measure of response bias (acquiescence) showed that these three dimensions accounted for almost all the variance. The authors point out that their dominance dimension is comparable with the "control" dimension of semantic differential studies and that the same dimensions have been obtained in studies of a variety of non-verbal expressions of emotion including facial expressions. In summary, therefore, it seems that the language of emotion of experience can be ordered in terms of dimensions comparable with those of facial expression/impression.

The same conclusions seem to hold for other languages and cultures. Block (1957) obtained the same dimensions with Norwegians as with Americans, although there were some cultural differences in the relationships between semantic scales. Osgood (1962) concluded that his three dimensions held for 5 language/culture groups and more recently Osgood *et al.* (1975) have re-affirmed this on the basis of studies of 20 different language/culture communities. Osgood (1962) had also shown that semantic differentials in the two languages of bilingual subjects were as close as repeat tests on non-bilingual subjects. Davitz (1969) applied his affect content analysis to Ugandan youths (mean 14·8 years) and found they were very similar to United States youths (mean 15·6 years) in the items of affective experience volunteered in reports of happiness, sadness and anger. There were small differences in the relative frequencies of certain categories of response and Davitz was able to suggest cultural differences which could reasonably be responsible for them. Thus there seems to be very strong evidence that the underlying dimensions of emotion in language are common to a wide variety of languages and cultures, but weaker evidence for the universality of emotional categories in language.

The evidence for universality of facial expression/impression of emotions is now considerable. Ekman and his co-workers have systematically reviewed this evidence and contributed their own important studies (cf. Ekman *et al.*, 1969; Ekman *et al.*, 1972; Ekman, 1972, 1973b; Ekman and Oster, 1979). Although the emphasis in these studies have been on categories of emotion, Triandis and Lambert (1958) used Schlosberg's Lightfoot photographs and found that Greek observers gave dimension ratings close to United States values but showed differences in sorting the photographs into the six Woodworth categories. Saha (1973) has also found a close similarity in dimension ratings with Asian Indians using the Lightfoot photographs. Ekman (1972) described studies of elicited facial expressions in Japanese and United States subjects, video-recorded while watching films, which confirm that a number of similar expressions were emitted and interpreted similarly as to their unpleasant or pleasant nature across these two cultural/racial groups. The Tomkins and McCarter categories used by Izard (1971) for 9 literate cultures and by Ekman and Friesen (Ekman 1972) for 5 literate cultures were appropriately judged from photographs (cf. Table 13, p. 157, in Ekman *et al.*, 1972). Izard in fact tested for labelling (free naming) in 4 cultures as well as for recognition by selecting from a set of labels. He was able to classify the free responses into his 8 affect categories but found cultural differences in uses of particular words. He also gave a 12-item Emotion Attitude Questionnaire to 7 culture groups and concluded that there was more cross-cultural agreement than for other complex concept attitudes. However only two (African and Japanese) non-Caucasian groups have been involved in all these studies of literate cultures. The studies by Ekman and Friesen and by Heider and Heider reported by Ekman (1972) of two isolated pre-literate New Guinean cultures are therefore doubly significant in showing choice of the same facial expressions for the emotion categories of happiness, sadness, disgust and surprise to match situation stories rather than the verbal labels. There was some confusion between anger and disgust (Foré and Dani) and between fear and surprise (Foré). Ekman and Friesen were also able to obtain poses of these emotions from the Foré tribesmen and subsequently photographs of these faces were shown to United States subjects for recognition. Happiness, anger, disgust/contempt and sadness were judged accurately but fear and surprise were difficult for both judges and posers. This use of situation stories rather than verbal labelling gives some confidence that the category labels used by Ekman have some validity across cultures and may be isomorphic with affect-cognitive entities. A further significant point is that the Dani language was lacking in names for some of the emotion categories (Ekman, 1973b). Thus Oster and Ekman (1979) were able to conclude: "In sum there is unambiguous evidence of universality only for the expressions of happiness, anger, disgust, sadness, and combined fear/surprise." The study of Izard (1971) adds the categories of interest and shame to this list but Ekman and Oster consider that head position was the critical cue in the photographs used for these categories. Presumably blends of these facial expressions will also be universally recognized, for Nummenmaa (1964) and Ekman and Friesen (Ekman *et al.*, 1972) have found that the "primary" emotion elements in blended expressions can be detected in both Sweden and United States respectively.

This conclusion, of course, does not say that cultural/ethnic differences in detail may not exist and make recognition a hazardous affair. Ekman (1972) has emphasized that cultural differences in the eliciting stimuli, in display rules, and in the behavioural responses associated with particular expressions, may all affect the quality and intensity of the facial expression (both primary and blended) and its probability of occurrence. Thus the facial expressions of the Japanese subjects when interviewed about the films they had been observing in the study by Ekman (1973b) included more positive and less negative emotional features than did those of their United States counterparts. Display rules also involve management of facial expression and as Ekman and Friesen (1969a, p. 98) have suggested ". . . the face is likely to be the major non-verbal liar. . .". However it also "leaks" information, particularly through "micro-displays", i.e. momentary movements of the "true" feeling expression before either inhibition or masking by assumption of a simulated alternative expression can occur. Inhibition and masking may themselves be incomplete and so give partial or blended expressions. These factors will clearly apply in the recognition of live facial expressions across cultures and so complicate the disarmingly simple statement regarding the recognition of the four or five "primary" categories of typical facial expressions "frozen" at their peak moments in still photographs. To which must be added the necessity of distinguishing the differences in other more voluntary facial gestures and postures which are used for non-verbal signalling in the role of illustrators, regulators, adapters, and emblems of speech (Ekman and Friesen, 1969b). Ekman (1973b) has suggested that the emblematic uses of the "smile" for happiness, raised upper lip and wrinkled nose for disgust, jaw drop for surprise, and lips pulled back for fear, are typical in the United States. Such emblems as these are particularly noteworthy because they may be culturally ritualized elements of "true" emotional expressions. If so then there may well be similarities or comparable emblems across cultures. These emblems obviously shade into simulated expressions being used for masking or display control, and they may contribute to local "dialect" in expression such as that suggested as occurring in an area of the South Eastern United States by Seaford (1975).

It would seem that in the hands of Ekman and his co-workers the category approach to facial recognition of emotion has had considerable success. Yet at the same time the dimensional approach appears to have a validity which applies across cultures for the language of emotional experiences as well as for the facial expressions of emotion. It is interesting to see how these alternative (or complementary?) approaches fare in developmental studies.

3 THE DEVELOPMENT OF EXPRESSION AND IMPRESSION

In their recent review of this area Ekman and Oster (1979) asked when the facial categories (i.e. adult categories) of interest, surprise, sadness, fear and anger first appear in development. They concluded that there is no clear evidence for interest, that surprise rarely occurs before 1 year, that sadness has not been distinguished from the distress face, and that fear, sadness, and anger responses seem to involve neutral attention or distress faces. Recognizable happiness and disgust expressions are present along with distress early in the first year (cf. Herzka, 1979; Izard, 1979). Relevant studies of facial expression in infants and children since Darwin's fundamental descriptions (1872, 1877) have been reviewed by Charlesworth and Kreutzer (1973). The most evident fact is that most conform with Darwin's categorizations—anger, fear, affection/delight/joy involving smiling/laughing, discomfort/distress/ grief involving crying, surprise, shyness/coyness/shame, jealousy, and disgust/contempt/hatred. However these categories are founded on total body, facial, and vocal expressions, not just on the face. In the neonate unequivocal facial expressions in the first week of life may be restricted to crying, smiling, head-turning avoidance, pursing of lips for oral intake, and grimaces to taste (cf. Ruckmick, 1936). The collection of photographs of young infants published by Herzka (1979) adds very little to this list apart from attention or interest, yawning, and possible pre-speech movements—at least to the reader who has no vocal, body or situational information available. Sherman (1927) studied adult recognition of emotions experimentally elicited in very young infants and found no agreement in the absence of knowledge of the eliciting stimulus, but Ekman *et al.* (1972) have given good reasons for doubting the adequacy of the experiment. Goodenough (1931) used 8 still photographs of 10-month infants with expressions of astonishment, dissatisfaction, grimacing, satisfied smiling, roguish smiling, fear, pleasure, and crying, and found that judges could assign them to their appropriate situations choosing from a list of 12 descriptions. Recently Emde *et al.* (1978) have taken up this approach to see if photographs of infant expressions (3½ months) could be assigned to categories of emotion. With Ekman's seven primary categories only happiness and interest seemed relevant and identifiable, while Izard's nine categories gave agreement for enjoyment/joy, interest/excitement, and distress/ anguish. Emde *et al.* concluded that ". . . forced judgments using categories derived from adult peak emotional expression appear to be inappropriate for the 3-month old. . . ." However in both tests, when free-labelling was allowed, more discriminations were apparent. A further free-labelling study was conducted and the responses classified according to a lexicon of labels constructed by Izard (1971) for his emotion categories. Emde *et al.* then found that 86% of the responses could be classified and that *post hoc* addition of passive/bored and sleepy classes accounted for a further 10% of the labels. Confirmatory results with two further experiments were obtained and overall the response ranges were 26–39% enjoyment, 25–32% interest, 10–16% distress, 5–9% sleepy, 2–6% anger, 1–5% passive/bored, 0·1–3% surprise, 0·4– 2% shame, 0–0·5% disgust. Presumably these frequencies of responses reflect the sampling of the emotions in the infant as well as the possible clarity of expression/impression. These results still do not encourage the application of adult expression categories to the young infant and it seems more likely that the elements of adult expressions are being recognized but that they are not in the organized patterns that are isomorphic with the cognitive organizations for these categories in the adult judges.

Emde *et al.* proceeded to apply a multidimensional scaling approach in their infant study. They asked 25 women experienced with infants to sort 25 photographs of infants or verbal responses of mothers to their own infants' pictures and to label the groupings. Analysis for 2½-month infants gave two dimensions—hedonic tone and either activation or state—for both photographs and verbal responses. A third dimension—internally/externally oriented—appeared for sorting pictures of 3½-month infants and for both pictures and verbal response sorting in the case of 4½-month infants. It would seem that the adult can judge 4½-month infant expressions in terms of three dimensions comparable with those found for adult expression if the third dimension is taken as equivalent to acceptance/rejection or control dimensions. It seems reasonable to conclude that there are elements in infant facial expressions which correspond with those of the adult which give rise to three-dimensional ratings. Emde *et al.* were also able to show concordance between results from MDS and free-reponse labelling, i.e. that photographs classed in the same categories also clustered on the relevant dimensions. The authors, nonetheless, conclude that the categories of emotional expression ". . . undergo an epigenesis continuing through the first postnatal year and beyond". Clearly the basic elements of emotional expressions are evident, particularly smiling, brow-knitting, pouting, crying, disgust, laughing, attention, flushing, sulking, weeping (Charlesworth and Kreutzer, 1973; Ekman and Oster, 1979) and adults may name these. But they may not be of the same relative importance or in the same organized patterns as in adult expressions from which the emotional categories have been obtained (both experimentally and cognitively) in studies of facial expression.

When and how these adult patterns emerge remain to be answered as Ekman and Oster (1979) have noted. In the case of total body patterns, however, fear, anger, joy, and affection are evident at 2 years and shame, anxiety, elation, and hope are all clear by 5 years (Bridges, 1931, 1932; Sroufe, 1979). Instrumental learning clearly plays a role and is evident in the first year in the case of smiling and crying (cf. Ekman and Oster, 1979) and could well be important in the shaping of basic expressions into the adult categories. Imitation also plays a part throughout the period 4–16 years (cf. Kwint, 1934; Hamilton, 1973) and may operate even earlier being evident by the end of the first year (cf. Charlesworth and Kreutzer, 1973). Specific motor imitations of tongue and lip protrusion and mouth opening have been claimed to occur in the first few weeks after birth (Meltzoff and Moore, 1977). This early imitation involves visual discrimination but not necessarily affective recognition (cf. Jacobson, 1979). It may be initially a reflex response but it provides opportunities for entrainment and interactions (Schaffer, 1977) in which the mother imitates the infant (Pawlby, 1977) and so produces repetition and timing patterns (Fogel, 1977) which provide a natural system for shaping the infant's expressive system into the adult's modes of organization and use. Eibl-Eibesfeldt's (1973) descriptions of facial expressions of children born deaf–blind include smiling, laughing, crying in distress and anger, frowning, pouting, surprise, refusal head shake, clenched teeth, strong exhaling, and jerking the head back. These are, again, basic elements of adult expression categories. Other studies of blind children reviewed by Charlesworth and Kreutzer (1973) describe their expressions of fear, anger, sadness, and happiness, as normal with a possible deficiency in ability of older children to pose such expressions voluntarily. However Ekman and Oster (1979) have commented that the descriptions of the categories of emotional expression in these children are not sufficiently precise for proper assessment of the importance of learning for the fully organized normal patterns. For the present therefore the point remains that adults may play a role in shaping the facial expressions that develop in infancy and childhood into the familiar adult categories. In so doing they will be contributing to the development of corresponding reciprocal decoding responses, i.e. to the development of the perception of facial expressions of emotion.

Studies of the development of impression of facial affect have been reviewed by Izard (1971), Charlesworth and Kreutzer (1973) and Ekman and Oster (1979). Recognition of facial affect prior to 2½–3 years may be indicated by discriminatory orienting or affective responses. The earliest differential responses of looking at different facial expressions have been recorded at 4 months, when they may occur more to joy than to anger or neutral faces projected on slides (La Barbera *et al.*, 1976), and at 3 months when looking occurs to a "surprise" face following habituation to faces with happy and sad expressions (Young-Browne *et al.*, 1977). But differential affective responses are needed to determine whether such recognition was perception of affect expression or simply of stimulus differences. Even when negative affective responses and distress do occur they may simply be to the less familiar stimulus—the so-called stranger reaction (cf. Décarie, 1974). In general affect recognition, by affective responding or explicit reporting, improves, i.e. becomes increasingly like adult responses from 3 to 11 years of age. A face recognition study comparable with adult studies was made by Gates (1923) using 6 Ruckmick photographs for joy, pain, anger, fear, contempt and surprise. Children from 3 to 14 years were questioned about the pictures and it seemed that laughter was recognized by more than half the 3-year-olds, pain was recognized by 6 to 6·11 years, anger at 7 years, fear at 10 years, and surprise at 11 years of age. Scorn was recognized by only 43% of the 11-year-olds. Comparable results were obtained in a repetition of this study by Kellog and Eagleson (1931) with a United States negro sample.

Izard (1971) studied United States and French children from 2½ to 9 years of age, asking them to discriminate triads from 36 photographs from the Tomkins and McCarter series according to descriptive labels. They were also asked for their own labels for 18 of the photographs. Recognition of Izard's emotion categories improved steadily from 2–9 years in both cultures. Recogition of anger, enjoyment, surprise, and fear developed fastest, with disgust and contentment the slowest, and interest and distress falling between them. Overall, recognition developed ahead of labelling ability which was almost absent at 2 years and still well below recognition performance at 9 years. Izard gives developmental curves for both cultures. Ekman and Friesen (1971) took the opportunity to test 130 children of the isolated Foré tribe in New Guinea using photographs of six of their primary emotion faces. In matching paired photographs to stories, responses ranged from 76–100% correct and 6–7-year-olds were as good as 14–15-year-olds. Understandably perhaps, studies asking children to rate faces on dimensions seem not to exist. But Honkavaara (1961) tackled an aspect of this problem in a series of experiments with groups of subjects ranging from 5–6 years to 30–45 years of age. She used magazine pictures and found that young children responded to facial expressions with "matter of fact" answers and that responses in terms of emotional categories or dimensions became predominant between her 8–14-year and 15–23-year-old groups. Honkavaara concluded that sad and happy expressions acquired their unpleasant and pleasant characters only with mental maturity. Furthermore, perception of the emotional expression develops after perception of the action involved so that her children comprehended laughing and weeping faces before recognizing them as happy and sad expressions. Consequently some of her 3–4-year-old children could, and did, perceive the action and emotion as contradictory. Honkavaara saw this development of perception in terms of the concepts of Werner (1957), with a sequence from "dynamic-affective" perception of signals and events, through "matter-of-fact" perception of objects and their actions, to the "physiognomic mode" of perception of expression as emotional concepts, and finally to an "intersensory" mode of sensitivity to people and their personal styles. This sequence is reflected in the development of recognizing and labelling emotional categories in the previously cited study by Izard (1971).

Clearly the development of recognition of categories of emotion in faces involves both recognition and language processes. Davitz (1969) applied his verbal-item cluster-categories to descriptions of emotional experiences given by 7–8 to 13–14-year-old children in response to open-ended interview questions about their own experience of happiness, sadness, love, anger, and fear. He found the quantity of items mentioned within each category increased, especially at 10–11 years, probably as a result of language skills improvement. More importantly it appeared that the more a cluster was ephasized in adult descriptions, the earlier it tended to appear in the children's reports. In detail; happiness evoked Davitz' activation and comfort items with enhancement added by 6th-grade age (11–12 years); sadness evoked discomfort and hypoactivation responses with incompetence and dissatisfaction added by 6–8th grade; love evoked moving-toward items with comfort added by 4th grade (9–10 years). However, anger evoked moving-against and hyperactivation items in 8th-grade children (13–14 years), with a reverse order of emphasis in adults. Fear evoked tension and moving-away descriptions in the youngest children with inadequacy and hyperactivation appearing in 6–8th grades; these latter two categories are predominant in adult responses.

Thus much of the evidence from both cross-cultural and developmental studies is consistent with the view that perception of emotion in the face may involve both dimensional and categorical assessments. However the developmental evidence suggests that the specific natures of these assessments may be the result of cognitive structuring in development by the categories and intensities of stimuli presented to the child and by the kinds and degrees of coping responses required of it. The resultant cognitive patterns of impression are not necessarily, therefore, isomorphic with the processes of facial expression of emotion. Indeed the recognition or perception of emotion in the face may not be an immediately cognitive process and certainly not a language process. If this is the case then it may be profitable to essay a fresh approach to the problem which does not involve *a priori* implicit use of the categories or dimensions of emotions.

4 AN ETHOLOGICAL VIEW OF EXPRESSION/IMPRESSION

The alternative approach is to ask what involuntary gestures does the face show and for what purposes? This is not simply the question of what possible movements can the face make. Studies of individual muscle actions such as those of Duchenne (1862), Hjortsjö (1970), and Ekman and Friesen (1976) inevitably lead to consideration of movements of visible morphological features since these are what the observer senses and perceives. These studies have also employed intuitive labelling or the familiar categories of emotion for correlation both with muscle actions and feature movements. An early attempt at such correlations by Allport (1924) still bears examination along with those of Izard (1971), Ekman, Friesen and Tomkins (1971) and Ekman *et al.* (1972). Hjortsjö (1970) gives facial features for 24 emotional conditions which he groups into 8 sets roughly corresponding with angry, happy, sly, mournful, enquiring, frightened, contemptuous and nauseated. More recently Ermiane and Gergerian (1978) have proposed a set of correlations of facial patterns with complex emotional, mood, attitude, and personality categories. These approaches tend to beg the question as to the meaningfulness of the information available to the receiver. Human ethological studies that attend to unit features of facial expression tend not to recognize patterns that correspond with emotion categories, but rather to recognize the patterns described in infant studies of expression already listed (smiling, laughing, crying, frowning, pouting, grimacing etc.) or to use even more elemental groupings of movements and postures (cf. Grant, 1969, 1970; Blurton-Jones, 1971; Brannigan and Humphries, 1972; Eibl-Eibesfeldt, 1972, 1973; Young and Décarie, 1977). Andrew (1972) has provided a most rational analysis of the information contained in mammalian displays and earlier had applied it to the evolution of facial expressions in primates including man (1963a,b). In particular Andrew has shown how movements for the protection of the ears and eyes and of the respiratory and alimentary entrances can account for the grimace and the grin face and for distress vocalizations. Similarly he suggests that incipient functional movements can account for other expressions such as disgust from oro-nasal rejection movements, threat from mouth opening for biting, and approach for social interaction from mouth and lip movements for feeding. Movements that enhance sensory or intake capabilities constitute alert responses. This approach is compatible with the mimetic theory of expression of Piderit and Wundt (see description by Allport, 1924), in which functional and sensori-motor reactions such as those to sweet or bitter tastes come to be given to other stimuli which are analogous in that they are perceived as being acceptable or unacceptable respectively. It is also compatible with the developmental theory of Peiper (1935, 1963) which derives infant facial expressions from combinations of movements of mouth, eyes, and nose, which either decrease or increase receptive ability, together with "spreading reactions" of these two tendencies into parts of the face not directly stimulated or involved, e.g. closing eyes in response to a bitter taste. Peiper's descriptions of infant expressions are consistent with these views: "The mouth and eyes assume a defensive position at the beginning of a bad mood as well as in crying and screaming. The facial expressions of defiance, negation and stubbornness correspond to those signifying refusal of food. The laughing infant opens his mouth and eyes, but a certain defensive position of the eyes may also occur. That smiling is connected with the reactions to food intake is doubtful. Affirmation, attention, astonishment, and fear open the sensory organs." (1963, p. 143.) These expressions together with the basic food acceptance and rejectance patterns are all evident in the neonate and early infant photographs assembled by Herzka (1979). In the case of adult facial expressions Hjortsjö (1970) has based his analysis on the actions of dilator and sphincter musculature of the facial orifices controlling stimulus intake. In conjunction with direction of gaze, pupil size, lower jaw position, and head movements, Hjortsjö used these muscle systems to construct expressive patterns for 24 emotional conditions. However, the assumption of his 24 emotional conditions once again begs the question of what emotions are shown by facial expressions. The system of Ermiane and Gergerian (1978) uses a similar approach but is just as assumptive in the emotional and personality categories which it assigns to facial patterns.

In an attempt to avoid prior assumptions of emotional categories it seems better simply to categorize the functional patterns of facial movements which occur and which might convey information about emotional states or at least be interpreted as such by the observer. Table 4 presents a list of such categories with tentative designations. This list draws on previously cited descriptions of the facial expressions of human infants, adults, and non-human primates (for which see also Van Hooff, 1962, 1967, 1972, 1976; Bolwig, 1964; Jolly, 1972, Table 17; Chevalier-Skolnikoff, 1973; Redican, 1975; Marriott and Salzen, 1978, Table 1). Of course the list would be more satisfactory if it were for total body patterns of which facial expressions are but part. This is especially true for attack which in man is by striking with the fist (often holding a weapon) rather than by simple biting. (Anger is less well recognized in facial recognition studies using still photographs which are often of the tense-mouth or clench-teeth effort expression rather than the open mouth shout-face). The descriptions also follow Andrew (1963b) and Van Hooff (1967) in assuming that smiling is a specific human display derived from the fear or protective grimace and that laughing is another display derived from the primate play attack face (see also Van Hooff, 1972). They can be regarded respectively as protective and attacking intention movements coupled with relaxation or relief movements. Their ambivalent character and relation to crying and relief/relaxation were early noted by Crile (1915) and thoroughly explored by Ambrose (1961, 1963). Indeed the play face itself may be an ambivalent expression of open-mouth attack and open-mouth scream

TABLE 4

Functional categories of facial expressions in emotion

The Table lists and describes eight categories of facial action which are functional and which contribute to the expression of emotion. The theoretical basis of this classification of functional expressions is described in the text.

Category	Description
Attend	Phasic and involuntary attention with open eyes, raised brows, and spreading reaction of open mouth. Head pulled back. (Surprise) Focal attention with stare, frown, and spreading reaction of tense mouth. Head forward. Tonic voluntary action. (Interest)
Incorporate	Lip and tongue protrusion with mouth opening, directed gaze and head advancement for oral intake
Attack	Focal attention with tense mouth or open mouth of intention bite with tense lips and expiration (shout). Pallor
Reject	Raised upper lip with nostril dilation, depression of mouth corners and ejection action of tongue with lower lip eversion. Spreading reaction of eyes close or gaze aversion with head turning and lateralization of rejection
Retreat	Aversion of gaze, head turning and retraction, eyes close (cut-off or hide), panting, flushing, sweating, dry mouth, and lip-licking
Protect	Eyes close, lips retract, close glottis with expiration (scream) or hold breath and clench teeth (grimace). Lacrimation
Relax	Relaxation from the other facial actions especially from Protection (smile) and Attack (laugh or play face). Relaxation oscillations of muscular, autonomic, and respiratory systems
Tire	Open mouth and glottis for inhalation, spreading reactions to brow raise and eyes open, but flaccid eyelid droop and jaw drop. Residual effort may give frown/oblique brow and clenched teeth with retracted lips

giving the neutral position of lip tension of the play face. The relation between smiling and laughter is complex but there are good reasons for believing that they have separate origins (Van Hooff, 1972) and may still have separate functions of greeting and play respectively. Lockard *et al.* (1977) recently studied 141 adult dyad interactions and confirmed that affiliative smiling did indeed occur in greeting and departure interactions while laughter was confined almost exclusively to recreational contexts. Harper *et al.* (1978) cite a study by Beekman which found that in mixed- and same-sex dyadic encounters women smiled and laughed more than males yet reported that their feelings were of discomfort and defensive abasement. Males who smiled and laughed reported feeling sociable, friendly and affiliative. Such reports agree with the submissive and appeasement functions of the primate grin-face and support the homologous nature of the human smile. But these data for smiling are confounded with laughter. A low-intensity laugh is very like the smile and indeed smiling has been regarded as low-level laughter because of their similarities in incidence, form and eliciting situation, e.g. Ambrose (1961, 1963), Bolwig (1964). It is likely that smiling and low-level laughing have not been properly distinguished in infant studies of smiling. Thus Cicchetti and Sroufe (1976) in studying Down's syndrome infants called an open mouth with motor activity an "active smile", and noted that "This reaction has the appearance of a low-level non-audible laugh". I suspect that they were indeed low-level laughs and that many studies of infants have been scoring laughs with inaudible respiratory actions as smiles. These probably include the so-called "open-mouth smiles" and so it may not be true that laughing only develops after smiling as is widely accepted in the literature (e.g. Sroufe and Waters, 1976). Van Hooff (1972) has considered this point too and noted that few workers have paid attention to the actual form of the expressions they were categorizing as "smile" or "laugh". He recalled Washburn's (1929) descriptions of early smiling and notes that there is a "round-mouth smile" with open mouth and lips not much retracted, which may be equivalent to the play face, and a "croissant smile" with mouth-corner retraction, which may be equivalent to the grin face. The recent paper by Oster (1978) although attending to detailed muscle involvement in infant smiling still fails to separate these two expressions of true smiling and low-level laughing. She uses the action of *zygomaticus major* as a criterion but this is involved in laughing as well as in various forms of smiling. Indeed Figure 2b in Oster's paper is an excellent picture of a round-mouth laugh although it is labelled as a smiling infant, and the same is true in her Figure 5. Cheyne (1976) has studied the forms and functions of smiling in preschool children and has discerned three common smiles—closed, upper, and broad—which occur differentially in solitary activity, in interpersonal exchange, and in play respectively. The so-called "broad smile", according to the present suggestion, is in fact low-intensity laughing—the play face. The recognition of low-level laughing distinct from smiling would also explain why Sroufe *et al.* (1974) obtained clear trends in the development of laughing in infants if they combined data for "active smiles" along with "laughter". These trends were identical with those plotted for laughter alone by Sroufe and Wunsch (1972). If "smiling" scores were also included, then the trends were no longer apparent. All this evidence favours the view that low-intensity laughing is different from smiling and has not been distinguished in studies of infant smiling and laughing. It means that laughing appears in development earlier than has been recognized, and possibly as early as smiling. From Washburn's (1929) review and data it would seem both could occur in the first week after birth. Washburn, in fact, gave detailed descriptions of face, body, and vocal actions for smiling and laughing and noted that "Even the early smiles were very often accompanied by vocalization". Smiling accompanied by vocalization or squeals was in fact taken as laughter by other observers and by the mothers of the infants. Washburn's criterion for laughter was a repetitive vocalization. But the descriptions of head and body movements seem to confirm that the "open-mouth smile" of the infant was indeed like low-intensity laughing with unvoiced or non-repetitive vocalization. Many studies of infant behaviour and cognitive development have used an undefined "smiling" response as a measure and may well bear re-examination with this distinction between true smiling and low-intensity laughing. The distinction is important because of the different uses of smiling in social greeting and laughter in play.

In addition to these two specialized affect displays of "smiling" and "laughing", two others can be recognized, namely "crying" and "shouting" in distress and anger. These are vocalizations accompanying the protective face and the open-mouth attack-face respectively. In both, the calls increase in duration and amplitude with increasing intensity of affect; with high frequency or pitch dominating in crying–screaming distress and low pitch in the shout–bellow of anger. Andrew (1963b) has described the prolonged calls to intense thwarting such as distress and social isolation for a variety of primates and has suggested that they are related to the short grunt-like calls given as low-intensity calls to novel and interesting objects, close social contact, and food recognition. Andrew's sound spectographs of human infant vocalizations suggest that crying and the attention "Ooo" may be related in this way. Wolff (1969) believes that the first non-cry vocalizations may arise from incipient crying. Both crying and shouting could be high-intensity excitement calls involving thwarting (of flight and attack respectively) and their differences could be due to the different postures and tensions of the respiratory and vocal apparatus associated with protective and attack patterns. Both these vocalizations and their behaviours may become mixed in distress and anger giving complex displays both in man and in other primates (cf. Andrew, 1963b; Wolff, 1969, Plates 10, 11). Of course the evolution and development of weeping provides an additional feature of the crying display in man (cf. Bindra, 1972; Charlesworth and Kreutzer, 1973). Andrew also gives reasons for believing that the "cry mouth" of man with the drawing down of the mouth corners is a special display due to the action of the *triangularis* muscle in protruding the lower lip and the *platsyma* muscle in pulling down the mouth corners—the latter originally serving a function in relation to intense vocalization but now serving a display function antithetical to that of the mouth corner raising produced by *m. zygomaticus major* in smiling and laughing. However, Oster and Ekman (1978) have described the "horseshoe mouth" of infants as due largely to the action of *m. triangularis* and have noted that it does not precede crying which involves protrusion of the lower lip. It may be that the "horseshoe mouth" is derived from the intention rejection mouth rather than from the protective grimace since this would be more consistent with the descriptions given by Oster and Ekman. In which case the "horseshoe mouth" is a dislike or disappointment face rather than a "cry face". A possible fifth specialized display is the "surprise" face of phasic attention to sudden or unexpected stimuli. The enlarged eyes and open mouth could serve as a frightening display to other species while signalling potential danger to conspecifics. In this way it too could be a specialized affect display but it quickly gives way to, or blends with, expressions appropriate to the nature of the stimulus when this is apprehended.

Thus the specialized derived displays and facial expressions of emotion in man can be seen as patterns of intention movements and postures of the classes of behaviour given in Table 4. These classes of behaviour clearly cannot correspond with the so-called categories of emotion used in so many studies of facial expression. However some equivalences are suggested in Table 2 for the classes used by Ekman *et al.* (1972), Izard (1971), Allport (1924) and Darwin (1872). It can be seen that some of the proposed functional classes of expressive behaviour cut across the categories of emotion. It is interesting that the proposed functional classes have close equivalents in the earlier classification of basic emotions proposed by McDougall (1921) and both classifications are shown in Table 5. This similarity may be because McDougall based his affect classes on the feelings associated with classes of "instinctive" behaviour and the present proposal is based on intention movements of instinctive behaviours or consummatory responses. I have elsewhere (Salzen, 1978, 1979) defined emotion as the signalling behaviour resulting from the thwarting and end-of-thwarting of such consummatory behaviours. This approach is closer to McDougall's view but distinguishes this emotional behaviour from the feelings of the performance

TABLE 5
Categories of behaviour and emotion

The Table compares the functional categories of facial expression of Table 4 with corresponding instinctive behaviour and emotion categories recognized by McDougall. The relations between functional behaviours and emotional expressions is evident from this comparison.

Facial actions of expression	McDougall (1921)	
	Instinctive behaviour	Emotion
Attend	Curiosity	Wonder
Incorporate	Parental	Tender emotion
Attack	Pugnacity	Anger
Reject	Repulsion	Disgust
Retreat	Flight	Fear
Protect	Self-abasement	Subjection
Relax	Self-display	Elation
Tire	—	—

of the consummatory behaviour which may not themselves be emotional in the commonly understood sense of the word emotion. On this basis the perception of emotion in the human face is in fact the perception of these thwarting and end-of-thwarting reponses. As far as the face is concerned Table 4 summarizes these responses and it is perhaps sufficient to note that the relaxation/relief patterns of smiling and laughing are end-of-thwarting patterns that have become indicative of happiness and joy. However these various intention movements and postures may occur in blends either in space or time and so give the more familiar complex affect displays of facial expression. Figure 1 gives a paired interaction table of the functional expressions and shows how the products of such pairings could be interpreted in the terms commonly used for emotional expressions. Clearly within each pairing there may be different intensities for each pattern element. Combinations of more than two patterns are not by any means impossible. Hence Fig. 1 can give only an incomplete picture of what emotions can be perceived in human facial expresions. But it seems a more veridical approach to the problem than the conventional category approach reviewed in the earlier parts of this chapter. Figures 2–6 are a selection of photographs from the Frois–Wittman series which I have used to illustrate the functional categories of facial expression listed in Table 4. The Figures

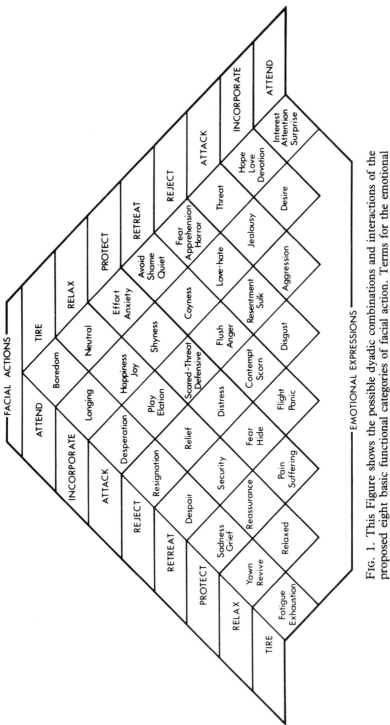

FIG. 1. This Figure shows the possible dyadic combinations and interactions of the proposed eight basic functional categories of facial action. Terms for the emotional categories that might correspond with these facial actions are proposed and entered in each cell of the combination table. For a description and definition of the functional categories of facial action see Table 4.

give some idea of how this type of categorizing could be applied to available materials used for research on the facial expressions of emotion.

This functional analysis of facial expression of emotion can account for the three commonly measured dimensions of emotion. Thus the unpleasant/pleasant dimension corresponds with the thwarting/end-of-thwarting involved in all emotions. The activation dimension may reflect the level of arousal of the tendencies which have been thwarted and the attention/rejection dimension may reflect the nature of the arousing stimulus, i.e. a stimulus for approach or avoidance behaviours. Frijda (1969) used two sets of photographs from the Lightfoot and Nelly series and correlated ratings by 3–5 judges of specific facial features with dimensions obtained from factor analyses of ratings on 27 or 28 scales by 12 subjects. The four dimensions were pleasantness, social acceptability or evaluation, level of activation, and interest. It is clear from Frijda's data that defensive mouth postures, smiling/laughing, and frowning, correlated highly with the pleasantness dimension. Mouth opening, along with general expressiveness and muscular activity, correlated well with the dimension of activation. Eye-opening,

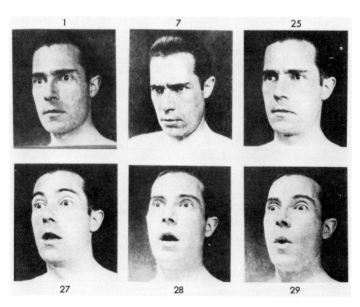

FIG. 2. Six pictures selected from the Frois–Wittman series showing Attend facial ctions (cf. Table 4). The pictures and numbers are taken from Hulin and Katz (1935). Numbers 1, 7, 25 represent variations of Tonic Attention (Interest) and numbers 27, 28, 9 represent variations of Phasic Attention (Surprise).

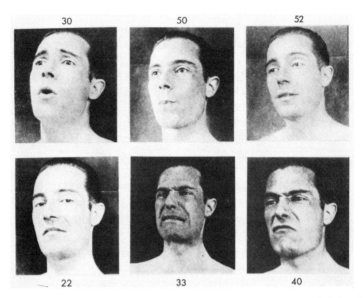

FIG. 3. Six Frois–Wittman pictures showing Incorporate and Reject facial actions (Table 4). Numbers 30, 50, 52 represent variations of Incorporate (Love and Desire) and numbers 22, 33, 40 represent variations of Reject (Dislike and Disgust).

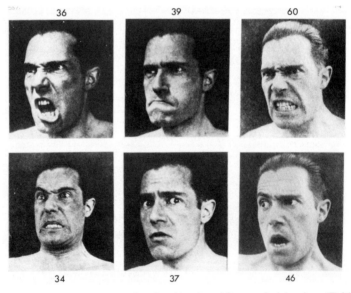

FIG. 4. Six Frois–Wittman pictures showing Attack and Retreat facial actions (Table 4). Numbers 36, 39, 60 represent variations of Attack (Anger and Determination) an. numbers 34, 37, 46 represent incipient Retreat combined with Reject, Attend an. Attack (Apprehension and Fear).

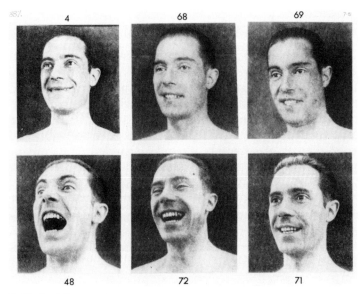

FIG. 5. Six Frois–Wittman pictures showing Relax facial actions (Table 4). Numbers 4, 68, 69 represent intensity variations of Protect–Relax (Smile) and numbers 48, 71, 72 represent intensity variations of Attack–Relax (Laugh).

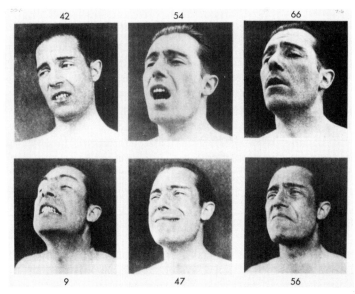

FIG. 6. Six Frois–Wittman pictures showing Protect and Tire facial actions (Table 4). Numbers 42, 54, 66 represent variations of Tire with Incorporate and Protect (Disappointment and Grief) and numbers 9, 47, 56 represent variations of Protect with Effort Distress).

along with attention and muscular activity, correlated moderately with the interest dimension. The correlations of the mouth and eye opening with these dimensions is not inconsistent with the present functional analysis of expression.

Studies of recognition of emotion from specific parts of the face have divided it into mouth, eyes, and brow regions. Results, reviewed by Ekman *et al.* (1972) have favoured upper, lower or neither region as superior for recognition. Conflicting results have been obtained for the same emotion category and results may even depend on the individual judge (Frois–Wittman, 1930; Kushner and Forsyth, 1977). As Ekman *et al.* point out, Frois–Wittman's results suggest that parts of the face contribute to patterns of expression and need to be considered in combinations. This, too, is expected from the present functional approach to categories of expression and a combined rating system for face parts such as FAST developed by Ekman *et al.* (1971) should be more effective for recognition of expressions. Boucher and Ekman (1975) have pursued the regional identification question and have obtained evidence of good recognition of disgust and happiness from the cheeks/mouth and from the eyes/eyelids with cheeks/mouth region. Decreasing levels of recognition for fear and sadness were obtained from the eyes/eyelids, cheeks/mouth, and brow/forehead regions, while moderate levels of recognition for surprise and low levels for anger were also obtained from these three regions. These results again can be understood in terms of the functional elements involved. An obvious rejection mouth signals disgust, smiling and laughter signal happiness, and the less obvious blended functional categories signal fear, sadness and surprise and involve more than one region. Without a "shout" open-mouth attack face anger may be difficult to distinguish from attention and the tense-mouth or clenched teeth of effort. It would be interesting, and probably more fruitful, to use such face region recognition tests for the identification of the present functional expression categories rather than for the conventional emotional categories.

5 PERCEPTION OF EMOTIONAL EXPRESSIONS

Clearly the present hypothesis of emotional expression involves particular aroused motivational systems, their releasing and thwarting stimulus situations, the aroused reponse tendencies, and the associated thwarting responses. The hypothesis includes all the factors which Frijda (1973) has postulated as contributors to his concept of emotion Thus Frijda (p. 327) has written: "An emotion may be defined as complex psychological event composed of three components: (1) A situational "valence-for-the subject"; (2) An immediate behavioural tendency, consisting of a strong or weak increasing or decreasing interaction with that valence, and thus embodying a resultant "stance" toward that valence; (3) A change in the pattern of probabilities of subsequent behaviours–a changed "readiness" profile." The present hypothesis also implies that facial expressions of emotion can only be perceived as the specific response tendencies shown in Table 4, their paired combinations shown in Fig. 1, and their more complex higher-order combinations. But these can be interpreted with certainty only in relation to the full bodily orientation and intention patterns and the stimulus situation which has provided the releasing stimuli for the specific aroused behaviour tendencies and the thwarting circumstances, i.e. incompatible tendencies or inadequate stimuli for response performance.

The literature on recognition of facial expressions shows that the face alone is most significant in expressing happiness (Jenness, 1932a). In reviewing the accuracy of recognition of face photographs Ekman *et al.* 1972) felt that for spontaneous behaviour accuracy has been shown with certainty only for positive versus negative emotional states. It may be that the special displays of smiling and laughter contribute greatly to this distinction. In the case of posed expressions, Ekman *et al.* concluded that their primary emotions were distinguishable and noted that such posing probably resulted in extreme expressions based on the spontaneous ones. The relative identifiability of these categories of emotion seems to vary with the particular photographs or expressions used (cf. Jenness, 1932a, b; Harper *et al.*, 1978). In most cases happiness is the most and anger is a less well recognized expression. The relative importance of bodily versus facial movements in the intention and orientation movements involved in these emotion categories (see Table 2) might explain this finding, particularly if the "shout-mouth" expression is not used in the photograph studies. However Gitter *et al.* 1972a) found that happiness and pain were the most, and fear and sadness the least, well judged faces. But so much depends on the particular stimuli used. In general, relative identifiability of isolated facial expressions should depend on the presence and clarity of the specific displays of smiling and laughing (happiness), screaming (fear), crying (sadness), shouting (anger), rejecting (disgust/contempt), attending (interest/surprise). Reviews of the importance of the face versus other cues—vocal, bodily and contextual—include those of Frijda (1969), Ekman *et al.* (1972) and Ekman and Oster (1979). It is not surprising that they show no simple findings. When judgments are to be in terms of categorical emotions so much depends on the information built into these separate stimulus parameters by the experimenter. There are interactions between the "obviousness" of the clues, their concordance or discordance, the specific judgment required, and even the character of the judge and the emotion which he is required to judge. In the past this kind of test too often has produced the answer built into it by the experimenter. Watson (1972) has attempted to control these factors and their interactions in a study using face photographs for neutrality, sadness, happiness, anger, and anger/disgust expressions in relation to different verbal contexts. She found that in general the facial cues were more determinative than the context. The discussion of these interacting factors by Ekman et al. (1972) remains valid and it can only be said that in natural circumstances great attention is paid to the facial expressions of emotion but that this attention is not exclusive.

The extent to which training can improve recognition of facial expressions has been the subject of argument (cf. Jenness, 1932a; Honkavaara 1961). Ekman and Friesen (1975) have produced a guide book to help people make judgments in accordance with the authors' own emotional category system. Certainly a conscious analytic approach to identification of facial expressions such as FACS can be learned (Ekman and Friesen, 1976). Rosenthal et al. (1979) have shown that performance on their Profile of Non-verbal Sensitivity (PONS) test can be improved by practice and training. Whether such learning is important in normal life remains obscure. There are consistent reports of positive but low correlations of intelligence with ability to recognize facial expressions (see reviews by Jenness, 1932a; and Davitz, 1964). Yet Rosenthal et al. (1979) could find little relation between general intelligence and sensitivity to non-verbal signals. Although Levy et al. (1960) found little difference in pleasantness judgments made by college students and mental retardates in response to photographs of facial expressions Izard (1971) reports emotion recognition ability as a significant predictor of academic achievement, reading, and arithmetic tests in children. The relationship between the development of verbal abilities and the labelling of facial expression has already been discussed. Izard (1971) has shown that this labelling invariably lags behind recognition But Izard's "recognition" test required the child to match a photograph to an emotion label. Totally non-verbal tests of recognition of facial expressions are rare. Some studies have used similarity sorting tasks (e.g. Gladstones, 1962; Stringer, 1967), others have required identification of the eliciting situation (e.g. Goodenough, 1931; Coleman, 1949 Buck, 1976) or matching with stories involving situations (e.g. Dashiel

1927; Ekman and Friesen, 1971). Honkavaara (1961) used questioning methods with children in order to explore the associations between facial expressions, stimulus situations, experienced feelings, and labelling. Although the stimuli and methods lack some controls and experimental rigour her findings are in many ways more interesting than methodologically more secure studies of the recognition and labelling of photographs. She provides some evidence that 3–6-year-old children had no preference between photographs of laughing and crying people and that they recognized such photographs as "laughing" or "crying" more often than as "happy" or "sad". From this and various other enquiry tests of children Honkavaara concluded that children first develop perception of expressive actions as "matter of fact" perceptions to which they may assign wrong or contradictory feelings. They then develop recognition of these expressions as emotions without themselves experiencing the same affect (physiognomic mode of perception). Introspection of sadness, for example, appeared later in development than recognition of sadness.

Empathy (see Aronfreed, 1970, for a restrictive definition) develops in children (cf. Hamilton, 1973; Greenspan *et al.*, 1976; Hoffman, 1975, 1978a) but the precise chronology depends on the specific affect and the degree of specificity of the affective stimulus under consideration. Most studies of empathy include the stimulus situation as well as the observed affective expression and so could be regarded as examples of vicarious affect to the eliciting stimulus situation (see Aronfreed's discussion of his point). The inclusion of such examples in empathy (e.g. see Hoffman, 1978b, for a concept of conditioned affect arousal in empathic affect) will result in an apparently earlier appearance in development. Hamilton's (1973) study appeared to show that empathic facial expressions to pleasant and unpleasant filmed models increased with age in nursery and older children. But this type of congruency of expression is established early in the infant–caretaker interactions (cf. Schaffer, 1977) in which the affect-eliciting situations are common to both participants. Adult introspections of the process of perceiving or recognizing facial expressions suggest a variety of intuitive methods which are commonly non-analytic and include imagining associated body postures or the situations, or sympathetic mimicry of the expressions (cf. Jenness, 1932a; Coleman, 1949; Frijda, 1953). These are comparable with the "empathic" classes of responses defined by Hoffman (1978b) as "motor mimicry" and "imagining oneself in the other's place". All these modes of "empathic" responding are subsumed in the last of the three constituents of recognition of emotion proposed by Frijda (1969), namely, (1) situation reference—the situational interpretations which subjects volunteer when asked to describe facial expressions (see Frijda, 1953); (2) action anticipation—predictions of the likely further actions of the person showing the emotion; (3) emotional experience—equivalent experience through imagination of the feeling, through verbal labelling, or through motor imitation. Frijda regards recognition by the first two processes as the primary recognition of expression and he has written: "That is, if expressive activity is perceived in a functional sense as activity of approach, sensory readiness or closure, generalized tenseness and the like, this perception is perception of the expressive meaning. There is nothing "behind" the expressive activity which is expressed: rather emotional experience is in part, the consciousness of this functional activity or its intention (p. 193)." I suggest that the functional categories of facial expression in Table 4 have the functional sense indicated by Frijda and are the perceived activities and expressions with nothing "behind" them, i.e. they and their combinations are the emotions. Instead, therefore, of assuming or introspecting categories of emotion such as those of Table 2 one should study the situations and the action flow involving these functional expressions between individuals. This has been done by Marriott and Salzen (1978) for facial expressions in squirrel monkeys (see their Table II) and by Van Hooff (1973), using a structural analysis, for the social behaviours and signals of chimpanzees. This provides a form of validity testing that does not involve circular cognitive constructs of emotional introspective experience. Frijda considers that his third constituent of recognition (by emotional experience) involves meaning responses to, or a coding of, the behavioural significance given by the first two processes. It is not therefore, the source of this significance or meaning. These experience or meaning responses must be acquired and so must involve conceptual cognitive structuring in the development of physiognomic and empathic modes of perception (cf. Honkavaara, 1961) and in the development of labelling abilities (cf. Izard, 1971). There is evidence that memory and discrimination of facial expressions, such as "happy", "sad", and "angry" expressions, can be mediated in the right cerebral hemisphere (cf. Suberi and McKeever, 1977; Campbell, 1978; Levy and Bryden, 1979). It seems likely that the conceptual emotional experience element of recognition will involve left hemisphere mediation. I suggest that it is the development of such conceptual cognitive mediating processes that converts the perception of the thwarting and end-of-thwarting functional expressions listed in Table 4 and their combinations as listed in Fig. 1, through their situational reference and action anticipation associations and consequences, into the comprehended "classical" emotional categories and dimensions. The process of this categorizing can be apprehended from the relationships between the functional categories and the emotional categories indicated in Table 2 and Fig. 1. These cognitive structures of emotional experience and meaning, being acquired in the individual's development, are shared approximately among individuals and cultures and differ where the situational references and action anticipations are significantly different within and between cultures respectively (cf. Ekman's, 1972, treatment of elicitors and the consequences for the consistencies and differences of facial expressions between cultures). For the same reasons then, the recognition of the so-called primary emotion categories of facial expressions (Table 2) will be subject to individual and cultural differences whereas the affective functional response categories (Table 4) should be more consistently identifiable both alone and in their admixtures (Fig. 1). These functional expression categories and their admixtures are the perceived emotional expressions of people, while the emotional categories are the cognitive constructs of these perceptions.

8 Theoretical Aspects of Face Recognition

Hadyn D. Ellis

1 INTRODUCTION

In this chapter I propose to examine some of the work that has been carried out to explain the processes that intervene between encountering a person and deciding whether or not we can identify him. Stated as succinctly as that, the task sounds as though it may be an easy one. It will soon be evident, however, that knowledge of the cognitive processes mediating face recognition is patchy and often confused—indeed, so incomplete and inadequate that one of the primary purposes of what follows will be to attempt to identify areas of research that have yet to be tackled. Another aim will be to collate and interpret relevant research most of which is already published, but some as yet unpublished experiments will also be described.

A Evolution

It may be that, as some have observed, our capacity for discriminating among and identifying within the general category of objects called faces represents more or less the ultimate in our classificatory abilities. Most of us can discriminate among an almost infinite number of faces and we can probably identify several thousands, even if we are unable to provide a name for each one. Bahrick *et al.* (1975) demonstrated that the vast memory for faces is also durable: people asked to identify photographs of class mates' faces when mixed with other faces displayed a very high success rate 15 years later, and even after a 50-year lapse about three quarters of the faces were correctly classified. In the laboratory also it is particularly easy to demonstrate a fairly high recognition rate for large numbers of photographs of strangers seen briefly, even after quite long intervals (Goldstein, 1977).

How our facility for processing and storing faces evolved is not exactly known. Obviously, accurate recognition of other members of the same species is important for any animals that live in social groups. For many species olfactory identification is an important means of classifying group members from strangers and high dominance from low dominance animals. The higher primates, however, appear to rely more on vision to make such classifications. A group of higher primates may comprise a very large number of individuals and clearly it is essential that every member of the group be able rapidly to identify and classify any of his fellows. Although the face is by no means the only clue to identity, its involvement in emotional expression probably means that, for higher primates at least, the face provides a most important indication of individuality (Wilson, E.O., 1975). This view perhaps, is reinforced by Gallup's (1977) observations on the ability of animals to recognize their own image. He discovered that such self-awareness only occurred in higher primates, and, although Gallup does not himself draw this conclusion, it may be conjectured that self-recognition may be a function of a more widely based ability to differentiate among conspecifics.

Rosenfeld and Van Hoesen (1979) have demonstrated the ability of rhesus monkeys to learn two-choice discrimination tasks with photographs of other rhesus monkeys as discriminative stimuli. They found that this capacity extended to occasions when the stimulus animals remained constant but their pictures were altered in size, illumination, colour and even pose. These observations suggest that even at a comparatively low level of primate development there is a capacity to abstract the essential characteristics of a face so that it can be recognized despite various transformations applied to it. In Man, of course, the face is the paramount means of identification and there have been strong selection pressures to improve its efficiency (Geschwind, 1979): voice, gait, clothing etc. can all act as aids to the recognition process, but none of them provides quite such useful evidence as the face.

B *Face specificity*

It has been argued that our ability to perceive and store faces is so unusually good that we must have evolved a special face-processing mechanism for the task (Yin, 1969, 1978; Whiteley and Warrington 1977; Teuber, 1978; Geschwind, 1979). Others have pointed to the possible ·biological need for the young infant to possess an innate face processor to enable imprinting on the mother to occur (Tzavaras *et al.*, 1970).

The doubtfulness of most of these arguments has been explored elsewhere (Ellis, 1975). For the present I will confine myself to another and rather more powerful source of evidence favouring the notion of face specificity. There are accounts of brain-damaged patients whose most salient symptom is their inability to recognize people they have known intimately (e.g. Charcot, 1883; Bodamer, 1947; Hécaen and Angelergues, 1962). If it could be demonstrated that the only deficit to be observed in such patients is a difficulty in processing faces then this would constitute almost unshakeable evidence for the idea of a mechanism specialized for the processing of faces.

Both Meadows (1974) and Ellis (1975) have reviewed the published research on patients suffering from prosopagnosia, which is characterized by this inability to recognize faces, and arrived at the same conclusion: namely, that the disability does not appear to occur independently of other handicaps. In a sense, the name prosopagnosia may be misleading for it draws attention only to the face-memory problem (Greek, prosopon = face, agnosia = not knowing). A detailed examination of the various cases of prosopagnosia reveals that, in addition to their difficulty with remembering faces, most patients display a variety of other symptoms that may be related to it. Often, for example, there is also observed to be a disorder in topographical memory so that patients are unable to locate their way around the hospital (Beyn and Knyazeva, 1962); others show difficulty in discriminating among different animal species (Macrae and Trolle, 1956); yet another has been observed to have difficulty in discriminating one food from another (Pallis, 1955).

Prosopagnosia then could be a more general deficit in the ability to make difficult discriminations from memory within classes of complex patterns, and as such will be most noticeable when the sufferer attempts common everyday perceptual judgments. Thus, one would predict that patients with prosopagnosia should show a deficit in identifying individual members of any class of objects that previously they were able to differentiate to a high degree of proficiency. Bornstein (1963), reports that such was the case with an ornithologist who, following brain injury, lost not only her ability to recognize faces but also was unable to identify different birds. Similarly, a farmer who acquired prosopagnosia was thereafter unable to recognize his individual cattle (Bornstein *et al.*, 1969).

An interesting observation by Bateson (1977) is of relevance here. He tested the claims of a student that she could identify some 450 Bewick's swans by names she had given each of them. Bateson photographed a large number of these swans each of which the student named, and tested her ability to identify a sample of them at a later date. He found her reliability in naming to be virtually perfect. This is a striking demonstration of the human capacity for making and storing discriminations among highly similar objects, and suggests that such a facility is not unique to the handling of face patterns.

C *A two-stage model of face recognition*

The exact nature of the problem of how people can recognize faces may be elusive. It is clear from the review of the literature on prosopagnosia that face recognition must involve at least two processing stages. In the first a face is categorized as a face, and in the second it is either categorized as a particular, familiar face or that of a stranger (Ellis, 1975; Whiteley and Warrington, 1977).

Sometimes faces are seen by brain-damaged patients as being not only unfamiliar but also strange and distorted—a condition known as metamorphosia that has also been observed in other types of patients, (for example, those suffering from amphetamine psychosis, Ellinwood, 1969). It is possible that some such process of distortion occurs at an earlier level in translating input into a form that can be used in the memory search procedure that must precede identification. Obviously the distortion is not great enough to disrupt the classification of a percept as a face rather than some other object, but it may be sufficient to render useless any search through stored representations of familiar faces.

Alternatively, it may be that in prosopagnosia the face-memory store itself is destroyed or impaired; but this is a less parsimonious explanation of the condition for it fails to account for the associated disorders mentioned above. It is perhaps worth mentioning at this point that, although prosopognosia is usually a permanent condition, there are reports of prosopagnosia which is quite transitory in nature. Agnetti *et al*. (1978) have recently reported one such case in whom prosopagnosia appeared as a symptom of epileptic attack. This patient was able to give the investigators an interesting and vivid account of what prosopagnosia must be like.

> I was sitting at the table with my father, my brother and his wife. Lunch had been served. Suddenly . . . something funny happened: I found myself unable to recognize anyone around me. They looked unfamiliar. I was aware that they were two men and a woman; I could see the different parts of their faces but I could not associate those faces with known persons. . . . Faces had normal features but I could not identify them.
>
> Agnetti *et al*., 1978, p. 51

Further discussion of the organization of face memory will be postponed until later in the chapter but it should be made clear that we know very little about how faces are stored. Indeed research into the area has been scant owing largely to the fact that the recall techniques that have been extensively employed to study the organization of verbal memory are inappropriate for the detailed study of memory for complex visual material including memory for faces.

2 FACE PROCESSING

The arguments for the existence of face-specific processing mechanisms are not very compelling. What is acceptable is the proposal that we have acquired certain skills in processing faces because of their importance as sources of sociobiological information. Our ability to discriminate and store faces is usually unmatched by our facility with any other types of stimuli (Meadows, 1974). As the example of the girl recognizing swans shows, however, experts in many fields may display equally astounding feats of perceptual learning. According to this view faces are not unique objects in the sense that they are processed by a special system: rather, they probably represent the degree to which people can process visual information when motivated to do so.

Let me return to the two-stage model of face identification outlined earlier. It was argued on the evidence drawn from reports of prosopagnosia patients that the visual information-processing system, at an early stage, categorizes the input into what Rosch *et al.* (1976) would call a "basic" level category (i.e. faces) and then proceeds to the "subordinate" level (i.e. differentiating one's own face, friend's face, prime minister's faces etc.) It could be argued that prosopagnosia may be interpreted as being a malfunction in the process of moving from "basic" to "subordinate" levels of processing. This is quite well illustrated by the quotations from the patient of Agnetti *et al.* He was quite able to classify the objects before him as faces and was even able to distinguish female from male faces but was temporarily unable to recognize them as familiar faces.

A related question that has been raised by a number of investigators is how does this fundamental processing occur? Are the features of a face arranged in a sequence of feature descriptions? Or does the mechanism involve a wholistic or gestalt match between input and stored representation? Susan Carey and Rhea Diamond have argued that face processing by adults involves a configurational or wholistic strategy but that young children may adopt a piecemeal or feature extraction approach (Carey and Diamond, 1977; Diamond and Carey, 1977; see

Carey's chapter in this volume, for further details). Either theoretical persuasion can easily be incorporated into the two-stage model outlined above, but notice that all of the approaches that will be reviewed in the next section involve implicitly the idea of a one-stage process of face recognition.

A *Serial versus parallel processing*

The general consensus among investigators who have examined the possible means by which faces are processed is that they are analysed, at least in part, by a sequential process of feature extraction, usually sampled in a top to bottom order. Such a view is consistent with the general notion that patterns are stored as a set of feature descriptions (see Frisby, 1979). Results to support this view in full or in part have been offered by Bradshaw and Wallace (1971), Matthews (1978), Orenstein and Hamilton (1977), Smith and Nielsen (1970), and Walker-Smith (1978).

Bradshaw and Wallace (1971) employed a task in which pairs of usually identical Identikit faces were scanned by subjects looking for a pair in which the faces were different. Differences could be on 2, 4 or 7 facial features which, according to a simple parallel model, should lead to equally fast detection as all features are scanned simultaneously. A simple serial model in which search stops as soon as a critical difference is noted, however, would predict that on average the faces differing on 7 features would be discriminated more quickly that those differing on 4 features and faster still than those differing on just 2 features. The results supported this particular model, in that the greater the number of feature differences the shorter were found to be the decision latencies.

Smith and Nielsen, using sequentially presented pairs of schematic faces differing on a varying number of features, concluded that "different" judgments were the result of a serial processing of the second face that terminated when a feature was encountered which was different from one in the first face. The latency of "same" judgments, however, was unaffected by the number of critical features and Smith and Nielsen argued that this suggested parallel processing for the decision of "sameness". Thus they propose two processing systems, a serial self-terminating one for "different" judgments and a parallel one for "same" judgments. It should be noted that Orenstein and Hamilton (1977) have argued that the apparent parallel processing for "same" judgments may also be explained by the notion of serial processing. Furthermore, as Townsend (1971) and others have pointed out, it is usually impossible unequivocally to decide from latency measures whether a process is serial or parallel in nature. Usually it is possible to offer special cases of both kinds of processing to account for almost any results.

According to Matthews (1978) the perception of faces involves a mixture of serial and parallel processing: outer facial features are processed together in parallel and inner features are then scanned in a sequential manner. The idea that two separate processes occur may have much to commend it even if the precise nature of each of them cannot unambiguously be determined. But Matthews' views are not shared by other investigators. However, I do not intend to discuss here why there should be discrepancies among the various proposals that have been made because they are based on such different experimental situations that to attempt any reconciliation would involve too great a diversion from the main path of this review.

Instead, I will argue that perhaps none of the models is at all appropriate for an understanding of how faces are normally processed. The problem with all of the work mentioned above is that each investigator has necessarily used artificial faces as stimuli (Identikit faces, Photofit faces or schematic faces). Use of such faces is essential for this kind of research because they allow alterations to be made to discrete facial features leaving other features constant. Unfortunately, as some of the investigators acknowledge, these stimuli may encourage the use of a serial-processing strategy. Subjects could quickly learn that the best way to detect differences between such faces is to make a feature-by-feature comparison until a mismatch is found. Matthews' (1978) results suggest that the implementation of such a strategy may follow a preliminary assessment of similarity based on a global impression, but this will probably depend on how dissimilar are the features. None of the studies has attempted to select feature differences according to any common metric (e.g. by ensuring that all differences involve the same number of "just noticeable differences" regardless of the particular feature involved) and, even if they had done so, they would be still open to the criticism that the presentation of artificial faces could cause subjects to use atypical cognitive strategies.

Models of face processing based upon the unnatural manipulation of facial features are unlikely to represent what happens when we normally encounter and discriminate faces. This leaves us ineluctably in a Catch-22 position—for without the use of artificial faces it seems that we cannot resolve the serial/parallel processing question, and by using them we are only likely to produce wrong answers.

The use of pictures of real as opposed to artificial faces leads us to consider what constitutes a facial feature. Shepherd (1977, and Shepherd *et al.*, this volume) has presented evidence from multidimensional scaling analyses on face-similarity judgments that there are three principal dimensions along which faces can conveniently be arranged. These are face shape, age, and hair length. It is appropriate to ask whether these dimensions, or clusters of features, form the basis of any cognitive process involved in the rapid classification of faces. If these are considered as "natural features" then it is clear that work should be undertaken in which these are varied rather than that arbitrarily selected features are chosen.

B *Spatial frequency approach*

There are alternative approaches to the problem of pattern recognition which do not involve the concept of feature descriptions and consequently they avoid questions of serial versus parallel processing. Spatial frequency analysis is one such approach, the essence of which is that there are channels in the visual system that are sensitive to the different orientations and spatial frequencies contained within a two-dimensional visual array. The outputs of these channels are used to compute the total distribution of orientations and spatial frequencies in the array rather like a Fourier transform (Campbell and Robson, 1968).

Harmon and Julesz (1973) have shown that masking by "noise bands" that are close to the spectrum of frequencies contained in a face are effective in preventing it being recognized. This work has recently been extended by Tieger and Ganz (1979) who demonstrated the fact that a grid-like mask of 2·2 cycles per degree is particularly effective in reducing the recognizability of faces. Masks of a higher and lower frequency are less likely to interfere with recognition. Interestingly, the optimum masking frequency does not correspond directly either to the sensitivity of the visual system or to the predominant spatial frequencies contained within a face. Tieger and Ganz speculate that at some later stage in processing a weighting or filtering of relative spatial frequencies takes place so that middle-range frequencies are emphasized. Unfortunately the results of Tieger and Ganz do not entirely correspond with those found by Woodhouse (1976). Woodhouse approached this problem by selectively filtering out certain spatial frequencies found in a face by a method using laser diffractometry. She established a critical range of frequencies at the low end of the scale that were sufficient for recognition, but then went on to show that this range did not alter with viewing distance. In other words, the critical frequencies were not cycles per degree but rather were cycles per face. Woodhouse claims that minimum information necessary for facial recognition include spatial frequencies up to about 4 cycles per face. Applying this approach to the results of Tieger and Ganz, we find that their faces were masked best by patterns of about 20 cycles per face. Thus there is a large discrepancy between the results of the studies and this will have to be resolved before the spatial-frequency approach to face recognition can proceed.

It is too early to tell whether the spatial frequency approach to face perception is likely to provide better answers than those based on assumptions of feature testing. Equally, it is unclear whether questions about serial and parallel processing can be translated into language appropriate to the spatial frequency approach or whether they become entirely redundant concepts. What is clear at the moment, however, is that the spatial frequency approach has a long way to go before it can be said to represent a unified position.

C *Information extraction*

It would seem that the overall processing of faces is rapid, for we achieve complete identification almost instantly despite the potentially large data bank of known faces that we have to search. Contextual cues probably help the search process and when these are inappropriate, as say when encountering a neighbour while on holiday in a different town, errors or delays in recognition may occur.

According to Simpson and Crandall (1972) we are able to extract information about facial expression from a 20 millisecond view as accurately as from much longer inspection times. But it is also true that the longer the inspection time the more durable is the memory representation for a face (Alexander, 1972; Forbes, 1975; Ellis *et al.*, 1977). Ellis *et al.* (1977) found a log–linear relationship between viewing duration and recognition rate. Clearly for up to 4 seconds (and, according to Forbes' data, probably well beyond 4 seconds) it is possible either that more and more information is extracted which increases the probability of subsequent recognition (e.g. by allowing eye movements to different facial areas, Walker-Smith *et al.*, 1977), or that somehow the increased time automatically leads to a stronger and more permanent memory representation.

Long exposure durations would obviously allow more opportunity for elaborative or deeper levels of processing of the faces than would short durations. But at first glance one would not necessarily expect a linear relationship between exposure duration and recognition accuracy; rather it would seem more likely that discontinuities would occur as subjects changed from a shallow level of processing following short inspections to a deeper level following a longer inspection period. Unfortunately, the studies published to date do not allow a suitably fine-grain analysis to be performed on the responses of individual subjects. It is conceivable that individual results would show discontinuities (but occurring at different points on the abscissa) so that by averaging across subjects an apparent continuity is evident. Be that as it may, ultimately a satisfactory theory of face recognition will have to incorporate an explanation as to why recognition is improved by increased looking time.

3 FACIAL PROTOTYPES

Returning now to the question as to how faces are identified, I want to report some work recently completed by Donald Christie and myself which attempted to investigate the possibility that faces are processed with reference to prototype faces. The assumption behind this research was that there may exist in memory a selection of prototypical faces sampling the range of faces normally encountered, and that incoming faces are first roughly categorized by type and then more specifically anlaysed in terms of deviations from the appropriate prototypical face. This idea has also been tentatively explored by Reed (1972) and Malpass (1975).

This kind of approach to face recognition arises from the research of Posner and his associates into schemata formation (Posner, 1973). According to Posner (1973), "a prototype serves as an internal representation of a whole set of individual patterns" (p. 54); further, such a system can provide an "economical storage system which can deal with a multitude of individual experiences without overloading the memory" (p. 56). Such a system has been demonstrated for the classification of novel and simple stimuli such as dot patterns where the prototype pattern from which stimulus patterns are derived is classified as a member of the group as effectively as the patterns previously encountered (Posner and Keele, 1968).

Christie and I applied a similar approach to examine face processing. We first collected groups of 5–9 faces that were consistently sorted together as being similar. (They were derived from the cluster analysis described by Davies, Shepherd and Ellis, 1979b). Twenty such groups of faces were used. Each group was processed by a technique, first used by Galton (1879), which involves photographically superimposing the faces in such a way as to produce a single, composite face that in some ways represents an average or prototypical face for the group. An illustration of some of these prototype faces is given in Fig. 1.

Ten groups of faces were randomly allocated to act as target faces and ten as distractor faces. Four faces were selected from each of the target groups to be presented as test faces.

The first experiment using these stimuli involved the following procedure. The 40 test faces were first presented singly in a tachistoscope. They were then mixed with 40 new faces: these were made up of the 10 composite target faces, 10 faces drawn from the target clusters, 10 faces from the distractor clusters, and the 10 distractor composite faces.

It was argued that if subjects had derived prototype information from the original set of faces, they would be liable to misclassify the "relevant" composite faces in the recognition run. That is to say they should show a tendency to say they had seen those particular composites when in fact they had merely seen some of the faces from which they were constructed.

The results indicated no such pattern of errors. Subjects in both groups were as easily able to dismiss the "relevant" composites as the other distractor faces. The same result was noted in an analysis of the latencies of decisions.

Thus this experiment provides no support for the idea that individuals derive their own prototypes from an inspection of groups of similar faces and therefore erroneously categorize faces as having been seen before.

A second experiment was conducted to explore further the extraction of prototype information by a study of classification behaviour. Subjects were required to classify a set of faces into one of 4 categories following a paired-associate learning paradigm. The 4 categories were based on the similarity clusters used earlier, so that each category (A,B,C and D) contained 4 highly similar faces. Although not told of the classification rule, all subjects learned to categorize to criterion the 16 randomly presented faces into the 4 groups within about a dozen trials.

Following the learning session, some subjects were tested immediately and some were tested at intervals of 2 or 4 days. The testing session involved tachistoscopic presentations of faces to be categorized as quickly as possible. These faces were the original 16 plus the corresponding 4 prototypes and 4 other faces, one drawn from each of the face groups.

Results were computed for latency and accuracy of classifications and are rather too involved to detail here. The expectation was that, if prototypes had been established in the learning session by a process akin to that involved in the Galton photographic method, composite faces

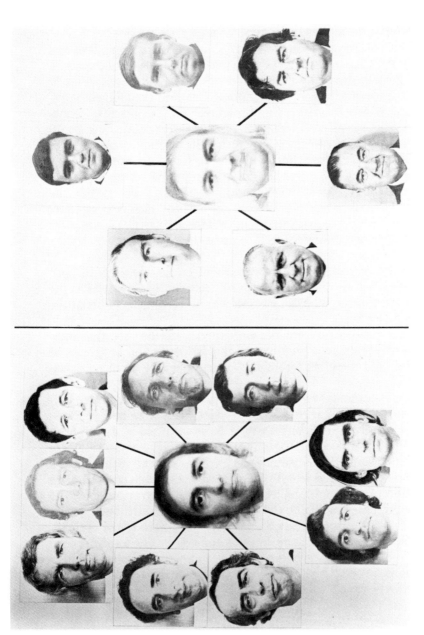

FIG. 1. Two examples of the Galton method for constructing face prototypes. In each case the central "face" was derived by photographically superimposing the surrounding faces that had been previously rated as being similar to one another.

would (a) be "correctly" classified as belonging to groups A,B,C or D; and (b) be so classified as quickly or more quickly than the original faces and certainly more quickly than the new faces. The results were just about opposite to those predicted: subjects were more likely to mis-classify the composite faces and even took longer to reach a decision on them than for the new faces. These data, then, give no support for the idea that people extract schema or prototype faces from an experience of particular types of individual faces.

Although one can never unreservedly accept negative results, the conclusion I wish to draw from these two experiments is that when examining faces people do not normally extract prototype patterns. This implies that faces may be processed rather differently from the sort of simple, abstract stimuli commonly employed to demonstrate proto-type or schema formation (Posner, 1973; Rosch *et al.*, 1976). This may be because face perception is geared to differentiate individual differ-ences rather than to discern commonalities.

People do talk of facial stereotypes, however. They sometimes appear to be reducing face-individuality by combining different exemplars under the same label (such as a typical bank manager's face, or a typical Scotsman's face). However, when Jean Shepherd and I attempted to test people's willingness to nominate stereotypical faces from an array of 184 faces, the results were rather disappointing. Subjects found the task of selecting any faces as being typical of any category to be difficult, and there was little consistency across their selections. Moreover, when some concordance was observed, subjects often gave quite different or even conflicting labels ("stately-home owner" and "manual worker" given to the same face, for example).

These observations confirm the belief that, in general, face percep-tion involves a process of differentiation rather than categorization. This does not mean that the system never makes errors. Davies *et al.* (1979b) showed quite clearly that, when presented with faces similar to those previously encountered, subjects are quite likely to misidentify them. For some reason, such errors do not occur when the original target face is also present.

Light *et al.* (1979) also found that faces rated as "typical" rather than "unusual" were more likely to be rated as similar to other faces in the pool used, and were less likely to be well remembered. These observa-tions may help to explain why faces rated as pleasant/unpleasant, attractive/unattractive, unique etc. are better remembered than those intermediate on these scales (Peters, 1917; Shepherd and Ellis, 1973; Going and Read, 1974).

Light *et al.* discuss their results in terms of "a facial prototype" to which "typical" faces are more similar than are "unusual" faces. This use of the term "prototype" is akin to that employed by Rosch and her co-workers but is somewhat different from the notion of facial prototypes unsuccessfully explored by Christie and myself. Extrapolating from the argument of Light *et al.*, a single facial prototype may exist which represents some sort of average of faces encountered. Faces that are similar to the prototype are not so well remembered as those that are very different from it—deviancy, of course being along any one of a number of facial feature dimensions (see Shepherd *et al.*, this volume). This idea, which is reminiscent of Helson's Adaptation-Level Theory (1964), is interesting and merits further investigation because it may reveal information about the organization of face memory. If the internal representations of faces are not stored in a haphazard fashion, then some means of classifying them must be employed and Shepherd's (1977) finding that facial similarity can be meaningfully and reliably analysed by multidimensional scaling methods to reveal 3 or 4 basic dimensions (or clusters of features) could prove a useful adjunct to the arguments put forward by Light *et al.*

4 KNOWLEDGE OF INDIVIDUAL FACES

Turning from considerations of the ways in which our total repertoire of faces may be organized, I want to discuss how we store information about a single face. Unfortunately, most laboratory experiments on face memory have involved the presentation of a static, fixed photographic view of a face which has to be later identified from among other photographs showing faces with a similar pose and expression. Such a technique is convenient and may reveal a good deal about pattern recognition and pictorial memory, but it is unarguably artificial. Leaving aside the difficulties of extrapolating to real faces information derived from experiments using photographed faces, when we meet a person we see his or her face from a range of angles and adopting a variety of expressions.

There are two aspects of this point that are quite distinct. The one concerns our ability to recognize people first seen in one situation, pose etc. when we next encounter them under different circumstances. This will be discussed in the next section. The other aspect concerns the internal representation of a face (or, indeed, any object) which we have experienced from various angles and in a number of different circumstances. The question here concerns just how such a variety of information is encoded. Do we store some sort of prototypical information about a single face and transform input so as to make it comparable with the standard image? Or do we instead store a whole complex of images or description to cover every contingency?

Whatever the actual mechanism for storing multiple information about a particular face may be, it is worth exploring the possibility that it involves a process of schema or prototype formation to represent the most typical view, expression, context etc. for that face. Clearly efforts should be directed at discovering more about this process. Interestingly, "S" the famous mnemonist studied by Luria (1968) could not easily remember faces. He complained that they were too mobile and changeable for him to construct a clear image.

A *Transformations of faces*

The first aspect to the problem raised earlier concerns our ability to cope with various transformations of a single face as we look at it and at a later date recognize it as being the same face when it is presented in an entirely new context, and viewed from a different angle.

This process is of particular interest when considering the development of knowledge about a particular face. An illustration of our ability to cope with transformations of faces was provided by an experiment performed by Davies *et al.* (1978b) in which some faces were presented full face and tested for recognition in three-quarter profile view and vice versa.

Interestingly, not only were subjects able to recognize transformed faces quite adequately but they performed at a level equivalent to that when recognizing untransformed faces (full pose at presentation and test; or three-quarter pose at presentation and test). This finding demonstrates a flexibility in face recognition which is quite impressive. It is obvious that we normally cope with other types of transformations when viewing faces: we can recognize reasonably well a face that has changed expression between presentation and test (Galper and Hochberg, 1971); and we appear to be quite good at detecting invariance over long time intervals when quite drastic changes in facial features occur (Pittenger and Shaw, 1975).

That is not to say that all transformations can be easily handled. Unusual or "unnatural" ones such as inverting the face (Yin, 1969), or showing a positive print followed by a negative print (Galper, 1970) produce a marked deterioration in performance. These observations are really not very surprising: any complex pattern subjected to a transformation not normally encountered will be difficult to identify (Rock, 1974). It is possible that Yin's (1969) contention that face recognition is unusually disrupted by inversion is correct (although Toyama, 1975, did not find this to be the case), but this may merely mean that the greater the facility for processing a certain kind of pattern, the greater the impairment when a severe transformation is encountered.

In a recent experiment Jan Deregowski and I attempted to discover whether white, European subjects could recognize black faces that had undergone a small transformation in pose with the same ease that similar subjects had been able to recognize white faces (Davies *et al.*, 1978b). As far as possible the procedure employed was the same as in the Davies *et al.* study.

The results were quite unambiguous: white subjects were unable to accommodate small transformations in pose in the types of faces with which they were not familiar. I do not think that this result occurred simply because of the general difficulty white people have in remembering black faces (Malpass and Kravitz, 1969; Shepherd *et al.*, 1974, also see Shepherd, this volume). When black faces were presented for recognition in the same pose as that in which they had appeared at the initial presentation stage, subjects averaged a hit rate of 75%. When pose did change, however, performance fell to near 50% or chance level. Thus it would seem that we acquire the ability to recognize faces of a type with which we have some experience despite various transformations applied to them. This facility does not readily generalize to alien facial types. In keeping with this conclusion, it was further demonstrated that African subjects find particular difficulty in recognizing white faces transformed in pose between study and test yet handle such transformations of black faces relatively easily (Ellis and Deregowski, 1981).

B *External representation of faces*

Patterson (1978) and others have expressed some concern over the fact that so much research into the process of face recognition is based on the use of photographs. This is obviously a very expedient technique but at best it can only tell us something about the basic pattern analysis involved in face identification and, before we can learn the whole story, research using real faces will probably be necessary.

Where investigations using multiple still photographs of faces have been conducted some interesting facts have emerged. Dukes and Bevan (1967), for example, presented pictures of 20 people and required subjects to learn their names. During training, some subjects saw every target person in the same pose and wearing the same clothing, while others saw the targets at different times in various poses and dress. The first group of subjects proved to be superior at recalling the names of the target people when they were later presented, provided the pictures used at test were the same as those employed during the training trials. When completely new photographs were used for testing name recall, the group of subjects who had been trained on a variety of photographs of each target person were better at identifying them. Dukes and Bevan argued from these results that the experience of seeing a variety of views of somone enables generalization to occur which facilitates identification. If we consider this finding in the light of the previous section on facial transformations, it is obvious that a variety of information about a face, i.e. the normal process when becoming acquainted with a new person, leads to a better internal representation which in turn facilities subsequent recognition.

This conclusion would never have been reached from the usual procedure of presenting subjects with a single photograph of a face and testing their recognition ability by later showing the identical picture mixed with pictures of other faces.

C *Caricatures*

Perkins (1975) offered the suggestion that a caricature of a face is more likely to be recognized than its true representation. The basis of his thesis is that cartoonists have long exaggerated the more salient or unusual features of an individual's face and the public have responded by readily recognizing the person. Perkins suggested that this process may reveal something about the normal mechanism of face recognition. Perhaps we store faces encoded in some form of a caricature, a "super fidelity" representation.

Attractive though this idea is (see Frisby, 1979), there is no empirical support for it. Hagen *et al.* (1978) attempted to test whether unfamiliar faces shown initially as photographs would subsequently be recognized better from the same photographs, from different-pose photographs or from caricatures of the target faces. The results indicated that the caricatures elicited the worst overall performance which means that the "super fidelity" hypothesis gains no support from the only experiment yet to test it. The reason that newspaper caricatures are so recognizable may involve a complex interaction between the usefulness of exaggerating prominent features and a complicity between the cartoonist and his audience in which they agree on a code to denote the person being caricatured. An example of this is offered by Perkins himself. President Ford was regularly depicted as having a low forehead and this was one of his more "recognizable" features. Photographs clearly show, however, that in fact Ford had, if anything, a rather high forehead and so it is unlikely that anyone would have easily recognized him from a caricature alone unless somehow "educated" to do so. Thus caricatures may go beyond physical information about a face to include other information. Such a process is unlikely to aid the identification of relatively unknown faces but may well be useful in triggering recognition of very familiar faces. This point will be raised again shortly when I shall discuss the possible internal representations of familiar as opposed to unfamiliar faces.

Before leaving this topic, it is probably relevant to note that, in general, line drawings of faces are not so identifiable as photographs (Davies *et al.*, 1978b). There would seem to be a fairly direct relationship between the amount of detail shown and the likelihood of identification. This would obviously militate against the effectiveness of caricature sketches. Added to this is the problem of faces being experienced in one form (real life, film or photograph) and being presented for recognition in some other form. Generally this is thought to reduce indentification (Patterson, 1978).

5 ORGANIZATION OF FACE MEMORY

We know very little about the nature of the internal representations of faces or about the way in which face memory is organized. Likewise, although it is clear that we are able to access stored representations very quickly, the mechanism for achieving this is not yet understood. What evidence has been produced on these and related matters is limited in value because of the disproportionate amount of research that has been undertaken into the ability to recognize photographs of strangers' faces, usually seen only once before. There has been little research into the acquisition of memory for a face seen repeatedly, from different angles and in different contexts. There has been some work, however, involving the presentation of familiar or famous faces, and this has advanced somewhat our knowledge of the organization of faces in memory.

A *Familiar faces*

Not surprisingly, pictures of famous people are better recognized than are pictures of strangers when the usual presentation/test paradigm for estimating face memory is employed (Ellis *et al.*, 1979b). During the presentation of a set of famous faces it is possible for subjects to encode them both visually and verbally, whereas this is not so easy with the faces of nameless strangers.

As I mentioned earlier, familiar faces also have to be represented rather differently because we know them not from single, static images but as a result of a number and variety of exposures, including probably exposures to pictures and films as well as live encounters.

Further evidence for differences in encoding familiar and unfamiliar faces comes from other experiments reported by Ellis *et al.* (1979b). They showed that the faces of well-known, public figures could be recognized quite well by subjects given the central part of the face with the periphery masked (see Fig. 2). The alternative condition of masking only the central part of the face produced a significantly inferior identification rate. In contrast, when pictures of the faces of strangers were presented whole and then shown with either the inner or outer features masked there was no difference in subjects' ability to recognize them.

Presumably, in the establishment of internal representations of familiar faces some additional weighting is given to inner rather than outer features. This may occur because the inner features are expressive and thereby command more attention over time. The fact that no such advantage was found for the encoding of strangers' faces suggests that the process is not simply due to a disproportionate initial examination of the eyes, nose and mouth compared with the hair and general face shape. (This point is examined in more detail by Shepherd *et al.*, this volume).

The suggestion that familiar and unfamiliar faces may be represented and organized rather differently gains some circumstantial support from the finding made by Warrington and James (1967) that there was no correlation between the ability of neurological patients to recognize unfamiliar faces following a single exposure to them and the ability to identify the faces of well-known personalities. Furthermore, although Carey and Diamond (1977) have shown that young children are less able than older ones at identifying a face that has undergone change of headgear and emotional expression, this inability does not occur when the faces are familiar to begin with (Diamond and Carey, 1977; Samuels, reported by Teuber, 1978). Young children may be distracted by various transformations of strangers' faces but seem capable of dealing with similar changes applied to faces for which, presumably, they already have robust internal representations.

Access to stored representations of familiar faces appears to be possible in adults despite fairly severe transformations of the test pictures. In an experiment which I recently conducted, a set of photographs of the 30 well-known individuals used by Ellis *et al.*(1979b) were presented to different groups of subjects. One group saw the photographs in normal presentation; for another group the photographs were

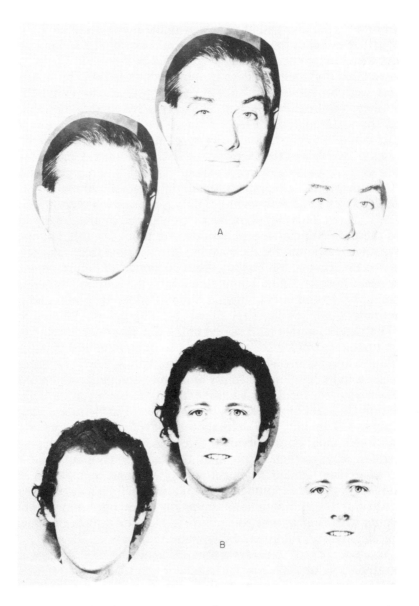

FIG. 2. Examples of the faces used by Ellis *et al.* (1979) to examine the recognition of A, a famous face (James Callaghan) and B, an unknown face (reproduced from *Perception*, 1979, 8, 433).

inverted; while for another group very blurred images were shown. The number of subjects who correctly identified each face was computed for these 3 conditions. Similar scores for the same faces shown with either inner or outer features masked were derived from an earlier study (Ellis *et al.*, 1979b), and the accuracy with which each face was recognized under these five transformations was established. See Fig. 3 for illustrations of the transformations.

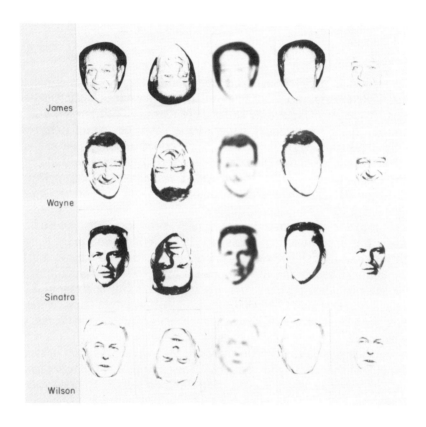

FIG. 3. The transformations shown in these four examples were made on 30 famous faces and the identifiability of each of these faces was independently assessed following every transformation.

Correlation coefficients were computed between each of the five transformation conditions and revealed some interesting relationships. The most relevant finding for the present discussion was that scores for the normal or untransformed faces significantly correlated with all of the transformed conditions ($p < 0.01$ in every case). In other words, access to representations of familiar faces, while disturbed by various transformations, show a similar ranking of success: the easiest faces to identify remain most accessible across all of the transformations studied. The reason for this finding may be that one aspect of increasing familiarity with a face is that it requires less and less evidence to trigger recognition, or, to put it another way, that the threshold of identification is a function of familiarity—not unlike some conceptions of the way in which words are recognized (e.g. Morton's, 1969, logogen model).

B Face semantics

There are other parallels between face identification and word recognition. Like words, faces can be familiar to a greater or lesser degree. Indeed Bruce (1979) has gone so far as to identify the common use of unfamiliar faces for memory experiments with the use of nonsense syllables to study verbal memory. Unfamiliar faces, however, are meaningful and so should not be considered equivalent to nonsense syllables. But Bruce's related argument, in essence that the representations of familiar faces be viewed as being parallel to semantic memory for verbal stimuli, is an interesting one.

The concept of "semantic" memory as opposed to "episodic" memory was introduced by Tulving (1972) as an admittedly rough attempt to distinguish between, say, knowing a word and knowing that it had just occurred in the context of a list of words to be remembered. There are problems perhaps in applying this kind of analysis to face memory but, as Bruce (1979) points out, there is a certain attractiveness in extending the concept of semantic memory to include the corpus of familiar faces.

Using a visual search procedure, Bruce revealed some rather intriguing aspects of the way in which internal representations of familiar faces may be organized and accessed during directed search. In one experiment she presented subjects with a face that was either one of a set of predefined target faces (four recent British Prime Ministers), or a distractor face which could be a familiar actor, an unfamiliar politician or a familiar politician. The distractor faces were further divided into those that were visually similar or dissimiliar to the targets.

The results of this experiment indicated that familiar non-target politicians took longer to reject than actors. This effect was independent of visual similarity but there was also a main effect for similarity: similar faces gave rise to longer rejection latencies than dissimilar faces. In another experiment where there was only a single target face (again of a politician) the effect of semantic category was present only for similar distractor faces.

Bruce has used these results to derive the model shown in Fig. 4. The most noteworthy feature of the model is that when searching faces for a particular person a semantic analysis and a visual analysis can proceed in parallel and both may pass information to a decision-making process.

If we accept the argument illustrated by the model in Fig. 4 then it would seem that for some purposes faces may be organized in long-term memory both by category and by physical features. Thus, classification by attributes like profession is paralleled by classification by visual similarity, the particular aspects of which have yet to be specified. One piece of evidence that may be relevant to this argument was recently provided by Marzi and Berlucchi (1977). They showed that familiar faces were better identified when individual faces were shown tachistoscopically in the right visual field (RVF), whereas generally results with unfamiliar faces indicate superior recognition for those shown in the left

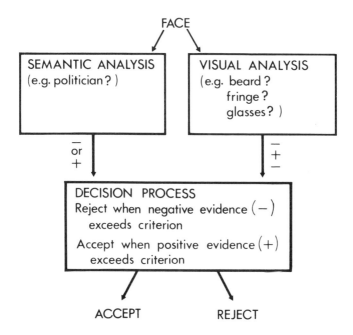

FIG. 4. Bruce's (1979) model of the rejection process in which both visual and semantic properties of the face are examined in parallel (reproduced with the permission of the author and the *Quarterly Journal of Experimental Psychology*).

visual field (LVF) (e.g. Ellis and Shepherd, 1975; Rizzolatti *et al.*, 1971). Stimuli falling in the RVF are relayed immediately to the left, usually language-superior hemisphere, while those ocurring in the LVF pass to the right hemisphere which is normally considered to be dominant for visuo-spatial processing. The findings of Marzi *et al.* (1974) suggest possible anatomical bases for a semantic and physical analysis of face stimuli, but it would be wise to remain cautious about applying the results of hemisphere asymmetry studies to normal information processing—not least because the results of Marzi and Berlucchi, although supported by results of an experiment performed by Umilta *et al.* (1978) may not be entirely generalizable. Leehey and Cahn (1979) found a left visual field or right hemisphere advantage for both familiar and unfamiliar faces following bilateral presentation of two faces. Their observations complicate the argument somewhat, and, before the notion of anatomically separate centres for the representation of semantic and physical data concerning faces can be taken any further, it will be necessary to explain the discrepancy between Leehey and Cahn's findings and those of Marzi and Berlucchi. In a similar vein the findings of Levy *et al.* (1972) will need to be considered. They showed that when familiar face stimuli were constructed from the left half of one face and the right half of another and these tachistoscopically shown to commissurotomized patients, at test the patients pointed to the left hand face (seen by their right hemispheres), but named the right hand face (seen by the left hemisphere). These observations suggest that, whereas the right hemisphere may be regarded as being superior at the physical analyses of faces, the left hemisphere not only can make a physical analysis but also provide related verbal information. The fact that prosopagnosia so often involves bilateral brain injury may also be significant here, for like the evidence from the study by Levy *et al.* it suggests that face processing may be carried out in different brain areas and that this type of processing may not be the same in each case.

C *Internal representation of faces*

The foregoing discussion touched upon the whereabouts and manner in which faces may be internally represented but did not go so far as to analyse the actual form of the representation. As yet only one study specifically addressing this topic has been published. Anderson and Paulson (1978) presented a study from which they argued that faces are represented in the same way as verbal information—that is to say by a single propositional code rather than by an imaginal code.

Anderson and Paulson reached this conclusion after performing a series of experiments in which it was shown that subjects' response latencies to decide whether Identikit faces were familiar (i.e. one of a number learned earlier), varied according to how many other faces shared the same facial features. Obviously it would be possible to explain that finding simply in terms of the difficulty of discriminating among faces sharing the same features. But a subsequent experiment showed that when faces and facial features were associated with labels and verbal descriptions which could also be shared by other faces, response latencies were affected both by the number of other faces sharing the facial features, and by the number of other faces sharing the same descriptors. According to Anderson and Paulson, these results are consistent with the idea that all information concerning a concept, including relevant verbal and visual data, is represented in the same code and is related in a network of interlaced conceptual nodes.

It is difficult to evaluate this explanation, particularly in view of the unresolved controversy currently being debated concerning the viability of single versus plural forms of representing knowledge (Pylyshyn 1973; Kosslyn and Pomerantz, 1977). What can be noted, however, is the pronounced artificiality of Anderson and Paulson's experiments, involving as they do unnatural face stimuli and designs untypical of the real life acquisition of information about people. These facts make it difficult to interpret or to evaluate their conclusions in relation to other work touching on the question of the internal representation of faces. In addition, Anderson and Paulson's ideas do not readily correspond with inferences that may be drawn from the experiments of Bruce, Levy *et al.* or Marzi and Berlucchi. In all of these other cases there is implied a distinction between physical and semantic knowledge about a face. Whether these studies can be incorporated into Anderson and Paulson's scheme has yet to be determined.

It seems to me that, at present, the principal lessons to be learned from Anderson and Paulson's work concern (1) the emphasis on acquisition of face knowledge; and (2) the importance of considering that, in becoming familiar with a person's face, we normally also acquire a variety of other information about him. How semantic knowledge is integrated with knowledge of his physical features is an important topic for future investigations aimed at discovering whether the various types of information are stored together in the same manner, or whether they are stored separately and are related by some cross-referencing system.

) *Context effects*

According to Watkins *et al.* (1976) one of the problems facing a network theory of memory like that assumed by Anderson and Paulson is that it does not predict that recognition memory for faces will be affected by the context in which they are originally encountered. This is because it is assumed that during presentation of any item, including a face, a tag is attached to the corresponding memory node indicating that it was encountered, and at the recognition stage of the experiment a match may be made between this input and the appropriately tagged node. Thus successful recognition will be largely independent of the context originally surrounding the face.

Watkins *et al.* (1976), however, demonstrated that recognition memory for faces is affected by context. When pairs of faces are shown initially, recognition is slightly better if, at the recognition stage, the same pairs are repeated rather than if the faces are shown in different pairs. Similar results were reported by Winograd and Rivers-Bulkeley (1977). Watkins *et al.* argue that findings such as these are inconsistent with tagging theory but are predictable from the standpoint of the episodic approach to memory (Tulving, 1972). This theory, which was briefly alluded to in the discussion of Bruce's work, envisages all memories as involving a new set of traces for every experience, and, as such, predicts that context effects will occur because each event is related to its surrounding contextual events. Unfortunately, the argument of Watkins *et al.* is somewhat weakened by the fact that the context effects they report are small. Indeed, the data reported by Winograd and Rivers-Bulkeley are actually ambiguous since hit and false alarm rates are roughly correlated—suggesting that context effects reflect changes in criterion rather than memory strength.

The debate concerning the nature of internal representations of information and the means by which they are accessed is by no means resolved. What is of interest to us here is that in recent years the arena has been extended to include non-verbal information, such as faces, and this has enriched an area of study that hitherto was not noted for its theoretical sophistication (Ellis, 1975; Baddeley, 1979; Bruce, 1979). Hopefully, this trend will continue so that research into the means by which faces are perceived, stored and retrieved will be less like the activity of blind men feeling different parts of an elephant vainly trying to discern its form.

6 CONCLUSIONS

We are now in a position, if not to detail the actual shape that an eventually successful theory of face recognition will assume, at least to specify many of the factors that such a theory will have to encompass.

The first point to make is that in perceiving a face it initially has to be categorized as such and then has to be checked for evidence of famili arity. Except in patients with prosopagnosia, familiar faces can usually be identified despite changes in context, pose, expression and age. This means that internal facial representations are somehow equipped with transformational rules that permit unique configurations to be correctly classified. These representations give greater weighting to evidence from inner compared with external facial features. There is as yet only equivocal evidence as to how the representation of other physical aspects of a familiar face are linked to other knowledge concerning the person. These may be separately stored and under some circumstances accessed in parallel (Bruce, 1979), or, less probably, they may be converted to some common representation which combines physical and semantic information (Anderson and Paulson, 1978).

Up to a point, unfamiliar faces are processed in the same manner: they must first be categorized as faces and then analysed for familiarity. Either prior to, or following, a negative decision there then may follow a more detailed analysis of outer as well as inner features which may be done in a piecemeal or configurational fashion, and possibly some sort of attributional judgments concerning characteristics such as likeableness may then occur. The longer the inspection period the more elaborate the analysis may be and this in turn will affect either the durability or the accessibility of the stored face representation. The greater the variety of experience with a new face the more flexible its representation tends to be (Bevan and Dukes, 1967). However, we still know very little about the chain of events involved in becoming increasingly familiar with a face and what this might imply for theories of face recognition. It seems, however, that the recognition of relatively unfamiliar faces drawn from races that we are accustomed to viewing enjoys an advantage over the recognition of alien types of faces, in that we are able to cope with small transformations in such faces between initial view and test whereas memory for alien faces is easily disrupted by such a procedure.

Of course, many of the above considerations apply to other objects in the visual world for, despite some evidence to the contrary, there is no compelling reason to expect face processing to be radically different from the processing of other categories of meaningful objects, and the eventual solution to the problem as to how we recognize faces will follow satisfactory answer to the question of how we identifying visual patterns in general. That is not to say faces are not special, rather the conclusion preferred is that in pattern-recognition terms they are no more special than other classes of object, each of which is likely to enjoy an appropriate and unique organization in memory. What makes faces so interesting is that they are universally significant and invariably compelling.

Applications

9 Psycho-legal Aspects of Face Identification

Kenneth A. Deffenbacher and Julie Horney

INTRODUCTION

This chapter has two principal concerns. Our primary concern shall be to describe current scientific knowledge of variables affecting face identification when using the two major pretrial procedures. Mindful of Wells' (1978) distinction between system variables and estimator variables, we shall first summarize research relevant to performance of testimony and lineup tasks as such. Whether these task characteristics are referred to as system variables or process variables, they are ones that are (or potentially can be) under the direct control of criminal justice systems. The interest here is in discovering which particular identification procedures are the most efficient and/or the least biased. Although the effects of various individual difference variables such as sex, age, anxiety, and confidence can only be estimated *post hoc* for any real criminal situation, this does not mean their effects may not be powerful ones. Despite their effects often being difficult to estimate, judicial finders of fact should also be made aware of what light experimental psychology may shed on individual difference or estimator variables as they affect persons giving testimony or viewing lineups. Our second concern shall be to relate these two bodies of research to certain national systems of identification procedures and associated rules regarding admissibility of evidence in cases of eyewitness testimony. In this regard we shall try to point out any inconsistencies there might be between current legal practice and psychological findings. In some of these instances we may also suggest alternative practices judicial systems might consider. We shall conclude with commentary

regarding what the proper role might be for the experimental psychologist as expert witness.

2 FACIAL IDENTIFICATION WITH PRETRIAL PROCEDURES

In this section we shall be first discussing the sorts of task characteristics
that have been shown to affect face identification accuracy of witnesses
giving testimony or viewing lineups or photospreads. Inasmuch as some
amount of testimony is almost invariably given to police before an
eyewitness views a lineup or photospread, we shall adopt this arbitrary
ordering in our discussion. Experimental studies of testimony giving
have documented the effects of some seven different variables on
accuracy and completeness of response. These variables include type of
questions, order of questions, type of items probed, form of response
permitted, bias manipulations, interrogator characteristics, and retention interval. Research with lineups and photospreads, on the other
hand, has addressed the relative efficacy of lineups and photospread
and has recorded the effects of facial similarity, various sorts of bias
manipulations, and retention interval.

A *Task variables affecting giving of testimony*

There exist two principal formats for obtaining testimony from witnesses, the narrative, often referred to as free narrative, and the
interrogative. The former procedure involves free recall of details of the
incident, either orally or in writing. It is of the form, "Tell us all you can
remember." There are a variety of forms of interrogative question. All
four forms of interrogative that have been studied experimentally involve cued recall; they differ only in the manner in which the cues are
presented and in the extent to which the cues are informative. Two
forms of interrogative question are perhaps best labelled as controlled
narrative (cf. for example, Loftus, 1979). Both of these interrogative
types put more constraint on the witness' responses than the free
narrative. Examples would include: "Now describe the person you saw
at the very beginning of the incident"; "Mention in detail everything
about the face of the person you saw." The first example would be
labelled by Marquis *et al.* (1972) as an open-ended interrogative involving moderate guidance of the witness. The second would be referred
by Marquis *et al.* as an open-ended interrogative involving high
guidance. Leading questions and multiple-choice questions are likewise
interrogative in nature. They both put a great deal of constraint on the
witness's testimony by limiting it to a yes or no answer in the former case

and a choice of two or more verbally stated alternatives in the latter. While the eyewitness obtains much better cueing of his or her memory with these two procedures, the potential for biasing of response or even of memory for the incident is clearly greater as well. "The person had blue eyes, did she not?" "Was his nose long, moderately long, or short?"

Research from the early part of this century showed the narrative type of question to result in more accurate testimony than the interrogative across all types of items probed, details of persons, actions, objects, and background (Whipple, 1909). Two modern studies suggest, however, that the accuracy advantage for free narrative may hold only for more difficult items (Marquis *et al.*, 1972; Clifford and Scott, 1978). Both studies define "difficult" items as those not spontaneously mentioned in free recall by non-experimental subjects. As might be expected, within the interrogative class of questions, open-ended interrogatives produce greater accuracy of responding than multiple-choice or leading (Marquis *et al.*, 1972; Lipton, 1977). Recent studies (Marquis *et al.*, 1972; Lipton, 1977) as well as the older literature are in agreement, though, that the interrogative form of questioning is more complete. That is, the range of responses made to it is greater. The more recent research differs in its findings from the classical only in the magnitude of the completeness advantage of the interrogative form, finding an advantage of as much as 200%. Among interrogative question types, multiple-choice and leading questions have been found to result in greater completeness than open-ended ones.

There is clearly a trade-off between accuracy and completeness when using the two major questioning procedures. Witnesses queried in the free narrative manner obviously are adopting a very conservative response criterion. A detail is not mentioned unless they are quite sure of it. This accounts both for their low completeness scores and high accuracy, inasmuch as details not mentioned do not detract from their accuracy scores. Witnesses queried in the interrogative fashion, on the other hand, are constrained to respond with details they might not always be so certain about. This will raise their completeness scores but their error rates as well. It is interesting to note that if one's criterion were instead total number of details accurately reported, the interrogative question format comes off better. Consider an example from Lipton's (1977) data. His free narrative subjects had a mean completeness score of 21% with an accuracy of 91%, for a total of 19% of all details accurately reported. Subjects queried by open-ended interrogative, however, showed a completeness of 32% with an accuracy of 82%, yielding a total of 26% of all details accurately reported.

The issue then becomes whether both question formats need be used for a given witness, and, if so, in which order. There are two reasons why the narrative form should also continue to be used. First, it produces extraordinary accuracy for those items that are mentioned by the witness, as high as 96% in some instances (Marquis *et al.*, 1972). Second, it puts a minimum of constraint on the witness's responses and does not suggest details to the witness about which he or she is unsure, with the result that such details are mistakenly incorporated into memory for the event. If the free narrative format is to be used, then, it would seem that it should occur before any interrogative questioning.

Indeed there is empirical evidence to support this notion. Cady (1924), among others, had suggested that the order free narrative–interrogative should be more productive of accurate testimony than the reverse order. In perhaps the first study actually to manipulate the order of query, Snee and Lush (1941) found that the narrative–interrogatory sequence produced more correct and fewer "don't know" interrogatory responses than the reverse order, while resulting in the same error rate. The narrative–interrogatory order resulted in only 61% as many correct narrative responses as the reverse order but it more than compensated for this by producing only 47% as many erroneous narrative responses as the other sequence. One recent study (Clifford and Scott, 1978) has reported that form of the initial query makes no difference in accuracy of responses to a final interrogatory query. This last result does not mitigate the need to employ the free narrative technique first, however. The free narrative is as indicated earlier more accurate than the interrogative for more difficult details, and Clifford and Scott tested memory only for "easy" details. A most difficult item to recall verbally is a face (e.g. Shepherd *et al.*, 1978a), and given the centrality of faces as defining characteristics of persons viewed, the criminal justice system needs all the accuracy that is possible.

Though laboratory tests of verbal recall of faces indicate that it is poor, one could well inquire whether it is any better in those studies of testimony previously cited, studies employing either a live or filmed simulation of a criminal event. Research reviewed by Whipple (1909) reported accuracy rates as high as 85–90% for persons, actions, and objects, with description of pesons (presumably including their faces) always being more accurate than memory for their actions. However two modern studies have reported much lower accuracies for descriptions of personal appearance and have shown person descriptions to be more poorly recalled than action descriptions (Marshall, 1966; Clifford and Scott, 1978). Inasmuch as the 36·5% correct recall for person descriptions in Clifford and Scott's experiment is rather similar in size to some of the figures reported by Shepherd *et al.* (1978a) for verbal recall of faces, we are inclined to believe the modern findings. Of course, given the poor recall of faces and physical appearance more generally, proper recognition tests, lineups and photospreads, are needed to supplement testimony giving.

Only two studies seem relevant to the question of whether oral or written testimony produces greater accuracy and completeness (Marshall, 1966; Lipton, 1977). Marshall found that witnesses who gave a free narrative orally recalled about two items less on average (115 items possible) than did witnesses who wrote their narratives. Lipton, on the other hand, found no differences in accuracy or completeness between oral and written testimony. Given Marshall's small effect and Lipton's lack of effect, we do not believe that police need concern themselves with changing the predominant practice of taking oral depositions.

Thus far we have been concerned with reviewing psychology of testimony research that has had as its goal discovering the most effective procedures for eliciting eyewitness report. Equally important, however, is to have knowledge of those conditions that are not just ineffective but which may cause miscarriage of justice by creating response bias and memory bias in the witness. Perhaps the single most researched bias manipulation is that of the leading question. Binet (1900) found accuracy rates of 62% for moderately suggestive and 39% for strongly suggestive leading questions. If a leading question is phrased so as to elicit a yes or no answer, then a witness could achieve a score of 50% just by guessing. Two more recent studies (Marquis *et al.*, 1972; Lipton, 1977) have found leading question accuracy rates of 81% and 72%, respectively. It could be that the leading questions of these two modern studies include less suggestive language and cover more central details of the incident and that these factors account for the higher accuracy rates than those Binet found. In any event, there is no doubt that the presence of even one leading question could lead to biasing of a response or even of memory, with potentially serious consequences. Clifford and Scott (1978) nicely document the susceptibility of witnesses to the lure of at least one leading question; only 4% of their witnesses were not misled by at least one leading question of the four embedded in a 44-item questionnaire.

Type of bias has an effect on accuracy of testimony, too. Lipton (1977) found an accuracy of 83% for neutral-bias questions (open-ended interrogatives), 76% for positive-bias questions, and 52% for negative-bias questions, all values being significantly different from one another. The positively biased interrogatives were leading questions suggesting a correct answer and multiple-choice questions that included a correct alternative. Negatively biased interrogatives were leading questions suggesting an incorrect response and multiple-choice questions not including a correct alternative.

Other types of bias manipulations having effects on accuracy of testimony have been demonstrated in the work of Elizabeth Loftus. Wording of the leading question has long been known to be important, but Loftus and Palmer (1974) and Loftus and Zanni (1975) showed just how important it could be. In both studies subjects answered questions about films of automobile accidents they had viewed. Loftus and Palmer found that the question, "About how fast were the cars going when they smashed into each other" consistently elicited a higher estimate of speed than when "smashed" was replaced by other verbs such as "collided". Loftus and Zanni showed that witnesses who were asked questions employing the definite article "the" were more likely to report having seen something, whether or not it had actually occurred in the film, than those asked questions that substituted the indefinite article, "a". Loftus (1975) further showed that whether a question asked immediately after an event contained a true or a false presupposition, an eyewitness was more likely to report later having seen the presupposed object.

There are two other manipulations that could be classified as biasing but which we have chosen to discuss separately as interrogator characteristics. Two studies are relevant here. Marshall (1966) found that having a high prestige interrogator increased the length of reports given by both law students and police trainees but only the latter group increased their accuracy of reporting as a result of the manipulation, bringing their accuracy up to approximately that of the law students. Marquis et al. (1972) attempted to vary the atmosphere created by the interrogator. Either a positive, supporting atmosphere was created or a negative, challenging one. Marquis and colleagues found no effect of atmosphere and noted that a positive atmosphere did not make leading questions any more tempting.

Last, but not least, there is the consideration of how retention interval may affect accuracy of testimony. How much additional accuracy is lost by delaying testimony giving beyond the immediate? Though there are methodological problems with some of the older research (cf for example, Whipple, 1909), based on such research, a reasonable estimate of average accuracy loss would be about 0·3% per day. A loss of about 0·25% per day on average can be gleaned from some of Marshall's (1966) data, while Lipton (1977) found that the loss was approximately 0·6% per day for his witnesses. At any event, the forgetting curve implied here are not as steeply declining as one might expect from the classical Ebbinghaus forgetting functions, based on one person's learning of many nonsense syllable lists. But then details of a single eyewitnessed event are not nonsense.

B *Task variables affecting lineups and photospreads*

Perhaps the most fundamental research question here is that of the relative efficacy of lineups and photospreads. Experiments reported in three British publications (Dent, 1977; Dent and Stephenson, 1978; Hildendorf and Irving, 1978) and one American publication (Egan *et al.*, 1977) have directly compared performance with photographs and lineups. Which procedure is more efficacious may possibly depend on whether an American-style lineup or a British-style identity parade is employed. Egal *et al.* had their eyewitnesses view two target persons through a one-way mirror in a simulated crime situation. Witnesses made identifications either from a live five-person lineup (including a target person) or from packs of black and white photos that included a full-length, head-on view and a full-face view of each of the same five persons that appeared in the lineup. These witnesses made an anonymous yes or no recognition decision for each person viewed by marking individual response sheets. Egan *et al.* found that the false alarm rate (rate at which innocent persons are indicted) was not differentially affected by viewing procedure. However, viewing the corporeal lineup produced a significantly higher hit rate (rate at which guilty persons are indicted), 98%, versus 85% for those viewing photographs. In statistical decision theory terms, then, Egan *et al.*'s witnesses showed greater sensitivity at discriminating guilty from innocent when a corporeal lineup, American-style, was used. Not inconsistent with these results are those of Hilgendorf and Irving (1978) who found that when the person seen at the "crime" was not included, eyewitnesses were much more likely to commit false alarms on facial photos (80%) than on an identity parade (25%). Hilgendorf and Irving employed a parade conducted according to standard British Home Office recommendations.

At variance with the just cited findings are those of Dent (1977) and Dent and Stephenson (1978). In the former experiment, ten- and eleven-year-olds attempted to identify the "criminal" either from coloured slides (full face, profile, and full length) projected to life size or from an identity parade. The latter procedure is much more confrontational than the American one; the British require the witness to go up and down the line, looking each squarely in the face, and if the suspect is recognized, to tap him or her on the shoulder. Dent found that the children had the same false alarm rates with photographs as with a live parade (32%). The hit rate, however, was more than twice as high with the coloured photos (29% versus 12%, the latter being quite close to the chance rate of 11%). The fourth experiment reported in Dent and Stephenson (1978) yielded the same sort of superiority of photographs over live parade, using university student witnesses this time. Dent attributes the inferiority of the parade condition to the manifestly greater anxiety and stress experienced by witnesses. We are inclined to agree but do not know how to account for the fact that similar styles of parade in Hilgendorf and Irving's study resulted in much higher accuracy (75%).

A frequent concern with the use of lineups and photospreads is whether the retention interval is so long that the reliability of eyewitness response will be seriously affected. How long is too long since the crime? Two studies seem particularly relevant: a straightforward laboratory study by Shepherd and Ellis (1973) and the more direct simulation of a crime and pretrial procedure employed in the previously described study of Egan et al. (1977). Direct comparisons of identification rate are difficult; differences are best described in terms of d', the index of discriminability derived from statistical decision theory (Banks, 1970). Shepherd and Ellis measured recognition accuracy in a two-alternative, forced-choice test at 3 minutes, 6 days, and 35 days. The d' index was 1·73 (89% hit rate), 1·24 (81%) and 0·78 (71%) respectively, where chance would be represented by a d' value of zero (i.e. a 50% hit rate). In the Egan et al. study, d' was 1·39 after 2 days, 1·01 after 21 days and −0·14 after 56 days. Based on these two studies there is evidence of a modest amount of facial forgetting even after a few minutes and evidence of some further loss after two days. However, loss over the next three weeks is proportionately much slower, in keeping with classical forgetting functions. Even after three to five weeks, then, memory for faces is still substantially above chance performance. By eight weeks, though, performance has apparently deteriorated to a chance level. Interestingly, Shepherd and Ellis noted that memory for undistinctive faces, those of moderate attractiveness, was at chance after only five weeks. But they also found no evidence for a steady increase in the forgetting of more distinctive faces, those of high and low attractiveness. That is, after an initial loss during the first three minutes, performance on these faces remained in the 80–85% range over the next five weeks. So delaying a photospread or lineup would be less crucial if the suspect's face were rather distinctive.[1]

[1] Though the distinctiveness of individual target faces was not assessed, Shepherd et al. (1980), in a very recent series of experiments, found no significant increase in forgetting in the interval from one week to four months; identification did, however, decline to chance level after a year.

The subjects in the previous two studies did not suffer the disadvantage of retroactive interference (RI) conditions, being exposed to additional faces shortly after viewing the target faces. Davies *et al* (1979a) exposed their witnesses to additional faces 30 minutes later, while Carr *et al.* (1979) exposed more faces a mere 15 seconds later. Neither set of investigators found any interference with memory for the target faces themselves at an immediate test of memory. Carr *et al.* found significant interference with memory for exact temporal context of occurrence, however, a matter of considerable forensic import. Furthermore, Carr *et al.* found after a two-week retention interval that there was interference not only with memory for temporal context but also significant interference with memory for the faces themselves. These two types of RI together resulted in an additional 10% error. So the usual tendencies to forget faces may be compounded by viewing additional faces very shortly after viewing the target face(s) in question.

As we have already indicated, facial distinctiveness seems to increase long-term memorability. But of course for fair lineups and photospreads to be conducted, there must be limits on the relative distinctiveness of faces present. Put another way, there should be modest inter-face similarity in a given lineup or photospread. How much similarity is appropriate? Ultimately judges and juries must decide, but Wells *et al.* (1979a) have provided a very nice procedure for assessing the relative amount of inter-face similarity. A group of subjects who have never seen the suspect is given the verbal description of his or her facial and other physical characteristics that the witness(es) provided the police. These non-witnesses are then asked to pick him or her from the photospread or a photo of the lineup. There is greater inter-face similarity the more nearly there is equiprobability of choice across the faces present. A more practically useful metric is obtained by inverting the probability of the suspect being chosen by the non-witnesses; this probability is D/N, where D is the number of choices of the suspect and N is the number of non-witnesses making a choice. The quantity N/D is referred to as the functional size of the lineup or photospread. Wells *et al.* used this technique in an actual bank robbery case, where the defendant had been identified from a six-person lineup. Of 41 non-witnesses making a choice, 25 identified the defendant, yielding a functional size for the lineup of only 1·64. A functional size somewhat closer to 6·00 would have indicated a more fair lineup and greater inter-face similarity.

It is of concern not just to know the relative amount of inter-face similarity in a lineup or photospread but also to know what its effects are on accuracy as assessed by hit and false alarm rates. There have been three studies that have involved manipulation of the similarity variable.

Laughery *et al.* (1974) used three different definitions of target item–decoy item similarity in three separate experiments and found that in general the greater the target–decoy similarity, the poorer the recognition performance. Typically, their high similarity conditions produced lower hit rates and higher false alarm rates than did their low similarity conditions. Employing a rather crude definition of similarity, Patterson and Baddeley (1977) found the same pattern of results, a somewhat lower hit rate in the high similarity condition and a false alarm rate nearly twice as high. Employing perhaps the most quantitatively sophisticated definition of similarity yet devised, Davies *et al.* (1979b) likewise found lowered accuracy when target faces were embedded in arrays of high similarity decoys. However, though high target–decoy similarity produced a false alarm rate twice that of low similarity, there was no difference in hit rates between the two similarity conditions.

Research concerning bias manipulations of lineups and photospreads yields itself to a four-way classification, leading photospreads, biased instructions, guided recollection of the crime, and photo-biased lineups. Buckhout *et al.* (1975) manipulated both the degree of instructional bias and the degree to which the photospread was leading or suggestive. Telling the witnesses that the perpetrator was actually in the photospread produced no greater accuracy than simply asking if they recognized anyone in the photos, provided that the photospread was not also biased by printing the suspect's photo at an angle and with a different expression. Instructional bias and photospread bias combined to yield a decidedly higher indictment rate of the suspect, 61%, as opposed to the 40% rate obtained in the conditions where the two types of bias did not combine. Hilgendorf and Irving (1978) manipulated only instructional bias, instructions that either encouraged witnesses by telling them that lineup identification was rather easy or discouraged them by noting that it was often rather difficult. No differences in lineup accuracy were found as a function of instructional differences of this sort. The content of these instructions may have been overridden by the powerful situational characteristics of the confrontational, British-style parade.

Malpass and Devine (in press) likewise manipulated instructional bias. They told one group of eyewitnesses that it was certain that the vandal was in the American-style lineup, and no mention was made of the possibility of rejecting the entire lineup. Another group was told that it was not certain the vandal was present and that they were free to reject the lineup. The biased instructions increased the tendency to choose someone from the lineup when it was not at all required. These instructions also reduced accuracy by increasing the false alarm rate, particularly when the vandal was absent from the lineup. Malpass and Devine's unbiased instructions, on the other hand, reduced choosing and false alarms without decreasing hits. Hence, they argue, unbiasing of police lineup procedures should occur sufficiently that rejection of the lineup becomes a realistic option for the eyewitness. Davies *et al.* (1979b) performed a similar instructional manipulation in a laboratory picture recognition task and found that unbiased, strict criterion instructions reduced the false alarm rate by about 40%.

Malpass and Devine (1981) have tested whether an interview guiding recollection of a staged vandalism, the vandal, and the witness's reactions to them might not improve accuracy after a lengthy retention interval. Even though such a procedure introduces opportunities for biasing the witness's recollections, Malpass and Devine found that the recollective interview increased the percentage of correct identifications from 40 to 60, after a five-month retention interval.

Two studies have investigated the effects on accuracy of a photo-biased lineup, one where a witness has viewed a set of photographs prior to the lineup (Brown *et al.*, 1977; Hilgendorf and Irving, 1978). Brown *et al.* noted that prior viewing of mugshots of persons actually encountered at the crime scene does indeed increase their chances of indictment, regardless of whether the witness had been aware a crime was occurring at the time. However, they also noted that prior viewing of the mugshots of innocent persons significantly increased their chances of indictment. The effect was particularly striking when witnesses did not know until later a crime had occurred: Here innocent persons seen only in mugshots were as likely to be indicted as criminals who had been viewed only at the crime scene. Hilgendorf and Irving have confirmed Brown *et al.*'s findings in that they obtained a false alarm rate under photo-biased conditions that was twice as high as that obtained under unbiased lineup conditions.

C *Individual differences affecting facial identification*

There would seem to be as many as eight dimensions on which individuals differ than can affect face identification performance with pretrial procedures. Some of these, age, race, sex, trait anxiety level, and degree of eyewitness identification training are relatively constant in their effects for any given person, at least over a reasonable span of time. Other characteristics such as level of violence and crime seriousness, level of awareness a crime had occurred, and confidence in identification response would appear situationally specific.

Whipple's (1909) review of classical studies of eyewitness testimony documents the fact that children are more suggestible than adults with regard to recall of facial and other details, but it is still not clear just how much more suggestible they are. The classical research also documents that in young children relatively low completeness and accuracy of testimony are coupled with high confidence. Between the ages of 7 and 18, however, completeness scores increase by as much as 50%, while accuracy increases by a similar amount with the interrogatory form but only by about 20% with the narrative form of questioning.

Three very recent studies and two of slightly greater vintage, taken together, confirm that memory for faces is developmentally sensitive across the life span (Cross *et al.*, 1971; Ellis *et al.*, 1973; Smith and Winograd, 1978; Blaney and Winograd, 1978; Brigham and Williamson, 1979; see also Carey, this volume). That is, recognition memory for adult faces increases to adulthood and declines later in life (age 60–80). Interestingly, a comparison of d' scores (statistical decision theory's unbiased measure of discriminability) from the two studies by Winograd indicates that the geriatric subjects and 10-year-olds both have about 70% of the memory sensitivity for faces that young adults do.

Regarding race of eyewitness, there appear to be three commonly held assumptions by law enforcement personnel who are directly involved with eyewitness identification (Brigham and Barkowitz, 1978): (1) own-race faces are better recognized than other-race faces; (2) degree of racial prejudice is negatively correlated with accuracy of cross-racial identification; (3) amount of cross-racial experience is positively correlated with cross-racial identification accuracy. It turns out that there is virtually no empirical evidence for the last two assertions (e.g. Malpass and Kravitz, 1969; Cross *et al.*, 1971; Brigham and Barkowitz, 1978; see also Malpass and Shepherd, this volume). There is considerable evidence for the first assertion, however. That is, if both white and black subjects are tested for recognition memory for black faces as well as white, a race of subject by race of picture interaction typically is found. The nature of the interaction is not firmly fixed, though. Some studies (e.g. Malpass and Kravitz, 1969; Cross *et al.*, 1971) have found an own-race bias only in whites. Others (e.g. Malpass *et al.*, 1973; Shepherd *et al.*, 1974) have found the own-race bias to be present in both whites and blacks. Still other studies (Malpass, 1974; Brigham and Williamson, 1979) have found an own-race bias of greater magnitude in blacks. In any event, two studies (Elliott *et al.*, 1973; Malpass *et al.*, 1973) have found evidence that an own-race bias can be overcome with *specific* training in making other-race discriminations (see also Malpass, this volume). This finding would seem to dovetail with Goldstein and Chance's (1980) suggestion that other-race discriminations are a function of race-specific face schemata that develop incrementally over time.

Whipple (1909) reports two investigators as finding female superiority in accuracy and completeness of testimony and one finding greater male accuracy but greater female completeness. Lipton (1977), however, found greater female accuracy but no sex differences in completeness. These results must be qualified on two counts. First, there is evidence that females are less accurate (Clifford and Scott, 1978) and less complete (Kuehn, 1974) in their recall than males under more violent conditions. Second, Powers *et al.* (1979) have found that each sex is more accurate and more resistant to suggestion concering testimonial details oriented to their own sex.

Two recent reviews of the literature on sex differences in facial memory conclude that though the literature is not perfectly consistent, females seem generally superior to males, especially on female faces (Ellis, 1975; McKelvie, 1978; see also Shepherd, this volume). We concur. We have found ten studies reporting no overall sex superiority, six studies reporting females to be better on female faces while males do equally well on both types, seven studies showing an overall female superiority (Ellis *et al.*, 1973; Paskaruk and Yarmey, 1974; Yarmey, 1974; Yarmey, 1975; Brigham and Barkowitz, 1978; Dent and Stephenson, 1978; Deffenbacher *et al.*, 1981), and only one study reporting a male superiority (Deffenbacher *et al.*, 1978).

Regarding the effects of level of violence and crime seriousness, we have already cited results indicating greater male accuracy and completeness under more violent conditions. To this must be added the fact that both sexes are less accurate under violent than under non-violent conditions (Clifford and Scott, 1978). It also appears that if a witness knows of a crime's seriousness at the time, a highly serious crime results in more accurate identification of the suspect than a non-serious one (Leippe *et al.*, 1978), where seriousness is defined in terms of monetary value of a stolen article.

We have just seen that greater situational stress results in lowered accuracy. Are the effects of chronically higher felt stress, trait anxiety, similar? Though not all investigators have found significant negative correlations of trait anxiety and accuracy at face recognition (e.g. Deffenbacher *et al.*, 1978), some have (Siegel and Loftus, 1978; Zanni and Offermann, 1978). The former investigative team noted correlations of −0·20 between accuracy and anxiety and −0·25 between accuracy and self-preoccupation. The latter team found accuracy and neuroticism to be correlated as highly as –0·51. Consonant with these results are those of Buckhout *et al.* (1974) and Mueller *et al.* (1979) who found that persons reporting less stress or anxiety were more accurate at face identification.

The degree of experience or training in eyewitness identification would not seem generally to be related to accuracy, except in so far as it may reduce an own-race bias (Elliott *et al.*, 1973; Malpass *et al.*, 1973). Tickner and Poulton (1975) showed that though police officers reported more alleged thefts than did civilians, they were not better in number of true detections of people and actions. Bull and Reid (1975) noted that police suffered the same short-term memory capacity limitation as did civilians, even when they were recalling information ostensibly of importance to them. In a field situation, Clifford and Richards (1977) found that police were no more accurate than civilians at recalling details of a target person after a 15-s exposure to him; they were more accurate after a 30-s exposure, however (30-s retention intervals). Finally Woodhead *et al.* (1979) found that a three-day, intensive training course (isolated-feature-oriented) produced no improvement in face recognition ability. Given that several effective face encoding strategies have been documented in a number of laboratory studies (e.g. Winograd, 1978; Courtois and Mueller, 1979; Deffenbacher *et al.*, 1981), it is just possible that different training programmes than those heretofore employed would produce a training effect (see Malpass, this volume). It is also possible that a training effect may require tremendous amounts of very specific practice, something probably rarely if ever achieved in real life.

Accuracy at identifying faces is, of course, lower when the eyewitness was unaware a crime was occurring at the time (Brown *et al.*, 1977; Deffenbacher *et al.*, 1978). Furthermore, as we noted earlier, the chances of indicating an innocent are raised considerably—such that a criminal not seen also in mugshots and an innocent seen only in mug-shots are equally likely to be indicted (Brown *et al.*, 1977).

Though Lipton (1977) reported a correlation of +0·44 between accuracy of testimony and witness confidence, the preponderance of published data would indicate no relationship between accuracy and confidence (Brown *et al.*, 1977; Clifford and Scott, 1978; Leippe *et al.*, 1978; Wells *et al.*, 1979b). The Wells *et al.* study is particularly important because it showed not only that there was no relationship between eyewitness self-rated confidence and eyewitness accuracy for some 42 cross-examined witnesses, but also that there was no relationship between witnesses' confidence and jurors' accuracy in deciding whether witnesses were mistaken or not in their identifications. These findings of zero or near-zero correlation are not necessarily contradicted by more recent work (Deffenbacher *et al.*, 1981; Malpass and Devine, 1981). Both studies found between-subjects correlations of accuracy and confidence about +0·50. However, these higher correlations may be of limited forensic generality, for both original viewing and testing conditions were reasonably optimal. Furthermore, Deffenbacher *et al.* found the range of within-subjects correlations to be from –0·05 to +0·60. Even under rather optical conditions, then, the correlation of accuracy and confidence may be zero for some witnesses.

3 FACIAL IDENTIFICATION AND LEGAL PRACTICE

Members of the legal community have long been sensitive to the short-comings of eyewitness identification evidence. As early as 1904 a British committee investigating a highly publicized conviction based on mistaken identity noted eyewitness identification evidence is perhaps the least reliable class of evidence (Watson, 1924). The legal scholar Wigmore stated in 1931: "No part of the field of proof has been so defective in its use of the common sense of psychology. And at no point is the danger greater of condemning an innocent person." (Wigmore, 1931, pp. 550–551.)

Awareness of identification problems did not lead immediately to solutions. In the United States the Supreme Court did not directly deal with the identification issue until its *United States v. Wade* decision in 1967. In England two convictions of innocent men led recently to the formation of another committee to study the law and procedure relating to identification. The Devlin Report (1976) issued by this committee was followed by the Bryden Report (1978) resulting from a similar investigation in Scotland. Most of the key issues are thus still being debated today.

There are essentially three different methods by which protection against wrongful convictions can be built into a system. Legislation is the most direct method, but it has also been the least used in countries with the common law tradition. Those countries have instead relied heavily on judicial decisions to provide protections. Countries with highly centralized police forces, such as England and Scotland, have also relied upon administrative police rules, whereas there are no national rules on identification for the locally controlled police of the United States. Model rules exist in the United States, but these have no official status. In reviewing the specific ways in which the three methods have been used we shall first consider attempts to deal with the problem of suggestive procedures and then consider attempts to deal with the inherent problems of eyewitness identification.

A *Protections against suggestive procedures*

Most of the responses of various legal systems to the problem of eye-witness identification have involved efforts to make identification procedures less suggestive. The various procedures dealt with are the questioning of witnesses, identification by lineups, photospreads and informal procedures, and identification in court.

The first stage in the identification process is the questioning of witnesses by police in order to obtain descriptions of the offender. Although psychologists have extensively studied the effects of different questioning approaches on accuracy and completeness of descriptions, relatively little attention has been paid to this stage of the process by those in the legal system. In Scotland, the Bryden Committee did consider a proposal from the psychology department at Aberdeen University that police should encourage all witnesses to give complete verbal descriptions by providing checklists of terms commonly used to describe persons' features. The proposal was rejected, however, because the committee feared such a checklist might result in uncertain witnesses trying to answer every question regardless of how much they remembered (Bryden, 1978).

In light of what psychologists know about testimony, it might be appropriate for the police to first use free narrative questions and then interrogative questions. It should be clear that only answers to the narrative questions would later be used as evidence, while answers to interrogative questions would be valuable in furthering the police investigation. It is important to note that the potential for active police biasing would exist only in those cases in which the police already have a suspect.

One key issue with regard to descriptions has been their later use to confirm or cast doubt upon identifications made by lineup or photospread. The Devlin and Bryden Committees recommended that the prosecution provide the defense with copies of descriptions given by witnesses. Recognizing the possibility of biased descriptions the Devlin Committee further recommended that the only descriptions admissible in court should be those given during the first interview with the police (before the witness has seen the accused, seen a photo of the accused, or heard descriptions given by other witnesses). The Bryden Committee concluded that the descriptions most valuable for evidence are those given spontaneously and that these should be separately noted as such by the police.

Most of the legal attention to identification procedures has focused on the lineup or identity parade. It is especially critical that adequate procedures be developed because as Williams and Hammelmann (1963) have noted, jurors may be unduly influenced by the appearance of fairness which is inherent in the procedure. In England and Scotland, police rules govern parade procedures, and perhaps the most important matter covered in the rules is the composition of the parade. The English rules require at least eight other persons besides the suspect (if practicable) who are "as far as possible of the same age, height, general appearance (including standard of dress and grooming) and position in life" (Devlin, 1976, p. 159). The Scottish rules only call for five stand-ins but they go further in encouraging similarity of appearance by suggesting that any physical abnormality a suspect might have should be concealed. The police should, for example, furnish glasses for all participants if the suspect wears glasses or a patch for all if the suspect has lost an eye. As of 1978 the Scottish rules stated that the suspect should wear the clothes in which the witnesses originally saw him or her, but the Bryden Committee concluded that it was undesirable for an identification to be influenced by clothing and recommended that this rule be deleted. Model rules in the United States (LaSota and Bromley, 1974) approve the wearing of such clothing by the suspect but only if it is also worn by each of the other participants.

Sometimes a witness may request to hear a participant in a parade speak or to see the person walk. Here there is some disagreement as to the proper procedure. The Scottish rules (Bryden, 1978) as well as the model United States police rules (LaSota and Bromley, 1974) require that in such cases every member of the parade be requested to perform the same action. The Devlin Committee in England, however, noted that "the parade is a fair test of appearance only; the participants are not selected for similarity of speech or gait" (Devlin, 1976, p. 122). There-fore, it would not be fair for identification to be based on such characteristics. Concluding that it would be appropriate for a witness to confirm an identification by checking speech or gait, they reco-mmended that such a request be allowed for only one member of the parade and only after that member has been identified by the witness.

One very important check on the suggestiveness of a lineup or parade is the after-the-fact determination of functional size from a photograph, as described earlier (Wells *et al.*, 1979a). Bytheway and Clarke (1976) suggested what could be an even more valuable procedure if combined with the Wells *et al.* analysis. They proposed having the actual parade viewed by non-witnesses who are asked to pick out the police suspect. This procedure could additionally control for the tendency for a suspect to stand out because of nervousness, a condition not necessarily captured in a photograph.

Finding enough persons of similar appearance for a lineup can sometimes be difficult for the police, especially in sparsely populated areas. A number of years ago Wigmore (1937) recommended an alternative procedure involving the use of a large number of films of people going through standard movements. A suspect would be filmed and his or her film would be shown to witnesses with approximately 25 others. The proposal was never taken very seriously because of the tremendous costs involved, but as noted recently ("Comment", 1971) the video technology available today makes such a plan more realistic. In fact one very large set of standard tapes could be supplied to all police departments. Not only would this plan allow for much larger lineups, but it would also make it possible to systematically control the similarity of lineup participants. Procedures such as those developed by Davies et al. (1979b) could be used to classify faces and those closest to the suspect on a large number of dimensions would be chosen for comparison. Before such an approach is recommended, however, there should be research to weigh the benefits of increased similarity and more comparisons against any costs in accuracy due to non-corporeal viewing.

English, Scottish and United States model rules are in general agreement that any lineup or parade should be viewed by only one witness at a time and that the conclusion of one witness should not be heard by others who are going to view it. The English and Scottish rules further state that the witnesses should not see any parade participants beforehand.

One notable variation in procedures has already been mentioned. The English rules are the only ones requiring that the witness make an identification by touching the person selected (although an especially nervous witness may be allowed to point to the person instead). It is interesting to speculate whether this procedural difference is related to a difference in rate of identification. Data presented to the Devlin Committee indicated that for all parades held in England and Wales during 1973 no one was identified in 47% of the cases (Devlin, 1976, p. 163). In Scotland, however, during a one year period only 18% of the parades resulted in no identification (Bryden, 1978, p. 74).

A major issue of concern regarding witnesses is the pressure they may feel to make an identification—pressure which derives from the assumption that the police have a suspect in the parade. Impressed by evidence from psychologists, the Devlin Committe recommended that the officer in charge of a parade explain to each witness that the person who committed the crime is not necessarily present and that the witness should touch someone only if certain it is the right person. The Bryden Committee, believing that tentative identifications should not be totally discouraged, recommended that if no positive identification is made the witness should be asked if anyone in the parade resembles the person seen.

The inclusion of "blank parades" or parades without suspects is another procedure sometimes proposed as a means of reducing pressure on the witness (Lefcourt, 1978). The Devlin Committee considered such a proposal but noted that if the suspect is in the first parade and is identified there is little point in holding a second except to confuse the witness. If there is no suspect and no identification in the first parade, the witness may feel even greater pressure to make an identification in the second.

There seems to be widespread agreement today that parade proceedings should be recorded very carefully. Both the Devlin Committee and Bryden Committee recommended standard report forms. They also felt that photographing the parade would be beneficial, but because of police concerns about participants not wishing to be photographed, they proposed that limited trials be conducted before incorporating this requirement into the police rules.

Parade procedures used by police in Australia, Canada, and Ireland are very similar to those in England and Wales (Devlin, 1976). Although the procedures of Italy and Mexico are not unusual in substance, it is important to note that these and other non-common-law countries have for many years had specific identification procedures in their criminal or penal codes (Murray, 1966). Typical Swedish procedures, while not mandated by law or rules, provide an interesting substantive contrast (Devlin, 1976). In Sweden the suspect is placed in a room with a number of other people, all of whom carry on conversations and in general behave in a casual manner. The rationale for this approach is that it puts the suspect at ease and also allows the witness to observe characteristic mannerisms. It is also the case in Sweden that if the original observation during the crime took place in poor lighting or other less than optimal conditions, then the identification procedure is conducted under conditions as similar to those as possible. A comparison of such procedures with more traditional parades could be a fruitful area of study for psychologists.

In the United States, the problem of eyewitness identification has been addressed primarily through court decisions. In the landmark *United States v. Wade* (1967) case the Court declined to lay down any rules for the conduct of lineups, but did conclude that the defendant has the right to have counsel present at a lineup. The presence of counsel would provide safeguards in two ways. First it would serve to prevent abuse of the lineup procedure, and second it would enhance the ability of the defense to question the reliability of identification evidence during cross-examination. This right, however, has been seriously undermined by a later decision (*Kirby v. Illinois*, 1972) in which the Court limited the right to counsel to lineups conducted after formal charges of some kind are filed. As Sobel (1972) noted, this later ruling means that the defendant does not have the right to counsel when it is most needed. In the cases with the greatest danger of convicting the innocent—those with eyewitness identification evidence only—the police must hold the lineup before formal charges are filed in order to justify the filing of charges.

Even if counsel is not required, all lineups must still meet a "due process" standard in order for the identification evidence to be admissible. In *Stovall v. Denno* (1967) the Supreme Court ruled that due process of law is denied if a procedure is "unneccessarily suggestive and conducive to irreparable mistaken identification" (p. 301). In deciding which cases meet this standard the Court has certainly had the opportunity to provide guidelines on what constitutes a fair procedure, but instead of focusing on procedures, the Court has focused on the accuracy of the identification. Thus in *Neil v. Biggers* (1972), a case which some have viewed as undermining the due process protection (Pulaski, 1974), the Court listed five factors to be considered in determining whether an identification was reliable. These five are:

1. the opportunity of the witness to view the criminal at the time of the crime;
2. the witness' degree of attention;
3. the accuracy of the witness' prior description of the criminal;
4. the level of certainty demonstrated by the witness at the confrontation;
5. the length of time between the crime and the confrontation. (*Neil v. Biggers*, 1972, p. 199)

Although psychologists would agree with the relevance of four of the five factors, the fourth, certainty of the witness, is an important exception. Research cited earlier (Brown *et al.*, 1977; Clifford and Scott, 1978; Leippe *et al.*, 1978; Wells *et al.*, 1979b) has indicated little or no relationship between accuracy and confidence.

As a result of the emphasis on reliability of the identification, most lineup cases reviewed by appellate courts in the United States have been upheld. Sobel (1979) has described a number of cases in which very suggestive procedures were used, but which have been found by the courts to meet the standards of due process.

There is clear agreement across national systems that lineups and parades are generally the least suggestive of identification procedures. It is also reasonably clear that there are circumstances which prevent the use of a lineup, as, for example, when there is no specific suspect. The Devlin Committee suggested that it may then be reasonable to use alternative procedures which still involve the witness picking someone out of a group. If, for example, the police suspect the offender is a member of a particular group the witness may be taken to a place where that group is known to spend time.

The United States model rules (LaSota and Bromley, 1974), reflecting court decisions, provide for a one-to-one confrontation or showup if a suspect has been arrested or temporarily detained within two hours of the offense and a lineup cannot be arranged immediately. The rationale for allowing a showup is that it is important to the ongoing police investigation and that the accuracy to be gained from an immediate identification outweighs any loss of accuracy due to suggestiveness of the procedure. Psychological research could perhaps provide data to determine whether the loss of accuracy in the few hours or day or so needed to arrange a lineup outweighs the loss due to the suggestive showup procedure.

There is agreement in England and Scotland that photographs should not be used for identification if a personal identification is possible (Devlin, 1976; Bryden, 1978). The primary use of photographs is in the investigation stage when there is no suspect; witnesses look through the police photo files or "mug books" to try to identify the offender. There is an awareness, in line with the data of Brown *et al.* (1977), that viewing a suspect's photograph affects the validity of a later personal identification. For this reason both the English and Scottish rules provide that if one witness makes a positive identification from photographs, any other witnesses should not be shown photographs but should view a parade which includes the suspect.

The Devlin Committee deemed the procedure of asking a witness if the person in the dock is the person who committed the crime such a suggestive one that it should be allowed only if preceded by a parade identification. The only exception would be if the judge determined that a parade was impracticable or unnecessary (as when the accused refused to participate, or when identity was not in question). The Bryden Committee disagreed, arguing that a witness who could not make an identification during a parade but who decides upon entering the court that he or she does recognize the defendant should then be able to make the identification.

In the United State, in-court identifications are generally held to be inadmissible if suggestive pretrial procedures have been used. The Supreme Court ruled, however, that they would be admissible if the prosecutor establishes by "clear and convincing evidence that the in-court identifications were based upon observations of the suspect other than the lineup identification" (*United States v. Wade*, p. 240). Justice Black argued in this case that this would inappropriately force judges to act as psychologists and try to understand the witness's subconscious minds. What has actually resulted is that courts evaluate the accuracy of the pretrial identification, and if satisfied with it, then rule that the in-court identification has an independent source (Pulaski, 1974). Guidelines provided in the *Wade* decision for determining an independent source are very similar to those used to assess reliability when determining whether the identification procedure meets the due process standard.

B *Protections against the inherent problems of identification*

Although many measures have been adopted to reduce the suggestiveness of identification procedures, the basic problem still exists that numerous factors not under the legal system's control influence the reliability of eyewitness identification. Traditionally, adversary systems have relied upon cross-examination of the witness as the primary safeguard. Three other possible safeguards are the requirement of corroboration, the use of judicial warnings, and the use of expert testimony.

One position is that eyewitness identification is so unreliable that a defendant should never be convicted on uncorroborated identification evidence. Wall (1965) suggested three possible versions of a corroboration rule. The strongest rule would provide that a person could not be convicted on identification evidence alone, no matter how many witnesses identified the person. Goldstein (1977) has argued for such a rule in light of the inherent invalidity of face recognition. Wall believed this rule would often prevent conviction of the guilty and considered it excessive. A second rule might prevent convictions on identification by a single witness. This rule, Wall noted, would prevent conviction even if a witness had observed the offender for an extended period of time. The third possible rule would disallow conviction solely on identification evidence if the original identification procedure was unduly suggestive.

In Scotland the second type of corroboration rule is law. Not only identification evidence but any evidence must be corroborated before the prosecution can proceed. Identification by a second witness, however, is considered corroboration. In rejecting such a statute for England, the Devlin Committee noted that in many of the cases of mistaken identification the defendant was wrongly identified by two or more witnesses. They concluded that this corroboration rule would still not provide adequate protection, while a stricter one would impose an unfair burden on the prosecution.

Although unwilling to endorse a corroboration rule, the Devlin Committee stil felt that in most cases eyewitness evidence alone should not be enough for a conviction. Therefore, they recommended passage of a statute which would require the judge to direct the jury that they should not convict on eyewitness evidence alone unless there are exceptional circumstances. The judge should point out any such circumstances (e.g. extended observation by the witness) and if he or she finds no evidence of another sort to corroborate the identification, then he or she should direct the jury to return a not guilty verdict (Devlin, 1976, p. 150).

After the Devlin Committee recommendations, a case arose (*R v. Turnbull*, 1976) in which the Lord Chief Justice took the opportunity to lay down guidelines to the trial judge similar to those proposed by the committee. These guidelines in addition stressed the need to refer to the possibility that a number of witnesses can be mistaken and to the fact that a witness is very convincing does not mean he or she is not mistaken.

The Supreme Court of the Republic of Ireland has required a similar warning in all cases in which identity is an issue. In *The People v. Casey* (1963) they ruled that the jury should in such cases be warned that there have been many cases of erroneous identification—even when the honesty of the witness was not in question and when the witness had an adequate opportunity for observation. Australian court decisions also have favoured the giving of such instructions (Bates, 1977).

Although some United States courts have formulated model instructions for the judge to give the jury (e.g. *United States v. Telfaire*, 1972), Woocher (1977) argued that judicial warning would probably be an inadequate protection against wrongful conviction in the United States. The United States judge has much less latitude in commenting on the evidence than does the English judge, and therefore could only call the jury's attention to the problem but not explain all the dangers. Woocher also noted that even if judges were allowed to comment on the evidence they could not provide the necessary information because of their lack of expertise in the area.

The solution to the problem which Woocher (1977) has proposed is to rely on expert testimony by psychologists. United States courts have not been in agreement, however, on the admissibility of expert testimony on identification issues. The key legal issues with regard to admissibility have been the status of the scientific field of inquiry involved and the encroachment into the province of the jury. One judge in refusing to allow expert testimony ruled that identification issues are within the understanding of the jury, and therefore the aid of the psychologist is not needed (Goodrich, 1975). Loftus (1979), however, has presented data indicating that the general population is not very knowledgeable with regard to factors affecting identification accuracy.

Wilson (1975) and Woocher (1977) have reviewed cases and rules on expert testimony and argued that a good case can be made for the admissibility of expert testimony on identification evidence. There is, however, some difference of opinion as to what the exact role of the expert witness should be. Wall (1965) has suggested that a psychologist could administer tests to witnesses to determine the ability of a witness to observe and remember accurately. He or she would then testify, offering an opinion regarding the test findings. Another possibility is for the expert witness to consider all the relevant factors in a particular case and then give an estimate of the likelihood that a witness's identification is accurate (Wells, 1978). Woocher (1977) and Loftus (1979) have contended that this approach should not be used if the expert witness is to avoid invading the province of the jury. They propose rather that the expert should point out the relevant factors to the jury, explain how those factors operate for a typical witness, and let the jury draw its own conclusions regarding the accuracy of the particular witness in the particular circumstances involved.

Wells (1978) and Clifford (1979) point out two difficulties with either of the latter approaches. First, if there are any interaction effects among relevant variables, and Clifford contends interactions are the rule rather than the exception, it becomes almost impossible to estimate the effect of the many variables in any given case. Second, they suggest that conflicting data and biased data make it inappropriate to clearly state general principles. Hastie *et al.* (1979) more optimistically contend that the experts in the field are at least in agreement on the methods used and results obtained in identification research. Clifford (1979) and Wells (1978) have argued that it would be much more appropriate for psychologist expert witnesses to deal only with system variables, and thus to present evidence on the suggestiveness of procedures. The psychologist might then conduct experiments such as those described by Wells *et al.* (1979a) to determine the functional size of a lineup.

A more general problem regarding expert testimony is that of competing expert witnesses. Woocher (1977) asked what will happen when prosecutors begin to introduce their own experts to counter the testimony of the defendant's expert. The process could become very time-consuming and confusing to a jury, if experts cite contradictory studies or emphasize different factors as relevant. Woocher concluded that while the harm from introducing psychological testimony may in fact outweigh the benefits in many situations, the tremendous impact of eyewitness identification and the number of wrongful convictions which result tip the balance in favour of allowing the expert to testify.

A final question to ask is what impact psychological testimony will have on judges and jurors. Loftus (1979) described one case in which the jury convicted the defendant in spite of expert testimony on problems of identification. An interview with a juror after the verdict was rendered disclosed that the jurors did not believe the performance of a witness in a psychology experiment was the same as that in an actual crime situation. This anecdote may weaken the argument that the psychologist will have too much influence on the jury, but it also points out that psychologists will probably have to address the generalization issue squarely in their testimony if they are to be effective.

4 CONCLUSIONS

The role of the psychologist as an expert witness testifying in criminal trials has already been discussed. It must be noted here, however, that psychologists in this role have a rather limited potential for producing an impact on the criminal justice system in terms of its treatment of eyewitness identification. They are limited just as trial judges are by the fact that very few cases are actually disposed of by trial (Levine and Tapp, 1973). The impact of psychologists would be much greater if their efforts were directed at the changing of statutes, judicial decisions, and police rules. They should therefore actively campaign to educate judges, legislators, administrators, and law reform groups on the relevance of face identification research to the legal system. Such efforts apparently were well received by the influential Devlin and Bryden Committees.

Finally, in their roles as researchers, psychologists must be knowledgeable about the legal system in order to design and interpret research that will in fact be relevant. The research we have reviewed is evidence of progress in this direction. There is still a need, however, for more experiments employing close simulations of real incidents and actual police procedures, for more field experiments such as the one carried out by Clifford and Richards (1977), and for more data on actual cases of the sort provided by Kuehn (1974). The concern for the future is to carry out enough of these converging operations to ensure greater generalizability of psychological findings.

10   Face Recall Systems[1]

Graham M. Davies

1   INTRODUCTION

In the early 1880s, a young Frenchman working in the office of the
Prefecture of Police was becoming increasingly exasperated by the
inability of orthodox verbal descriptions to provide a guide to the
identification of criminals. Much to the amusement of his colleagues, he
began to clip isolated facial features from photographs of criminals in
the Department's archives and to arrange these systematically by size
and shape. The young man was Alphonse Bertillon (1853–1914), the
great forensic scientist and inventor of anthropometry and the standardized "mugshot" (Rhodes, 1956). The photographs of features, once
classified and labelled, formed the basis of the first face recall system,
portrait parlé.

Portrait parlé was originally designed to help the detective retain
information about a criminal whose identity and appearance were already known (Thorwald, 1965). However it was also used as an aid for
witnesses to describe accurately the appearance of unknown suspects
and continues to be so to this day (Allison, 1973). The modern detective
confronted with a "good" witness is more likely to turn to a newer
generation of face recall systems which aim to provide a pictorial

The studies by Hadyn Ellis, John Shepherd and the author described in this chapter were
funded by grants from the Social Science Research Council and the Police Scientific Development
Branch of the Home Office. Thanks are due to my colleagues and to Ken Laughery and Monica
Barnbrough for permission to cite unpublished work. Tony Kitson, Bob Ashcroft and Pat
Dunleavy provided invaluable information on the operational use of face recall tools. Illustrations
of Photofit composites are reproduced with permission of Sirchie Fingerprint Laboratories Inc.
and Mr. Jacques Penry. The views expressed in this chapter are those of the author and do not
necessarily represent the policy of the Police Department, Home Office.

likeness of the suspect rather than an elaborate verbal description. The present paper surveys the range of such face recall systems, describes the laboratory research they have generated, and, through a consideration of the shortcomings revealed, suggests how such systems might develop in the future.

2 FACE RECALL SYSTEMS

A *An overview*

All face recall systems break the face down into component features. The number of features included varies as does mode of representation: line drawing or photographic likeness. An operator assists the witness in selecting each feature component in turn from a range of representative alternatives. The selected components are then integrated into a composite face by a variety of techniques. The best known of these systems are the Identikit and Photofit. As these are also the best researched their structure will be described in some detail.

i *The Identikit*
The Identikit was one of the first, and most successful face recall systems and is still used extensively in America and elsewhere. The individual features are portrayed as line drawings which are printed on transparent acetate sheets.[1] The main feature components in the standard kit, with the approximate number of variants in parentheses, are as follows: hairlines (130); eyes (102); chins (52); lips (40); and noses (37). Additional overlays cover such accessories as eyebrows, scars, glasses, age lines, beards and hats. A composite face is achieved by superimposing the transparent sheets. The length of the face can be adjusted and additional detail added by hand with a chinagraph pencil. The variations of each feature are coded for ease of transmission and filing.

Training manuals (McDonald, 1960) recommend that the witness first provide a general description of the suspect from which the operator assembles a first composite. With the exception of hairstyles, scrutiny of features in isolation is discouraged. Witness and operator work on the individual features in the composite, exchanging element until a satisfactory likeness emerges.

---

[1] The line-drawn version has now been superseded by a version using photographic representations of the features. However, as all research and operational experience has been derived from the line system, this is the kit described in the text.

ii Photofit

Photofit is the system which replaced Identikit in the United Kingdom and is now used in 27 other countries. The components of Photofit are photographs of individual features, printed on thin card. The features included in the male kit, together with the approximate number of variants, are as follows: hairline and ears (195); eyes and eyebrows (99); nose (89); mouth (105); and chin and cheeks (74). Additional kits are designed to extend coverage to include white females, Afro-Asian and Arab faces. As with the Identikit, there is also a range of accessories (hats, glasses, beards etc.) designed to be used in conjunction with the features. A composite face is compiled by fitting the chosen features into a special frame which also provides the facility for altering the length of the face. Additional detail can be added to the composite by drawing on the transparent cover of the frame. Feature variations are coded and classified according to a system of facial topography developed by the system's inventor, Jacques Penry (Penry, 1971). All kits are supplied with a handbook known as the Visual Index and a folding chart depicting a range of face shapes.

There is no one prescribed method for compiling a Photofit. Home Office surveys (King, 1971; Darnbrough, 1977) suggest most police operators begin by securing a verbal description. They then either refer the witness to relevant portions of the Visual Index or select plausible features themselves. Most operators first establish the chin and hairline—the face frame—showing the witness the folding chart if necessary. The internal features and accessories are then added under the witness's guidance. Following assembly of the initial composite, features can be exchanged until a satisfactory likeness is achieved.

iii Minolta Montage Synthesizer

The Minolta Montage Synthesizer extensively used by the Japanese police uses a sophisticated system of optical blending to achieve a composite likeness. In contrast to other systems, no range of features is supplied with the kit which is designed to operate in conjunction with a library of standardized mugshots. The witness begins by selecting a mugshot which bears some resemblance to the target. Up to three features of the existing mugshot may then be changed by blending in features from other mugshots, selected by the witness (see Duncan and Laughery, 1977, for an interesting account of development work featuring this system).

iv Other projector systems

Other systems which have also used optical projection include the

Vaicom system and Mimic. The latter stores drawings of different features on film strips which are then projected on to a screen to achieve a whole face effect. The division of the face in Mimic is similar to Identikit; a novelty of the system is the incorporation of a polaroid camera for the production of an instant likeness (see Allison, 1973, for a full description).

v Strip systems

A number of systems dissect the face into a series of horizontal strips which can then be exchanged in the manner of a child's "heads, body and legs" game. The French *Portrait Robot* uses a threefold division of the face: hair, eyes/nose and mouth/chin. All elements are photographs of actual faces. The American Identiface uses a fourfold division (hair; eyes, nose, and mouth/chin) and line drawings for components. Similar systems were formerly employed by the West German and Italian police, using a fivefold division of the face.

vi Sketch artists

The use of sketch artists has been the traditional alternative to the face-recall kit (Harmon, 1973). Today, there is an increasing tendency to see these methods as complementary rather than opposing. Many sketch artists use the illustrations of features in the kits as a guide to their witnesses. Artists themselves are also sometimes brought in to render a more life-like picture from a composite image. Most kits include the option of pencil work and this can sometimes involve the operator in an extensive reworking of the whole image.

B *Operational effectiveness*

Information on the development and operational effectiveness of face recall kits is difficult to obtain, beyond accounts of sensational cases (Jackson, 1967; Owens, 1970; Cole and Pringle, 1974). The British Home Office, to their credit, have published periodic surveys of user reaction to the kits and have made some effort to establish their effectiveness in operational use. Venner (1969) estimated that the Identikit, which was then standard equipment, had played an important role in clearing up 5–10% of the cases in which it was employed. A later survey on Photofit reported by Darnbrough (1977) dealt with series of 728 cases involving the use of the kit. After two months, some 140 had been cleared up, of which the investigating officers estimated some 25% had been greatly assisted by the availability of the Photofit likeness.

Such surveys can provide useful information but need to be complemented by laboratory research into the scope and accuracy of the systems (Venner, 1969). Until recently, manufacturers were reluctant to release kits for laboratory study, but this position is now changing and extensive studies have been undertaken of the Identikit and Photofit which are described in the next two sections. In both instances, the investigators were concerned with three major issues: (i) to establish the limits of accuracy of the system under controlled laboratory conditions; (ii) to study whether performance fluctuated in contexts which normally influence facial recognition accuracy; (iii) to find correlates of successful performance with the system concerned.

3 LABORATORY STUDIES

A *The Identikit*[1]

As part of a larger project described elsewhere in this volume, Laughery *et al.* (1977) carried out an extensive study comparing the relative effectiveness of the sketch artist and the Identikit in registered facial appearance.

All studies involved three phases: (i) pairs of subjects (witnesses) who had been informed that recall would later be required, talked informally to a target person for 7–8 minutes; (ii) witnesses immediately constructed likenesses of the target from memory, one working with a sketch artist and the second with an Identikit technician; (iii) artist and technician constructed a likeness with the target present. This latter procedure provided a measure of the optimum performance of the system, devoid of any contaminating effects associated with the witnesses' recollections.

In all studies, large numbers of target persons were employed and the resulting likenesses were assessed for similarity by two different measures. The first and main measure, *rated similarity*, involved panels of judges assessing the similarity of the individual sketches and Identikits to a photograph of the target, using a rating scale. A subsidiary measure involved a *computerized algorithm;* measurements were taken across key features in the likeness and used as a basis for a computerized search of a mug file consisting of photographs of all the targets employed. The success of the algorithm in detecting the target served as a measure of the accuracy of the likeness.

The Identikit is manufactured by the Identi-Kit Company, 17985 Sky Park Circle, Suite C, California 92714, USA.

Laughery performed three studies, each using a different population as targets: the first used white males, the second, white females and the third, black males. All studies involved large numbers of targets (likenesses from 51 different targets were used in the initial study) and large undifferentiated populations of witness subjects. A number of different technicians and artists were employed to control for operator effects.

The results from the major experiment on white male targets set the pattern for all studies. Figure 1 illustrates the range of likeness achieved by the two systems. The rating data showed a significant advantage overall for the sketches compared to the Identikit. Sketches made with the target present were rated significantly better than those from memory, but there was no corresponding difference for Identikits. Neither system provided a particularly effective basis for the computerized search; in the case of the Identikit, overall performance was no better than chance.

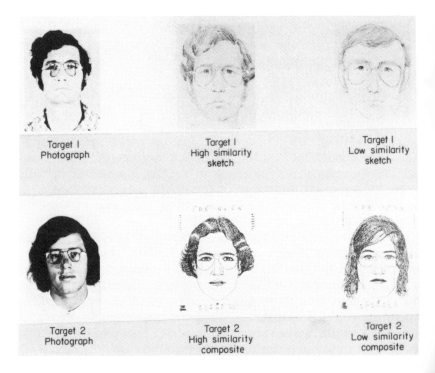

FIG. 1. Examples of Identikit composites and artists' sketches receiving high and low ratings (from "Sketch artist and Identikit procedures for recalling faces" by K.H. Laughery and R. Fowler. Copyright (1980) by the American Psychological Association. Reprinted by permission).

An identical pattern emerged from the study involving white female targets: sketches received better ratings than Identikits, sketches with target present (termed "from view") were superior to those made with the target absent (termed "from memory") but no parallel effect emerged for Identikits. The computerized search based on the Identikits again produced chance results.

A third study involved black male targets. Here again sketches were rated significantly more like their targets than the Identikits. However, on this occasion, both sketch and Identikit likenesses made from view received higher ratings than those from memory, though the effect was much larger in the case of sketches. Neither form of representation, however, provided a satisfactory basis for locating a target via computerized search.

As the majority of ratings were secured from common panels of judges, it was possible to make some comparison of the relative similarity of likeness achieved of the three target populations. As Fig. 2 illustrates, highest average ratings were achieved on white male targets, followed by white females with black males showing the lowest rating. As Laughery *et al.* note, all operators were white males and, thus, the data may illustrate the influence of the same experiential factors which lead to higher recognition performance on same-race and same-sex faces. In the case of the Identikits, a contributory factor may lie in the range and variety of features provided to model the target population: an effect for the code as well as the encoder. Further light might be shed on this by examining the performance of the witnesses as a function of

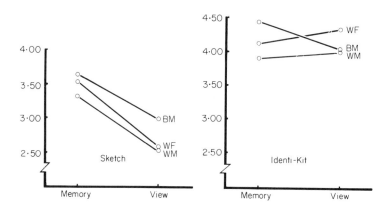

FIG. 2. Mean rated accuracy of Identikit constructions and artists' sketches of white male (WM), white female (WF) and black male (BM) targets. Ratings on 6-point scale; lower score represents better likeness. (Redrawn from Laughery *et al.*, 1977.)

their race and sex but, unfortunately, Laughery *et al.* do not report the means of these subpopulations.

Laughery *et al.* also examined whether an intention to recall had any effect upon image quality. As before, witnesses met and talked with the target who was always one of several white males. Half the subjects knew that they would later have to reconstruct his appearance while the remainder believed they would merely be asked to rate his personality. No consistent effects were found for expectancy on the quality of either the Identikits or sketches, though once again sketches were superior in overall quality. Laughery *et al.* attribute the finding to the inadequate manipulation of the variable concerned but this negative effect for awareness should also be seen in the light of a similar finding for Photofit discussed below.

Laughery *et al.* also administered a number of tests of imagery and academic aptitude in the hope of finding a useful predictor of success at composite or sketch construction. No consistent relationships emerged across studies between rated accuracy of a construction and the witnesses' scores on the visual imagery scale of the Betts test (Sheehan, 1967), the Gordon's Controllability of Imagery Questionnaire (Gordon, 1949), or the SAT test of academic aptitude.

The studies of Laughery *et al.* show a consistent advantage for the sketch compared to the Identikit in reproducing the likeness of a target under laboratory conditions. This difference in the rated quality of image need not mean that the Identikit is not an effective guide to locating a face within a mug file. This latter fact was demonstrated by Laughery and Smith (1978) who showed that the most highly rated composites from their initial experiment enabled judges to identify the target in a file of 46 faces on 51% of occasions. However, good sketches were still more effective (71% accuracy), while poorly rated composites produced results no better than chance.

B *Photofit*[1]

The Photofit system has been the subject of an extended series of laboratory tests by the author and his colleagues (Ellis *et al.*, 1976).

An initial study concerned two simple tests of encoding accuracy (Ellis *et al.*, 1975b). In the first, subjects attempted to construct in Photofit a white male face which was itself a Photofit composite. Con-

---

[1] Photofit is manufactured by Messrs John Waddington of Kirkstall Ltd., Commercial Road Leeds, LS5 3AJ, and is marketed outside the UK by Sirchie Fingerprint Laboratories Inc., P.C Box 269, Moorestown, NJ 08057, USA.

struction, made with the aid of a technician, was from view, or immediately after a 10-second observation. Accuracy on this simple task was surprisingly low, and no subject completed a face entirely correctly in either condition. Accuracy was higher when the task was done from view than from memory.

Subjects who had performed particularly well or badly in the first experiment were selected for a second, more realistic, experiment. Here, subjects were required to successively construct from memory one of two sets of three photographs of white males. Each target was again shown for 10 seconds and then immediately constructed with the help of the operator. The accuracy of the resulting constructions was assessed by panels of judges. They were provided with examples of attempts at each one of the six faces which they then attempted to identify among an array of 36 alternative faces. First-choice accuracy on this test was just 1 in 8 (12·5%) which improved to 1 in 4 (25%) if second and third choices were taken into account. These subjects who had made the most accurate copies in the initial experiment also produced more recognizable likenesses of real faces (see Fig. 3).

A second study by Davies *et al.* (1978a) examined the effect of delay between observation of the face and construction in Photofit. In their first experiment, subjects made constructions from memory of two coloured photographs showing white male faces, each of which had been seen for 10 seconds. Operators assisted subjects to construct one face immediately following observation, while a second was made after a lapse of one week.

The accuracy of the resulting constructions was assessed by (i) a decoding task similar to that used by Ellis *et al.* (1975b), (ii) a rating scale similar to that employed by Laughery *et al.* (1977), and (iii) a forced choice sorting task where judges allocated the composites to one or other of the target photographs. Overall accuracy on the decoding task was again low with only 16% of Photofits being identified correctly, a figure increased to 30% when second and third choices were taken into account. No effect was found for delay, nor did either of the other measures produce a significant delay effect.

This failure to show an effect for delay was repeated in a second experiment, where three weeks separated initial and delayed constructions. Following a 10-second observations of a coloured photograph of a white male, separate groups of subjects constructed this face in Photofit and then attempted to recognize it among a sequence of 36 mugshots projected briefly on to a screen. This latter condition provided a measure of trace strength for the face independent of the accuracy of the Photofit. Additional groups of subjects were employed at each delay

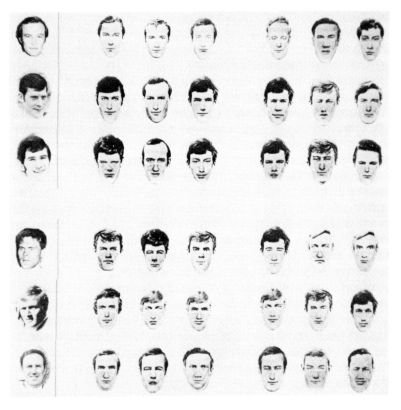

FIG. 3. Examples of the range of Photofit likenesses produced by witnesses of 6 target faces shown in left-hand column. The first three constructions (columns 2, 3 and 4) are those made by good encoders, the remaining three (columns 5, 6 and 7) were made by witnesses rated as poor encoders in the prior experiment. (From Ellis *et al.*, 1975b.)

interval who merely performed the recognition test to control for any effects of construction on recognition accuracy.

Both experimental and control subjects registered a significant decline in recognition accuracy with a three-week delay. However, for experimental subjects, this was not accompanied by any significant decline in the rated likeness of their Photofit constructions, nor was the judged fidelity of construction related to probability of success on the recognition test. In the light of the recognition data, Davies *et al* concluded that trace strength had undergone a real decline over the three-week interval, but this had failed to be reflected in Photofit accuracy due to the insensitivity of the system.

A third study by Ellis *et al*. (1978a) examined further the ability of Photofit to reflect fluctuations in trace strength and availability. In a first experiment, subjects observed a video recording of a white male reading a passage on snakes. Half of the subjects were instructed to attend to the passage while the remainder were told to look at the face. Subsequently, all witnesses answered questions on the passage and cooperated in making a Photofit impression.

Subjects instructed to attend to the passage showed higher test scores than those told to observe the face. However, the converse was not found: Photofits produced by face-oriented subjects were rated no better likenesses than those made by passage-oriented subjects. Thus, despite a measurable shift in orientation, the kit failed to show a measurable decrement in construction accuracy, a finding reminiscent of Laughery *et al*. (1977) in their study of expectancy.

This first experiment of Ellis *et al*. (1978a) also included a manipulation of exposure interval (15 seconds versus 2 minutes) which again failed to show a measurable effect. A second experiment, therefore, included a condition of construction from view. As with the Identikit, no difference in ratings emerged for likenesses made from view and those from memory.

A final experiment compared Photofit and sketching as methods of achieving a likeness. However, the drawings were produced not by professional artists, but by the witnesses themselves. Subjects produced likenesses from photographs of two male targets, one of whom was always the subject of a sketch and the second, a Photofit. Half the subjects performed with the targets in view and the remainder from memory, immediately following a 10-second exposure to the targets. The average ratings of similarity accrueing to sketches and Photofit composites are shown in Fig. 4. As can be observed, Photofits again achieved no higher ratings when composed from view than from memory. When composed with the target face present, Photofits elicited significant lower ratings than subjects' own attempts to sketch the face. However, when both types of likeness were made from memory, Photofits were marginally superior, largely due to the steep decline in the quality of the drawings.

Studies have also been conducted on the influence of sex and race of witness on performance with the Photofit kit. A study on the effect of sex of target and sex of witness was reported by Ellis *et al*. (1976). Male and female witnesses constructed likenesses of a male and female target from memory, following a 10-second exposure to each target face. The resulting composites were assessed for similarity by ratings and a forced choice sorting task. No differences in accuracy due to either the sex of

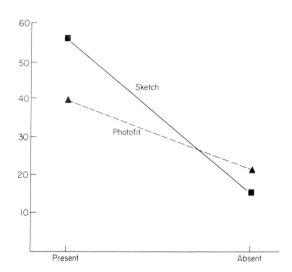

Fig. 4. Mean rated likeness of witnesses' sketches and Photofit composites made in the presence of a photograph of the target or from memory. Ratings on a 100-point scale; higher score represents better likeness. (Redrawn from Ellis *et al.*, 1978a.)

the target or the sex of the witness were found, a surprising result in view of the sex effects normally found in face recognition studies (see Shepherd, this volume).

The influence of race of target and witness were examined in an experiment by Ellis *et al.* (1979a). White Scottish and black African students made Photofits from memory of one black and one white face following a 15-second exposure. The target faces were drawn systematically from a range of 20 coloured photographs, half of which depicted black faces and half white. The resulting composites were assessed for likeness by a sorting task in which white judges attempted to allocate the composites to the appropriate faces. Figure 5 shows the average accuracy achieved as a function of race of the witness, and race of target.

Overall, the average accuracy of composites of white targets (45%) was almost twice as high as for black (23%). Differences in accuracy were also found due to the race of the witness, but these were confined to composites of white targets. Photofits of white targets by black witnesses were sorted significantly less accurately than the corresponding composites produced by white witnesses. Superiority in recognizing members of one's own race have been reported by a number of investigators (Malpass and Kravitz, 1969; Shepherd *et al.*, 1974). The failure to find a complementary effect with composites of black targets could be due to the use of exclusively white judges in the sorting accuracy task or

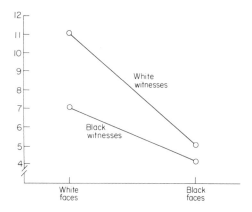

FIG. 5. Accuracy of sorting of Photofit composites produced by black and white witnesses of photographs of black and white target faces. Accuracy scores are from a maximum of 20 and a chance rate of 2. (Redrawn from Ellis *et al.*, 1979a.)

to the limitations imposed on image quality by the more restricted range of features available in the Afro-Asian Kit.

A number of attempts have been made by the same researchers to identify correlates of high constructive accuracy with Photofit, but these have not met with success. On the assumption that success on Photofit involves the differentiation of features from a total *gestalt*, Davies *et al.* (1978a) correlated the rated accuracy of the Photofit produced by their subjects with scores on the Embedded Figures Test (Witkin *et al.*, 1962): no significant relationships emerged. Nor was judged accuracy related to performance on a test of recognition memory for 30 faces.

As in the studies of Laughery *et al.* (1977), no relationship has emerged between competence at Photofit and scores on tests of mental imagery. Good and poor constructors on Photofit in the study of Ellis *et al.* (1978a) were tested retrospectively on the Gordon's Controllability of Imagery Questionnaire: no difference was found between the groups. A study reported by Ellis *et al.* (1976) compared extreme scorers on the visual imagery scale of the Betts Test: again, no difference in Photofit performance was found when image quality was measured by ratings and sorting accuracy. Finally, witnesses' own rated confidence in the accuracy of their constructions showed no correlation with assessed accuracy as measured by sorting or ratings.

Thus, the only measure to emerge with any predictive validity whatever is competence in using the kit to reproduce a facsimile of an existing Photofit face (Ellis *et al.*, 1975b). The major factor militating against predicting performance on Photofit is the very high variability in image quality in composites produced by the same subject for different target faces. One study reported no significant correspondence (Ellis *et al.*, 1975b) while another found a near-significant negative correlation between the rated accuracy of composites produced by the same subjects (Davies *et al.*, 1978a).

C *Relevance of laboratory studies to field experience*

Although conceived and carried out quite independently, the studies of Laughery *et al.* on Identikit and Ellis *et al.* on Photofit show many striking similarities, both in approach and pattern of results. Neither system emerges from these laboratory studies as a particularly effective tool for constructing resemblance. In particular, their low sensitivity is demonstrated by the failure of either system to show a consistent superiority when construction is made in the presence of the target rather than from memory. Under continuous viewing conditions, optimal performance should be possible with both systems; the fact that this fails to produce the expected superiority suggests that the limitations on performance lies not in the witness but in the kits.

The fact that both types of kit are failing to transmit all available information is confirmed when independent measures suggest a fluctuation in performance and the kits do not. In Laughery's studies, this is reflected in those experiments where witnesses working with a sketch artist show the expected fluctuations in performance but those working with the Identikit do not. In the experiments on Photofit, the studies on delay (Davies *et al.*, 1978a) and directed attention (Ellis *et al.*, 1978a) both include indices designed to measure trace strength independent of Photofit performance. In both cases, these showed changes indicating that the experimental manipulation has indeed been successful, but had failed to be echoed in Photofit performance.

This, of course, is not to say that either system is totally insensitive or necessarily inadequate at transmitting an accurate likeness under laboratory conditions. Nor is there any reason for believing that any of the other systems currently in production would be capable of any better performance: the Identikit and Photofit have been singled out simply because they are the only systems to have been rigorously studied. Both Photofit (Ellis *et al.*, 1975b; Davies *et al.*, 1978a) and Identikit (Laughery and Smith, 1978) are capable of generating images which enable others to identify the faces concerned at well above chance levels. Further, both systems do, on occasion, show the expected sensitivity to experimental manipulations: Identikit when working with black targets from memory and view and Photofit, with black and white encoders working with white targets.

Given the low sensitivity of such systems in the laboratory, how are they likely to fare in operational use? Clearly, as analogues of field practice, the present studies all enjoy low ecological relevance and this must raise a question over the generality of the findings. This point has been put forcefully by Penry (1976):

> Laboratory-style facial memory testing is bound to operate on a different academic level without the genuine stimuli of threat, severe shock or acute fear. . . If the face to be recalled has been confronted in a personally menacing or shocking or in anyway emotive situation, its imprint is far more likely to be vivid, detailed and long lasting.
>
> Penry, 1976, p.3.

Clearly, none of these studies involved an element of threat or shock, but a Home Office survey (Darnbrough, 1977) suggests that only 21% of Photofits made by the police are associated with such crime as rape and murder; many arise from non-emotive contexts such as theft or fraud.

Furthermore, there is no evidence that witnesses to crimes involving personal threat are any more accurate in their recall than those associated with non-emotive incidents. On the contrary, a survey by Kuehn (1974) suggested that recall by witnesses of suspects involved in crimes of violence was significantly poorer than for other types of crime. A further complicating factor in constructing facial appearance may be the adverse character traits attributed by witnesses which may seriously distort the composite.

The operation of this latter factor was highlighted in a study by Shepherd *et al.* (1978b) in which witnesses were shown a photograph of a famous multiple murderer. Half were told his true identity and something of his life of crime while the remainder were informed that the portrait was of a lifeboat captain who had been decorated for bravery at sea. Judgments of character traits were seriously distorted by the context in which the face had been observed and this was reflected in the Photofits subsequently produced by subjects. Composites of the target produced by "murderer" oriented witnesses were rated significantly less good-looking and of lower intelligence compared to those made by "lifeboatman" witnesses. Thus, there is no evidence to support the belief that better composites will arise from violent crimes; whatever evidence is available points the opposite way. Indeed, special techniques such as the use of hypnosis (Kleinhauz *et al.*, 1977) may be necessary to obtain accurate information from sensitive witnesses under these conditions.

Another possible source of artefact concerns the training of the technicians: no system can hope to function effectively with incompetent operators. In the case of the Identikit studies, at least one of the team of operators had taken the training course sponsored by the Identi-Kit Company. The Photofit operators had received no formal training, but were highly experienced: one operator completed 215 composites over a 15-month period whereas Darnbrough's survey suggests the great majority of police technicians complete less than 25 a year. Further, a comparison between one of the operators used by the research team and an experienced police professional yielded no difference in rated quality of likeness (Ellis *et al.*, 1978a).

One potential criticism which bears rather more consideration concerns the nature of the accuracy criteria employed in the laboratory studies. It could be argued that they are too high: all that is being attempted is a "type" likeness which will eliminate irrelevant suspects, rather than form the basis of a unique identification. This argument is a tempting one and there is certainly evidence from the Photofit studies that misidentifications do not form a random pattern. However, in the absence of a satisfactory typology, an argument in favour of "types" looses a lot of its force. Confronted with a Photofit and a photograph of the criminal it is possible to see that the composite has captured some features correctly (see Baddeley, 1979, for an example). However, without knowledge of the suspect, it is not at all obvious which aspects of the composite are likely to be correct and which positively misleading.

Clearly, work is needed to identify the dimensions which are likely to be satisfactorily registered by the witness (see Shepherd *et al.*, this volume, for some suggestions) and thus translated into composite performance. However, it is apparent that at least a minority of composites do not allow witnesses to identify the targets even in the presence of a photograph. Davies *et al.* (1978a) selected two targets which were physiognomically distinct. When judges were provided with Photofit composites representing them and asked to assign each to a picture of one or other target, nearly a third were assigned at chance levels or less. The study of Laughery and Smith (1978) exhibited a similar lack of differentiation with low-rated Identikits.

Penry is, of course, correct to point to the inevitable limitations on realism which accompany laboratory studies: they cannot hope to mimic the strains and tension of an actual criminal investigation. However, it seems likely that such stresses will reduce, rather than enhance, performance. One possible compensating factor may be the greater determination of both witness and technician to produce a recognizable likeness. There is certainly evidence that police operators often take a great deal of time over composite production (Venner, 1969; Darnbrough, 1977) but none that extended interviews necessarily produce good composites (e.g. Duval, 1979). Finally, it is important to emphasize that in police investigations, a composite is only one element of evidence, but combined with other information, even a poor likeness, may be sufficient to provide the missing link in the chain of evidence leading to the criminal. To this extent, the limited accuracy of composite systems under laboratory conditions may provide a somewhat over-pessimistic picture of their effectiveness in police hands. There is, however, much room for improvement and the experimentalist can further assist by exploring some of the psychological assumptions which have guided the design and deployment of existing tools. By eliminating sources of unintentional artefact it should be possible to develop more refined and effective face recall systems.

4 PSYCHOLOGICAL FACTORS IN SYSTEM DESIGN

It is convenient to group the issues raised over the structure and usage of recall tools under four headings. The first issue is concerned with the operating characteristics of existing systems, the second and third, the software conventions, and the fourth, the implicit theoretical model of face encoding which underlies them.

A *Interference effects in face recall*

One possible explanation of low recall may be that the very act of perusing numerous features in search of alternatives interferes with the witnesses' memory of the original face (Duval, 1979). A study by Laughery *et al.* (1974) reported that recognition of whole faces was impaired when a large number of faces were scanned prior to the target face. However, the effects observed by Laughery *et al.* may be specific to the paradigm involved (Forbes, 1975; Davies *et al.*, 1979a) and do not address the problem of whether fragmented faces would have greater or lesser effects upon memory.

A study by Davies and Christie (in press) examined whether interference could be produced by isolated Photofit features. A white male was seen in a short film talking to the camera about his life. Subsequently, subjects attempted to recognize his eyes and mouth in arrays of alternatives. In the interval between study and test, witnesses searched through sets of eyes or mouths extracted from the Photofit Library or indulged in an irrelevant filler task. No interference effects were found, nor was there any effect when the interpolated features were embedded in a Photofit face made up to resemble that of the target.

Another method of approaching the same problem is to examine the effects of face construction upon later recognition. If exposure to irrelevant features inteferes with memory, then subsequent identification should be impaired. Davies *et al.* (1978a) found no effect upon recognition of prior construction of a Photofit face of the target. A similar finding was also reported by Hall (1977), who examined the effect of completion of a *portrait parlé* description of a suspect on subsequent identification parade performance.

In the same study, however, Hall did report a near-significant decrement in identification following collaboration with a sketch-artist. Hall attributes the effect not to exposure to competing visual stimuli as such, but rather to the excessive demands made by the artist on witnesses' powers of recall which led to an actual distortion of the original memory (cf. Loftus *et al.*, 1978; Clifford and Scott, 1978).

The sketch-artists in the Hall study were deliberately briefed to ask for elaborate details on the subject's appearance. A study by Laughery and Fowler (1977) suggested that more skillful and circumspect questioning need not have such damaging effects. They reported a very high rate of recognition for a target face which had been made with the Identikit or sketched by an artist six months to a year prior to the test. A subsequent study by Mauldin (1978) included control subjects who were not involved in composite construction prior to recognition. He reported a significant *facilitation* of recognition due to composite construction, irrespective of whether composites were made just prior to, or two days before, test.

This range of results suggested that face recall systems can produce varying effects upon subsequent recognition, depending upon the style and sensitivity of the operator in how far he chooses to extend witnesses' retrieval powers. In this respect, the results from face recall tools are not different from those for verbal interrogation which produce the same variety of effects (e.g. Marshall *et al.*, 1971; see also Deffenbacher and Horney, this volume). Clearly, however, no evidence has been produced of any unique difficulties associated with face recall systems as such, or with their reliance on exposing witnesses to multiple versions of different features.

B *Mode of representation*

Face recall systems use a variety of modes for representing features. Users have complained about the less than life-like appearance of line-drawn systems (Laughery *et al.*, 1977). The use of photographic representation has led to speculation that members of the public will interpret a composite as a specific individual rather than as an approximate likeness (Simpson, 1955; Venner, 1969). Davies *et al.* (1978b) compared identification accuracy for individuals shown as photographs, detailed line drawings in the manner of Identikit, or outline drawings. Irrespective of whether famous or unknown people were used as targets, photographs led to markedly higher identification rates than line drawings.

It can, of course, be argued that in the latter study, subjects were dealing with perfect images. Will the specificity factor work against photographic likeness when dealing with less than perfect images? There is little evidence to support this view. When the more specific information has been removed from Photofit likenesses by photographic means (Ellis *et al.*, 1976) or by computer-aided techniques (D.A. Riley, personal communication) identification rates were reduced rather than increased. Finally, Laughery and Smith (1978) found that poorly rated detailed sketches were better recognized than Identikits receiving comparable ratings: a result they interpret in terms of the more life-like image associated with the sketches.

It appears that in this respect, Photofit offers significant advantages over the traditional Identikit, a point tacitly acknowledged by the recent introduction of the photographic version of the latter system. However, Photofit does contain one feature which inhibits rather than enhances its life-like qualities: the presence of sharp gradations of contrast between features which emerge as lines in the photographed composite. Ellis *et al.* (1978b) found that not only were Photofit images less well recognized than ordinary faces, but that a similar drop in recognition accuracy occurred for normal faces when both study and test photographs had a Photofit-like grid superimposed upon them.

Thus, existing studies seem united in suggesting that, irrespective of the level of accuracy, the more like a real face the composite becomes, the greater the probability of identification. Any increase in the specificity of the image is more than compensated for by the gain in realism.

C *Range and representativeness of features*

A second source of difficulty may lie in the choice and range of features involved in the systems. Home Office surveys (Venner, 1969; Darnbrough, 1977) reveal that a large proportion of operators resort to pencil amendments to modify existing features to conform to witnesses' requirements. Analysis of protocols generated in the laboratory also suggests that witnesses sometimes express dissatisfaction with the range of features available, particularly hairstyles (Ellis *et al.*, 1976; Laughery *et al.*, 1977). One interpretation of the low intra-subject consistency in producing good or poor likenesses with Photofit is that the kit contains the features for making some faces but not others.

Manufacturers have been reluctant to release information as to how features were selected. According to Sondern (1964), the Identi-Kit Company took 50 000 photographs of faces and then took representative features from them. However, to judge from operators in the field and in the laboratory, this selection process does not seem to have been entirely successful. Ellis and Shepherd analysed the Photofit Library by asking members of the public to sort features into like piles and analysing the resulting similarity matrices by multidimensional scaling and hierarchical clustering analysis. This revealed that while the dominant structure employed for sorting some features (e.g. noses, hair and forehead) showed some correspondence to the Penry Classification, others were quite different (e.g. eyes, mouths). These analyses also revealed some redundancies and obvious gaps in the range of features available. Such findings are consistent with the results of Darnbrough's recent survey which suggests that nearly a third of Photofit Operators sometimes experience difficulty in finding features which correspond with witnesses' demands. A considerable body of anthropometric work now exists (e.g. Shepherd *et al.*, 1977; Duncan and Laughery, 1977) and there seems no reason why more representative ranges of features should not be generated. However, the whims of fashion will always cause a problem with hairstyles—during the recent spate of longer male styles, many operators had to resort to female kits to achieve a reasonable likeness!

A second problem concerns the choice of features included in kits. The actual division of the face appears to reflect convenience of construction rather than any psychological analysis as to which attributes witnesses attend. Evidence on the issue of the saliency of different features is reviewed elsewhere (see Shepherd *et al.*, this volume). These findings suggest that no one feature or set of features is necessarily salient under all circumstances. This would imply that as few constraints as possible should be placed upon the witnesses' abilities to manipulate features independently; it should be possible to manipulate not only features, but also the distances between them (Garneau, 1973). In this respect, systems based on horizontal strips, which include only limited degrees of freedom over choice and placing of individual features, are likely to lead to coarser, less accurate, images than those which permit greater freedom over such matters as face length and shape.

D *Global versus analytic processing*

Perhaps the greatest assumption made by existing systems is that subjects necessarily remember faces is terms of their constituent features. Analysis of witnesses' spontaneous descriptions reveal evidence that such global attributes as age, expression and imputed character figure significantly (Shepherd *et al.*, 1978b; Clifford and Bull, 1978). There is evidence that judgments based on such attributions are more effective for recognition purposes than those based directly on feature information (Bower and Karlin, 1974; Patterson and Baddeley, 1977). Most significantly, training techniques which emphasize memorizing faces in terms of features alone have been conspicuously unsuccessful in producing improvements in recognition accuracy (Woodhead *et al.*, 1979; see also Malpass, this volume).

There is evidence from laboratory studies that subjects who adopt a global strategy may be constrained in their performance on existing feature building systems. Duval (1979), related the judged similarity of composites generated by Laughery's subjects to their reported methods of remembering faces. Subjects who reported relying on a global-holistic strategy produced composites of lower rated quality than those relying on features alone.

Face recall kits also encourage a strategy of selecting features piece-meal and divorced from the context of the face as a whole. Duval reported that subjects who strove to perfect each isolated feature in turn produced poorer composites than those who worked on groups of features. Some reasons for this are provided in a study by Davies and Christie (in press). Subjects rated the likeness of sample features drawn from the Photofit kit to those in a target face. Judgments were made from view or from memory, and with the features in isolation or in the context of a Photofit face composed to resemble the target. All sets of judgments were intercorrelated except judgments on isolated features from memory. The fact that the effect is confined to memory suggests that the locus of the subjects' difficulties lies in disentangling and mentally comparing a feature from the integrated representation of the total face.

The view that face recognition may involve both feature analysis and more global processing is also supported by some information processing studies (see Baddeley, 1979, and Ellis, this volume). It suggests that face recall systems should be tried which permit the witness to operate on the basis of the total gestalt. One such system is "Facefit" (Fisher, 1977) which uses line drawings of faces which vary systematically along four dimensions: age (young/old), face shape (oval/round), hair (bald/hairy) and expression (sad/happy). Facefit in its present form is essentially a research device. Its operational use is restricted by the low degree of realism of the simple line drawings and the limited range of dimensions. Nevertheless, Facefit demonstrates that a global approach to face recall is achievable and should be accommodated within future systems.

5 HOW GOOD CAN FACE MEMORY BE?

Laboratory study of the constraints on face recall performance suggest that a number of modifications should be incorporated in future recall systems if they are to surpass the levels of accuracy of existing systems. They should use photographic quality as a basis of representation. They should include a full range of alternative features and provide a high degree of flexibility in their positioning. The systems should not be overconcerned about exposing witnesses to the alternative features available, but should permit them to operate on the basis of a total face as well as to build up from isolated features.

To achieve this degree of flexibility clearly demands that manufacturers move away from acetate sheets and cardboard and join the microchip revolution. A prototype of the new generation of electronic systems, being developed for the British Home Office, was recently described by Kitson et al. (1978). This uses a small computer and a graphics display terminal to display a face on a TV monitor. The data base consists of the existing Photofit Library stored on disc. Alternative features can be displayed as a strip down the side of the screen or in the context of the composite face. Faces can be built up in orthodox feature-by-feature manner or a range of whole faces can be displayed and modified; joins between sections are eliminated by a blending routine. In addition to changes analogous to those in Photofit, additional distortions (stretching; shortening) can be carried out on individual features and their relative position altered. Some examples of products of this new systems, together with conventional Photofits of the same targets are displayed in Fig. 6.

With the development of an appropriate library of features, systems such as the one described should permit a major improvement in the quality of likeness achievable by a witness. However, there is every reason for believing that while image quality can be improved, face recall will never reach the standards of accuracy of face recognition. The reasons for this lie not only in the general abstractive and reconstructive nature of memory processes (Davies et al., 1978c). There is also the unique social role of the face which makes recall particularly vulnerable

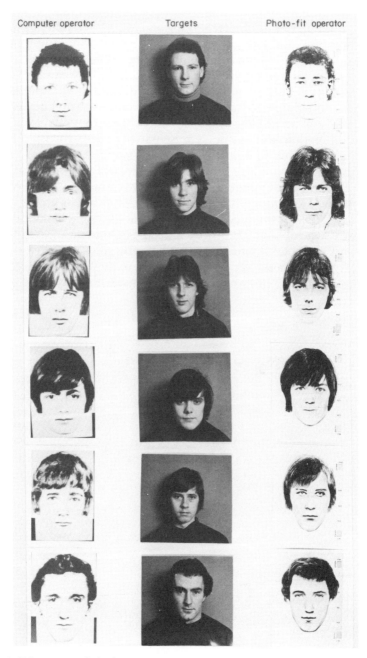

Computer operator   Targets   Photo-fit operator

FIG. 6. Likenesses of six faces produced by experienced operators working in the presence of a photograph of the target using the experimental computer system (column 1) and the conventional Photofit system (column 3).

to the powerful effects of stereotyping and attribution (see Clifford and Bull, 1978; and Shepherd, this volume).

Whatever their ultimate limits, computer-driven systems are just over the horizon rather than currently available. Police scientists are compelled to operate in the realm of the here and now. In the absence of rigorous comparative testing, it would be invidious to nominate a "best buy" from among existing systems. No one extant kit offers the necessary combination of realistic representation, comprehensive feature library and flexibility of operation which laboratory study suggests is necessary for high levels of success. However, it is clear that, judged by these criteria, some systems fall appreciably further short of perfection than others. Depending upon their skills, sketch artists are capable of producing some of the very best and some of the worst likenesses from witnesses' descriptions. Probably a good photographic-based system combined with pencil amendments offers the greatest chance, but no guarantee, of success. We have moved on some way from Bertillon's "speaking portrait" but what is being said is still not fully understood.

11 Computer-guided Recognition and Retrieval of Facial Images

Kenneth R. Laughery, Ben T. Rhodes, Jr and
George W. Batten, Jr

1 INTRODUCTION

This chapter addresses the use of computers in dealing with the mug-file problem. The problem involves searching a large set of faces, the *data base*, to find a match to a referent or target face. The data base may consist of front-bust photographs, profile photographs, or both. The target face to be matched may be in the memory of a person, as in the case of a witness to a crime, or it may be a photograph, as is sometimes obtained in bank robberies or cheque-cashing episodes.

The use of a computer as a tool in dealing with the mug-file problem would appear to be a natural application of the power of the device. Searching large files of information, executing complex matching algorithms for each item in the file, and keeping track of the many pattern-match outcomes are tasks that computers handle extremely well in comparison to people. There have been several research and proto-type developments efforts in this area. The purpose of this chapter is to critically review these efforts and to propose some profitable directions for future work.

Developing a system to recognize images is a *pattern recognition* problem. There are two major steps in pattern recognition. The first is *feature selection* which is the choice of features to serve as the basic information units. The second is the development of an *algorithm* which can recognize patterns similar to those of a specified target image.

Three useful distinctions emerge in characterizing the research and prototype development efforts to date. The most important of these is the nature of the target image that serves as input to the search algorithm. One type of image is the target photograph as obtained from bank-robbery or cheque-forging situations. Another input is an image generated from a witness's memory, such as a sketch, Identikit composite, or image generated with the aid of a computer. This distinction is important because the nature of the target representation versus the representation in the data base has implications for design of the overall system. The second distinction is in the ways of coding faces. The types of coding are herein referred to as *syntactic* and *geometric*. In the syntactic approach facial information is categorical. For example, a forehead might be classified into receding, vertical or bulging. Geometric information consists of measurements between points on the face. Examples are nose length and mouth width. The third distinction concerns the pose position of faces in the mug-file: front and profile positions have been used.

Although the goal of a recognition/retrieval system is to obtain *the* image in the mug-file which matches the target, system designers must settle for less in most cases. Thus, they use pattern recognition algorithms which deliver a subset of the mug-file. *Matching algorithms* select the subset by determining all those images for which chosen features match those of the target. *Sequencing algorithms* determine a measure of similarity between the target and each image, and order the file accordingly. Some recent systems use a combination of matching and sequencing algorithms.

The remainder of this chapter is divided into three sections. The first two review research and development efforts in which the computer is used in a support role. The first concerns the construction of facial images from a witness's memory. The second deals with cost-effective procedures for locating points on a facial photograph. The third section deals with issues that are the main thrust of this paper, namely, pattern recognition methods for selecting faces in the file.

2   THE COMPUTER AS AN AID IN FACIAL CONSTRUCTION

An interesting and potentially important application of computers in the facial memory area is their use as a support device in constructing facial images. One of the limiting aspects of determining memory for faces is the response problem: most people are not capable of generating (drawing) a facial image that accurately reflects their memory for the face. Davies contribution to this volume discusses a number of devices that have been developed to cope with this problem in law enforcement applications. In this section, efforts that enlist the computer as an aid to construction of facial images will be described.

A *Gillenson and Chandrasekaran: the Whatsisface system*

Gillenson and Chandrasekaran (1975) have developed a computer-based system that permits a non-artist to create a facial image on a graphic display. The system has pre-stored, line-drawn facial features, an average face as a starting point, and a heuristic strategy that guides the user in the construction of the facial image.

The feature set in the Whatsisface system comprises 17 features, seven of which are paired (e.g. eyebrows) for a total of 24. These features can be separately selected and manipulated. The number of features was guided by two considerations: too many features would be intractable, while too few would require many variations on each feature.

The heuristic strategy begins by displaying an average face. The user estimates the target's age, and facial lines are added as appropriate. The gross facial shape is adjusted by vertically and horizontally stretching the face. Next, gross changes in individual features or groups of features are made. At this point a "retrieval phase" is initiated in which the features are individually altered in a prescribed order from most to least important: the hairline is first, then the chin, and so forth. The user can interrupt and alter this order. Several types of changes can be made on the features, including position, size, rotation and intensity. A new feature replacement is brought in only when a major shape change is necessary.

The actual user responses in the Whatsisface system are restricted. The user presses typewriter keys and provides size information by adjusting dials (see Gillenson, 1974, for further details).

In an effort to assess the system, a number of people created two images of targets, one using Whatsisface and the other a paper and pencil sketch. All target faces were male Caucasian adults with no facial hair or glasses. The time required to compose Whatsisface images ranged from 45 minutes to 2 hours. A "jury" then evaluated the images by attempting to select the target photograph on the basis of the sketch or Whatsisface image. The results showed significantly better images using the Whatsisface system.

In this study, all target faces were in view during construction. A less formal effort was made to construct a target image from memory. The results were described as quite poor. While the general shape and feature placement was not bad, the image "simply did not look like him". It was noted that the heuristic strategy seemed deficient for constructing images from a witness's memory.

B *Rhodes and Klinger: the Sketch system*

Rhodes and Klinger (1977) have reported preliminary work on a facial construction system that can be viewed as an extension of Whatsisface. The interface between the user and the machine with Whatsisface consisted of one-character keyboard symbols and analogue devices. Rhodes and Klinger developed an interactive system, Sketch, focusing on conversational dialogues between the user and the machine. The user communicates through a keyboard in a restricted but flexible, natural language. The machine responds by altering the displayed image, or communicating back to the user through text messages, or both.

An example of a user statement to Sketch is "Draw the eyes wider". Sketch permits the use of predicate modifers: the statement, "Draw the eyes much wider" would lead to greater changes than the former statement. If a user message cannot be interpreted, clarification is requested. Sketch maintains an elaborate data structure relating features and contextual associations used in the dialogue.

Sketch is more restricted than Whatsisface in graphic display capabilities and other hardware facilities. It has only eleven features, which can be modified in position, size and location. Rotational transformations and variable intensities are not available.

While the system has been implemented on a computer and faces have been generated, no assessment of effectiveness has been reported.

C *Wiederhold: the computerized montage*

The Minolta Montage Synthesizer is a device produced in Japan for constructing facial images by blending features from different photographs. The Synthesizer has three parts: an optical "blender", a closed-circuit television camera, and a television monitor. The optical blender enables partial images from separate sources to be combined, producing a composite image. A "base" facial photograph is placed in an input port of the device. Filters block out parts of the base image while simultaneously reflecting parts of secondary faces located at three input ports. The composite image passes to the television camera. The size and brightness of each secondary image can be adjusted to obtain a good blend.

Wiederhold (1976) developed a computer simulation of the Minolta Montage Synthesizer. Her simulation includes a collection of photographs; a set of filters corresponding to facial features; and methods for assigning pictures and filters to input locations, combining the base and secondary photographs, blending filtered areas into surrounding regions, and vertically adjusting features.

Photographs are represented by recording the light intensity from each point in a 128 × 128 matrix. Each element in the matrix contains a number between 0 and 63, with 0 representing a black area and with lighter regions receiving progressively higher numbers. This digital approximation to the photograph may be viewed as a 128 × 128 checkerboard with each square an appropriate shade of grey. The filters in the system are also stored as 128 × 128 matrices with each element in the mirrored area given a value of one and with all other elements set to zero. Filter elements near the borders of the mirrored area are given values between zero and one to obtain a smooth transition from one feature to another. Vertical displacement of features can be made when necessary.

The simulated synthesizer contains a picture file and a filter file. A base photograph is selected and displayed on a television monitor. Substitutions of features from secondary photographs are made by multiplying each element of the photograph by the corresponding element of the filter. Thus, a zero value (black) results from areas of the filter that are designated zero, and intensity values in the mirrored area of the secondary photograph (the feature region) remain. Complementary computations are done on the base image. The filtered base and secondary matrices are combined to form the composite image. Features blend because of the smooth filter transitions at the borders of the mirrored areas.

Wiederhold's system operates by soliciting and reacting to operator commands. Currently, there are 10 standard commands, but others can be added easily (see also Batten and Wiederhold, 1977).

No studies have been carried out to assess the potential of Wiederhold's system for generating images with witnesses. However, one point should be noted. The primary advantage of the simulator is that selection and alignment of pictures and filters is simple, fast and repeatable.

D *Summary*

The above three efforts represent interesting and promising activities. Certainly the development of computer systems for constructing better facial images from a witness's memory would represent a valuable contribution to the general problem of facial identification; however, Whatsisface, Sketch and Wiederhold's simulator must be regarded as experimental prototypes. Further development will be necessary before their potential can be realized.

3 MEASUREMENT OF FACIAL IMAGES

Several research efforts have used the computer in locating and measuring distances between points in facial images. The use of such geometric information is based on the assumption that certain points in a facial image can be located with accuracy. Once located, the positions of each point (fiducial) can be recorded in a suitable coordinate system. It is convenient if the coordinate system is placed in a standard position relative to the facial features, but the coordinates can be measured relative to any coordinate system and transformed later.

The methods by which images are obtained usually preclude determination of absolute facial size, which in any case, is not crucial for facial recognition. Rather, one must adjust the scale of each image so that it can be compared with others. Adjustment is easily done by choosing the scale factor for each image so that some facial distance (referent) has a preassigned value (e.g. 1·0). Kaya and Kobayashi (1972) refer all distances to nose length. We prefer intrapupillary distance as the referent, since the pupils are easily located with precision.

Points typically located during measurement are the corners and pupils of the eyes; the rightmost, leftmost, and lowest points on the nose; the corners, highest, and lowest points on the mouth; points on the chin line; and points on the sides of the face. Some of these points, such as those on the sides of the face, are difficult to locate with reproducible accuracy.

Since manual measurement of images is slow and error-prone, several groups have investigated automating the process. There has been considerable progress, and undoubtedly automation will be important in the future. To date, however, automatic systems have not been as useful for measurement as interactive man–machine systems.

A *Automatic measurement*

Automatic measurement begins with conversion of an image into a form that can be processed in a digital computer. The image area is subdivided into a large number of regions called *picture elements* or *pels*, usually forming a two-dimensional rectangular array. The average intensity within each pel is converted to a number. The numbers arranged in a matrix from a digital representation of the image.

When 128 lines are to be resolved in both horizontal and vertical directions, there must be at least $128 \times 128 = 16384$ pels per facial image. Modern computer memories are sufficiently large for storing a single image, but considerable computation is needed to manipulate such an image. At the present it is impractical to store an entire mug-file (thousands of images) in digital form if rapid retrieval is required.

The resolution used by most workers in facial recognition is about 128×128 lines, which is nearly one-fourth that used by American television stations. Intensity resolution has varied from 8 to 256 grey levels (3 to 8 bits per pel). It appears that 32 levels (5 bits per pel) is adequate for facial image processing. Indeed, Harmon's (1971) work suggests that even fewer levels may be sufficient.

Some of the earliest work in automatic measurement of facial features was done by Bisson (1965a; 1965b). The first of these reports, which describes efforts to determine the outside corners of the eyes, illustrates both the methods and the difficulties in such image processing. Processing was done in the following four steps:

a. the top, bottom, and sides of the iris were located;
b. points along the upper and lower eyelids were found;
c. parabolas were fitted to the eyelid lines;
d. the intersections of the parabolas were found and used as the corners of the eyes.

Steps (a) and (b) employ the following technique. A vertical strip centred at abscissa x is evaluated from average intensities within the strip above and below ordinate y. Figure 1 illustrates what would be expected near the lower edge of the iris. Let $I_A(y)$ and $I_B(y)$ be the average intensities in the regions A and B (above and below y) respectively. Since the iris is dark (intensity $\simeq 0$), the function $R(y) = I_A(y) - I_B(y)$, called a *signature*, has a minimum at y corresponding to the lower edge of the part of the iris within the strip. The centre of the strip is moved to determine the lowest point of the iris. This technique is used for other edges of the iris and for the eyelids. Most failures in this work were due to lack of contrast in certain regions, particularly near the outer corners of the eyes. This approach generally requires some initial estimates about the size and positions of the components to be determined. Such estimates are usually easy to make when dealing with facial images.

In his second report Bisson (1965b) discusses the use of the technique for locating facial features. Examples are shown, but no statistical information on the success of the method is given.

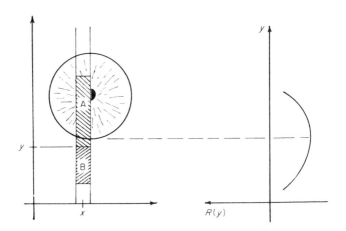

FIG. 1. Automatic location of the iris.

Sakai *et al.* (1969) used a complex algorithm to extract lines from images prior to pattern detection. The algorithm begins by determining points at which the gradient of the intensity exceeds a certain value. These points determine lines in the image, and the lines are extended as far as possible by examining the nature of the gradient near endpoints of already determined lines. Final recognition of faces is done by matching the line image to a template with five parts corresponding to the eyes, the nose, the mouth, the contour of the face, and an area in which no lines should be present. Although they indicate that the algorithm succeeded in locating faces in many different pictures, they give no success-rate statistics.

The first successful automatic measuring algorithm appears to be that of Sakai *et al.* (1972). Line images are produced by thresholding the "9 × 9 Laplacian" of the image. This simple technique produces very good line images. Facial features are then located using a signature technique with $R(y)$ equal to number of dark pels across the strip. Features are located in the following order: top of the head; sides of the face; nose, mouth, and chin; then the chin contour. Once these have been determined, some refinements are made, and the positions and dimensions of various features are determined. The whole process is done with a considerable amount of feedback. A diagram showing the logical flow within the algorithm is reproduced in Fig. 2.

The algorithm was applied to about 800 photographs including images of young and old, male and female, persons with and without glasses and hats, and those with tilt and turn. Of the 607 faces with no glasses or beard, 562 were successfully measured. Failures occurred

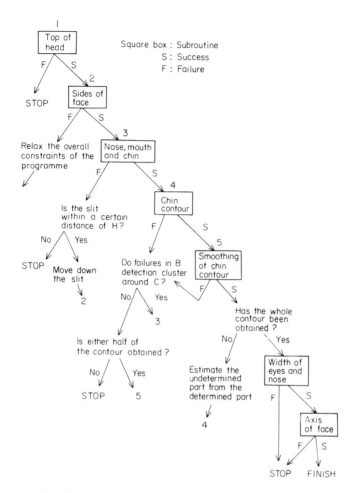

FIG. 2. Algorithm for automatic location of facial features.

most frequently in searching for the eyes (18 cases); the chin contour (15 cases); and the nose, mouth and chin (10 cases).

Bromley (1977) developed a similar feature-measuring algorithm. It s based on a line detection scheme using an optimum filter for detecting dges in images. This filter happens to be a cascade of the Laplacian perator with a low-pass filter, so it is related to the one used by Sakai *et l.* (1972).

The order of processing the features is different from that of Sakai *et l.* First the left and right sides of the face and the face centre line are etermined. The signature (similar to that of Sakai *et al.*) along the centre line is used to find the top of the head, the hairline, the mouth position, and the chinline. Eyebrow and eye positions are located using signatures along lines positioned to the left and right of the centre line. The algorithm locates the tip of the nose and the end points of the mouth, then determines the facial outline by a searching outward in various regions of the face. The algorithm was applied to nine images without glasses or beards. The feature location capability was classified as "good" in eight cases, "fair" in the other; the outlining capability was classified as "good" in four cases, "fair" in two, "poor" in two, and "bad" in one.

B *Interactive measurement*

Batten and Rhodes (1978) describe a man–machine system used to obtain measurements from several thousand images. The system comprises a computer-controlled projector, a digitizing tablet, and a minicomputer with sufficient mass storage to save the measurements.

Digitizing tablets are computer-peripheral devices which determine the coordinates of a stylus placed in the image area. These coordinates in digital form, are transmitted to the computer for processing. The computer software is organized so that all operator communication to the computer is via the tablet. A special message area on the tablet is used for selecting specific images and recording unusual features such as scars. The operation is quite efficient since the operator handles only the stylus.

A CRT terminal for the computer is used for audible and visual feedback to the operator. Each time the stylus is used to mark a point or select a message cell, the computer generates an audible beep using the "bell" of the terminal. Multiple beeps indicate an operator error, such as specification of an illegal image number. These audible signals are important for efficient operator performance. Visual information, such as the image number, and the next point to be measured allow the operator to check operation of the projector system and to pick up at the next measurement point after an interruption.

With this system, an operator can easily measure two pictures per minute. It does not appear that modifications of this system would lead to significantly faster interactive measuring (see also Rhodes and Bargainer, 1976).

C *Summary*

Facial images can be measured accurately and economically on available interactive systems. Measurement precision exceeds that of manu measurement. Some automatic measuring systems have been demonstrated. These automatic systems are not yet completely reliable, but it appears that they will be very useful in the future.

4 PATTERN RECOGNITION SYSTEMS

The major steps in constructing a pattern recognition system are feature selection and algorithm design. The basic approach to the mug-file problem is for the system to compare features from the target with those in the data base being searched. As noted earlier, the nature of the target image relative to the images in the data base is crucial, since this relationship is a major determinant of the difficulty of the overall procedure.

When the target image is a photograph taken under the same standard conditions as the mug-file, features of the same person will be quite similar. A series of studies by Goldstein *et al.* (1971, 1972), Harmon *et al.* (1979), Harmon *et al.* (1978), and Kaya and Kobayashi (1972) have treated the target image as one of the photographs from the mug-file. Using this assumption they predict, and achieve with small samples, high performance in terms of hit rates for their prototype systems.

Bledsoe (1964), and Rhodes and Prasertchuang (1977) have considered the problem where the target image is a non-standard photograph such as might be available in bank robbery and forgery cases. In this case it is necessary to mathematically "rotate" the face before features can be compared to mug-file images. No evaluation is available for Bledsoe's system. Favourable, but very preliminary results were obtained by Rhodes and Prasertchuang using a variation of the algorithm of Townes (1976).

Townes (1976), and Della Riccia and Iserles (1977, 1979) developed systems which can begin with an Identikit image generated by a technician working with a witness. Townes also worked with images drawn by a sketch artist. The quality of this type of image depends on the skill of the technician and the memory of the witness, so these systems are not expected to achieve the performance levels predicted for photographs of targets. Even though the orientation of the face is the same, Townes felt that these non-photographic images required a mathematical correction before geometric values could be compared. He reached this conclusion from an analysis of measurements of sketches and Identikit images collected by Laughery and Fowler (1980). His correction procedure used regression equations obstained from this data to adjust for bias in these techniques of generating images.

A *Feature selection*

Several factors are important in the selection of the features to be used in a pattern recognition system. The most important are

  a. the usefulness of the features in discriminating among faces;
  b. the ease of obtaining suitable "values" or "codes" for the features;
  c. the stability of the feature, since faces change over time;
  d. the efficiency of the system, which includes the economics of data collection, storage, and application.

The usefulness of sets of features can be studied with concepts of information theory. Facial features which are unique for each person, such as fingerprints are, would be ideal, since they would provide definitive discrimination. To date, no one has identified such a feature set for faces. The approach taken by most researchers is to use features such as the width of the lips, which are known to vary from person to person.

The precision and accuracy of measuring (and coding) a feature are important in terms of the useful information provided and the cost of using the feature. Precise and accurate measurement of a feature with less information content may be more cost-effective than imprecise measurement of a feature with more information content. This kind of system optimization can only be accomplished with extensive evaluation of the alternatives available. While the researchers working in facial pattern recognition appear to be aware of this problem, extensive comparisons of the efficiencies of feature sets for large populations of faces have not been made because of the time and expense involved.

Once a set of features has been measured (coded) for a larger set of faces, statistical analyses can be performed to identify a subset of features which tend to be independent and summarize the information in the original set. The number of features used is an important parameter for a pattern recognition system. It influences the cost of data collection, storage and computer processing time. In general, researchers with high quality images such as photographs taken under standard conditions have used more features than those working with descriptions provided by a witness. The criterion of "information provided per unit cost" appears to have been used by most researchers. Such cost considerations have also influenced the type of coding used with a feature.

  i *Syntactic coding of features*

A person can look at a face and describe certain features using words which are descriptors of that feature. For example, Goldstein *et al.*

(1971) use "receding", "vertical", and "bulging" as descriptors for the forehead. They also use "long", "average", and "short" as descriptors for the length of nose. One advantage of syntactic coding is that descriptors can be selected which are natural for people to use. With some training (calibration) people can make reasonably reproducible classifications.

Goldstein *et al.* (1971) developed a complete syntax for coding facial information which is outlined in Table 1. There are a total of 21 features, with the number of descriptors for each feature ranging from two to five. They selected these 21 features from a set of 35 based on an experiment in which ten trained observers coded their descriptions of 256 facial images. The 21 features were selected on the basis of their reliability and independence.

Syntactic coding is also a useful way to record information about facial accessories. For example, Della Riccia *et al.* (1977) include as features, moustache, beard, eye colour, marks or scars, and eyeglasses.

TABLE 1
A coding for facial features

	Feature	Descriptors
1	Hair coverage	Full, receding, bald
2	Hair length	Short, average, long
3	Hair texture	Straight, wavy, curly
4	Hair shade	Dark, medium, light, grey, white
5	Forehead	Receding, vertical, bulging
6	Cheeks	Sunken, average, full
7	Eyebrow weight	Thin, medium, bushy
8	Eyebrow separation	Separated, meeting
9	Eye opening	Narrow, medium, wide
10	Eye separation	Close, medium, wide
11	Eye shade	Light, medium, dark
12	Nose length	Short, medium, long
13	Nose tip	Upward, horizontal, downward
14	Nose profile	Concave, straight, hooked
15	Upper lip	Thin, medium, thick
16	Lower lip	Thin, medium, thick
17	Lip overlap	Upper, neither, lower
18	Lip width	Small, medium, large
19	Chin profile	Receding, straight, jutting
20	Ear length	Short, medium, long
21	Ear protrusion	Slight, medium, large

ii Geometric coding of features

Another approach to coding facial features is in terms of distances, angles, areas and other mathematical functions. The basic elements for geometric information are coordinates of points. For example, the feature "length of nose", is the distance between "top of nose" and "bottom of nose". Most existing systems use trained people to locate these points.

A system which uses geometric coding usually combines basic measurements into features which summarize information about the images. Two of the early facial pattern recognition studies, Bledsoe (1964, 1966) and Kaya and Kobayashi (1972), used geometric coding of features; the latter used 10 distances to code 9 features, each feature being a distance divided by a referent, the nose length.

Kaya and Kobayashi collected data for these 9 features from images of 62 Japanese adults aged between 20 and 30 years. Their analyses of this data illustrate the techniques used in building a pattern recognition algorithm. They made replicate photographs and measurements of each face, then used the means the variances to normalize the data. A principal components analysis of the normalized data indicated that 92% of the variation could be explained by five components. These components can be considered higher-level features which summarize information from the basic features. Such summary features are efficient for computer analysis, but they are usually meaningless abstractions to a human observer.

Townes used a similar set of distances shown in Fig. 3. Instead of scaling each distance to a single referent such as nose length, he considered all possible ratios less than one and selected those which had the best correlation with his target image.

B *Algorithms*

Several researchers including Townes, Bledsoe and Della Riccia began by developing a similarity measure and using it in a *sequencing algorithm*. Algorithms of this type require geometric coding of features. The objective of this approach is to sequence the photographs in the mug-file on the basis of similarity to the target. A function of $\Sigma(t_i - x_i)^2$ or $\Sigma|t_i - x_i|$ is used as a measure of the "distance" from the target $(t_1, t_2 . . .,t_k)$ to another image $(x_1, x_2, . . .,x_k)$. Images with small values for these sums are similar to the target. For example, suppose a target has two feature values $(t_1 = 6, t_2 = 5)$ and an image in the mug-file has $(x_1 = 6, x_2 = 5)$ for the same features. The distance between the image as measured by these sums is zero. Another mug-file image with featur

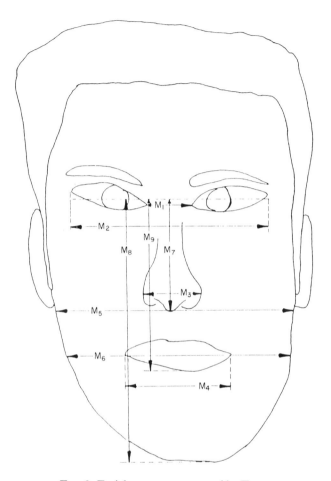

Fig. 3. Facial measurements used by Townes.

alues (7,3) would give $(6 - 7)^2 + (5 - 3)^2 = 5$ for the first sum and $|6 - 7| + |5 - 3| = 3$ for the second sum. Algorithm design must consider the precision and accuracy of measurements and develop appropriate scales for components of the feature vector $(x_1, x_2, \ldots, x_k)$.

Another type of algorithm is a *matching algorithm*, which is used with syntactic data and can be used with geometric data. The computer is programmed to select matching features in a specified order. An illustration is (1) select all "long noses", (2) from the set of all "long noses" select all "receding foreheads", etc. Algorithm design is concerned with the sequence in which selections are made and how to minimize errors in the description of a face. Goldstein *et al*. (1972) considered a variety of approaches in developing an "automatic-feature-selection" algorithm which selects the feature most likely to discriminate at each step. They also used an interactive mode of operation combining human judgment with automatic feature selection. This mode provided superior performance in their experiments.

Kaya and Kabayashi (1972) used a matching algorithm with their geometric feature codes. They selected a "window", which they called β, for determining when two geometric features match. To illustrate, if $\beta = 0 \cdot 5$ and the target's feature value is 6, then all images which have values between $5 \cdot 5$ and $6 \cdot 5$ are matches. A larger β permits more of the mug-file population to "fit the window" and be treated as matches for that feature, while a smaller window increases the probability than an error in coding a feature will cause the correct image to be missed during the search. Variations in the order in which features are considered and the size of the window will give different algorithm performance. Some researchers, Harmon, Townes, and Lenorovitz included, have considered using the confidence of the witness about certain features to influence the size of β or the order of feature matches.

Lenorovitz (1975) developed a computer-witness interactive system using a matching algorithm with synactic coding of features. His study is unique because he used Identikit images for the mug-file. Using scaling procedures, he developed a complete syntax for coding Identikit images. In his study a witness interacted with the system, through another person who served as computer operator. A face from the file was shown to the witness who responded either by identifying the face as the target or by indicating on the basis of the syntactic code how the target differed from the displayed face. Non-matches served to eliminate unlikely alternatives from the file. Another face was then shown and the process repeated. This "pruning" operation continued until the target was identified or the file was reduced to 50 or fewer alternatives. In the latter case, a linear search through the remaining alternatives was carried out. Lenorovitz compared results of the interactive system to results obtained with a straightforward linear search through the entire mug-file. The system led to a significant reduction in the number of faces viewed, a greater number of correct identifications, and fewer false identifications.

Harmon *et al*. (1979) used both a matching algorithm (population reduction by window mismatch) and a sequence algorithm (similarity based Euclidean distance) with geometric feature codes of profile images. Only the subset of the file chosen in the matching step was used in the sequencing step. With this approach they achieved "nearly perfect" identification for a population of over 100 faces, when the target image was a tracing of a photograph (see also Harmon and Hunt, 1977).

C *Summary*

It appears that either matching or sequencing algorithms can be used to recognize and retrieve facial images. What appears to be critical to system performance is the information content of the coded features and the precision of the target image relative to the file being searched. When the target image is quite different from the images in the file (which is usually the case for witness generated images), wide windows must be used to compensate for the lack of precision. In this case a syntactic code may be adequate and may be the only code that can be justified. When the target images are photographs, geometric coding of features appears to be a better approach if it is economically justified.

5 SUMMARY AND CONCLUSIONS

This chapter has reviewed work involving the computer as a tool in recognizing and retrieving facial images. Researchers have been very creative in this area and potential applications in law-enforcement, security, and anti-terrorism are important. Assessment of cost-effectiveness of systems using these ideas requires consideration of the cost of alternatives, a cost which can be very high. Those who can justify sophisticated information retrieval systems for identifying people are likely to include facial recognition as one component, perhaps in the form suggested by Fig. 4. Nguyen (1976) has described such a system, but it has not been tested.

It is reasonable to expect such systems to include components for assisting witnesses in describing criminals, and for coding and measuring images. When such components have been developed, the incremental cost of adding them to a system will be small.

A *Assessment of the current status*

i *Witness-computer generation of facial images*
Prototype systems have produced facial images of promising quality. There is a need for interactive systems which give better results than those obtained using the construction methods discussed by Davies in this volume. Unfortunately, researchers using computers have not concentrated their attention on the most important application, obtaining better images from a witness.

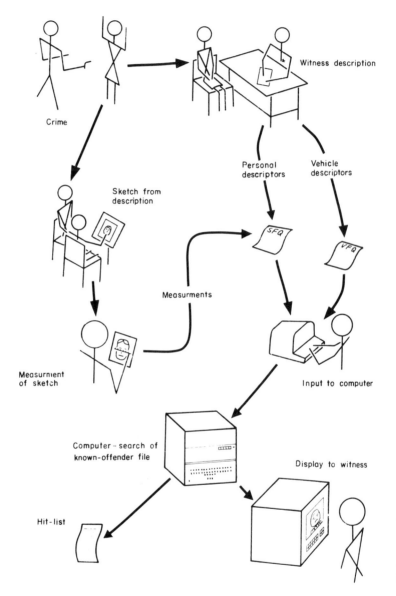

Crime

Witness description

Personal
descriptors

Vehicle
descriptors

Sketch from
description

SFQ

VFQ

Measurments

Measurment
of sketch

Input to computer

Computer - search of
known-offender file

Display to witness

Hit - list

FIG. 4. A system for investigation of crime.

ii Coding of facial information

Interactive systems for rapid, accurate coding and measuring of facial images have been demonstrated. Such systems make it economical to establish the large data bases for statistical studies which are needed for better feature selection and system optimization. They may also be incorporated in identification systems in the field.

The development of automatic systems is an area of active research. Some of these efforts have been reasonably successful, but human supervision and inspection of measurements will be with us for some time.

iii Pattern recognition

Work on feature selection and the statistical nature of image quality is urgently needed. Design methods for matching and sequencing algorithms are sufficiently developed if statistical information is available. This information is also needed for optimum design of data bases: it makes no sense to make and store very precise, detailed measurements of thousands of images if target information is imprecise. Designs will have to be tailored to particular applications.

Adaptive algorithms using witness input are promising. The success of the interactive system of Lenorovitz (1975) and the adaptive mode of the automatic-feature-selection system of Goldstein *et al.* (1972) are steps in this direction.

B *Future directions*

Much of the work to date involved teams, with many researchers making contributions to one facet of the problem. Development of systems for computer-guided recognition and retrieval of facial images requires the coordinated efforts of people with various expertise. One person, Leon Harmon, deserves recognition for his pioneering contributions and for his ability to bring the skills of other specialists to bear in a continuing series of advancements in facial recognition.

Researchers will continue to find creative ways to use computers in the fascinating area of facial identification. How rapidly these developments will find real-world applications depends on the steps listed above. System design will require evaluation of the many alternatives that are available. Hardware limitations will decrease because information technology is rapidly developing. We expect to see important applications once a significant system design effort is mounted.

12   *Training in Face Recognition*

Roy S. Malpass[1]

1 INTRODUCTION

Recognition of individuals previously encountered is unquestionably an important social skill. Successful recognition can be flattering, and recognition failures can be both embarrasing and socially costly. Successes and failures are within the social experience of most of us, some associated with considerable affective intensity. Maintaining contact and position in ones community requires one to recognize and accord individuality to a moderately large number of persons. Some of the persons in our lives are important for the resources they represent to us while others are important for the damage they can do. It should be very useful to remember who represents which. There are certain professions or social environments which even a naive analysis suggests would make demands on face recognition accuracy. Politics is one of these, and any profession which requires maintaining positive relations between oneself and a large group of potential constituents or clients should be expected to make similar demands. Other professions, such as law enforcement, are expected to make greater than usual demands on recognition memory. While these expectations are widely held, there is little evidence that the expected superiorities in recognition memory for faces in fact occur. This chapter addresses the questions of whether there is evidence from either natural environment training conditions or from laboratory research on face recognition training supporting a

[1] The author would like to thank Kenneth Laughery for loaning us the sets of photographs used in our training study, and Terri Scanlon, James Laraby, Charles Miller and Dan Dwyer for their participation as experimenters in the training study.

superiority of face recognition ability in those receiving the training conditions.

A *What use is face recognition training?*

The basic uses are social ones, as outlined above. A positive effect of training would be of potential practical utility in a variety of everyday settings as well as in specialized occupations. Beyond these, however, knowledge of variations in the face recognition performances of groups trained in laboratories or in their occupations could contribute to our understanding of the psychological processes underlying face recognition and enhance our understanding of cognition.

B *How good can face recognition be?*

It is difficult to answer this question, since the conditions of observation, test, and the time delays involved in empirical investigations vary widely. Studies performed under laboratory conditions are of little use in forming an answer. Such studies generally employ a number of inspection faces, with exposure time, delays between inspection and recognition, ratios of inspection faces to recognition foils, orienting tasks and time allowed for recognition judgments, all calculated to produce average recognition performances approximately half way between chance performance and perfect performance. The logic of this makes sense in the laboratory: one wishes to avoid either ceiling or floor effects so that individual and group differences can be observed. This same laboratory control makes laboratory studies very artificial, and an invalid basis for estimating levels of recognition performance in everyday life. Knowing how good recognition can be is important, since that can help us decide whether we should expect very much improvement from recognition training. A naturalistic study of long-term recall and recognition for persons, names and faces was undertaken by Bahrick *et al.* (1975) using materials taken from high school yearbooks in the possession of subjects who graduated from high school as many as 50 years prior to the study. Subjects were able to identify photographs taken from their own high school yearbook among 5 foils taken from other yearbooks with an accuracy of 90% after an average of 34 years since graduation, with the last reported review of the material occurring 2–5 years prior to the recognition test. Of course the pictures had been viewed many times, and recognition for the photographs of years ago is not the same as recognition for the person in the present. Still, this is a high level of performance. On the other hand, the persons-to-be-recognized were not strangers in the first place, as is the case in most recognition studies and in much of everyday life.

Another source of information about the general level of face recognition accuracy comes from studies of eyewitness identification which have used live "offenders" (compared to "offenders" presented on film, videotape, or in colour slides) and either real persons or photographs in the subsequent identification. For a set of 12 such studies, with median inspection time of 55 seconds (mean = 83 seconds, SD = 87 seconds) and median delay between inspection and identification of 14 days (mean = 24 days, SD = 41 days), the median percentage of correct recognition is 71% (mean = 70%, SD = 22%). Percentage of identification errors ranged from 0 to 53%, and errors of omission from 0 to 19%, but it was not always possible to find the appropriate data on errors or types of errors made. Chance expectation in most cases was approximately 20%. The studies included in this group are Buckhout *et al.* (1975); Buckhout *et al.* (1974); Brown (1934); Brown *et al.* (1977); Covey *et al.* (1978); Egan *et al.* (1977); Hall and Ostrom (1975); Lindsay and Wells (1979); Lindsay *et al.* (in press); Malpass and Devine (1981; in press); Wells *et al.* (1979). Given changes in the persons-to-be-recognized between study and test (Patterson and Baddeley, 1977), changes in context (Watkins *et al.*, 1976), changes in pose and variations in incentives to make an identification (Malpass and Devine, in press); 71% recognition is certainly respectable. But it is not spectacular. Recognition seems already fairly good but there also appears to be ample room for improvement.

C *Why should we think face recognition training could be effective?*

On one hand we might expect that by the time one reaches adulthood ones ability to recognize faces will be at its maximum: the social utility of recognition will have induced persons to become as good at it as they can become and the amount of experience with the skill will have been very great indeed by that time. This is not, of course, to rule out individual differences. However, there are three circumstances which imply the possibility of improving faces recognition by either laboratory or naturalistic training.

1. *Special experience.* If groups of individuals sharing an occupation or type of experience perform in a manner superior to others.

2. *Differential recognizability.* If certain classes of faces are recognized better than others, in the absence of stimulus bound bases for the differential (inherent difficulty, Clifford and Bull, 1978). This could be considered a special case of 1, above.

3. *Instruction and orienting tasks.* If instructions or the tasks which orient observers to the faces, produce variations in recognition accuracy.

i Special experience

There is very little evidence on the first point with specific reference to face recognition. Howells (1938) reports superiority of store clerks over either university students or adult farm people. Billig and Milner (cited in Clifford and Bull, 1978) found police to be no better than non-police in recognizing white or black faces, but that is the extent of the literature. A number of studies exist on memory for other kinds of objects and events, and taken together there is only minor evidence for superiority of police over non-police (Tickner and Poulton, 1975; Clifford, 1976; Clifford and Richards, 1977; Clifford and Bull, 1978). Were there strong evidence that some naturally existing groups possessed superior face recognition abilities it would be tempting to assume that others could attain the higher levels of performance through training. The alternative explanation, that better face recognizers self-select into the group would, of course, have to be examined.

ii Differential recognizability

There is substantial evidence that some classes of faces are more difficult to recognize than others. Recognition for persons whose "race" is different from that of the subject is generally inferior to recognition for faces of the subjects own "race".

First, a note on terminology. All ways of referring to "racial" groups in connection with face recognition studies are awkward to some degree or imply acceptance of one or another theory of race. We will use the terms "black", "white" and "oriental" to designate "racial" group membership. Race in this context is used as a folk concept, not as a technical term. No precise meaning is intended. We acknowledge that at the borders of these categories no clear decision on category membership can be made. Our intent is to refer to the physical appearance of stimulus faces, on the one hand, and the social group membership of subjects/observers on the other. We feel sure that the reader will know what is intended by the use of these terms, and that their imprecision is empirically not very important even though the theoretical issues we avoid may be interesting and important.

Findings differ slightly from study to study (see Shepherd, this volume, for a detailed review). Many studies find that both black and white subjects recognize own-race faces better than they do other race faces (Malpass *et al.*, 1973; Luce, 1974; Shepard *et al.*, 1974; Chance *et al.*, 1975; Feinman and Entwistle, 1976; Brigham and Barkowitz, 1978). Others find that white subjects have difficulty with black faces but that black subjects perform equally well with both sets of faces (Malpass and Kravitz, 1969; Cross *et al.*, 1971; Malpass, 1974). Just the reverse was found in elderly white and black subjects by Brigham and Williamson (1979). Three kinds of hypotheses are generally offered as possible explanations for these findings:

    a. *Inherent difficulty hypothesis:* that black and oriental faces are inherently more difficult to recognize (are more homogeneous, for example) than white faces.

    b. *Differential attitude hypothesis:* that subjects have more favourable attitudes towards members of their own group, and that attitude is related to recognition.

    c. *Differential experience hypothesis:* that subjects will have had more social experience with members of their own group, and therefore will be better at recognizing them. The latter two suggest that an own race versus other race differential might be trained out of existence by modifying attitude or experience.

The *inherent difficulty hypothesis* appears to have little support. If it were true, black and oriental faces would have to be uniformly less well recognized, and this is not the case: the level of recognition depends on the race of the observer as well. Further, there is no evidence that any of these facial groups are more or less homogeneous than the other (Goldstein and Chance, 1976, 1978b; Goldstein, 1979a,b). Also, while verbal descriptions elicited by white and black faces from white and black observers differ (Ellis *et al.*, 1975), no one makes the case that the structure of the descriptions is more or less complex for any group.

The *differential attitude hypothesis* has received no support in studies that do not allow inspection preferences or response bias to operate (Lavrakas *et al.*, 1976; Brigham and Barkowitz, 1978; Yarmey, 1979a). That there are few published studies of attitude and face recognition may in itself be illuminating. Seeleman (1940) studied recognition for American white and American black faces among "pro-negro" and "anti-negro" whites, predicting that "pro" subjects would perform better in the recognition of black faces than would the "anti" subjects. The two subject groups were equated on their responses to a questionnaire about their experience with Negroes and the geographical location of their residence. Seeleman (1940, p. 24) reports the following per cent correct recognition data: Pro-Negro subjects viewing white faces, 68.3%; Pro-Negro subjects viewing black faces, 75·4%; Anti-Negro subjects viewing white faces, 67·8%; Anti-Negro subjects viewing black faces, 65·7%. The major difference is the elevation of the performance

of pro-Negro subjects viewing black faces. Since this level of responding is considerbly above performance of either group for white (own-
race) faces one should examine the possibility of response bias operating
such that pro-Negro subjects simply identify more black faces as having
been seen before, thus increasing the number expected to be correctly
identified by chance alone. The recognition task used by Seeleman was
a yes/no task, in which the number of faces identified as having
been seen before was not controlled. Only the number of faces correctly
identified plus those correctly rejected is reported, so that we cannot
reanalyse to evaluate the response bias interpretation. The response bias
interpretation is sufficiently plausible to prevent us from concluding
that an attitude–recognition relation exists on the basis of Seeleman's
data. Malpass et al. (1973), for example, found that "other-race" faces
are incorrectly identified approximately 14% more frequently than
"own-race" faces.

Galper (1973) investigated an idea similar to Seeleman's: that
American white students in a black studies course, having chosen close
association with black students, black history and black culture, function as members of a black reference group, and perform recognition
tasks similarly to black subjects. Her data show a differential recognition effect for white subjects in a psychology course, but not for white
subjects in the black studies course, supporting her initial contention.
However, subjects were shown the initial display of faces in a matrix of 4
rows of 8 faces each, with white faces being in a 24:8 majority for half the
subjects, and a 8:24 minority for the other half. Subjects were allowed 5
minutes to study the 4×8 matrix of faces, with the expectation that
they would be tested for their recognition performance later. Thus the
time spent inspecting faces of the two racial groups was free to vary. It is
plausible to suppose that the white students in the black studies course
were highly motivated to perform well with recognizing black faces, and
accordingly gave more time to inspecting black faces as compared with
white faces in preparation for the subsequent recognition test, thus
offsetting the expected recognition performance deficit. While attitude
may have had an effect in this study, it is not clear that the effect has
been on recognition per se, but perhaps on details of inspection. Again,
these data cannot be taken as showing an attitude–recognition relationship. The study is further confounded by the possibility of differential
experience with blacks between the two subject groups, on which no
data are presented.

Finally, a number of attempts have been made to relate recognition
scores with questionnaire measures of interracial experience (Malpass
and Kravitz, 1969; Lavrakas et al., 1976; Brigham and Barkowitz,

1978). Lavrakas *et al.* found a marginal relationship between recognition and the quality of interracial contact (number of other-race friendships), while the other studies have failed to find an experience–recognition relationship. *Differential experience* is clearly implicated in differential recognition as it is the most obvious difference between groups of black and white subjects in this group of studies (Malpass and Kravitz, 1969; Cross *et al.*, 1971; Elliott *et al.*, 1973; Malpass *et al.*, 1973; Luce, 1974; Malpass, 1974; Chance *et al.*, 1975; Brigham and Barkowitz, 1978; Malpass, 1979). While it may be the most salient factor on which groups are contrasted, it appears unrelated to differential recognition when the analysis focuses on within-group variation. It may be that individual differences in inter-racial experience within groups are not sufficiently broad to show the relationship.

If differential experience is the basis for differential recognition, then it should be possible to provide experience (training) to offset the deficit. Note, however, that this training is aimed at bringing a group of facial stimuli which are subject to a prior experience deficit up to expected levels of recognition by providing additional experience. This is not the same as arguing that recognition for faces of ones own group can be improved by training.

iii Instructions and orienting tasks

There may be theoretical bases for anticipating training effects in face recognition. If we could discover the specific encoding and retrieval processes used in facial recognition, we could perhaps enhance recognition performance by intense instruction in the more efficient application of the technique. There is substantial evidence that "deep processing" instructions result in greater recognition when given during the study phase of a recognition experiment (Patterson and Baddeley, 1977; Strnad and Mueller, 1977; Mueller *et al.*, 1978; Bower and Karlin, 1979; Courtois and Mueller, 1979; Mueller and Wherry, 1979; see also Goldstein, this volume). The "deep processing" approach was developed by Craik and Lockhart (1972) in the area of verbal memory. The assumption behind the depth of processing view is that events processed at many "levels" will be encoded in a more elaborate associative context, and that this will result in "more elaborate, longer lasting and stronger traces" (Craik and Lockhart, 1972). Instructions directing subjects to specific facial features, or to judgments of sex would be considered to produce shallow processing, while instructions orienting subjects to personological aspects of the face (e.g. the persons honesty) produce deeper processing.

Weaker but encouraging evidence suggests that similar instructions are effective if given at the test phase along with instructions to recall the study context. Watkins *et al.* (1977) and Winograd and Rivers-Bulkeley (1977) both show negative effects on recognition of changing the context in which a target face is displayed from study to test trials. Smith (1979) shows (for verbal material) that instructing subjects at test to recall the (different) environments in which study trials occurred returns retrieval to usual levels (the environmental reinstatement effect). Malpass and Devine (1981) administered a 5-minute interview designed as an environmental reinstatement of events taking place 5 months earlier during a staged vandalism, and found a resulting improvement from 40% to 60% correct identification of the vandal.

Thus there is evidence that instructional manipulations at study or test phases can improve recognition performance over the "normal" case. Presumably if one could induce subjects to always instruct themselves in similar ways, their overall recognition performance would improve. The question of recognition training, however, seems distinct from the instructional manipulation question. Consider a distribution of recognition performances for a given individual observer, where each performance represents some combination of inspection time, inspection instruction, study–test environment similarity, retrieval instruction, arousal level of the observer, and so on. It may be true that if we could induce observers to self-administer special instructions, self-induce arousal, etc. that would result in their best performances. Strictly interpreted, however, the training question concerns how to produce an enhancing effect on the entire distribution of performances for observers, across tasks, and other environmental conditions.

2 TRAINING IN FACE RECOGNITION

There is very little information available on face recognition training. Few training strategies have been tried, and none have been tried systematically for periods of time that are more than miniscule in comparison to the weight of an individual's past experience. The beginnings of a research literature on face recognition training exists. There are two types of training that we will consider: training aimed at erasing a deficit in recognition (improving individuals' recognition for faces of another "racial" group) and training aimed at improving face recognition in general, focusing of ones own "race". Elliott *et al.* (1973) investigated the effectiveness of paired associate discrimination training for increasing recognition performance of white subjects for either white or oriental faces. Subjects were given either practice or no practice with either white or oriental faces, and were subsequently tested for recognition of white or oriental faces. Subjects were given sets of cards containing either white or oriental faces, each face paired with a number. They were given 10 cards at a time, and their task was to learn which number was paired with each face. Two minutes' study time was allowed, following which, each picture in the set was displayed singly for 4 seconds during which time the subject was asked to respond with the number paired with the face earlier. Trials were corrected: if the subject failed to provide the correct number the experimenter provided it. This continued either for 10 trials or until the subject attained two consecutive errorless trials. This procedure was then repeated for two additional sets of 10 cards each. Following training, subjects were given a face recognition task in which there were 20 white or oriental faces in a study set, each presented singly for 3–4 seconds. The test set contained these 20 faces and an additional 60 foils. Each face was responded to with a simple "Seen before" versus "Not seen before" judgment. False alarms were constrained by instructions. The findings were very clear. Subjects given no practice were superior in their recognition for white faces compared with oriental faces. Paired-associate training on either white or oriental faces failed to produce an increase in recognition for white faces, nor did training on white faces result in an increase in recognition for oriental faces. Training on oriental faces did, however, increase performance for oriental faces. These results are interpreted in the context of the development of a face schema for oriental faces, and subjects learning both how individual oriental faces differ from each other and how much they differ from the oriental group central tendency on the various features. Whatever theoretical account one prefers, paired-associate training had a significant effect on recognition for oriental faces immediately following training. How long this effect would persist through time is an important but unanswered question.

Malpass *et al.* (1973, experiment I) attempted to improve recognition for own or for other-race faces for both black and white subjects. They used a series of verbal training tasks which included (i) describing faces so that another person could recognize the face from the description, (ii) recognizing faces from descriptions and (iii) noting similarities and differences among triads of faces. Recognition was measured using a yes/no recognition task with sets of 20 study faces (10 white, 10 black) and 80 test faces (20 old, 60 new). Subjects were given 0, 2, 4 or 8 one-hour training sessions, one week apart. While increasing training effected performance on the verbal training tasks, especially recognition of faces from decriptions, there was no effect of verbal training on recognition for either own or other race faces.

Other studies have attempted to eliminate a recognition deficit for other-race faces through training. Malpass *et al.* (1973, experiment II) report a study of recognition training for own (white) and other race (black) faces. Subjects were shown 25 groups of four faces, each one individually, for 2 seconds each with a one-second interstimulus interval. Following this, they were shown four 4-alternative forced choice groups, each one containing one of the four study faces and foils. A time of 10 seconds was allowed for subjects to choose the one old face from each 2 × 2 display. The entire series of 100 faces was analysed in 5 blocks of 20 faces each. Recognition performance for white faces was superior to that for black faces on the first and fourth training blocks, but on the fifth block this ranking reversed (not statistically significantly). Thus at the end of a moderately short training experience, a differential recognition effect no longer appeared. Lavrakas *et al.* (1976) also provided evidence of effectiveness of training in eliminating differential recognition, and, in addition, show that the effect is transitory. Recognition was tested using the following procedure: American white subjects were shown three American black study faces for 1·5 seconds each, after which they were shown three recognition slides containing one of the previously shown faces plus five same-race foils, in a 2 × 3 arrangement. They were asked to verbally indicate the position of the face they had seen before. There were six sets of three, for a total of 18 faces in the recognition test. Different faces were used in the pre-test and post-test phases for all subjects, and the particular set seen at any given phase was counterbalanced across subjects.

Lavrakas *et al.* (1976) used two training tasks: a conjunctive concept learning task, and a simple concept learning task. Subjects were asked to learn face concepts containing black faces constructed using the Identikit. Again the results were straightforward. Both concept learning tasks resulted in an increase in recognition performance for black faces on an immediate post-test, but this improvement did not persist and on a one-week delayed post-test the performance of trained subjects was not superior to that of untrained ones. Three different training procedures, then, have produced a short-term increase in recognition performance for sets of faces for which there was a previous performance deficit. Nothing very specific can be said about the nature of the changes made in the subjects and we have essentially no information on the larger questions of what training strategies produce greater training effects, and the relation of amount of training to persistence of the training effect. Presumably the skills acquired in training would have to be practised in the subject's everyday social environment to be maintained. Thus if the conditions that led to a performance deficit for a particular subset of faces still prevail one would not expect the effects of a short training experience with that subset to persevere for long.

Additional data are available on attempts to train people for improved recognition of own-race faces. Woodhead *et al.* (1979) investigated the effects on face recognition and face matching of a face recognition training programme based on the work of Penry (1971). A pretest was given, followed by the training course, consisting of "three days of instruction at an intensive level, including lectures, slide and film demonstrations, discussions, practical work of handling course and case history materials, and field exercises" (Woodhead *et al.*, 1979, p. 334). A face recognition post-test (structured as the pretest) was given four days after the pretest and after training. The first of three experiments used 24 study faces and 48 foils in the recognition measures. Subsets of the study faces appeared in the test phase either unchanged in pose and not disguised, or changed in pose or disguised. While recognition performance was best for unchanged faces and worst for disguised faces, there was no evidence of a training effect. Two additional experiments were carried out, both involving matching rather than strictly recognition tasks. In the first of these, subjects were provided with one photograph each of 4 males, full face, unsmiling, and were asked to find these four individuals in a series of 240 photographs in which each of the four individuals photographed would appear 4 times, in varying poses and with various expressions. While accuracy was fairly high (80%+, with very few false alarms, $d' = {\sim}3.90$) there was no evidence of an effect due to training. The second experiment was like the first, except that the task was made more difficult by providing each subject 16 target faces in a 2×8 array, each of which would appear only once in the subsequent series of 240 faces (but again in poses and with expressions varying from the original). Under these conditions there was evidence of a significant decrement in recognition matching following the training experience.

Why is it that while training can improve recognition for other-race faces (for which there is an initial deficit) training for own-race produces no effect, or possibly a decrease in recognition performance? Two explanations are frequently offered: (1) that face recognition performance is overlearned and continually practiced so that it is unlikely to improve further, and (2) that the methods used in the training procedures are unnatural, and therefore do not enhance natural processes (Malpass, 1975; Ellis *et al.*, 1975; Woodhead *et al.*, 1979).

3 NEW DATA ON TRAINING FOR OWN-RACE RECOGNITION

Four different training procedures were used in a study recently completed in our laboratory. The subjects were white college students, and the training photographs were all of white males. All subjects were given a pretest prior to training and a post-test at end of the last training session. Training sessions were held for one hour on each of two days for each of 6 weeks (a total of 12 one-hour training sessions for each subject).

A *Feature analysis training*

Subjects were shown illustrations taken from Penry (1971) of the range of variation of a variety of facial features. For example, according to Penry, eyes could be large or small, hooded or lidless, brown or blue. Penry provides illustrations and explanations of these features, and their variations. In the first training session a large number of Penry's illustrations of facial features were shown to the subjects, with examples drawn from our own samples of face photographs. After this initial exposure, training sessions were concerned with making subjects familiar with particular features and their variations. At all sessions, new features were introduced and a review was made of features examined in previous sessions. Subjects spent the remaining time in each session examining face photographs and discussing which feature variations a particular face represented. Six subjects participated in this training condition.

B *Global personality sorting*

Following Craik and Lockhart (1972), a number of studies of face recognition have shown recognition increments following orienting tasks which ask subjects to make personological judgments of the person photographed (e.g. honesty) compared with other judgments in which surface features are focused upon (e.g. race, sex) (Bower and Karlin, 1974; Patterson and Baddeley, 1977; Strnad and Mueller, 1977; Mueller *et al.*, 1978; Courtois and Mueller, 1979; Mueller and Wherry, 1979). Based on these findings, one training condition required subjects to make personological judgments about faces. Subjects were asked to place faces into categories according to their location of the face on a personological dimension (such as "intelligent/stupid"). They could use as many categories as they wished, with the restriction that they must use at least three. They then sorted sets of 90 faces in this way.

Upon completion of this sorting task, they were given another personological dimension on which to sort, and another set of face photographs.
An experimenter inspected the categories following each sort. The
photographs used were black and white photographic prints, measuring
approximately 5 × 7·6 cm. Eleven subjects participated in this training
condition.

C *Global facial judgments*

As a contrast with both the feature analytic and personological
approaches taken in the first two training groups, we employed a
training procedure that was neither analytical, verbal, or aimed at
inferences based on facial appearance. Rather, we displayed for the
subjects 4 photographs of individuals chosen so as to be different in
their appearance, but similar in overall head shape. Subjects inspected
these photographs for approximately one minute after which the inspection faces were removed from view. Subjects were then asked to go
through sets of approximately 90 training faces and place each one in a
pile indicating the one of the four inspection faces to which it was most
similar. Subjects were instructed to concentrate on the overall physical
appearance of the faces. The faces or face categories were not labelled,
and no labels were requested from the subjects. Eight subjects participated in this training condition.

D *Repeated face recognition tests*

A fourth group of 15 subjects was given a series of repeated recognition
tests using transparencies made from the same faces sorted by the two
"global" training groups. There was no performance feedback of any
kind, and no attempt at instruction.

During both the pretest and the post-test subjects were presented
with a set of study faces and subsequently with a set of test faces
containing the study faces and an equal number of foils. The study set
contained 20 white faces which were serially presented by projection on
a white matte screen for approximately 1 second each, with a 1-second
interstimulus interval. Test trials followed after a 2-minute delay,
during which instructions were given about the recognition response
format. Test faces were also presented by projection, serially for 7
seconds each. The faces used were selected from the sets used by
Malpass and Kravitz (1969), Malpass *et al.* (1973), and Malpass (1979).
Subjects used a response form requesting a judgment on a 6-point scale
for each face in the test, from "I'm sure I have not seen this face before"

to "I'm sure I have seen this face before" (Banks, 1970). This 6-point rating scale yields d' values at each of 5 criterion levels. In the present data analysis the a' index (Grier, 1971), a non-parametric analogue of d', was used. The middle criterion level was used in each case. Four separate sets of study and test faces were used, with an approximately equal number of subjects within groups seeing each of the four subsets. The faces used in the pretest and post-test were different for each subject.

E *Results*

The data were analysed using a 2 (pretest–post-test) × 4 (types of training) unweighted means analysis of variance (Winer, 1962, pp. 375–377), with pretest–post-test a repeated measure. The only significant result was that post-test a' scores were lower than pretest scores ($0.724 < 0.777$; $F_{1,36} = 8.20$, $p < 0.01$). Thus, training had a negative effect on recognition performance, a result foreshadowed by Woodhead *et al.* (1979). Since there are no other studies that we are aware of that have examined training effects over even this relatively short time period we should be tentative in interpretation until there is replication. A negative training effect is not entirely surprising, however. Subjects were aware that they were participating in training aimed at improving their face recognition, and we encouraged all but those in the repeated recognition testing group to be more analytical about looking at faces in their everyday life. One can argue that this might induce subjects to attend selectively, or intentionally to faces. This in turn might reduce the amount of information available about the face by engaging subjects in an inspection and coding process that is deliberate and slower than normal processes, and which has not reached a high degree of efficiency. Theoretical clarification of face recognition processes is required before progress can be made with face recognition training.

4 CONCLUSIONS

Face recognition is an important social and cognitive skill. While there is reason to presume that substantial lack of experience with subsets of faces (other-race faces) can produce decreased recognition for those faces, there is little evidence that special experience can produce an increase in recognition ability. While there is evidence that recognition training can bring about short-term improvement of recognition for other-race faces there is no evidence that a relatively short training programme can increase recognition performance for own-race faces; indeed, the evidence points in the opposite direction. There are a number of possible interpretations. These include that (i) training is completely trivial compared with a lifetime of face recognition experience, and can't be expected to change anything; (ii) encoding and recognition strategies are formed early in life and are resistant to change; and (iii) our understanding of face recognition processes is insufficient to form a basis for planning effective face recognition training programmes. There is an insufficient body of literature available for an evaluation of these and other alternatives to be made. Much more analytical/theoretical treatments of the basis for recognition training procedures are needed if the next round of training research is to take us beyond present knowledge.

References

Abelson, R.P. and Sermat, V. (1962). Multidimensional scaling of facial expressions. *Journal of Experimental Psychology*, **63**, 546–554.

Agnetti, V., Carreras, M., Pinna, L. and Rosati, G. (1978). Ictal prosopagnosia and epileptogenic damage of the dominant hemisphere. A case history. *Cortex*, **14**, 50–57.

Alexander, J.F. (1972). Search factors influencing personal appearance identification. *In* "Personal Appearance Identification" (A. Zavala and J.J. Paley, Eds). C.C. Thomas, Springfield, Illinois.

Allison, H.C. (1973). "Personal Identification". Holbrook Press, Boston.

Allport, F.H. (1924). "Social Psychology". Houghton Mifflin, Boston.

Allport, G.W. and Kramer, B.M. (1946). Some roots of prejudice. *Journal of Psychology*, **22**, 9–39.

Ambrose, J.A. (1960). The smiling and related responses in early human infancy: An experimental and theoretical study of their cause and significance. PhD thesis, University of London.

Ambrose, J.A. (1963). The age of onset of ambivalence in early infancy: Indications from the study of laughing. *Journal of Child Psychology and Psychiatry*, **4**, 167–187.

Anderson, J.R. and Paulson, R. (1978). Interferences in memory for pictorial information. *Cognitive Psychology*, **10**, 178–202.

Andrew, R.J. (1963a). Evolution of facial expression. *Science*, **142**, 1034–1041.

Andrew, R.J. (1963b). The origin and evolution of the calls and facial expressions of the primates. *Behaviour*, **20**, 1–109.

Andrew, R.J. (1972). The information potentially available in mammal displays. *In* "Non-verbal Communication" (R.A. Hinde, Ed.). Cambridge University Press, Cambridge.

Argyle, M. (1967). "The Psychology of Interpersonal Behaviour". Cox & Wyman, London.

Argyle, M. and Cook, M. (1975). "Gaze and Mutual Gaze". Cambridge University Press, Cambridge.

Aronfreed, J. (1970). The socialization of altruistic and sympathetic behaviour: some theoretical and experimental analyses. *In* "Altruism and Helping Behavior" (J. Macaulay and L. Berkowitz, Eds). Academic Press, New York.

Assal, G. (1969). Régression des troubles de la reconnaissance des physionomies et de la mémoire topographique chez un malade opéré d'un hématome intracérébral parieto-temporal droit. *Revue Neurologique*, **121**, 184–185.

Assal, G., Zander, E., Kramin, H. and Buttet, J. (1976). Discrimination des voix lors lesions du cortex cérébral. *Archives Suisse de Neurologie Neurochiurgie et Psychiatry*, **119**, 307–315.

Attenborough, D. (1979). "Life on Earth". Collins, B.B.C., London.

Baddeley, A.D. (1976). "The Psychology of Memory". Harper and Row, New York and London.

Baddeley, A.D. (1978). The trouble with levels: A re-examination of Craik and Lockhart's framework for memory research. *Psychological Review*, **85**, 139–152.

Baddeley, A. (1979). Applied cognitive and cognitive applied psychology: The case of face recognition: *In* "Perspectives on Memory Research" (L.G. Nilsson, Ed.). L. Erlbaum, New Jersey.

Bahrick, H.P., Bahrick, P.O. and Wittlinger, R.P. (1975). Fifty years of memory for names and faces: A cross-sectional approach. *Journal of Experimental Psychology: General*, **104**, 54–75.

Baker, E. (1967). Perceiver variables involved in the recognition of faces. PhD thesis, University of London.

Banks, W.P. (1970). Signal detection theory and human memory. *Psychological Bulletin*, **74**, 81–99.

Bates, F. (1977). Australian draft legislation on identification parades. *Journal of Criminal Law*, **41**, 61–70.

Bateson, P.P.G. (1977). Testing an observer's ability to identify individual animals. *Animal Behaviour*, **25**, 247–248.

Batten, G.W. and Rhodes, B.T. (1978). UHMFS: The University of Houston mug file system. Proceedings of the 1978 Carnahan Conference on Crime Countermeasures. Lexington, Kentucky.

Batten, G.W. and Widerhold, T. (1977). A computer simulation of the minolta montage synthesizer. Mug File Project (Report Number UHMUG–14), University of Houston.

Bay, E. (1950). Agnosie und Funktionswandel. *Monographien aus dem Gesamgebiete der Neurologie und Psychiatrie*, **73**, 1–94.

Beck, U., Ashayeri, H. and Keller, H. (1978). Prosopagnosie und Farberkennungstörung bei Rückbildung von Rindenblindheit. *Archiv für Psychiatrie und Nervenkrankheiten*, **225**, 55–66.

Beloff, H. and Coupar, S. (1968). Some transactional perceptions of African faces. *British Journal of Social and Clinical Psychology*, **7**, 169–175.

Beloff, J. and Beloff, H. (1961). The influence of valence on distance judgements of human faces. *Journal of Abnormal Psychology*, **62**, 720–722.

Benson, D.F., Segarra, J. and Albert, M.L. (1974). Visual agnosia-prosopagnosia. *Archives Neurology*, **30**, 307–310.

Benton, A.L. (1980). The neuropsychology of face recognition. *American Psychologist*, **35**, 176–186.

Benton, A.L. and Van Allen, M.W. (1968). Impairment in facial recognition in patients with cerebral disease. *Cortex*, **4**, 344–358.

Benton, A.L. and Van Allen, M.W. (1973). "Manual: Test of Facial Recognition". Neurosensory Center Publication No. 287. Department of Neurology, University Hospitals, Iowa City, Iowa.

Berent, S. (1977). Functional asymmetry of the human brain in the recognition of faces. *Neuropsychologia*, **15**, 829–831.

Bergman, T., Haith, M.M. and Mann, L. (1971). Development of eye contact and facial scanning in infants. Paper presented at the meeting of the Society for Research in Child Development, Minneapolis, April 1971.

Bertelson, P. (1978). Personal communication (June).

Berlyne, D.E. (1958). The influence of complexity and novelty in visual figures on orienting responses. *Journal of Experimental Psychology*, **55**, 289–296.

Berscheid, E. and Walster, E. (1974). Physical attractiveness. *In* "Advances in Experimental Social Psychology" (L. Berkowitz, Ed.), vol. 7. Academic Press, London and New York.

Beyn, E.S. and Knyazeva, G.R. (1962). The problem of prosopagnosia. *Journal of Neurology, Neurosurgery and Psychiatry*, **25**, 154–158.

Biejk-Docter, M.A. and Elshout, J. (1969). (Field dependency and memory with reference to socially and not-socially relevant material). *Nederlands Tijdschrift voor de Psychologie en haar Grensgiebeden*, **24**, 267–279.

Bindra, D. (1972). Weeping. *Bulletin of the British Psychological Society*, **25**, 281–284.

Binet, A. (1900). "La suggestibilité". Schleicher, Paris.

Bisson, C.L. (1965a). Measurement by computer of the distances on and about the eyes (Report No. PRI–18). Panoramic Research, Inc., Palo Alto, California.

Bisson, C.L. (1965b). Location of some facial features by computer. (Report No. PRI–20). Panoramic Research, Inc., Palo Alto, California.

Blaney, R.L. and Winograd, E. (1978). Developmental differences in children's recognition memory for faces. *Developmental Psychology*, **14**, 441–442.

Bledsoe, W.W. (1964). The model method in facial recognition. (Report No. PRI–15). Panoramic Research, Inc., Palo Alto, California.

Bledsoe, W.W. (1966). Man–machine facial recognition. (Report No. PRI–22). Panoramic Research, Inc., Palo Alto, California.

Block, J. (1957). Studies in the phenomenology of emotions. *Journal of Abnormal and Social Psychology*, **54**, 328–363.

Blurton-Jones, N.G. (1971). Criteria for use in describing facial expressions in children. *Human Biology*, **43**, 365–413.

Bodamer, J. (1947). Die Prosop-Agnosie. *Archiv fur Psychiatrie und Nervenkrankheiten*, **179**, 6–53.

Bolwig, N. (1964). Facial expressions in primates, with remarks on a parallel development in certain carnivores. (A preliminary report on work in progress). *Behaviour*, **22**, 167–192.

Borges, M.A. and Vaughn, L.S. (1977). Cognitive differences between the sexes in memory for names and faces. *Perceptual and motor skills*, **45**, 317–318.

Boring, E.G. and Titchener, E.B. (1923). A model for the demonstration of facial expression. *American Journal of Psychology*, **34**, 471–485.

Bornstein, B. (1963). Prosopagnosia. *In* "Problems of Dynamic Neurology" (L. Halpern, Ed.). Hadassah Medical Organization, Jerusalem.

Bornstein, B., Sroka, H. and Munitz, H. (1969). Prosopagnosia with animal face agnosia. *Cortex*, **5**, 164–169.

Boucher, J.D. and Ekman, P. (1975). Facial areas and emotional information. *Journal of Communication*, **25**, 21–29.

Bower, G.H. and Karlin, M.B. (1974). Depth of processing pictures of faces and recognition memory. *Journal of Experimental Psychology*, **103**, 751–757.

Bower, T.G.R. (1976). Repetitive processes in child development. *Scientific American*, **235**, 38–47.

Bradshaw, J.L. and Wallace, G. (1971). Models for the processing and identification of faces. *Perception and Psychophysics*, **9**, 443–448.

Brannigan, C.R. and Humphries, D.A. (1972). Human non-verbal behaviour, a means of communication. *In* "Ethological Studies of Child Behaviour" (N.G. Blurton-Jones, Ed.). Cambridge University Press, Cambridge.

Bridges, K.M.B. (1931). "The Social and Emotional Development of the Pre-school Child". Kegan Paul, London.

Bridges, K.M.B. (1932). Emotional development in early infancy. *Child Development*, **3**, 324–341.

Brigham, J.C. and Barkowitz, P. (1978). Do "They all look alike?" The effect of race, sex, experience and attitudes on the ability to recognize faces. *Journal of Applied Social Psychology*, **8**, 306–318.

Brigham, J.C. and Williamson, N.L. (1979). Cross-racial recognition and age: When you're over 60, do they still "all look alike?" *Personality and Social Psychology Bulletin*, **5**, 218–222.

Broman, M. (1978). Reaction-time differences between the left and right hemispheres for face and letter discrimination in children and adults. *Cortex*, **14**, 578–591.

Bromley, L.K. (1977). Computer-aided processing techniques for usage in real-time image evaluation. Master's thesis, University of Houston.

Brooks, R.M. and Goldstein, A.G. (1963). Recognition by children of inverted photographs of faces. *Child Development*, **34**, 1033–1040.

Brooks, V. and Hochberg, J. (1960). A psychophysical study of "cuteness". *Perceptual and Motor Skills*, **11**, 205.

Broverman, I.K., Vogel, S.R., Broverman, D.M., Clarkson, F.E. and Rosenkrantz, P.S. (1972). Sex-role stereotypes: A current appraisal. *Journal of Social Issues*, **28**, 59–78.

Brown, A.L. (1975). The development of memory: Knowing, knowing about knowing, and knowing how to know. *In* "Advances in Child Development and Behavior" (H.W. Reese, Ed.), vol. 10. Academic Press, New York.

Brown, E., Deffenbacher, K. and Sturgill, W. (1977). Memory for faces and the circumstances of encounter. *Journal of Applied Psychology*, **62**, 311–318.

Brown, H.B. (1934). An experience in identification testimony. *Journal of Criminal Law, Criminology and Police Science*, **25**, 621–622.

Bruce, V. (1979). Searching for politicians: An information-processing approach to face recognition. *Quarterly Journal of Experimental Psychology*, **31**, 373–395.

Bruner, J.S. (1957). On perceptual readiness. *Psychological Review*, **64**, 123–152.

Bruner, J.S., Goodnow, J.J. and Austin, G.A. (1956). "A Study of Thinking". Wiley, New York.

Brunswick, E. (1956). "Perception and the Representative Design of Psychological Experiments". University of California Press, Los Angeles.

Bryden, W.J. (1978). "Identification Procedure under Scottish Criminal Law". Her Majesty's Stationery Office, Edinburgh.

Buck, R. (1976). A test of non-verbal receiving ability: Preliminary studies. *Human Communication Research*, **2**, 162–171.

Buckhout, R., Alper, A., Chern, S., Silverberg, G. and Slomovits, M. (1974). Determinants of eyewitness performance on a lineup. *Bulletin of the Psychonomic Society*, **4**, 191–192.

Buckhout, R., Figueroa, D. and Hoff, E. (1975). Eyewitness identification: Effects of suggestion and bias in identification from photographs. *Bulletin of the Psychonomic Society*, **6**, 71–74.

Bull, R.H.C. and Reid, R.L. (1975). Recall after briefing: Television versus face to face presentation. *Journal of Occupational Psychology*, **48**, 73–78.

Bush, L.E. (1973). Individual differences multidimensional scaling of adjectives denoting feelings. *Journal of Personality and Social Psychology*, **25**, 50–57.

Buzby, D.E. (1924). The interpretation of facial expression. *American Journal of Psychology*, **35**, 602–604.

Bytheway, W.R. and Clarke, M. (1976). The conduct and uses of identification parades. *Journal of Criminal Law*, **40**, 198–205.

Cady, H.M. (1924). On the psychology of testimony. *American Journal of Psychology*, **35**, 110–112.

Campbell, F.W. and Robson, J.G. (1968). Application of Fourier analysis to the visibility of gratings. *Journal of Physiology*, **197**, 551–556.

Campbell, R. (1978). Asymmetries in interpreting and expressing a posed facial expression. *Cortex*, **14**, 327–342.

Carey, S. (1978). A case study: Face recognition. In "Explorations in the Biology of Language" (E. Walker, Ed.). Bradford Books, Montgomery, Vermont.

Carey, S. (1980). Maturational factors in human development. In "Biological Bases of Mental Processes" (D. Caplan, Ed.). MIT Press, Cambridge, Massachusetts.

Carey, S. and Diamond, R. (1977). From piecemeal to configurational representation of faces. *Science*, **195**, 312–314.

Carey, S. and Diamond, R. (1980). Maturational determination of the developmental course of face encoding. *In* "Biological Bases of Mental Processes" (D. Caplan, Ed.). MIT Press, Cambridge, Massachusetts.

Carey, S., Diamond, R. and Woods, B. (1980). The development of face recognition—A maturational component? *Developmental Psychology*, **16**, 257–269.

Carmichael, L. (1926). The development of behavior in invertebrates experimentally removed from the influence of external stimulation. *Psychological Review*, **33**, 51–58.

Caron, A.L., Caron, R.F., Caldwell, R.C. and Weiss, S.E. (1973). Infant perception of the structural properties of the face. *Developmental Psychology*, **9**, 385–399.

Carr, T.H., Deffenbacher, K.A. and Leu, J.R. (1979). Is there less interference in memory for faces? Paper presented at the annual meeting of the Psychonomic Society, Phoenix, Arizona.

Carroll, J.D. and Arabie, P. (1980). Multidimensional scaling. *Annual Review of Psychology*, **31**, 607–649.

Carroll, J.D. and Chang, J.J. (1970). Analysis of individual differences in multidimensional scaling via an N-way generalization of "Eckart-Young" decomposition. *Psychometrika*, **35**, 283–319.

Carter, L.F. (1948). The identification of "racial" membership. *Journal of Abnormal and Social Psychology*, **43**, 279–286.

Chance, J.E. and Goldstein, A.G. (1976). Recognition of faces and verbal labels. *Bulletin of the Psychonomic Society*, **7**, 384–386.

Chance, J.E. and Goldstein, A.G. (1979). Reliability of face recognition. *Bulletin of the Psychonomic Society*, **14**, 115–117.

Chance, J.E. and Goldstein, A.G. (in press). Depth of processing in response to own- and other-race faces. *Personality and Social Psychology Bulletin*.

Chance, J., Goldstein, A.G. and McBride, L. (1975). Differential experience and recognition memory for faces. *Journal of Social Psychology*, **97**, 243–253.

Chance, J., Goldstein, A.G. and Schicht, W. (1967). Effects of acquaintance and friendship on children's recognition of classmates' faces. *Psychonomic Science*, **7**, 223–224.

Charcot, J.M. (1883). Un cas de suppression brusque et isolée de la vision mentale des signes et des objets (formes et couleurs). *Progrès Medical*, **11**, 568.

Charlesworth, W.R. and Kreutzer, M.A. (1973). Facial expressions of infants and children. *In* "Darwin and Facial Expression. A Century of Research in Review" (P. Ekman, Ed.). Academic Press, New York and London.

Chevalier-Skolnikoff, G. (1973). Facial expression of emotion in non-human primates. *In* "Darwin and Facial Expression. A Century of Research in Review" (P. Ekman, Ed.). Academic Press, New York and London.

Cheyne, J.A. (1976). Development of forms and functions of smiling in preschoolers. *Child Development*, **47**, 820–823.

Chi, M.T.H. (1977). Age differences in memory span. *Journal of Experimental Child Psychology*, **23**, 266–281.

Christie, D.F.M. (1979). A comparison of the dimensions of similarity among male and female faces, using multidimensional scaling techniques. Unpublished manuscript, University of Aberdeen.

Cicchetti, D. and Sroufe, L.A. (1976). The relationship between affective and cognitive development in Down's syndrome infants. *Child Development*, **47**, 920–929.

Clifford, B.R. (1976). Police as eyewitnesses. *New Society*, **22**, 176–177.

Clifford, B.R. (1979). The relevance of psychological investigation to legal issues in testimony and identification. *Criminal Law Review*, 153–163.

Clifford, B.R. and Bull, R. (1978). "The Psychology of Person Identification". Routledge & Kegan Paul, London.

Clifford, B.R. and Richards, V.J. (1977). Comparison of recall by policemen and civilians under conditions of long and short duration of exposure. *Perceptual and Motor Skills*, **45**, 503–512.

Clifford, B.R. and Scott, J. (1978). Individual and situational factors in eyewitness testimony. *Journal of Applied Psychology*, **63**, 352–359.

Cohen, L.B., Deloache, J.S. and Pearl, R.A. (1977). An examination of interference effects in infants' memory for faces. *Child Development*, **48**, 88–96.

Cohen, M.E. and Carr, W.J. (1975). Facial recognition and the von Restorff effect. *Bulletin of the Psychonomic Society*, **6**, 383–384.

Cohen, M.E. and Nodine, C.F. (1978). Memory processes in facial recognition and recall. *Bulletin of the Psychonomic Society*, **12**, 317–319.

Cole, P. and Pringle, P. (1974). "Can you Positively Identify this Man?" Andre Deutsch, London.

Coleman, J.C. (1949). Facial expressions of emotions. *Psychological Monographs*, **63** (whole No. 296), 1–36.

Coltheart, M. (1975). Faces. *New Behaviour*, April 1975, 14–15.

Comment, (1971). *Journal of Criminal Law, Criminology, and Police Science*, **62**, 363–375.

Cook, M. (1978). Eye movements during recognition of faces. *In* "Practical Aspects of Memory" (M.M. Gruneberg, P.E. Morris and R.N. Sykes, Eds). Academic Press, London and New York.

Coombs, R.H. and Kenkel, W.F. (1966). Sex differences in dating aspirations and satisfaction with computer-selected partners. *Journal of Marriage and the Family*, **28**, 62–66.

Cornell, E.H. (1974). Infants' discrimination of photographs of faces following redundant presentations. *Journal of Experimental Child Psychology*, **18**, 98–106.

Courtois, M.R. and Mueller, J.H. (1979). Processing multiple physical features in facial recognition. *Bulletin of the Psychonomic Society*, **14**, 74–76.

Covey, K., Scott, B., Miller, S., Adkins, D. and Williams, D. (1978). The impact of environmental surroundings on the witnesses' identification of a suspect. Unpublished manuscript, Department of Psychology, Oklahoma State University.

Craik, F.I.M. (1973). A levels of analysis view of memory. *In* "Communication and Affect: Language and Thought" (P. Pliner, L. Krames and T. Alloway, Eds). Academic Press, New York and London.

Craik, F.I.M. and Lockhart, R.S. (1972). Levels of processing: A framework for memory research. *Journal of Verbal Learning and Verbal Behaviour*, **11**, 671–684.

Crile, G.W. (1915). "The Origin and Nature of the Emotions. Miscellaneous Papers". W.B. Saunders, Philadelphia.

Cross, J.F. and Cross, J. (1971). Age, sex, race and the perception of facial beauty. *Developmental Psychology*, **5**, 433–439.

Cross, J.F., Cross, J. and Daly, J. (1971). Sex, race, age and beauty as factors in recognition of faces. *Perception and Psychophysics*, **10**, 393–396.

Darnbrough, M. (1977). The use of facial reconstruction methods by the police. Paper presented at the annual conference of the British Psychologica. Society, Exeter, Devon.

Darwin, C. (1872). "The Expression of the Emotions in Man and Animals" (2nd ed.) (Popular edition, 1904). John Murray, London.

Darwin, C. (1877). A biographical sketch of an infant. *Mind*, **2**, 285–294.

Dashiell, J.F. (1927). A new method of measuring reactions to facial expression of emotion. *Psychological Bulletin*, **24**, 174–175.

Davies, G.M. (1978). Face recognition: Issues and theories. *In* "Practical Aspects of Memory" (M.M. Gruneberg, P.E. Morris and R.N. Sykes, Eds) Academic Press, London.

Davies, G.M. and Christie, D.F.M. (in press). Face recall: An examination of some factors limiting composite production accuracy. *Journal of Applied Psychology*.

Davies, G.M., Ellis, H.D. and Shepherd, J.W. (1977). Cue saliency in faces as assessed by the Photofit technique. *Perception*, **6**, 263–269.

Davies, G.M., Ellis, H.D. and Shepherd, J.W. (1978a). Face identification: The influence of delay upon accuracy of Photofit construction. *Journal of Police Science and Administration*, **6**, 35–42.

Davies, G.M., Ellis, H.D. and Shepherd, J.W. (1978b). Face recognition accuracy as a function of mode of representation. *Journal of Applied Psychology*, **63**, 180–187.

Davies, G.M., Shepherd, J.W. and Ellis, H.D. (1978c). Remembering faces: Acknowledging our limitations. *Journal of the Forensic Science Society*, **18** 19–24.

Davies, G.M., Shepherd, J.W. and Ellis, H.D. (1979a). Effects of interpolated mugshot exposure on accuracy of eyewitness identification. *Journal of Applied Psychology*, **64**, 232–237.

Davies, G.M., Shepherd, J.W. and Ellis, H.D. (1979b). Similarity effects in face recognition. *American Journal of Psychology*, **92**, 507–523.

Davitz, J.R. (1964). A review of research concerned with facial and vocal expressions of emotion. *In* "The Communication of Emotional Meaning" (J.R. Davitz, Ed.). McGraw-Hill, New York.

Davitz, J.R. (1969). "The Language of Emotion". Academic Press, New York and London.

Davitz, J.R. (1970). A dictionary and grammar of emotion. *In* "Feelings and Emotion. The Loyola Symposium" (M.B. Arnold, Ed.). Academic Press, New York and London.

Décarie, T. (Ed.) (1974). "The Infant's Reaction to Strangers". International Universities Press, New York.

Deffenbacher, K.A., Brown, E.L. and Sturgill, W. (1978). Some predictors of eyewitness memory accuracy. *In* "Practical Aspects of Memory" (M.M. Gruneberg, P.E. Morris and R.N. Sykes, Eds). Academic Press, London.

Deffenbacher, K.A., Leu, J.R. and Brown, E.L. (1981). Memory for faces: Testing method, encoding strategy and confidence. *American Journal of Psychology*, **94**, 13–26.

Deffenbacher, K.A., Leu, J.R. and Brown, E.L. (in press). Remembering faces and their immediate context. *Journal of Applied Psychology*.

Della Riccia, G. and Iserles, A. (1977). Automatic identification of pictures of human faces. Proceedings of the 1977 Carnahan Conference on Crime Countermeasures. Lexington, Kentucky.

Della Riccia, G. and Iserles, A. (1979). PATREC: A computer programme for automatic identification of patterns. Manuscript submitted for publication, 1979.

Dent, H.R. (1977). Stress as a factor influencing person recognition in identification parades. *Bulletin of the British Psychological Society*, **30**, 339–340.

Dent, H.R. and Stephenson, G.M. (1978). Identification evidence: Experimental investigations of factors affecting the reliability of juvenile and adult witnesses. *In* "Psychology, Law and Legal Processes" (D. Farrington, K. Hawkins and S. Lloyd-Bostock, Eds). Macmillan, London.

De Renzi, E. and Spinnler, H. (1966). Visual recognition in patients with unilateral cerebral disease. *Journal of Nervous and Mental Disease*, **142**, 513–525.

De Renzi, E., Faglioni, P. and Scotti, G. (1969). Impairment of memory for position following brain damage. *Cortex*, **5**, 274–284.

Devlin, Lord Patrick (1976). "Report to the Secretary of State for the Home Department of the Departmental Committee on Evidence of Identification in Criminal Cases". Her Majesty's Stationery Office, London.

Diamond, R. and Carey, S. (1977). Developmental changes in the representation of faces. *Journal of Experimental Child Psychology*, **23**, 1–22.

Dickey, E.C. and Knower, F.G. (1941). A note on some ethnological differences in recognition of simulated expressions of the emotions. *American Journal of Sociology*, **47**, 190–193.

Dirks, J. and Gibson, E. (1977). Infants' perception of similarity between live people and their photographs. *Child Development*, **48**, 124–130.

Dittmann, A.T. (1972). "Interpersonal Messages of Emotion". Springer, New York.

Dodwell, P.C. (1971). "Perceptual Processing: Stimulus Equivalence and Pattern Recognition". Appleton-Century-Crofts, New York.

Donini, F. (1939). Su di un caso di aprasia constructiva con grave disorientamento esospaziale e perdita della facolta del riconiscimento della fisinomia della persone. *Note Psichiatre*, **68**, 469–485.

Dorfman, D., Keeve, S. and Saslow, C. (1971). Ethnic identification: A signal detection analysis. *Journal of Personality and Social Psychology*, **18**, 373–389.

Drag, R.M. and Shaw, M.E. (1967). Factors influencing the communication of emotional intent by facial expressions. *Psychonomic Science*, **8**, 137–138.

Dricker, J., Butters, N., Berman, G., Samuels, I. and Carey, S. (1978). The recognition and encoding of faces by alcoholic Korsakoff and right hemisphere patients. *Neuropsychologia*, **16**, 683–695.

Duchenne, G.B. (1862). "Mécanisme de la Physionomie Humaine, ou Analyse Electro-physiologique de l'Expression des Passions". Jules Renouard, Paris.

Dukes, W.F. and Bevan, W. (1967). Stimulus variation and repetition in the acquisition of naming responses. *Journal of Experimental Psychology*, **74**, 178–181.

Duncan, F.H. and Laughery, K.R. (1977). The Minolta Montage Synthesiser as a facial image generating device. Mug File Project (Report Number UHMUG-4), University of Houston, Houston, Texas.

Dusenbury, D. and Knower, F.H. (1938). Experimental studies of the symbolism of action and voice. I. A study of the specificity of meaning in facial expression. *Quarterly Journal of Speech*, **24**, 424–435.

Duval, G.C. (1979). An analysis of strategies in remembering and generating faces. Mug File Project (Report Number UHMUG-5), University of Houston, Houston, Texas.

Egan, D., Pittner, M. and Goldstein, A.G. (1977). Eyewitness identification—Photographs vs. live models. *Law and Human Behavior*, **1**, 199–206.

Eibl-Eibesfeldt, I. (1972). Similarities and differences between cultures in expressive movements. *In* "Non-verbal Communication" (R.A. Hinde Ed.). Cambridge University Press, Cambridge.

Eibl-Eibesfeldt, I. (1973). The expressive behaviour of the deaf-and-blind-born. *In* "Social Communication and Movement" (M. Von Cranach and I Vine, Eds). Academic Press, New York.

Eiser, J.R. and Stroebe, W. (1972). "Categorization and Social Judgement" Academic Press, London and New York.

Ekman, G. (1955). Dimensions of emotion. *Acta Psychologica*, **11**, 279–288.

Ekman, P. (1972). Universals and cultural differences in facial expressions o. emotion. *In* "Nebraska Symposium on Motivation, 1971" (J. Cole, Ed.) University of Nebraska Press, Lincoln.

Ekman, P. (1973a). "Darwin and Facial Expression. A Century of Research ir Review". Academic Press, New York and London.

Ekman, P. (1973b). Cross-cultural studies of facial expression. *In* "Darwir and Facial Expression. A Century of Research in Review" (P. Ekman, Ed.) Academic Press, New York and London.

Ekman, P. and Friesen, W.V. (1968). Nonverbal behavior in psychotherap" research. *In* "Research in Psychotherapy" (J.M. Schlien, Ed.), vol. 3 American Psychological Association, Washington.

Ekman, P. and Friesen, W.V. (1969a). Nonverbal leakage and clues to decep tion. *Psychiatry*, **32**, 88–106.

Ekman, P. and Friesen, W.V. (1969b). The repertoire of nonverbal behaviour: Categories, origins, usage and coding. *Semiotica*, 1, 49–98.

Ekman, P. and Friesen, W.V. (1971). Constants across cultures in the face and emotion. *Journal of Personality and Social Psychology*, 17, 124–129.

Ekman, P. and Friesen, W.V. (1975). "Unmasking the Face. A Guide to Recognising Emotions from Facial Clues". Prentice Hall, Englewood Cliffs, New Jersey.

Ekman, P. and Friesen, W.V. (1976). Measuring facial movement. *Environmental Psychology and Nonverbal Behaviour*, 1, 56–75.

Ekman, P. and Oster, H. (1979). Facial expressions of emotion. *Annual Review of Psychology*, 30, 527–554.

Ekman, P., Sorenson, E.R. and Friesen, W.V. (1969). Pan-cultural elements in facial displays of emotion. *Science*, 164, 86–88.

Ekman, P., Friesen, W.V. and Tomkins, S.S. (1971). Facial affect scoring techniques (FAST): A first validity study. *Semiotica*, 3, 37–58.

Ekman, P., Friesen, W.V. and Ellsworth, P. (1972). "Emotion in the Human Face: Guidelines for Research and an Integration of Findings". Pergamon Press, New York.

Ellinwood, E.H. (1969). Perception of faces. *Psychiatric Quarterly*, 43, 622–646.

Elliott, D.N. and Wittenberg, B.H. (1955). Accuracy of identification of Jewish and non-Jewish photographs. *Journal of Abnormal and Social Psychology*, 51, 339–341.

Elliott, E.S., Wills, E.J. and Goldstein, A.G. (1973). The effects of discrimination training on the recognition of white and oriental faces. *Bulletin of the Psychonomic Society*, 2, 71–73.

Ellis, H.D. (1975). Recognising faces. *British Journal of Psychology*, 66, 409–426.

Ellis, H.D. and Deregowski, J.B. (1981). Within-race and between-race recognition of transformed and untransformed faces. *American Journal of Psychology*, 94, 27–35.

Ellis, H.D. and Shepherd, J.W. (1975). Recognition of upright and inverted faces presented in the left and right visual fields. *Cortex*, 11, 3–7.

Ellis, H.D., Shepherd, J.W. and Bruce, A. (1973). The effects of age and sex upon adolescents' recognition of faces. *Journal of Genetic Psychology*, 123, 173–174.

Ellis, H.D., Deregowski, J.B. and Shepherd, J.W. (1975a). Descriptions of white and black faces by white and black subjects. *International Journal of Psychology*, 10, 119–123.

Ellis, H.D., Shepherd, J.W. and Davies, G.M. (1975b). An investigation of the use of the Photofit technique for recalling faces. *British Journal of Psychology*, 66, 29–37.

Ellis, H.D., Davies, G.M. and Shepherd, J.W. (1976). An investigation of the Photofit system for recalling faces. Final report to the Social Science Research Council, Grant number HR 3123/1.

Ellis, H.D., Davies, G.M. and Shepherd, J.W. (1977). Experimental studies of face identification. *National Journal of Criminal Defense*, 3, 219–234.

Ellis, H.D., Davies, G.M. and Shepherd, J.W. (1978a). A critical examination of the Photofit system for recalling faces. *Ergonomics,* **21,** 297–307.

Ellis, H.D., Davies, G.M. and Shepherd, J.W. (1978b). Remembering pictures of real and "unreal" faces: Some practical and theoretical considerations. *British Journal of Psychology,* **69,** 467–474.

Ellis, H.D., Davies, G.M. and McMurran, M.M. (1979a). Recall of white and black faces by white and black witnesses using the Photofit system. *Human Factors,* **21,** 55–59.

Ellis, H.D., Shepherd, J.W. and Davies, G.M. (1979b). Identification of familiar and unfamiliar faces from internal and external features: Some implications for theories of face recognition. *Perception,* **8,** 431–439.

Ellis, H.D., Shepherd, J.W. and Davies, G.M. (1980). The deterioration of verbal descriptions of faces over different delay intervals. *Journal of Police Science and Administration,* **8,** 101–106.

Emde, R.N., Kligman, D.H., Reich, J.H. and Wade, T.D. (1978). Emotional expression in infancy: I. Initial studies of social signalling and an emergent model. *In* "The Development of Affect" (M. Lewis and L.A. Rosenblum Eds). Plenum Press, New York.

Engen, J., Levy, N. and Schlosberg, H. (1957). A new series of facial expressions. *American Psychologist,* **12,** 264–266.

Engen, T., Levy, N. and Schlosberg, H. (1958). The dimensional analysis of a new series of facial expressions. *Journal of Experimental Psychology,* **55,** 454–458.

Erdelyi, M.H. and Becker, J. (1974). Hypermnesia for pictures. Incremental memory for pictures but not for words in multiple recall trials. *Cognitive Psychology,* **6,** 159–171.

Ermiane, R. and Gergerian, E. (1978). "Atlas of Facial Expressions". L Pensée Universelle, Paris.

Exline, R. (1963). Explorations in the process of person perception: Visual interaction in relating to competition, sex and need for affiliation. *Journal of Personality,* **31,** 1–20.

Eysenck, M.W. (1978). Levels of processing: A critique. *British Journal of Psychology,* **69,** 157–169.

Fagan, J.F. (1972). Infants' recognition memory for faces. *Journal of Experimental Psychology,* **14,** 453–476.

Fagan, J.F. (1973). Recognition memory and forgetting. *Journal of Experimental Psychology,* **16,** 424–450.

Fagan, J.F. (1976). Infants' recognition of invariant features of faces. *Child Development,* **47,** 627–638.

Fagan, J.F. (1977). Infant recognition memory: Studies in forgetting. *Child Development,* **48,** 68–78.

Fagan, J.F. (1979). The origins of facial pattern recognition. *In* "Psychological Development in Infancy: Image to Intention" (M. Bornstein and W Kessen, Eds). L. Erlbaum, Hillsdale, New Jersey.

Fantz, R.L. (1966). Pattern discrimination and selective attention as determinants of perceptual development from birth. *In* "Perceptual Develop ment in Children" (A. Kidd and J.L. Rivoire, Eds). International Universities Press, New York.

Farnsworth, P.R. (1943). Attempts to distinguish Chinese from Japanese college students through observations of face-photographs. *Journal of Psychology*, 16, 99–106.

Farnsworth, P.R. (1965). A social effect on the perception of facial resemblance. *Journal of Social Psychology*, 65, 221–223.

Faust, C. (1955). "Die Zerebralen Herdstörungen bei Hinterhauptsverletzungen und ihre Beurteilung". G. Thieme Verlag, Stuttgart.

Feinman, S. and Entwistle, D.R. (1976). Children's ability to recognize other children's faces. *Child Development*, 47, 506–510.

Feleky, A.M. (1914). The expression of the emotions. *Psychological Review*, 21, 33–41.

Feleky, A.M. (1924). "Feelings and Emotions". Pioneer Press Company, New York.

Fernberger, S.W. (1927). Six more Piderit faces. *American Journal of Psychology*, 39, 162–166.

Fisher, G.H. (1977). The "Face-fit" system. Paper presented at the annual conference of the British Psychological Society, Exeter, Devon.

Fisher, G.H. and Cox, R.L. (1975). Recognizing human faces. *Applied Ergonomics*, 6, 104–109.

Fitzgerald, H.P. (1968). Autonomic pupillary reflex activity during early infancy and its relations to social and nonsocial visual stimuli. *Journal of Experimental Child Psychology*, 6, 470–482.

Flavell, H. (1977). "Cognitive Development". Prentice-Hall, Englewood Cliffs, New Jersey.

Fleishman, J.J., Buckley, M.L., Klosinsky, M.J., Smith, N. and Tuck, B. (1976). Judged attractiveness in recognition memory for women's faces. *Perceptual and Motor Skills*, 43, 709–710.

Flin, R.H. (1979). Personal communication (July).

Flin, R.H. (1980). Age effects in children's memory for unfamiliar faces. *Developmental Psychology*, 16, 373–374.

Fogel, A. (1977). Temporal organization in mother–infant face-to-face interaction. *In* "Studies in Mother–Infant Interaction" (H.R. Shaffer, Ed.). Academic Press, New York and London.

Fontenot, D.J. (1973). Visual field differences in the recognition of verbal and nonverbal stimuli in man. *Journal of Comparative and Physiological Psychology*, 85, 564–569.

Forbes, D.D.S. (1975). An investigation into pictorial memory with particular reference to facial recognition. PhD thesis, Aberdeen University.

Freedman, J. and Haber, R.N. (1974). One reason why we rarely forget a face. *Bulletin of the Psychonomic Society*, 3, 107–109.

Friedman, M.P., Reed, S.K. and Carterette, E.C. (1971). Feature saliency and recognition memory for schematic faces. *Perception and Psychophysics*, 10, 47–50.

Frijda, N.H. (1953). The understanding of facial expression of emotion. *Acta Psychologica*, 9, 294–362.

Frijda, N.H. (1969). Recognition of emotion. *In* "Advances in Experimental Social Psychology" (L. Berkowitz, Ed.), vol. 4. Academic Press, New York.

Frijda, N.H. (1970). Emotion and recognition of emotion. *In* "Feelings and Emotion. The Loyola Symposium" (M.B. Arnold, Ed.). Academic Press, New York and London.

Frijda, N.H. (1973). The relation between emotion and expression. *In* "Social Communication and Movement" (M. Von Cranach and I. Vine, Eds). Academic Press, London and New York.

Frijda, N.H. and Philipszoon, E. (1963). Dimensions of recognition of expression. *Journal of Abnormal and Social Psychology*, **66**, 45–51.

Frisby, J.P. (1979). "Seeing, Illusion, Brain and Mind". Oxford University Press, Oxford.

Frois-Wittmann, J. (1930). The judgment of facial expression. *Journal of Experimental Psychology*, **13**, 113–151.

Gallup, G.G. (1977). Self-recognition in primates—A comparative approach to the bidirectional properties of consciousness. *American Psychologist*, **32**, 329–338.

Galper, R.E. (1970). Recognition of faces in photographic negative. *Psychonomic Science*, **19**, 207–208.

Galper, R.E. (1973). "Functional race membership" and recognition of faces. *Perceptual and Motor Skills*, **37**, 455–462.

Galper, R.E. and Hochburg, J. (1971). Recognition memory for photographs of faces. *American Journal of Psychology*, **84**, 351–354.

Galton, F. (1879). Generic images. *Proceedings of the Royal Institution*, **9**, 161–170.

Ganz, L. (1978). Innate and environmental factors in the development of visual form perception. *In* "Handbook of Sensory Physiology" (R. Held, H.W. Leibowitz and H.L. Teuber, Eds), vol. 8. Springer-Verlag, Berlin.

Garneau, M.J.P. (1973). The visual perception of facial images. PhD thesis, University of London.

Gates, G.S. (1923). An experimental study of the growth of social perception. *Journal of Educational Psychology*, **14**, 449–461.

Geffen, G., Bradshaw, J.L. and Wallace, G. (1971). Interhemispheric effects on reaction time to verbal and nonverbal visual stimuli. *Journal of Experimental Psychology*, **87**, 415–422.

Geschwind, N. (1979). Specializations of the human brain. *Scientific American*, **241**, 158–168.

Gilbert, C. and Bakan, P. (1973). Visual asymmetry in perception of faces. *Neuropsychologia*, **11**, 355–362.

Gillenson, M.L. (1974). The interactive generation of facial images on a CRT using a heuristic strategy. Report to the National Science Foundation.

Gillenson, M.L. and Chandrasekaran, B. (1975). A heuristic strategy for developing human facial images on a CRT. *Pattern Recognition*, **7**, 187–196.

Gitter, A.G., Black, H. and Mostofsky, D. (1972a). Race and sex in the perception of emotion. *Journal of Social Issues*, **28**, 63–78.

Gitter, A.G., Kozel, N.J. and Mostofsky, D.I. (1972b). Perception of emotion: The role of race, sex and presentation mode. *Journal of Social Psychology*, **88**, 213–222.

Gladstones, W.H. (1962). A multidimensional study of facial expression of emotion. *Australian Journal of Psychology*, **14**, 95–100.

Gloning, K. and Quatember, R. (1966). Methodischer Beitrag zur Untersuchung der Prosopagnosie. *Neuropsychologia*, **4**, 133–141.

Gloning, K., Haub, G. and Quatember, R. (1967). Standardisierung einer Untersuchungsmethode der sogenannten "Prosopagnosie". *Neuropsychologia*, **5**, 99–101.

Going, M. and Read, J.D. (1974). Effects of uniqueness, sex of subject and sex of photograph on facial recognition. *Perceptual and Motor Skills*, **39**, 109–110.

Goldman, P.S. (1972). Developmental determinants of cortical plasticity. *Acta Neurobiologiae Experimentalis*, **32**, 495–511.

Goldstein, A.G. (1965). Learning of inverted and normally oriented faces in children and adults. *Psychonomic Science*, **3**, 447–448.

Goldstein, A.G. (1975). Recognition of inverted photographs of faces by children and adults. *Journal of Genetic Psychology*, **127**, 109–123.

Goldstein, A.G. (1977). The fallibility of the eyewitness. Psychological evidence. *In* "Psychology in the Legal Process" (B.D. Sales, Ed.). Spectrum, New York.

Goldstein, A.G. (1979a). Race-related variation of facial features. Anthropometric data I. *Bulletin of the Psychonomic Society*, **13**, 187–190.

Goldstein, A.G. (1979b). Facial feature variation: Anthropometric data II. *Bulletin of the Psychonomic Society*, **13**, 191–193.

Goldstein, A.G. and Chance, J.E. (1964). Recognition of children's faces. *Child Development*, **35**, 129–136.

Goldstein, A.G. and Chance, J.E. (1971). Visual recognition memory for complex configurations. *Perception and Psychophysics*, **9**, 237–241.

Goldstein, A.G. and Chance, J. (1976). Measuring psychological similarity of faces. *Bulletin of the Psychonomic Society*, **7**, 407–408.

Goldstein, A.G. and Chance, J.E. (1978a). Intra-individual consistency in visual recognition memory. Paper presented at the convention of the American Psychological Association, Toronto.

Goldstein, A.G. and Chance, J. (1978b). Judging face similarity in own and other races. *Journal of Psychology*, **98**, 185–193.

Goldstein, A.G. and Chance, J.E. (1980). Memory for faces and schema theory. *Journal of Psychology*, **105**, 47–59.

Goldstein, A.G., Johnson, K.S. and Chance, J.E. (1979). Does fluency of face description imply superior face recognition? *Bulletin of the Psychonomic Society*, **13**, 15–18.

Goldstein, A.G. and Mackenberg, E.J. (1966). Recognition of human faces from isolated facial features: A developmental study. *Psychonomic Science*, **6**, 149–150.

Goldstein, A.G. and Papageorge, J. (1980). Judgments of facial attractiveness in the absence of eye movements. *Bulletin of the Psychonomic Society*, **15**, 269–270.

Goldstein, A.G., Stephenson, B. and Chance, J.E. (1977). Face recognition memory: Distribution of false alarms. *Bulletin of the Psychonomic Society*, **9**, 416–418.

Goldstein, A.J., Harmon, L.D. and Lesk, A.B. (1971). Identification of human faces. *Proceedings of the IEEE*, **59**, 748–760.

Goldstein, A.J., Harmon, L.D. and Lesk, A.B. (1972). Man-machine interaction in human-face identification. *The Bell System Technical Journal*, **51**, 399–427.

Gombrich, E.H. (1972). The mask and the face: The perception of physiognomic likeness in life and in art. *In* "Art, Perception and Reality" (E.H. Gombrich, J. Hochberg and M. Black, Eds). John Hopkins University Press, Baltimore.

Goodenough, F.L. (1931). The expression of emotions in infancy. *Child Development*, **2**, 96–101.

Goodrich, G.H. (1975). Should experts be allowed to testify concerning eyewitness testimony in criminal cases? *Judges' Journal*, **14**, 70–71.

Gordon, R. (1949). An investigation into some of the factors that favour the formation of stereotyped images. *British Journal of Psychology*, **39**, 156–167.

Gorsen, C.C., Sarty, M. and Wu, R.W.K. (1975). Visual following and pattern discrimination of face-like stimuli by newborn infants. *Pediatrics*, **56**, 544–549.

Grant, E.C. (1969). Human facial expression. *Man*, **4**, 525–536.

Grant, E.C. (1970). An ethological description of non-verbal behaviour during interviews. *In* "Behaviour Studies in Psychiatry" (S.J. Hutt and C. Hutt, Eds). Pergamon, Oxford.

Green, D.M. and Swets, J.A. (1966). "Signal-detection Theory and Psychophysics". Wiley, New York.

Greenspan, S., Barenboim, C. and Chandler, M.J. (1976). Empathy and pseudo-empathy: The affective judgments of first and third-graders. *Journal of Genetic Psychology*, **129**, 77–88.

Grier, J.B. (1971). Nonparametric indexes for sensitivity and bias: Computing formulas. *Psychological Bulletin*, **75**, 424–429.

Groner, R. (1967). Dimensionen der Wahrenhmung von Gesichtern. *Zeitschrift für experimentelle und angewandte Psychologie*, **14**, 135–154.

Gross, N.M. (1972). Hemispheric specialization for processing of visually presented verbal and spatial stimuli. *Perception and Psychophysics*, **12**, 357–363.

Haaf, R.A. (1977). Visual responses to complex facelike patterns by 15- and 20-week-old infants. *Developmental Psychology*, **13**, 77–78.

Haaf, R.A. and Bell, R.Q. (1964). A facial dimension in visual discrimination by human infants. *Child Development*, **38**, 893–899.

Hagen, M.A., Perkins, D. and Kennedy, P.A. (1978). A refutation of the super-fidelity hypothesis for caricatures. Paper presented at the annual meeting of the Eastern Psychological Association, Washington D.C., March, 1978.

Hainline; L. (1978). Developmental changes in visual scanning of face and nonface patterns by infants. *Journal of Experimental Child Psychology*, 25, 90–115.

Haith, M.M. (1978). Visual competence in early infancy. *In* "Handbook of Sensory Physiology" (R. Held, H.W. Leibowitz and H.L. Teuber, Eds), vol. 8. Springer-Verlag, Berlin.

Hall, D.F. (1976). Obtaining eyewitness identifications in criminal investigations: Applications of social and experimental psychology. PhD dissertation, Ohio State University.

Hall, D.F. (1977). Obtaining eyewitness identifications in criminal investigations: Two experiments and some comments on the Zeitgeist in forensic psychology. Paper presented at the American Psychology-Law Conference. Snowmass, Colorado.

Hall, D.F. and Ostrom, T.M. (1975). Accuracy of eyewitness identification after biasing or unbiased instructions. Paper presented at the meeting of the American Psychological Association, Chicago.

Hamilton, M.L. (1973). Imitative behavior and expressive ability in facial expression of emotion. *Developmental Psychology*, 8, 138.

Hamsher, K. de S., Levin, H.S. and Benton, A.L. (1979). Facial recognition in patients with focal brain lesions. *Archives of Neurology*, 36, 837–839.

Hanawalt, N.G. (1944). The role of the upper and lower parts of the face as a basis for judging facial expressions: II. In posed expressions and "candid-camera" pictures. *Journal of General Psychology*, 31, 23–36.

Harmon, L.D. (1971). Some aspects of recognition of human faces. *In* "Pattern Recognition in Biological and Technical Systems" (O.J. Gruesser and R. Klinke, Eds). Springer-Verlag, New York.

Harmon, L.D. (1973). The recognition of faces. *Scientific American*, 229, 71–82.

Harmon, L.D. and Hunt, W.F. (1977). Automatic recognition of human face profiles. *Computer Graphics and Image Processing*, 6, 135–156.

Harmon, L.D. and Julesz, B. (1973). Masking in visual recognition: Effects of two dimensional filtered noise. *Science*, 180, 1194–1197.

Harmon, L.D., Kno, S.C., Ramig, P.F. and Randkiv, U. (1978). Identification of human face profiles by computer. *Pattern Recognition*, 10, 301–312.

Harmon, L.D., Khan, M.K., Lasch, R. and Ramig, P.F. (1979). Machine identification of human faces. *Pattern Recognition*, 13, 97–110.

Harper, R.G., Wiens, A.N. and Matarazzo, J.D. (1978). "Nonverbal Communication: The State of the Art". Wiley, New York.

Harris, G.J. and Fleer, R.E. (1972). Recognition memory for faces by retardates and normals. *Perceptual and Motor Skills*, 34, 755–758.

Harris, G.J. and Fleer, R.E. (1973). Serial recognition memory by retardates of half or whole faces in two orientations. *Perceptual and Motor Skills*, 36, 476–478.

Hastie, R., Loftus, E.F., Penrod, S., and Winkler, J.D. (1979). The reliability of eyewitness testimony: Review of the psychological literature. Unpublished manuscript, Harvard University.

Hastorf, A.H., Osgood, C.E. and Ono, H. (1966). The semantics of facial expressions and the prediction of the meanings of stereoscopically fused facial expressions. *Scandinavian Journal of Psychology*, 7, 179–188.

Hécaen, H. and Angelergues, R. (1962). Agnosia for faces. *Archives of Neurology*, 7, 92–100.

Hécaen, H. and Angelergues, R. (1963). "La Cécité Psychique". Masson et Cie, Paris.

Hécaen, H., Ajuriaguerra, J. De, Magis, C. and Angelergues, R. (1952). Le problème de l'agnosie des physionomies. *Encéphale*, 41, 322–355.

Hécaen, H., Angelergues, R., Bernhardt, C. and Chiarelli, J. (1957). Essai de distinction des modalités clinques de l'agnosie des physionomies. *Revue Neurologique*, 96, 125–144.

Heidenhain, A. (1927). Beitrag zur Kenntnis der Seelenblindheit. *Monatsschrift für Psychiatrie und Neurologie*, 65, 61–116.

Helson, H. (1964). "Adaptation-level Theory: An Experimental and Systematic Approach to Behaviour". Harper and Row, New York.

Herzka, N.S. (1979). "Gesicht und Sprache des Säuglings". Schwabe, Basel.

Hilgendorf, E.L. and Irving, B.L. (1978). False positive identification. *Medicine, Science and the Law*, 18, 255–262.

Hilliard, R.D. (1973). Hemispheric laterality effects on a facial recognition task in normal subjects. *Cortex*, 9, 246–258.

Himmelfarb, S. (1966). Studies in the perception of ethnic group members. I. Accuracy, response bias and anti-Semitism. *Journal of Personality and Social Psychology*, 4, 347–355.

Hirschberg, N., Jones, L.E. and Haggerty, M. (1978). What's in a face? Individual differences in face perception. *Journal of Research in Personality*, 12, 488–499.

Hjortsjö, C-H. (1970). "Man's Face and Mimic Language". (Translated by W.F. Salisbury). Nordens Boktryckeri, Malmö.

Hoff, H. and Pötzl, O. (1937). Über eine optisch-agnostische Störung des "Physiognomie-Gedächtnisses". *Zeitschrift für die Gesamte Neurologie und Psychiatrie*, 159, 367–395.

Hoffman, C. and Kagan, S. (1977). Field dependence and facial recognition. *Perceptual and Motor Skills*, 44, 119–124.

Hoffman, M.L. (1975). Developmental synthesis of affect and cognition and its implications for altruistic motivation. *Developmental Psychology*, 11, 607–622.

Hoffman, M.L. (1978a). Empathy, its development and prosocial implications. *In* "Nebraska Symposium on Motivation, 1977" (C.B. Keasy, Ed.). University of Nebraska Press, Lincoln.

Hoffman, M.L. (1978b). Toward a theory of empathic arousal and development. *In* "The Development of Affect" (H. Lewis and L.A. Rosenblum, Eds). Plenum Press, New York.

Hogarth, W. (1953). "The Analysis of Beauty" (J. Burke, Ed.). Oxford University Press, Oxford.

Honkavaara, S. (1961). The psychology of expression. Dimensions in human perception. *British Journal of Psychology, Monograph Supplement*, 32, 1–96.

Howells, T.H. (1938). A study of ability to recognise faces. *Journal of Abnormal and Social Psychology*, **33**, 124–127.

Hoyenga, K.B. and Hoyenga, K.T. (1979). "The Question of Sex Differences". Little, Brown and Company, Boston.

Hubel, D.H. and Weisel, T.N. (1970). The period of susceptibility to the physiological effect of unilateral eye closure in kittens. *Journal of Physiology*, **206**, 419–436.

Hulin, W.S. and Katz, D. (1935). The Frois-Wittman pictures of facial expression. *Journal of Experimental Psychology*, **18**, 482–498.

Hurwitz, D., Wiggins, N.H. and Jones, L.E. (1975). A semantic differential for facial attribution: The face differential. *Bulletin of Psychonomic Society*, **6**, 370–372.

Hyde, T.S. and Jenkins, J.J. (1969). The differential effects of incidental tasks on the organization of recall of a list of highly associated words. *Journal of Experimental Psychology*, **82**, 472–481.

Iliffe, A.H. (1960). A study of preferences in feminine beauty. *British Journal of Psychology*, **51**, 267–273.

Izard, C.E. (1971). "The Face of Emotion". Appleton-Century Crofts, New York.

Izard, C.E. (1979). Emotions as motivations: An evolutionary-developmental perspective. *In* "Nebraska Symposium on Motivation, 1978" (R.A. Dienstbier, Ed.). University of Nebraska Press, Lincoln.

Jackson, R.L. (1967). "Occupied with Crime". Harrap, London.

Jacobson, S.W. (1979). Matching behavior in the young infant. *Child Development*, **50**, 425–430.

Jahoda, G. (1954). Political attitudes and judgements of other people. *Journal of Abnormal and Social Psychology*, **49**, 330–334.

Jenness, A. (1932a). The recognition of facial expressions of emotions. *Psychological Bulletin*, **29**, 324–350.

Jenness, A. (1932b). Differences in the recognition of facial expression of emotion. *Journal of General Psychology*, **7**, 192–196.

Jolly, A. (1972). "The Evolution of Primate Behavior". Macmillan, New York.

Jones, B. (1977). Beauty: 6. *Sunday Times*, December 11, pp. 74–75.

Jones, B. (1979). Lateral asymmetry in testing long-term memory for faces. *Cortex*, **15**, 183–186.

Jones, E.E. and Kohler, R. (1958). The effects of plausibility on the learning of controversial statements. *Journal of Abnormal and Social Psychology*, **57**, 315–320.

Jones, L.E. and Hirschberg, N. (1975). What's in a face? Individual differences in facial perception. Paper presented at the convention of the American Psychological Association, Chicago.

Jones, L.E., Hirschberg, N. and Rothman, J. (with R. Malpass) (1976). The face atlas. Anthropometric, cosmetic, and physiognomic measurements of 200 male faces. Report (No. 1) to the National Science Foundation.

Kaess, W.A. and Witryol, S.L. (1955). Memory for names and faces: A characteristic of social intelligence? *Journal of Applied Psychology*, **39**, 457–462.

Kagan, J. and Klein, R.E. (1973). Cross cultural perspectives on early development. *American Psychologist*, **28**, 947–961.

Kanner, L. (1931). Judging emotions from facial expressions. *Psychological Monographs*, **41**, No. 3 (whole No. 186), 1–91.

Kauranne, U. (1964). Qualitative factors of facial expression. *Scandinavian Journal of Psychology*, **5**, 136–142.

Kaya, Y. and Kobayashi, K. (1972). A basic study on human face recognition. *In* "Frontiers of Pattern Recognition" (S. Watanabe, Ed.). Academic Press, New York.

Kellog, W.N. and Eagleson, B.M. (1931). The growth of social perception in different social groups. *Journal of Educational Psychology*, **22**, 367–375.

King, D. (1971). The use of Photofit 1970–1971: A progress report. *Police Research Bulletin*, No. 18, 40–44.

Kirby v. Illinois (1972). 406. U.S. 682.

Kitson, T., Darnbrough, M. and Shields, E. (1978). Let's face it. *Police Research Bulletin*, No. 30, 7–13.

Klein, D., Moscovitch, M. and Vigna, C. (1976). Attentional mechanisms and perceptual asymmetries in tachistoscopic recognition of words and faces. *Neuropsychologia*, **14**, 55–66.

Kleinhauz, M., Horowitz, I. and Tobin, Y. (1977). The use of hypnosis in police investigation. *Journal of Forensic Science Society*, **17**, 77–80.

Kohler, W. (1940). "Dynamics in Psychology". Liveright, New York.

Kosslyn, S.M. and Pomerantz, J.R. (1977). Imagery, propositions, and the form of internal representations. *Cognitive Psychology*, **9**, 52–76.

Kruskal, J.B. and Wish, M. (1978). "Multidimensional Scaling". Sage, Beverley Hills.

Kuehn, L.L. (1974). Looking down a gun barrel: Person perception and violent crime. *Perceptual and Motor Skills*, **39**, 1159–1164.

Kurucz, J. and Feldmar, G. (1979). Prosopo-affective agnosia as a symptom of cerebral organic disease. *Journal of American Geriatrics Society*, **27**, 225–230.

Kushner, R.I. and Forsyth, G.A. (1977). Judgment of emotion in human face stimuli: An individual differences analysis. *Journal of General Psychology*, **96**, 301–312.

Kwint, L. (1934). Ontogeny of motility of the face. *Child Development*, **5**, 1–12.

LaBarbera, J.D., Izard, C.E., Vietze, P. and Parisi, S.A. (1976). Four- and six-month-old infants' visual responses to joy, anger, and neutral expressions. *Child Development*, **47**, 535–538.

Landis, C. (1924). Studies of emotional reactions. I. A preliminary study of facial expression. *Journal of Experimental Psychology*, **7**, 325–341.

Landis, C. (1929). The interpretation of facial expression in emotion. *Journal of General Psychology*, **2**, 59–72.

Landis, T., Assal, G. and Perret, E. (1979). Opposite cerebral hemispheric superiorities for visual associative processing of emotional facial expressions and objects. *Nature*, **278**, 739–740.

Langdell, T. (1978). Recognition of faces: An approach to the study of autism. *Journal of Child Psychology and Psychiatry*, **19**, 255–268.

Langfeld, H.S. (1918). The judgment of emotions from facial expressions. *Journal of Abnormal Psychology*, **13**, 172–184.

Lasota, J.A. and Bromley, G.W. (1974). "Model Rules for Law Enforcement: Eyewitness Identification". Police Foundation, Washington, D.C.

Laughery, K.R. and Fowler, R.H. (1977). Factors affecting facial recognition. Mug File Project. (Report Number UHMUG-3). University of Houston.

Laughery, K.R. and Fowler, R.F. (1980). Sketch artist and Identikit procedures for recalling faces. *Journal of Applied Psychology*, **65**, 307–316.

Laughery, K.R. and Smith, V.L. (1978). Suspect identification following exposure to sketches and identikit composites. Proceedings of the Human Factors Society 22nd Annual Meeting, Detroit.

Laughery, K.R., Alexander, J.F. and Lane, A.B. (1971). Recognition of human faces: Effects of target exposure time, target position, pose position, and type of photograph. *Journal of Applied Psychology*, **55**, 477–483.

Laughery, K.R., Duval, G.C. and Fowler, R.H. (1977). An analysis of procedures for generating facial images. Mug File Project. (Report Number UHMUG-2). University of Houston.

Laughery, K.R., Fessler, P.K., Lenorovitz, D.R. and Yoblick, D.A. (1974). Time delay and similarity effects in facial recognition. *Journal of Applied Psychology*, **59**, 490–496.

Lavrakas, P.J., Buri, J.R. and Mayzner, M.S. (1976). A perspective on the recognition of other race faces. *Perception and Psychophysics*, **20**, 475–481.

Leehey, S. (1976). Face recognition in children: Evidence for the development of right hemisphere specialization. PhD dissertation, Department of Psychology, Massachusetts Institute of Technology.

Leehey, S.C. and Cahn, A. (1979). Lateral asymmetries in the recognition of words, familiar faces and unfamiliar faces. *Neuropsychologia*, **17**, 619–635.

Leehey, S., Carey, S., Diamond, R. and Cahn, A. (1978). Upright and inverted faces: The right hemisphere knows the difference. *Cortex*, **14**, 411–419.

Lefcourt, G.D. (1978). The blank line-up: An aid to the defense. *Criminal Law Bulletin*, **14**, 428–432.

Leippe, M.R., Wells, G.L. and Ostrom, T.M. (1978). Crime seriousness as a determinant of accuracy in eyewitness identification. *Journal of Applied Psychology*, **63**, 345–351.

Lenorovitz, D.R. (1975). Development of a prototype computer assisted system to be used as an aid in facial recognition tasks. PhD thesis, State University of New York at Buffalo.

Levin, H.S. and Benton, A.L. (1977). Facial recognition in "pseudoneurological" patients. *Journal of Nervous and Mental Disease*, **164**, 135–138.

Levine, F.J. and Tapp, J.L. (1973). The psychology of criminal identification: The gap from Wade to Kirby. *University of Pennsylvania Law Review*, **121**, 1079–1131.

Levitt, E.A. (1964). The relationship between abilities to express emotional meanings vocally and facially. *In* "The Communication of Emotional Meaning" (J.R. Davitz, Ed.). McGraw-Hill, New York.

Levy, J., Trevarthen, C. and Sperry, R.W. (1972). Perception of bilateral chimeric figures following hemispheric deconnection. *Brain*, **95**, 61–78.

Levy, L., Orr, T.B. and Rosenzweig, S. (1960). Judgments of emotion from facial expressions by college students, mental retardates, and mental hospital patients. *Journal of Personality*, **28**, 342–349.

Levy, N. and Schlosberg, H. (1960). Woodworth scale values of the Lightfoot pictures of facial expression. *Journal of Experimental Psychology*, **60**, 121–125.

Lewis, M., Kagan, J. and Kalafat, J. (1966). Patterns of fixation in the young infant. *Child Development*, **37**, 331–341.

Ley, R.G. and Bryden, M.P. (1979). Hemispheric differences in processing emotions and faces. *Brain and Language*, **7**, 127–138.

Lhermitte, F., Chain, F., Escourolle, R., Ducarne, B. and Pillon, B. (1972). Élude anatomo-clinique d'un cas de prosopagnosie. *Revue Neurologique*, **126**, 329–346.

Lhermitte, F. and Pillon, B. (1975). La prosopagnosie, role de l'hemisphere droit dans la perception visuelle (A propos d'un cas consecutif a une lobectomie occipitale droite). *Revue Neurologique*, **131**, 791–812.

Liggett, J. (1974). "The Human Face". Constable, London.

Light, L.L., Kayra-Stuart, F. and Hollander, S. (1979). Recognition memory for typical and unusual faces. *Journal of Experimental Psychology: Human Learning and Memory*, **5**, 212–228.

Lindsay, R.C.L. and Wells, G.L. (1979). What is an eyewitness identification error? The effect of line-up structure depends on the definition of a false identification. Unpublished manuscript, University of Alberta.

Lindsay, R.C.L., Wells, G.L. and Rumpel, C.M. (in press). Can people detect eyewitness-identification accuracy within and across situations? *Journal of Applied Psychology*.

Lindzey, G. and Rogolsky, S. (1950). Prejudice and identification of minority group membership. *Journal of Abnormal and Social Psychology*, **45**, 37–53.

Lindzey, G., Prince, B. and Wright, W. (1952). A study of facial asymmetry. *Journal of Personality*, **21**, 68–84.

Lingoes, J.C. and Roskam, E.E. (1973). A mathematical and empirical study of two multidimensional scaling algorithms. *Psychometrika Monograph Supplement*, **38**, no. 4, part 2.

Lipton, J. (1977). On the psychology of eyewitness testimony. *Journal of Applied Psychology*, **62**, 90–95.

Lissauër, H. (1890). Ein Fall von Seelenblindheit nebst einen Beitrag zur Theorie derselben. *Archive fur Psychiatrie*, **21**, 222–270.

Lockard, J.S., Fahrenbruch, C.E., Smith, J.L. and Morgan, C.J. (1977). Smiling and laughter: Different phyletic origins? *Bulletin of the Psychonomic Society*, **10**, 183–186.

Loftus, E.F. (1975). Leading questions and the eyewitness report. *Cognitive Psychology*, **7**, 560–572.

Loftus, E.F. (1979). "Eyewitness Testimony". Harvard University Press, Cambridge, Massachusetts.

Loftus, E.F. and Palmer, J.C. (1974). Reconstruction of automobile destruction: An example of the interaction between language and memory. *Journal of Verbal Learning & Verbal Behaviour*, **13**, 585–589.

Loftus, E.F. and Zanni, G. (1975). Eyewitness testimony. The influence of the wording of a question. *Bulletin of the Psychonomic Society*, **5**, 86–88.

Loftus, E.F., Miller, D.G. and Burns, H.J. (1978). Semantic integration of verbal information into a visual memory. *Journal of Experimental Psychology: Human Learning and Memory*, **4**, 19–31.

Loftus, G.R. (1972). Eye fixations and recognition memory for pictures. *Cognitive Psychology*, **3**, 525–551.

Luce, T. (1974). Blacks, whites, yellows: They all look alike to me. *Psychology Today*, November, **8**, 105–108.

Luria, A.R. (1968). "The mind of the mnemonist". J. Cape, London.

Luria, S.M. and Strauss, M.S. (1978). Comparison of eye movements over faces in photographic positives and negatives. *Perception*, **7**, 349–358.

Macoby, E.E. and Jacklin, C.N. (1974). "The Psychology of Sex Differences". Stanford University Press, Stanford, California.

MacRae, D. and Trolle, E. (1956). The defect of function in visual agnosia. *Brain*, **79**, 94–110.

Malpass, R.S. (1974). Racial bias in eyewitness identification. Paper presented at the meeting of the American Psychological Association, New Orleans, August, 1974.

Malpass, R.S. (1975). Towards a theoretical basis for understanding differential face recognition. Paper presented at the meeting of the Midwestern Psychological Association, Chicago.

Malpass, R.S. (1979). A cross-cultural face recognition field manual: Description and a validation study. *In* "Cross-cultural Contributions to Psychology" (L.H. Eckensberger, W.J. Lonner and Y.H. Poortinga, Eds). Swets & Zeitlinger, Lisse, The Netherlands.

Malpass, R.S. and Devine, P.G. (1981). Guided memory in eyewitness identification. *Journal of Applied Psychology*, **66**, 343–350.

Malpass, R.S. and Devine, P.G. (in press). Eyewitness identification: lineup instructions and the absence of the offender. *Journal of Applied Psychology*.

Malpass, R.S. and Kravitz, J. (1969). Recognition for faces of own and other race. *Journal of Personality and Social Psychology*, **13**, 330–334.

Malpass, R.S., Lavigueur, H. and Weldon, D.E. (1973). Verbal and visual training in face recognition. *Perception and Psychophysics*, **14**, 285–292.

Mandler, G. (1970). Thought processes, consciousness and stress. *In* "Human Stress and Cognition" (V. Hamilton and D.M. Warburton, Eds). Wiley, Chichester.

Mandler, G. (1980). Recognizing: The judgement of previous occurrence. *Psychological Review*, **87**, 252–271.

Mann, V.A., Diamond, R. and Carey, S. (1979). Development of voice recognition: Parallels with face recognition. *Journal of Experimental Child Psychology*, 27, 153–165.

Marcel, T. and Rajan, P. (1975). Lateral specialization for recognition of words and faces in good and poor readers. *Neuropsychologia*, 13, 489–497.

Marquis, K., Marshall, J. and Oskamp, S. (1972). Testimony validity as a function of question form, atmosphere, and item difficulty. *Journal of Applied Social Psychology*, 2, 167–186.

Marriott, B.M. and Salzen, E.A. (1978). Facial expressions in captive squirrel monkeys (*Saimiri sciureus*). *Folia Primatologica*, 29, 1–18.

Marshall, J. (1966). "Law and Psychology in Conflict". Bobbs-Merrill, New York.

Marshall, J., Marquis, K. and Oskamp, S. (1971). Effects of kind of question and atmosphere of interrogation on accuracy and completeness of testimony. *Harvard Law Review*, 84, 1620–1643.

Martin, J.G. (1964). Racial ethnocentrism and judgement of beauty. *Journal of Social Psychology*, 63, 59–63.

Marx, M.H. and Nelson, J.A. (1974). Sex differences in face-name recognition memory. Paper presented at the annual meeting of the Psychonomic Society, Boston, Massachusetts.

Marzi, C.A. and Berlucchi, G. (1977). Right visual field superiority for accuracy of recognition of famous faces in normals. *Neuropsychologia*, 15, 751–756.

Marzi, C.A., Brizzolara, D., Rizzolatti, G., Umilta, C. and Berlucchi, G. (1974). Left hemisphere superiority for the recognition of well-known faces. *Brain Research*, 66, 358.

Matthews, M.L. (1978). Discrimination of Identi-Kit constructions of faces: Evidence for a dual processing strategy. *Perception and Psychophysics*, 23, 153–161.

Mauldin, M.A. (1978). The effects of composite production, time delay and exposure duration on facial recognition. PhD thesis, University of Houston.

Maurer, D. and Salapatek, P. (1976). Development changes in the scanning of faces by young infants. *Child Development*, 47, 523–527.

Mazanec, N. and McCall, G.J. (1975). Sex, cognitive categories, and observational accuracy. *Psychological Reports*, 37, 987–990.

McCall, G.J., Mazanec, N., Erikson, W.L. and Smith, H.W. (1974). Same-sex recall effects in tests of observational accuracy. *Perceptual and Motor Skills*, 38, 830.

McCall, R.B. and Kagan, J. (1967). Attention in the infant: Effects of complexity, contour, perimeter, and familiarity. *Child Development*, 38, 939–952.

McDonald, H.C. (1960). "The Identi-Kit Manual". Townsend Company, (Identi-Kit Division), Santa-Ana, California.

McDougall, W. (1921). "An Introduction to Social Psychology" (14th edition). Methuen, London.

McGurk, H. (1970). The role of object orientation in infant perception. *Journal of Experimental Child Psychology*, 9, 363–373.

McKelvie, S.J. (1973). The meaningfulness and meaning of schematic faces. *Perception and Psychophysics*, **14**, 343–348.

McKelvie, S.J. (1976). The role of eyes and mouth in recognition memory for faces. *American Journal of Psychology*, **89**, 311–323.

McKelvie, S.J. (1978). Sex differences in facial memory. *In* "Practical Aspects of Memory" (M.M. Gruneberg, P.E. Morris and R.N. Sykes, Eds). Academic Press, London and New York.

Meadows, J.C. (1974). The anatomical basis of prosopagnosia. *Journal of Neurology, Neurosurgery, and Psychiatry*, **37**, 489–501.

Mehler, J. (1977). Personal communication.

Meltzoff, A.N. and Moore, M.K. (1977). Imitation of facial and manual gestures by human neonates. *Science*, **198**, 75–78.

Messick, S. and Damarin, F. (1964). Cognitive styles and memory for faces. *Journal of Abnormal and Social Psychology*, **69**, 313–318.

Milian, G. (1932). Cécité morphologique. *Bulletin de l'Académie de Médicine*, **107**, 664.

Milner, B. (1968). Visual recognition and recall after right temporal lobe excision in man. *Neuropsychologia*, **6**, 191–209.

Milord, J.T. (1978). Aesthetic aspects of faces: A (somewhat) phenomenological analysis using multidimensional scaling methods. *Journal of Personality and Social Psychology*, **36**, 205–216.

Miranda, S.B. and Fantz, R.L. (1974). Recognition memory in Down's syndrome and normal infants. *Child Development*, **45**, 651–660.

Morton, J. (1969). Interaction and information in word recognition. *Psychological Review*, **76**, 165–178.

Moscovitch, M., Scullion, D. and Christie, D. (1976). Early versus late stages of processing and their relation to functional hemispheric asymmetries in face recognition. *Journal of Experimental Psychology: Human Perception and Performance*, **2**, 401–416.

Mueller, J.H. and Wherry, K.L. (1980). Orienting strategies at study and test in facial recognition. *American Journal of Psychology*, **93**, 107–117.

Mueller, J.H., Bailis, K.L. and Goldstein, A.G. (1979). Depth of processing and anxiety in facial recognition. *British Journal of Psychology*, **70**, 511–515.

Mueller, J.H., Carlomusto, M. and Goldstein, A.G. (1978). Orienting task and study time in facial recognition. *Bulletin of the Psychonomic Society*, **11**, 313–316.

Munn, N.L. (1940). The effect of knowledge of the situation upon judgment of emotion from facial expressions. *Journal of Abnormal and Social Psychology*, **35**, 324–338.

Murray, D.E. (1966). The criminal line-up at home and abroad. *Utah Law Review*, **10**, 610–627.

Murstein, B.I. (1972). Physical attractiveness and marital choice. *Journal of Personality and Social Psychology*, **22**, 8–12.

Nash, H. (1969). Recognition of body-surface regions. *Genetic Psychology Monographs*, **79**, 297–340.

Neil v. Biggers. (1972). 409 U.S. 188.

Nguyen, H.H. (1976). A computer system for the mugfile problem. Master's thesis, University of Houston.

Nickerson, R.S. (1965). Short term memory for complex, meaningful, visual configurations: A demonstration of capacity. *Canadian Journal of Psychology*, **19**, 155–160.

Nisbett, R.E. and Wilson, T.D. (1977). Telling more than we can know: Verbal reports on mental processes. *Psychological Review*, **84**, 231–259.

Noton, D. and Stark, L. (1971). Eye movements and visual perception. *Scientific American*, **224**, 34–43.

Nottebohn, R. (1970). Ontogeny of birdsong. *Science*, **167**, 950–956.

Nowicki, S., Winograd, E. and Millard, B.A. (1979). Memory for faces: A social learning analysis. *Journal of Research in Personality*, **13**, 460–468.

Nummenmaa, T. (1964). The language of the face. *In* "Studies in Education, Psychology and Social Research", vol. 9. University of Jyväskylä, Finland.

Nummenmaa, T. and Kauranne, U. (1958). Dimensions of facial expression. Reports from the Department of Psychology, Institute of Pedagogics, Jyväskylä, Finland, No. 20.

Orenstein, H.B. and Hamilton, K.M. (1977). Memory load, critical features, and retrieval processes in facial recognition. *Perceptual and Motor Skills*, **45**, 1079–1087.

Osgood, C.E. (1952). The nature and measurement of meaning. *Psychological Bulletin*, **49**, 197–237.

Osgood, C.E. (1955). Fidelity and reliability. *In* "Information Theory in Psychology. Problems and Methods" (H. Quastler, Ed.). The Free Press, Glencoe, Illinois.

Osgood, C.E. (1962). Studies in the generality of affective meaning systems. *American Psychologist*, **17**, 10–28.

Osgood, C.E. (1966). Dimensionality of the semantic space for communication via facial expressions. *Scandinavian Journal of Psychology*, **7**, 1–30.

Osgood, C.E., May, W.H. and Miron, M.S. (1975). "Cross-cultural Universals of Affective Meaning". University of Illinois Press, Urbana.

Oster, H. (1978). Facial expression and affect development. *In* "The Development of Affect" (M. Lewis and L.A. Rosenblum, Eds). Plenum Press, New York.

Oster, H. and Ekman, P. (1978). Facial behavior in child development. *In* "Minnesota Symposium on Child Psychology" (A. Collins, Ed.), vol. 11. L. Erlbaum, Hillsdale, New Jersey.

Owens, C. (1970). Identi-Kit enters its second decade—ever growing at home and abroad. *Fingerprint and Identification Magazine*, November 1970, pp. 3–8; 11–17.

Pallis, C.A. (1950). Impaired identification of faces and places with agnosia for colour. *Journal of Neurology, Neurosurgery and Psychiatry*, **18**, 218–224.

Parrott, G.L. and Coleman, G. (1971). Sexual appeal: In black and white. *Proceedings of the Annual convention of the American Psychological Association*, **6**, 321–322.

Pasaruk, D. and Yarmey, A.D. (1974). Recognition memory for faces. Paper presented at the annual meeting of the Canadian Psychological Association, Windsor, Ontario.

Patterson, K.E. (1978). Person recognition: More than a pretty face. *In* "Practical Aspects of Memory" (M.M. Gruneberg, P.E. Morris and R.N. Sykes, Eds). Academic Press, London and New York.

Patterson, K.E. and Baddeley, A.D. (1977). When face recognition fails. *Journal of Experimental Psychology: Human Learning and Memory*, 3, 406–417.

Patterson, K. and Bradshaw, J.L. (1975). Differential hemispheric mediation of non verbal visual stimuli. *Journal of Experimental Psychology: Human Perception and Performance*, 1, 246–252.

Pawlby, S.J. (1977). Imitative interaction. *In* "Studies in Mother–Infant Interaction" (H.R. Schaffer, Ed.). Academic Press, New York and London.

Peiper, A. (1935). Die Entwicklung des Mienenspiels. *Monatsschrift für Kinderheilk*, 63, 39–91.

Peiper, A. (1963). "Cerebral Function in Infancy and Childhood". (3rd edition). (Translated by B. Nagler and H. Nagler.) Pitman, London.

Penry, J. (1971). "Looking at Faces and Remembering Them: A Guide to Facial Identification". Elek Books, London.

Penry, J. (1976). Penry facial identification technique. News Bulletin 1975–1976. John Waddington of Kirkstall Limited, Leeds.

Perkins, D. (1975). A definition of caricature and recognition. *Studies in the Anthropology of Visual Communication*, 2, 1–24.

Perrett, D.E., Rolls, E.T. and Caan, W. (1979). Visual cells in the temporal lobe selectively responsive to facial features. Paper presented at the European Conference on Visual Perception, Noordivijerhout, The Netherlands.

Peters, A. (1917). Gefühl und Wiedererkennen. *Fortschritte der Psychologie und ihrer Anwendungen*, 4, 120–133.

Peterson, L.P. and Peterson, M.J. (1959). Short-term retention of individual verbal items. *Journal of Experimental Psychology*, 58, 193–198.

Pevzner, S., Bornstein, B. and Loewenthal, M. (1962). Prosopagnosia. *Journal of Neurology, Neurosurgery and Psychiatry*, 25, 336–338.

Phillips, R.J. (1972). Why are faces hard to recognize in photographic negative? *Perception and Psychophysics*, 12, 425–426.

Phillips, R.J. (1979). Some exploratory experiments on memory for photographs of faces. *Acta Psychologica*, 43, 39–56.

Phillips, W.A. and Baddeley, A.D. (1971). Reaction time and short-term visual memory. *Psychonomic Science*, 22, 73–74.

Piderit, T. (1867). "Wissenschaftliches System der Mimik und Physiognomik". Detmold, Meyers.

Pittenger, J.B. and Shaw, R.E. (1975). Aging faces as viscal-elastic events: Implications for a theory of non-rigid shape perception. *Journal of Experimental Psychology: Human Perception and Performance*, 104, 374–382.

Plutchik, R. (1962). "The Emotions: Facts, Theories and a New Model". Random House, New York.

Posner, M.I. (1973). "Cognition: An Introduction". Scott, Foresman, Glenview, Illinois.

Pontius, A.A. (1976). Dyslexia and specifically distorted drawings of the face—A new group with prosopagnosia-like signs. *Experientia*, **32**, 1432–1435.

Posner, M.I. and Keele, S.W. (1968). On the genesis of abstract ideas. *Journal of Experimental Psychology*, **77**, 353–363.

Powers, P.A., Andriks, J.L. and Loftus, E.F. (1979). Eyewitness accounts of females and males. *Journal of Applied Psychology*, **64**, 339–347.

Pulaski, C.A. (1974). Neil v. Biggers: The Supreme Court dismantles the Wade trilogy's due process protection. *Stanford Law Review*, **26**, 1097–1121.

Pulos, L. and Spilka, B. (1961). Perceptual selectivity, memory and anti-Semitism. *Journal of Abnormal and Social Psychology*, **62**, 690–692.

Pylyshyn, Z.W. (1973). What the mind's eye tells the mind's brain: A critique of mental imagery. *Psychological Bulletin*, **80**, 1–24.

Quanty, M.B., Keats, J.A. and Harkins, S.G. (1975). Prejudice and criteria for identification of ethnic photographs. *Journal of Personality and Social Psychology*, **32**, 449–454.

Rayner, K. (1978). Eye movements in reading and information processing. *Psychological Bulletin*, **85**, 618–660.

Redican, W.K. (1975). Facial expressions in non-human primates. *In* "Primate Behavior: Developments in Field and Laboratory Research" (L.A. Rosenblum, Ed.), vol. 4. Academic Press, New York.

Reed, S.K. (1972). Pattern recognition and categorization. *Cognitive Psychology*, **3**, 382–407.

Regina v. Turnbull (1976). *Weekly Law Reports*, **3**, 445.

Reynolds, D. McQ. and Jeeves, M.A. (1978). A developmental study of hemisphere specialization for recognition of faces in normal subjects. *Cortex*, **14**, 511–520.

Rhodes, B.T. and Bargainer, J.D. (1976). A mini-computer system for retrieval of look-alikes from a mug file. Proceedings of the 1976 Systems Engineering Conference: AIIE, Atlanta, Georgia.

Rhodes, B.T. and Prasertchuang, K. (1977). Forgery application of a pattern recognition algorithm for facial images. Mug File Project (Report Number UHMUG-11), University of Houston.

Rhodes, H.F.T. (1956). "Alphonse Bertillon: Father of Scientific Detection". Harrap, London.

Rhodes, M.L. and Klinger, A. (1977). Conversational text input for modifying graphics facial images, Draft of a report, University of Houston.

Riley, D. (1979). Personal communication (September).

Rizzolatti, G., Umilta, C. and Berlucchi, G. (1971). Opposite superiorities of the right and left cerebral hemispheres in discriminative reaction time to physiognomical and alphabetical material. *Brain*, **94**, 431–442.

Rock, I. (1974). The perception of disoriented figures. *Scientific American*, 230, 78–85.

Rosch, E., Simpson, C. and Miller, R.S. (1976). Structural bases of typicality effects. *Journal of Experimental Psychology: Human Perception and Performance*, 2, 491–502.

Rosenfield, S.A. and Van Hoesen, G.W. (1979). Face recognition in the rhesus monkey. *Neuropsychologia*, 17, 503–509.

Rosenthal, R., Hall, J.A., Di Matteo, M.R., Rogers, P.L. and Archer, D. (1979). "Sensitivity to Nonverbal Communication: The PONS Test". Johns Hopkins University Press, Baltimore, Maryland.

Royal, D.C. and Hays, W.L. (1959). Empirical dimensions of emotional behavior. *Acta Psychologica*, 15, 419.

Ruckmick, C.A. (1921). A preliminary study of the emotions. *Psychological Monographs*, 30, 30–35.

Ruckmick, C.A. (1936). "The Psychology of Feeling and Emotion". McGraw Hill, New York.

Rudolph, H. (1903). "Der Ausdruck der Gemütsbewegungen des Menschen: Textbund und Atlas". Kühtmann, Dresden.

Russell, J.A. and Mehrabian, A. (1977). Evidence for a three-factor theory of emotions. *Journal of Research in Personality*, 11, 273–294.

Saha, G.B. (1973). Judgement of facial expressions of emotion—A cross-cultural study. *Journal of Psychological Research*, 17, 59–63.

Sakai, T., Nagao, M. and Fujibayashi, S. (1969). Line extraction and pattern recognition in a photograph. *Pattern Recognition*, 1, 233–248.

Sakai, T., Nagao, M. and Kanade, T. (1972). Computer analysis and classification of photographs of human faces. Proceedings of the First USA–Japan Computer Conference, pp. 55–62.

Saltz, E. and Sigel, I.E. (1967). Concept overdiscrimination in children. *Journal of Experimental Psychology*, 73, 1–8.

Salzen, E.A. (1978). Social attachment and a sense of security—A review. *Social Science Information*, 17, 555–627.

Salzen, E.A. (1979). The ontogeny of fear in animals. *In* "Fear in Animals and Man" (W. Sluckin, Ed.). Van Nostrand Reinhold, New York.

Scapinello, K.F. and Yarmey, A.D. (1970). The role of familiarity and orientation in immediate and delayed recognition of pictorial stimuli. *Psychonomic Science*, 21, 329–331.

Schaffer, H.R. (Ed.) (1977). "Studies in Mother–Infant Interaction." Academic Press, New York and London.

Schill, T.R. (1966). Effects of approval motivation and varying conditions of verbal reinforcement on incidental memory for faces. *Psychological Reports*, 19, 55–60.

Schlosberg, H. (1941). A scale for the judgment of facial expressions. *Journal of Experimental Psychology*, 29, 497–510.

Schlosberg, H. (1952). The description of facial expressions in terms of two dimensions. *Journal of Experimental Psychology*, 44, 229–237.

Schlosberg, H. (1954). Three dimensions of emotion. *Psychological Review*, 61, 81–88.

Schulz, L.S. and Straub, R.B. (1972). Effects of high-priority events on adjacent items. *Journal of Experimental Psychology*, **95**, 467–469.

Seaford, H.W. (1975). Facial expression dialect: An example. *In* "Organisation of Behavior in Face-to-Face Interaction" (A. Kendon, R.M. Harris and M. Ritchie-Key, Eds). Mouton, The Hague.

Seamon, J.G. (1980). "Memory and Cognition: An Introduction". Oxford University Press, New York.

Seamon, J.G., Stolz, J.A., Bass, D.H. and Chatinover, A.I. (1978). Recognition of facial features in immediate memory. *Bulletin of the Psychonomic Society*, **12**, 231–234.

Secord, P.F., Bevan, W. and Katz, B. (1956). The negro stereotype and perceptual accentuation. *Journal of Abnormal and Social Psychology*, **53**, 78–83.

Seeleman, V. (1940). The influence of attitude upon the remembering of pictorial material. *Archives of Psychology*, **36**, No. 258.

Sheehan, P.W. (1967). A shortened form of the Betts' Questionnaire Upon Mental Imagery. *Journal of Clinical Psychology*, **23**, 386–389.

Shepard, R.N., Romney, A.K. and Nerlove, S.B. (Eds) (1972). "Multidimensional Scaling: Theory and Applications in the Behavioural Sciences", vol. 1, Theory. Seminar Press, New York.

Shepherd, J.W. (1977). A multidimensional scaling approach to facial recognition. Paper presented at the annual conference of the British Psychological Society, Exeter, Devon.

Shepherd, J.W. and Deregowski, J.B. (1981). Races and faces: A comparison of the responses of African and Europeans to faces of the same and different races. *British Journal of Social Psychology*, **20**, 125–133.

Shepherd, J.W. and Ellis, H.D. (1973). The effect of attractiveness on recognition memory for faces. *American Journal of Psychology*, **86**, 627–633.

Shepherd, J.W., Deregowski, J.B. and Ellis, H.D. (1974). A cross-cultural study of recognition memory for faces. *International Journal of Psychology*, **9**, 205–212.

Shepherd, J.W. Ellis, H.D. and Davies, G.M. (1977). Perceiving and remembering faces. Technical report to the Home Office under contract POL/73/1675/24/1.

Shepherd, J.W., Davies, G.M. and Ellis, H.D. (1978a). How best shall a face be described? *In* "Practical Aspects of Memory" (M.M. Gruneberg, P.E. Morris and R.N. Sykes, Eds). Academic Press, London and New York.

Shepherd, J.W., Ellis, H.D., McMurran, M. and Davies, G.M. (1978b). Effect of character attribution on Photofit construction of a face. *European Journal of Social Psychology*, **8**, 263–268.

Shepherd, J.W., Davies, G.M., Ellis, H.D. and Freeman, J. (1980). Identification after delay. Final report to the Home Office Research Unit for Grant RES 522/4/1. Department of Psychology, University of Aberdeen.

Sherman, M. (1927). The differentiation of emotional responses in infants. 1. Judgments of emotional responses from motion picture views and from actual observation. *Journal of Comparative Psychology*, **7**, 265–284.

Shoemaker, D.J., South, D.R. and Lowe, J. (1973). Facial stereotypes of deviants and judgments of guilt or innocence. *Social Forces*, 51, 427–433.

Shrauger, S. and Altrocchi, J. (1964). The personality of the perceiver as a factor in person perception. *Psychological Bulletin*, 62, 289–308.

Siegel, J.M. and Loftus, E.F. (1978). Impact of anxiety and life stress upon eyewitness testimony. *Bulletin of the Psychonomic Society*, 12, 479–480.

Simpson, A. (1955). Aids to identification—A new method. *Police Journal*, 220–229.

Simpson, W.E. and Crandall, S.J. (1972). The perception of smiles. *Psychonomic Science*, 29, 197–200.

Smith, E.E. and Nielsen, G.D. (1970). Representations and retrieval processes in short-term memory: Recognition and recall of faces. *Journal of Experimental Psychology*, 85, 397–405.

Smith, A.D. and Winograd, E. (1978). Adult age differences in remembering faces. *Developmental Psychology*, 14, 443–444.

Smith, S.M. (1979). Remembering in and out of context. *Journal of Experimental Psychology: Human Learning and Memory*, 5, 460–471.

Snee, T.J. and Lush, D.E. (1941). Interaction of the narrative and interrogatory methods of obtaining testimony. *Journal of Psychology*, 11, 229–236.

Sobel, N.R. (1972). Eyewitness identification: Legal and practical problems. (1979 Supplement). Clark Boardman, New York.

Sondern, F. (1964). The box that catches criminals. *Readers' Digest*, April, pp. 37–44.

Sroufe, L.A. (1979). Socioemotional development. *In* "Handbook of Infant Development" (J.D. Osofsky, Ed.). Wiley, New York.

Sroufe, L.A. and Waters, E. (1976). The ontogenesis of smiling and laughter; A perspective on the organization of development in infancy. *Psychological Review*, 83, 173–189.

Sroufe, L.A. and Wunsch, J.P. (1972). The development of laughter in the first year of life. *Child Development*, 43, 1326–1344.

Sroufe, L.A., Waters, E. and Matas, L. (1974). Contextual determinants of infant affective response. *In* "The Origins of Fear" (M. Lewis and L.A. Rosenblum, Eds). Wiley, New York.

Stechler, G. (1964). Newborn attention as affected by medication during labor. *Science*, 144, 315–317.

St John, R.C. (1979). Lateral asymmetry in face perception. Research Bulletin, 495. Department of Psychology, University of Western Ontario, London, Canada.

Stollreiter-Butzon, L. (1950). Zur Frage der Prosopagnosie. *Archiv für Psychiatrie und Nervenkrankheiten*, 184, 1–27.

Stovall v. Denno (1967). 388 U.S. 293.

Strauss, S. (1978). Appearances, disappearances, nonappearances, and reappearances of various behaviors: Methodological strategies of experimentation and their implication for models of development. *In* "Dips in Learning and Developmental Curves" (T.G. Bever and J. Mehler, Eds). L. Erlbaum, Hillsdale, New Jersey.

Stringer, P. (1967). Cluster analysis of non-verbal judgements of facial expressions. *British Journal of Mathematical and Statistical Psychology*, **20**, 71–79.

Stringer, P. (1973). Do dimensions have face validity? *In* "Social Communication and Movement" (M. Von Cranach and I. Vine, Eds). Academic Press, London and New York.

Strnad, B.N. and Mueller, J.H. (1977). Levels of processing in facial recognition memory. *Bulletin of the Psychonomic Society*, **9**, 17–18.

Suberi, M. and McKeever, W.F. (1977). Differential right hemispheric memory storage of emotional and non-emotional faces. *Neuropsychologia*, **15**, 757–768.

Tagiuri, R. (1969). Person perception. *In* "The Handbook of Social Psychology" (G. Lindzey and A. Aronson, Eds). Addison-Wesley, London.

Tajfel, H. (1957). Value and the perceptual judgment of magnitude. *Psychological Review*, **64**, 192–200.

Tajfel, H. (1969). Social and cultural factors in perception. *In* "The Handbook of Social Psychology" (G. Lindzey and A. Aronson, Eds), vol. 3. Addison-Wesley, London.

Taylor, C. and Thompson, G.G. (1955). Age trends in preferences for certain facial proportions. *Child Development*, **26**, 91–102.

Teuber, H-L. (1978). The brain and human behavior. *In* "Handbook of Sensory Psychology" (R. Held, H.W. Leibowitz and H-L. Teuber, Eds), vol. 8. Springer-Verlag, Berlin.

The People (at the Suit of the Attorney General) v. Dominic Casey (1963). (No. 2). IR 33.

Thomas, H. (1973). Unfolding the baby's mind: The infant's selection of visual stimuli. *Psychological Review*, **80**, 468–488.

Thompson, D.F. and Meltzer, L. (1964). Communication of emotional intent by facial expression. *Journal of Abnormal and Social Psychology*, **68**, 129–135.

Thorwald, J. (1965). "The Mark of Cain". Thames and Hudson, London.

Tickner, A.H. and Poulton, E.C. (1975). Watching for people and actions. *Ergonomics*, **18**, 35–51.

Tieger, T. and Ganz, L. (1979). Recognition of faces in the presence of two-dimensional sinusoidal masks. *Perception and Psychophysics*, **26**, 163–167.

Toch, H.H., Rabin, A.I. and Wilkins, D.M. (1962). Factors entering into ethnic identifications: An experimental study. *Sociometry*, **25**, 297–312.

Tolch, J. (1959). Studies in the measurement and analysis of achievement with some visual symbols of speech. PhD thesis, Ohio State University.

Tomkins, S.S. and McCarter, R. (1964). What and where are the primacy affects? Some evidence for a theory. *Perceptual and Motor Skills*, **18**, 119–158.

Torgerson, W.S. (1958). "Theory and Methods of Scaling". Wiley, New York.

Townes, J.R. (1976). A computer algorithm for mug shot identification. EAI

Symposium on Automatic Imagery Pattern Recognition, College Park, Maryland.

Townsend, J.T. (1971). A note on the identifiability of serial and parallel processes. *Perception and Psychophysics*, **10**, 161–163.

Toyama, J.S. (1975). The effect of orientation on the recognition of faces: A reply to Yin. PhD thesis, University of Waterloo, Canada.

Trevarthen, C. (1980). Functional organization of the human brain. *In* "The Brain and Psychology" (M.C. Wittrock, Ed.). Academic Press, New York.

Triandis, H.G. and Lambert, W.W. (1958). A restatement and test of Schlosberg's theory of emotion with two kinds of subjects from Greece. *Journal of Abnormal and Social Psychology*, **56**, 321–328.

Tronick, E., Adamson, L., Wise, S., Als, H. and Brazelton, T.B. (1975). Infant emotions in normal and perturbated interactions. Paper presented at the meeting of the Society for Research in Child Development, Denver, April, 1975.

Tulving, E. (1972). Episodic and semantic memory. *In* "Organization and Memory" (E. Tulving and W. Donaldson, Eds). Academic Press, New York.

Tversky, E. (1974). Eye fixations in prediction of recognition and recall. *Memory and Cognition*, **2**, 275–278.

Tzavaras, A., Hécaen, H. and Le Bras, H. (1970). Le problème de la spécificité de déficit de la reconnaissance du visage humain lors de lésions hémisphériques unilatérales. *Neuropsychologia*, **8**, 403–416.

Tzavaras, A., Merienne, L. and Masure, M.C. (1973). Prosopagnosie, amnésie et troubles du langage per lésion temporale gauche chez un gaucher. *L'Encéphale*, **62**, 382–394.

Udry, J.R. (1966). A research note on children's concept of beauty. *Merrill-Palmer Quarterly*, **12**, 165–171.

Umilta, C., Brizzolara, D., Tabossi, P. and Fairweather, H. (1978). Factors affecting face recognition in the cerebral hemispheres: Familiarity and naming. *In* "Attention and Performance" (J. Requin, Ed.), vol. 7. L. Erlbaum, Hillsdale, New Jersey.

United States v. Telfaire (1972). 469 F2d 552.

United States v. Wade (1967). 388 U.S. 218.

Van Hooff, J.A.R.A.M. (1962). Facial expression in higher primates. *Symposium of the Zoological Society of London*, **8**, 97–125.

Van Hooff, J.A.R.A.M. (1967). The facial displays of the Catarrhine monkeys and apes. *In* "Primate Ethology" (D. Morris, Ed.). Weidenfeld and Nicolson, London.

Van Hooff, J.A.R.A.M. (1972). A comparative approach to the phylogeny of laughter and smiling. *In* "Nonverbal Communication" (R.A. Hinde, Ed.). Cambridge University Press, London.

Van Hooff, J.A.R.A.M. (1973). A structural analysis of the social behavior of a semi-captive group of chimpanzees. *In* "Social Communication and Movement. Studies of Interaction and Expression in Man and Chimpanzee" (M. Von Cranach and I. Vine, Eds). Academic Press, New York.

Van Hooff, J.A.R.A.M. (1976). The comparison of facial expression in man and higher primates. *In* "Methods of Inference from Animal to Human Behaviour" (M. Von Cranach, Ed.). Aldine, Chicago.

Venner, B.R.H. (1969). Facial identification techniques. *Police Research Bulletin*, No. 13, 17–20.

Vernon, M.D. (1955). The functions of schemata in perceiving. *Psychological Review*, **62**, 180–192.

Vinacke, W.E. (1949). The judgment of facial expression by three national-racial groups in Hawaii. I. Caucasian faces. *Journal of Personality*, **17**, 407–429.

Vinacke, W.E. and Fong, R.W. (1955). The judgment of facial expressions by three national-racial groups in Hawaii. II. Oriental faces. *Journal of Social Psychology*, **41**, 185–195.

Vurpillot, E. (1976). "The Visual World of the Child". (Translated by W.E.C. Gillham). International University Press, New York.

Walker-Smith, G.J. (1978). The effects of delay and exposure duration in a face recognition task. *Perception and Psychophysics*, **24**, 63–70.

Walker-Smith, G.J. (1980). Memorizing facial identity, expression and orientation. *British Journal of Psychology*, **71**, 415–424.

Walker-Smith, G.J., Gale, A.G. and Findlay, J.M. (1977). Eye-movement strategies involved in face perception. *Perception*, **6**, 313–326.

Wall, P.M. (1965). "Eyewitness Identification of Criminal Cases". C.C. Thomas, Springfield, Illinois.

Wallace, C.G., Coltheart, M. and Forster, K.I. (1970). Reminiscence in recognition memory for faces. *Psychonomic Science*, **18**, 335–336.

Warrington, E.K. and Ackroyd, C. (1975). The effect of orienting tasks on recognition memory. *Memory and Cognition*, **3**, 140–142.

Warrington, E.K. and James, M. (1967). An experimental investigation of facial recognition in patients with unilateral cerebral lesions. *Cortex*, **3**, 317–326.

Warrington, E.K. and Taylor, A.M. (1973). The contribution of the right parietal lobe to object recognition. *Cortex*, **9**, 152–164.

Washburn, R.W. (1929). A study of the smiling and laughing of infants in the first year of life. *Genetic Psychology Monographs*, **6**, 397–537.

Watkins, M.J., Ho, E. and Tulving, E. (1976). Context effects in recognition memory for faces. *Journal of Verbal Learning & Verbal Behavior*, **15**, 505–517.

Watson, E.R. (1924). "The Trial of Adolf Beck". Hodge, Glasgow.

Watson, J.S. (1966). Perception of object orientation in infants. *Merrill-Palmer Quarterly*, **12**, 73–94.

Watson, S.E. (1972). Judgment of emotion from facial and contextual cue combinations. *Journal of Personality and Social Psychology*, **24**, 334–342.

Wayman, R. and Scott, W.C. (1974). The role of facial areas in facial recognition. *Catalogue of Selected Documents in Psychology*, **4**, 115–116.

Wells, G.L. (1978). Applied eyewitness-testimony research: System variables and estimator variables. *Journal of Personality and Social Psychology*, **36**, 1546–1557.

Wells, G.L., Leippe, J.R. and Ostrom, T.M. (1979a). Guidelines for assessing the fairness of a line-up. *Law and Human Behavior*, **3**, 285–293.

Wells, G.L., Lindsay, R.C.L. and Ferguson, T.J. (1979b). Accuracy, confidence and juror perception in eyewitness identification. *Journal of Applied Psychology*, **64**, 440–448.

Werner, H. (1957). "Comparative Psychology of Mental Development". (Revised Edition). International Universities Press, New York.

Whipple, G.M. (1909). The observer as reporter: A survey of the psychology of testimony. *The Psychological Bulletin*, **6**, 153–170.

White, R.W. (1959). Motivation reconsidered: The concept of competence. *Psychological Review*, **66**, 297–333.

Whiteley, A.M. and Warrington, E.K. (1977). Prosopagnosia: A clinical, psychological, and anatomical study of three patients. *Journal of Neurology, Neurosurgery and Psychiatry*, **40**, 395–403.

Wiederhold, T.P. (1976). Facial image generation by computer. Master's thesis, University of Houston.

Wigmore, J.H. (1931). Corroboration by witness' identification of an accused on arrest. *Illinois Law Review*, **25**, 550.

Wigmore, J.H. (1937). "The Science of Judicial Proof". (3rd edition). Little, Brown, Boston.

Wilbrand, H. (1892). Ein Fall von Seelenblindheit und Hemianopsie mit Sections-Befund. *Deutsch Zeitschrift für Nervenheilkunde*, **2**, 361–387.

Williams, F. and Sundene, B. (1965). Dimensions of recognition: Visual vs. vocal expression of emotion. *Audio-visual Communication Review*, **13**, 44–52.

Williams, F. and Tolch, J. (1965). Communication by facial expression. *Journal of Communication*, **15**, 17–27.

Williams, G. and Hammelmann, H.A. (1963). Identification parades. *Criminal Law Review*, 479–490; 545–555.

Wilson, C.R. (1975). Psychological opinions on the accuracy of eyewitness testimony. *Judges' Journal*, **14**, 72–74.

Wilson, E.O. (1975). "Sociobiology, the New Synthesis". Harvard University Press, Cambridge.

Winer, B.J. (1962). "Statistical Principles in Experimental Design". McGraw-Hill, New York.

Winograd, E. (1976). Recognition memory for faces following nine different judgements. *Bulletin of the Psychonomic Society*, **8**, 419–421.

Winograd, E. (1978). Encoding operations which facilitate memory for faces across the life span. *In* "Practical Aspects of Memory" (M.M. Gruneberg, P.E. Morris and R.N. Sykes, Eds). Academic Press, London.

Winograd, E. and Rivers-Bulkeley, N.T. (1977). Effects of changing context on remembering faces. *Journal of Experimental Psychology: Human Learning and Memory*, **3**, 397–405.

Wiseman, S. and Neisser, U. (1974). Perceptual organization as a determinant of visual recognition memory. *American Journal of Psychology*, **87**, 675–681.

Witkin, H.A., Dyke, R.B., Faterson, H.F., Goodenough, D.R. and Karp, S.A. (1962). "Psychological Differentiation". Wiley, New York.

Witryol, S.L. and Kaess, W.A. (1957). Sex differences in social memory tasks. *Journal of Abnormal and Social Psychology*, **54**, 343–346.

Wolff, P.H. (1969). The natural history of crying and other vocalizations in early infancy. *In* "Determinants of Infant Behaviour 4" (B.M. Foss, Ed.). Methuen, London.

Wolff, W. (1942). The right and left face. *Ciba Symposia*, **3**, 1136–1138.

Woocher, F.D. (1977). Did your eyes deceive you? Expert psychological testimony on the unreliability of eyewitness identification. *Stanford Law Review*, **29**, 969–1030.

Woodhead, M.M., Baddeley, A.D. and Simmonds, D.C.V. (1979). On training people to recognize faces. *Ergonomics*, **22**, 333–343.

Woodhouse, J.M. (1976). The application of contrast sensitivity to studies on image detection and recognition. PhD thesis, University of Cambridge.

Woodworth, R.S. (1938). "Experimental Psychology". Methuen, London.

Wundt, W. (1907). "Outlines of Psychology". (7th edition). (Translated by C.H. Judd). Wilheim Engelmann, Leipzig.

Yarbus, A.L. (1967). "Eye Movements and Vision". (Translated by B. Haigh). Plenum Press, New York.

Yarmey, A.D. (1971). Recognition memory for familiar "public" faces: Effects of orientation and delay. *Psychonomic Science*, **24**, 286–288.

Yarmey, A.D. (1974). Proactive interference in short-term retention of human faces. *Canadian Journal of Psychology*, **28**, 333–338.

Yarmey, A.D. (1975). Social-emotional factors in recall and recognition of faces. Paper presented at the annual meeting of the Mid-western Psychological Association, Chicago.

Yarmey, A.D. (1978). The effects of attractiveness, feature saliency, and liking on memory for faces. *In* "Love and Attraction: An International Conference" (M. Cook and G. Wilson, Eds). Pergamon Press, Oxford.

Yarmey, A.D. (1979a). "The Psychology of Eyewitness Testimony". The Free Press, New York.

Yarmey, A.D. (1979b). Through the looking glass: Sex differences in memory for self-facial poses. *Journal of Research in Personality*, **13**, 450–459.

Yarmey, A.D. and Paskaruk, S. (1974). The influence of affect, ego-involvement and sex differences in recognition of faces. Unpublished manuscript, University of Guelph, Ontario, Canada.

Yin, R.K. (1969). Looking at upside-down faces. *Journal of Experimental Psychology*, **81**, 141–145.

Yin, R.K. (1970). Face recognition by brain-injured patients: A dissociable ability? *Neuropsychologia*, **8**, 395–402.

Yin, R.K. (1978). Face perception: A review of experiments with infants, normal adults, and brain injured persons. *In* "Handbook of Sensory Physiology" (R. Held, H.W. Leibowitz and H.L. Teuber, Eds), vol. 8. Springer-Verlag, Berlin.

Young, A.W. and Ellis, H.D. (1976). An experimental investigation of developmental differences in ability to recognize faces presented to the left and right cerebral hemisphere. *Neuropsychologia*, **14**, 495–498.

Young, G. and Décarie, T.G. (1977). An ethology based catalogue of facial/ vocal behaviour in infancy. *Animal Behaviour*, 25, 95–107.

Young-Browne, G., Rosenfeld, H.M. and Horowitz, F.D. (1977). Infant discrimination of facial expressions. *Child Development*, 48, 555–562.

Zanni, G.R. and Offermann, J.T. (1978). Eyewitness testimony: An exploration of question wording upon recall as a function of neuroticism. *Perceptual and Motor Skills*, 46, 163–166.

Zavala, A. and Paley, J.J. (Eds). (1972). "Personal Appearance Identification". C.C. Thomas, Springfield, Illinois.

Subject Index

A

Accuracy, 202–211, 214–215, 224–227, 231–240, 248–250, 272–273
  composite constructions, 231–240, 248–250
  confidence in, 214–215, 239
  estimation by expert witnesses, 224–225
  identity parade performance, 207–211
  limits to, 248–250, 272–273
  witnesses' testimony, 202–207, 227
Adolescents, 24–26
Affect, 69–70, 74–76, 150–151
Age, 126, 127, 212; *see also* Developmental trends
Anthropometric measurements, 76, 246
Anti-sematism, *see* Racial prejudice
Anxiety, 72–73, 213
Arousal, 89, 213, 278
Attention, 10–11, 13, 19, 57, 60–61, 68–69, 91, 98–99, 107, 117, 124–129, 150, 173, 187, 214, 234, 237, 246, 276, 282, 283
Attractiveness, 68, 74–78, 87, 99, 128, 208
Attributional judgments, 64, 75–76, 90–91, 99, 125, 128, 241, 247
Autism, impaired recognition and, 3, 115
Awareness, 102, 234, 237, 284

B

Babies, *see* Infants
Beards, *see* Paraphernalia
Beauty, *see* Attractiveness
Blank parades, 219
Brain damage, 32, 40–41, 44–46, 50, 172–175; *see also* Prosopagnosia
Bryden Report, 215–216, 218–219, 221, 225

C

Caricatures, 187–188; *see also* Line drawings
Certainty, 214–215, 239
Children, 16–24, 69, 151–152, 212
  boy/girl recognition, 69
  classification of emotions by, 151–152
  instructional effects, 19–20
  development of encoding skills, 18–20
  recognition performance, 16–18
  testimony reliability, 212
Chin, 12, 106–120, 125, 155, 259
Complexion, 106, 107, 127
Composite systems, 228–250; *see also* Photofit, Identikit
  laboratory studies, 231–240
  operational effectiveness, 230–231
  psychological factors, 243–244
Computer-guided face retrieval 251–269
  feature selection, 251, 262–264
  matching algorithm, 252, 265–267